CHILDREN AWAY FROM HOME

**MODERN
APPLICATIONS
OF
SOCIAL
WORK**

**A
SERIES
EDITED
BY
JAMES K.
WHITTAKER**

CHILDREN AWAY FROM HOME

A SOURCEBOOK OF RESIDENTIAL TREATMENT

EDITED BY
JAMES K. WHITTAKER (UNIVERSITY OF WASHINGTON)
AND ALBERT E. TRIESCHMAN
(WALKER HOME FOR CHILDREN)

WITH A FOREWORD BY GISELA KONOPKA
(UNIVERSITY OF MINNESOTA)

ALDINE·ATHERTON
CHICAGO AND NEW YORK

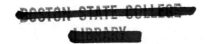

About the Editors

James K. Whittaker is Associate Professor, School of Social Work, and Special Consultant on Research and Training, Social Work Department, Child Development and Mental Retardation Center, University of Washington, Seattle, Washington.

Albert E. Trieschman is Executive Director of the Walker Home for Children, Needham, Massachusetts, and Staff Clinical Psychologist, Children's Hospital Medical Center, Boston.

First published 1972 by
Aldine • Atherton, Inc.
529 South Wabash Avenue
Chicago, Illinois 60605

ISBN 0-202-36010-5
Library of Congress Catalog Number 72-140014

Printed in the United States of America

Foreword

Love was a flower of slow nurture, justice was a fruit of
vigilant cultivation. The flower would wither and the fruit
would drop under the hands of a shiftless gardner.

—Morris L. West, *Daughter of Silence*

These words of Morris West give the essence of the significance of people
who work with children. They must have patience and knowledge, a sense
of justice and deep respect for every human being, as well as an all-en-
compassing love that goes beyond justice. This applies to all who work
with people, but especially to those who work with children who puzzle
us, annoy us, frighten us. This book was edited by two men who do not
look at such children as curious objects. They have lived with and cared
for these children who are important and vibrant to them. The whole field
of residential work needs the wisdom of such practitioners who can also be
scientific enough to be systematic in trying to understand children and develop ways of healing the hurt ones.

It is important that the editors have collected material, not only from
their own rich experience, but also from the literature written by others.
Too often, insights and practices in the institutional field are hailed as
great innovations when there is nothing really new about them. The collection of papers in this volume helps us to establish continuity and learn
where clarification is still needed.

Over and over, some of the same questions and objections are raised:
Why institutions at all? Would it not be best to keep all these children in
their own home and give only day care? Is individual treatment not sufficient? Sometimes the questions include attacks: Aren't those residential

treatment centers always too permissive? Aren't the children allowed to act out instead of being taught something?

Any child who can be kept in his own family without suffering too severely from the home situation or making the family suffer so much that the other members become disturbed, certainly should stay at home. If a community has excellent schools with special classes for disturbed children, provides enough child guidance clinics, opens opportunity for therapeutic day care centers, many more children can remain in their home environment than do today. Yet even under the best circumstances, there are children who must be granted total relief from the pressures of relationships that harm them over and over again; and there are families who simply cannot tolerate the aggressive outbursts of a child in pain, or the moody withdrawal combined with suicide attempts of a teenager, or the frequent silent tears of a mute nine year old incapable of expressing the terror that lives within him. Treatment institutions are not boarding schools; they are not substitute families—at least they should not be any of those. They are a special kind of group living that for every hour of the day provides help, support, understanding, and hopefully—when possible and necessary—insight and a moving out of the inner darkness and hate. They must not be places to which the child is being "removed" or "put away." They must be safe places where the tortured mind or soul can scream out its pain to be *heard* and then be helped.

In the normal environment, one cannot allow this pain to come out. It is too harmful to others. It does not always mean only a scream; it may mean a smashing of things close at hand, or hitting others, or many other actions that one cannot tolerate in everyday life. In a true treatment institution, staff must find and offer ways in which hurt and hate can be expressed without being harmful to the individual or others. It is necessary to open this opportunity, to better understand what produces the pain. In finding out, in helping the child to have the extraordinary experience of being *heard* and *understood,* the healing process can start. This is not "permissiveness" per se. It does not mean to allow everything. It only means that staff acts consciously and purposefully in relation to the particular problem of the child so that he becomes healthier. Repression alone would only mean keeping the sickness inside. It is necessary to assess the illness and to know when more or fewer limitations are necessary. The whole controversy about permissiveness is a false issue. It is as if one would argue whether it is right to allow a patient to stay in bed while he is physically ill or whether such permission will play into his laziness. How long a patient needs bed rest has changed according to physicians' knowledge of the needs of the body. Exactly this same attitude must prevail in relation to emotional disturbances. Permission to act out or the diminishing of demands is related to the particular illness and to the degree of illness. The healthier the child, the more demands can be made and the greater can be the expectation that the child can handle his emotions.

Our emotionally sick children, whatever the reason for their disturbance, have always *experienced* some rejection, some feeling that they are not worth anything. This has been frequently misunderstood, and it was thought that the *cause* of their illness has been rejection. Parents were made to feel very guilty. The causes of emotional illness vary widely reaching from somatic problems to environmental factors, both physical and in human relations. Frequently, we do not yet know about the causes. For instance, we are only beginning to learn of the relationship of biological chemistry to emotional disturbances. Yet these children have been rejected because of the way they behaved. Nobody can be blamed for this, but they do need a place where they can recover. They need a place that is more than a place to be held until they get their medicine or the doctor comes in to talk with them for an hour. The twenty-three hours outside of that one therapeutic interview become most significant. The people who are with the children all day are most important to them. Those twenty-three hours must help the child to regain self-respect, some self-confidence. A person can only move out of hate or isolation when he can think of himself as a worthwhile person. Only then can he begin to be master of his own instincts and emotions.

James Whittaker and Albert Trieschman have collected material from writers who have deep convictions about institutional treatment as a twenty-four hour responsibility. They themselves—one a psychologist and the other one a social worker—write as Jim Whittaker wrote to me in a letter:

> . . . from the vantage point of professionals who are used to working with children in the context of the life milieu—we are essentially child-care workers at heart!

They conceive of treatment as a total life experience. Like many of the other writers they have included in this book, they do not see the individual *versus* the group, but the individual *in* the group situation. They do not see permissiveness *versus* limitations, but permissiveness *within* the limitations of appropriate help. They do not see professional staff *versus* nonprofessional staff, but a *working together* of everyone whom the children need. And finally, they do not see the institution *versus* or outside of the community but they see it as an *integral* part of a community so that the child can move in and out according to his readiness. It is this integrative concept that makes the collection of articles and the dialogue of the writers most valuable.

In a period of considerable confusion about residential treatment, this book will help both the practitioner and the teacher gain clarity. Yet, best of all, it may help confused and disturbed children and youngsters regain their health in a community based on mutual respect.

Gisela Konopka
University of Minnesota

Preface

Good books, like good teachers, should raise as many questions as they answer. We believe that this volume meets those two purposes. Our dialogue attempts to raise some of what we feel are the crucial issues and related problems facing residential treatment today. The selected readings reflect some of the answers to those problems and issues. Our feeling is that a discussion of these problems and issues—whether one agrees with our position or with the view of an individual author—will ultimately result in better care and treatment for children: a goal to which we all ascribe. Hopefully, our book will set the stage for such a discussion.

We would like to thank the individual authors and publishers for permission to reprint their works. Space limitations prevented us from using all the articles we received permission to reprint. A more complete bibliography may be found at the end of this volume. Special thanks go to our publisher, Robert W. Wesner, who truly seeks to nurture a joint working relationship between author and publisher. Our thanks go also to our colleagues, many of whom are represented in this volume, for their helpful suggestions along the way. Syb Lemack and Eleanor Smith were responsible for the major preparation of the manuscript.

Finally, this project, as others, succeeded only through the understanding of our wives, Kathleen Whittaker and Nancy Trieschman, who provided a critical (and sometimes painful) review of our efforts, as well as the encouragement to try again.

Contents

CHILDREN AWAY FROM HOME

Dialogue

Introduction

The term *dialogue,* when referred to as a literary form, usually carries with it the connotation of two great persons sharing their respective wisdom and knowledge from the vantage point of having lived through almost all of a long and fruitful life. We can claim neither such wisdom nor longevity! The focus of our conversation is not on problems long since mastered in a distant past, but on problems that plagued us "then" and are still causing us some difficulty today. We are both currently involved in the active, day-to-day practice of residential treatment for emotionally disturbed children. Our conversation really represents a kind of continuous dialogue in which we daily find ourselves engaged. We feel there are no easy answers or stock solutions to the complicated problems of living with, caring for, and treating emotionally disturbed children. Our tentative "answers" to some of these difficult problems reflect not so much the wisdom that comes from an instantaneous revelation as they do the insight that has been painfully garnered from many trials and many errors. Our goal is not to present a foolproof blueprint for residential treatment (We don't believe that such a plan will ever exist), but to try to share with our readers the way in which we have attempted to approach the problems that confront all of us engaged in the practice of residential treatment.

Those readers who are familiar with our earlier work, *The Other 23 Hours,* know that we are both firmly committed to the philosophy of treating the

3

child in the life milieu. Toward this end, we have been intimately involved in the problems of training the "on-line" therapists—the child care workers. Both of us are convinced of the fact (having been often reminded by the children!) that there is no one "right way" in milieu treatment. Our ultimate goal is a model for treatment that is open to new ideas, basically eclectic in regard to theory—and most important of all—a model that will bear both the test of time and that of the children.

Finally, it has long been our contention that the "problems and issues" of residential treatment that are discussed at many national and regional conferences have more to do with the needs and strivings of the professional groups who run residential treatment centers than they do with the needs and problems of the children in care. We are attempting with this volume to reverse that trend. The problems and issues we chose to present—both in the dialogue and in the readings—are real to us and to many who are working in the field of residential treatment. We contend that solutions to these problems will only be reached when professional in-fighting is cast aside and a true dialogue is begun in conferences, professional journals, institutes, workshops, and staff meetings. We fully intend to continue our dialogue in all of these areas. Please join us.

Current Issues and Problems in Residential Treatment for Emotionally Disturbed Children

The Role of Residential Treatment

Whittaker: Some people in the field are saying that the growth of day care centers and the whole community mental health movement, with its emphasis on treating the troubled child in his natural environment, will replace residential treatment. Do you really think we'll be out of business in the next few years?

Trieschman: No. Even with earlier and more effective intervention in family difficulties closer to home, there will still be youngsters who need to be away from their families, both for their own sake and that of the family. I think that in the next decade the kinds of children who will come into residential treatment may be more severely disturbed, more psychotic, than those we are presently serving. Of course, if effective means of treatment closer to the family become more available, more children will be allowed to stay at home and receive help within their communities and within special classes in public schools so that there will be less need for what might crudely be called "parentectomies;" that is, the real separation of the child from his family.

Whittaker: Where are the professionals who will staff these community mental health centers to receive their training?

Trieschman: Part of what will keep residential treatment very much alive in the forseeable future is that the techniques required for working in communities, in family settings, and in day care centers are based on applications of mental health theory to everyday life circumstances—from serving meals in the day care center to planning activity programs, and helping with family activities.

Whittaker: If we're truly concerned with treating the child's problems in his natural family, we must be sure that our professional people have some knowledge about what it is actually like to live with an emotionally disturbed child for more than the fifty-minute therapy hour.

Trieschman: Exactly. The residential treatment center is the only laboratory that has developed the kind of ideas that actively extend mental health ideas to the natural circumstances of a day, a week, and a year. Our other engagement with illness and pathology has been in very much more restricted circumstances—a fifty-minute hour with two people in a room face to face or a specifically designed group that meets once a week. We have not been engaged in standard clinic operations in dealing with the natural circumstances of emotional disturbance.

Another important locus for mental health ideas to take hold will be the public schools, especially in the relationship of the community, the family, and the public school. One of the arguments for the longevity of the residential treatment facility is that it will be a place where the mental health professional (the social worker, the psychologist, and the psychiatrist) can be trained in techniques and modes of intervention he will need when he's called upon to talk to teachers and counselors in public schools and child care workers in day care centers.

Whittaker: The growth of the communty health movement has raised some question about the role of private residential treatment in the future. With so many private centers strapped for funds and smaller than public facilities, one wonders if there is going to be a continued need for private residential treatment of children.

Trieschman: Definitely yes. When discussing private residential treatment, the first topic is *funding.* Private residential treatment will still have an important claim to private charitable funds and continue to be a good investment for public funds that typically come to private residential treatment centers on a per capita basis primarily because of the role private facilities in general play in our society. Private treatment centers will continue to be ideal places for research and training. Large public institutions are always confined by the service requirements of the community. They can't be so selective about patients; they have to take the people who come to their doors; and they are usually staffed from civil service rolls, which means that they can't be so flexible about changing staff because they become committed to people on the basis of seniority and length of service. A private center whose staff want to try to work with a particularly difficult sub-group of children, can choose to accept only those children. Similarly, if they want to try a different way of treating a child's difficulties by introducing a new professional or if they want to experiment with a novel role, they can seek out people who have the desired kind of background or skills. They do not have to worry about eligibility lists. They can more easily develop innovative programs and study more circumspectly certain kinds of problems with more controls than could be achieved in a public institution, which must care for all the children in the community and is held to codified role descriptions and job descriptions and a civil service employment policy.

Whittaker: The residential treatment facility becomes, in effect, then, a kind of living laboratory that supplies the public treatment center with trained staff and innovative programs.

Trieschman: Yes, this is what has typically been the role of private agencies: they have filled needs that can't be easily filled by public agencies and they also have developed programs in small scale that can be useful to the large institution. Even economically one could demonstrate that it is less expensive to carry out that kind of research and development operation in a private setting than it is in a large public setting. This is true of other operations quite distant from mental health; the government chooses to farm out the development of a new rocket, because a private contractor can develop it less expensively than within the system.

Whittaker: Your thesis that private residential treatment is a catalyst for change and innovation has been borne out in fact in recent history in this country. The two theoretical models that perhaps have had the most impact on the field in general have been those developed in private residential treatment centers. I'm thinking of the model developed by Bruno Bettelheim at the Orthogenic School and the Life Space Model developed by Fritz Redl and David Wineman at their Pioneer House.

Trieschman: It's hard to imagine either of these models of treatment being spawned in a public hospital or in a state-operated detention center.

Whittaker: What do you think then should be the watchword for executives of private residential treatment centers at this time?

Trieschman: They must be carefully looking to their programs in terms of research, training, and service for the future. If they think that they can operate ten years from now exactly as they are today and if they continue to feel they can serve a small population well without awareness of what kind of transfer value their treatment has to other settings, residential treatment centers are going to be in difficulty.

One area right now that we all have to be working on very hard is the after care of our patients. What happens when these children return to the community can help us to learn how effective the ideas developed within a milieu are when the patients leave the milieu. This is also one of the ways that we can move ourselves into the larger community and make more relevant the concepts we have developed. Unless we begin to think about the implications of this question and start to work on them, we will lose our claim to public support and charitable interest.

Theory of Residential Treatment

Trieschman: Most people would dispute the idea that there is only one way to put into practice the theory of residential treatment. How might we develop a theoretical framework that would contain a complete description of residential treatment?

Whittaker: As of this moment there is no fully developed theory of residential treatment for disturbed children. There are quite clearly a number of different models in use across the country, each having its own advocates. One of the more deleterious effects of having this plurality of models has been that the person or agency seeking to open a residential treatment center has tended to look upon the theoretical framework that underpins the actual operation of the center as being something of an "either/or" proposition; that is, people have tended to talk in terms of "permissive" institutions versus those which stress "repression and self control." As one of the great writers in this field, Fritz Redl, has pointed out, permissiveness versus punishment is really a false dichotomy. Too often what we find in residential treatment is that an institution will begin with an erroneous idea of what permissiveness really means, interpreting it to be something a little to the left of absolute license in which, for purposes of catharsis and to resolve inner conflicts, children are allowed to express pent-up feelings and break up the furniture! This usually does not last very long before a system of complete repression and control sets in; under this model all of the resources of the institution would be geared to the goal of getting rid of noxious symptomatology. Behavior control becomes an end unto itself, often the only end; there is very little thought given to any kind of systematic approach to running a therapeutic milieu. Somewhere between these two models exists a kind of a "nonsystematic eclecticism:" people doing what they do simply because it works.

Trieschman: Very often one finds an institution swinging back and forth. After a period of repression and control, a new group of professionals will come in and tend to see all that was old as bad and begin to move very much closer to "permissiveness" or simply to overevaluate the ventilating of emotions. Permission, in the true sense, really implies that there is some structure that permits certain things to happen. There is no true permissiveness if everything is permitted. After the permissiveness (which has some sort of mystique because it's seen as the opposite of repression and control) fails, people who represent the old guard are empowered and the institution swings back toward repression and control again. The institution moves back and forth with more accommodation to the needs of the professional than to any real focus on the children's needs.

Whittaker: For example, one could take the efforts of some of the sociobehavioral theorists in the field today and put them at one pole, and at an extreme pole one might put the psychoanalytic group as exemplified by someone like Bettelheim. The point is I don't think the state of the knowledge, or the art, is such that we could attempt a complete synthesis of the two. But I do think that it behooves each camp—and also those of us in between—to pay attention to what the others are saying. I don't think that we can exist very much longer simply by setting up "strawmen" and then knocking them over saying that they don't fit into the same ethical framework.

Trieschman: This is exactly what happens, and people say either that all of psychoanalytic theory can be translated into behavior modification or all of behavior modification can be translated into psychoanalytic theory.

Whittaker: How would you describe, then, a working model of residential treatment that *does* take into account the different points of view that exist in the field?

Trieschman: If one starts with the need to change these children as the primary motivation and clear directive, he thinks of what will help effect the change—what he should "permit" or "repress," what techniques could be drawn from behavior modification, what techniques, skill, or understanding could be drawn from psychoanalytic theory.

Child Care Workers

Trieschman: Another polarity develops in residential treatment around roles in an institution. The medical people can be seen as the changers of children and the other people as mere attendants who take care of the rest of the time.

Whittaker: For "medical people" you could substitute social workers, clinical psychologists, really any professionals.

Trieschman: The kind of thing that most of us have encountered most frequently is the devaluation of the child care worker. This has been sufficiently belabored in my writing and that of a great many other people.

Whittaker: I would agree that more attention has been paid to the importance of the role of the child care worker in the past few years than in previous years, but in many circles professionals simply pay lip service to the idea that the child care worker is indeed the most important figure in the child's treatment. Simply because no one else wants to do it, child care workers have received the brunt of the task of working with emotionally disturbed children during the twenty-three hours of the day that they are not in therapy.

Whittaker: There is a fair amount of discussion about where the child care work fits into the professional bailiwick. Henry Maier has made the point that the child care work is a branch of social work. Others feel that the child care worker, following the European model of the *educateur,* really belongs in the field of special education. In short, there are simply 101 different answers to the whole problem of how you train child care workers. A number of academic programs have sprung up around the country in the past few years at the junior college level, the collegiate level, and even the graduate level. What is your feeling about all this? Do we really have an answer?

Trieschman: I worry about the way the question is very frequently put. It's always been, "Who would make a good child care worker?" "What kind of personality variables—MMPI profile or Rorschach protocol—would a good child care worker have?" "What would his background be?" I think the answer usually is that we work with who applies for jobs and can't quibble much about their basic personality unless there are two applicants. Refined selection techniques really only work when, for example, ten million persons are being inducted into the Army and they want to find which ones would make good espionage agents! We just don't have that kind of labor pool to draw from.

Trieschman: Another way the question often is asked is, "How could we professionalize the child care workers?" Child care work organizations are frequently debating this: "What kind of degree should we have, what kind of certificate should we have?" The answer to that question is that there are many different reasons for being in child care work, but if the pay scales are such that they won't sustain people who have a great deal of training and education, why do we bother to train and educate?

Whittaker: We are still not willing to match in salaries what we say the child care worker is actually worth to the treatment of the child.

Trieschman: How do we give some status to child care workers? They're called "therapeutic aides" or "counselors" or anything to make the role sound somewhat more professional. I don't think that elaborate selection techniques or degrees or terrific names for the role are what really will make child care work an important job. The only way to do that is by realistically discussing the tasks of child care work, specifying the functions. The functions should set the role description. What are the opportunities for intervention in the child's life outside of therapy? What are the alternatives that reasonable adults have to choose from to take advantage of the opportunities?

Whittaker: If we started with the idea that we could define the role of the child care worker by specifying his functions, we would ask, "How much decision-making power and treatment authority should the child care worker have?"

Trieschman: Yes, and now you're asking specifically how much decision-making power will be helpful to his operations with the child in the milieu, not how much decision-making power should he have to feel important in the system or how much decision-making power should he have to be called a professional?

I'm sure that medical doctors didn't attain their status by having someone say, "We'll give them a degree, or we'll tell the whole society it's an important role, or we'll put them in the right place on the organizational chart." They did it because they developed a network of skills, which is just another way of saying they developed some functions that were useful for their purpose, which was to alleviate suffering. Our purpose is to change children and so our functions have to be a network of skills and alternative actions that will take us towards that goal.

Whittaker: Yes, and there is something we should be doing on the organizational level to insure the child care workers that they will have salaries commensurate with their training.

Trieschman: We're going to have to attract them with real commitment to the importance of the tasks that they're doing, and in any culture one of the ways that is done is by paying good salaries.

Whittaker: Recent political campaigns have pointed out that there is literally no lack of idealism and manpower available on the college campus and among young people in general. A certain amount of public relations work will be necessary to tap this resource.

Trieschman: It's almost an ideal time to be trying to interest young people in working with children. The appeal of programs such as the Peace Corps and Vista and the concern the young people have with social action in general in this country is certainly not foreign to our interest in changing children and working with the "nitty-gritty" of their daily lives. People are going out to live in deprived areas of our own country and elsewhere; this type of motivated young person could be coming to work in the residential treatment situation. I know it's true that this idealism has some difficulties and some extremes and some emotionalism associated with it; despite these drawbacks it's certainly a very good beginning. My concern would be that if we talk only about status and selection, we will get some good people coming to our doors, but they will be very discouraged after six months or a year of working with us. They'll feel that they aren't where the action is.

Whittaker: There is another fault that should be laid at the door of the child welfare establishment. There is an old saying in social work that you couldn't wash dishes in a settlement house unless you had a master's degree, and the same thing is partially true of residential treatment. We simply do not have positions available for the young person who wants to try out the profession and see what's it's like. It's very hard for a person to get on-the-job experience and training in this field today.

Trieschman: Irving Goffman has written some interesting things about what happens to the self-concept of a mental patient who has lived for a period of time in an institution. More and more of him begins to be defined by the institutional structure. He sees that things are done more for the efficiency of the organization than for the change of the patients. It's a kind of deterioration of the self in an institution. One could do a parallel study of the progress of the self of a child care worker in an institution. A young person comes full of zeal and, perhaps, even too much idealism about how much children can be changed. Then he finds us suggesting that if a patient brings up a dream, he should not discuss it but should refer him to his therapist. We tell the child care worker, in effect, the most important thing is to keep the windows clean and the toys picked up and have the meals served on time. Not that these things aren't important, but he begins to wonder where the action is and begins to feel that he's not a part of it. He develops either a kind of institutional personality, as some patients do, where he goes along with the system, or else he begins to undercut it.

Communication Within the Institution

Trieschman: Typically, there is little real communication with the therapist and other professionals.

Whittaker: "Communication" is a rather ambiguous term. Everybody has a rather vague feeling that if we have a lot of it, it's somehow a good thing, and if we're lacking it, we had better be doing something about remedying the situation. What really counts is not the presence or absence of meetings, but some real thought and attention paid to *what gets said* and *who says it.* For example, to initiate something like a "gripe session" among your child care staff without really spelling out limits or purposes to such discussion can prove disastrous. We know this because we've tried it! The purposes of supervision should be spelled out almost in the same sense that we try to make clear to the children the treatment contract that we have with them. In many cases therapists have approached supervision of a child care worker in the same way that they approach therapy. I do not negate this model of supervision, but I think it should be made clear what the rules of the game are. So little has been written in this area and so little attention has been paid to it that in many ways we tend to hide behind rather glib statements and global generalities about how good it is to have people talking to one another, discussing the issues, and ventilating feelings.

Whittaker: Many institutions have operated on the assumption that staff meetings are strictly for professionals and the results of the meeting should be passed on to the child care worker. Others have felt that the child care work role is central to the organization and have invited the child care worker to the staff meetings. I don't pretend to have any single answer that will accommodate every residential treatment center, but these are problems that have to be solved. We have seen in our own organization that certain barriers can be set up by the fact of *who* gets invited to and excluded from the staff meeting.

Trieschman: There is always the problem with staff meetings that is parallel to the problems of supervision. We can either work on the "order-of-the-day" model, in which we get everybody together and pass out a prescription or have a kind of group therapy in which we tell how we feel about each other and how a child is getting to us and not getting to somebody else. Unless we are specific about *why* people have come together, they will digress from the work with the children and the meetings will become either therapy for the child care worker (which may be very profitable for him but may be relatively irrelevant to how well he's doing with the children) or a time for the worker to receive a list of things to do and not to do. Either way we lose the interest and motivation and sense of involvement of the staff. If the staff comes away from the meeting with a list, they say "Boy, I didn't get a chance to say any of the things that were really bothering me; all I got was a lot of plans for when my group can use the swimming pool or when we can go to the library or which bus we're supposed to use!" With group therapy for the staff the same kind of frustration is exhibited: "My goodness, all we did was talk about how Phyllis irritated everybody, and I don't think I know a bit more about what to do with Jimmy, and I'm not even sure I know what to do about Phyllis except that everybody else agrees with me; she's a pain in the neck!" A staff meeting that is mostly a gripe session is a rather unsatisfactory meeting for some of the staff. It is important to keep this in mind for supervisory conferences when some things can be taken up individually.

There has to be a compromise between the two extremes in meetings both for supervision and for staff. A certain amount of mechanical organization, order giving and prescription, is necessary to keep the environment organized; and a certain amount of the participation of the child care people might teach us a great deal about the children and how to work with them. The one thing that's required is that we keep some kind of balance.

A good rule is to keep channels of communication open at times other than formal supervisory times or staff meetings. Often the child care worker won't ask questions in the formal sessions but would while working with the children if he has some opportunity to have his questions answered or to share in the thinking about a particular child's behavior at that particular time. It would mean far more to him then than at a supervisory conference. An interesting finding in a recent study showed that the kind of supervisors that child care workers themselves tended to value the most were the persons who are either themselves involved in the life space treatment of children or those who had recently been child care workers.

Trieschman: This provides an opportunity for the child care worker to see how a person from the hierarchy—the director, the supervisor—would handle a situation and how he would talk to a child. Without that opportunity, the only person's work that is exposed to everyone elses eye is the child care worker's. Supervisors, directors, and even board people wander by and see him struggling with a child or trying to get a meal peacefully organized or trying to get a game started or dealing with a cursing angry child, but *no one* ever comes into the inner sanctum of the office and finds out what goes on in there. He feels it is only his work that is exposed, and exposure always means the possibility of criticism.

Whittaker: If we hold strictly to formal communication, we really lose the effect of all the communication the child has with those members of the residential treatment staff who are not seen in formal supervision. I'm thinking here of the conversations children have with cooks, truck drivers, and maintenance men. Often, to our chagrin, we assemble a staff of highly trained people whose major skill is being able to talk with children and we find that children gravitate to those members of the staff whom we hire to take care of the maintenance! This is a fact that has to be faced and is just one of the many reasons for including nonprofessional maintenance staff in the formal supervisory and communication structure.

Trieschman: This reminds me of the lament of therapists: "My patients sit in the waiting room and tell each other more significant things than they tell me when they come into the office!" If we provide loopholes in the environment, when children have particular weighty or troublesome thoughts in their heads and are fearful that somebody will overwork them if they tell them to the therapist or child care worker, they will begin to talk to the cook or to the maintenance men. Unless we have some way of including these people in our conversation, this valuable piece of information will be lost to us.

Introduction of New Staff

Whittaker: Many people involved in residential treatment centers have raised the question of how you introduce new staff into the therapeutic milieu.

Trieschman: Let's restrict our discussion to that specific point rather than talking about how to set up a whole training program. We should try to keep in mind two sets of variables when a new person comes into the environment to be a child care worker: one of them has to do with how the person fits himself into the group of children and the other on how he fits in with the group of other child care workers.

Whittaker: A typical method is for the child care worker to come in to observe the children and staff at work and ask questions for the first few days. But we tried this method at the Walker Home and found it somewhat ineffective.

Trieschman: The major difficulty we encountered was the completely "roleless" state that the person is in as an observer. He can be a problem to his colleagues who are busy getting children from school, to lunch, organizing games.

Whittaker: In the sense that they're in the way?

Trieschman: Yes, and the more experienced staff feel, "My goodness, why doesn't he help me, doesn't he see that this child needs a hand to get up to lunch!" The established child care worker may feel observed by the newcomer and feel mildly irritated that he's not doing something to help.

Whittaker: They also have something added to their task—the need to explain what they're doing.

Trieschman: Yes, one more person whom they have to remember and to whom they have to tell why they said this or why they said that.
This situation also somewhat shakes the children's impression of responsible adults—who care about them and help them—to have someone who seems to them somewhat short-circuited. They bump him, or they throw something at him, or they run by him in obvious disobedience to someone else and he says nothing! This strange being moved in practically like a Rorshach so that they have to project themselves on him to get something out. So he's at a disadvantage with the children.
The in-training observation method also poses disadvantages to a new counselor. Perhaps he feels either that he has to bite his tongue all the time because the things that he'd like to be saying or the things that he could be saying to get to know the children might put him into a position of being a critic of what other people have done. He is also reticent to ask staff why they said this or why they said that, something many people find difficult even after they know people fairly well but especially when they first come into an environment.

Whittaker: The new person probably feels a certain amount of embarrassment coming into a quite provocative kind of situation; the situation can be paralleled to walking into somebody's home in the middle of an argument.

Trieschman: I prefer the medical imagery to the home imagery. Sometimes a new counselor feels a little like someone who wandered into the operating room in a hospital and finds them short-handed and the patient in trouble. They sure wish they knew what they could do to help, but they just stand there afraid they're going to be in the way of a passed scalpel at some point!

Whittaker: Perhaps we might describe, then, the techniques that we have found helpful to alleviate this type of problem.

Trieschman: One of the best remedies is to discuss the problem openly with the new counselors. We would probably all agree that a certain amount of participant observation would be valuable to find out a little bit about the children, the rest of the staff, the institution, and the rules and regulations. There are these problems that come up, but what we've done at Walker Home is to discuss them openly with new and old staff. Most newcomers deal with this complexity of getting to know the children and getting to know the counselors by actually joining one group or the other. I've seen some new counselors come in and literally not have anything to do with the children except look at them and talk only to counselors and try to back away and escape any contact with the kids.

Whittaker: Yes, and spend a lot of time in the office reading records.

Trieschman: They read records and stay on the fringe of activities and try to align themselves with the adult group. The other group does just the opposite. They say, "Gee, I can't learn much that way," and they so completely join the children that they literally become like another one of the children. They come in and take off their coats and ties and roll up their sleeves and on the second day they dress in older clothes. Most of the time they sit on the floor excitedly playing a game so enthusiastically that it is hard to distinguish them from the children. They are really trying very hard to incorporate themselves into the child group.

The crucial thing, of course, is that they have to be a part of both groups because in true milieu treatment, the two operate very closely together. And it is no easy task to learn how to serve both. Presenting some of these problems helps the new counselor to see that there is a kind of role in between. We try to have them literally watch and participate with one counselor on a particular shift, a particular routine, or work with a particular child, so that they have an opportunity to emulate one person.

Whittaker: Almost like a big sister or big brother.

Trieschman: Yes, or a kind of senior counselor that you might have in an ordinary summer camp. We prepare them with some answers to the problems that we anticipate because they are going to be part of the broadening and helping environment right away. We know the children will ask them for special privileges and think they don't know the rules, so we literally teach a new person several ways to defer questions that he's not able to answer. For example, a child may ask for permission to go off campus to a neighborhood store; the new person doesn't yet know the institution's rules about that or what this particular child's problem is, but to avoid both antagonizing the child and getting into a "you-don't-trust-me" situation, we tell him to explain that he will have to check with the senior counselor.

Whittaker: I think a useful suggestion we've given new counselors is to say "I'm not really sure what the rule is on that point, but I'm going to ask you to come with me while I check that out."

Trieschman: I have never encountered the difficulty of having the new counselor become a carbon copy of the counselor with whom he works.

One other thing I should mention is that we have some particular life space duties that are important to the effective running of the milieu: care of the clothing, recess calling, working in the garden, and running activities. Some have to do with organizing the things and spaces in the environment; some have to do with programs in the environment. We found that it's very helpful to give the new counselor some specific tasks in the program with the children and to give him some specific tasks in relation to the care of the plant, equipment, and clothing. It's a very limited role definition but it helps to identify him to the children in relation to what he's doing in the milieu.

Whittaker: Each child care worker is identified with a particular activity, special skill, or something that is his speciality.

Trieschman: I think it helps him move into the system by helping to clarify the children's perception of him and also helps him to clarify his own role to himself. It's almost like a beginning kind of safe, limited role; a "piece of a role" that he takes on to help him move more comfortably in the environment. Otherwise we're in danger of having the children witness just another pair of eyes watching either to prevent them from doing something bad, or to mull over their problems. I've actually heard children say to a new counselor, "What are you looking at me for? Why do you keep watching me?"

Rules and Regulations

Whittaker: This raises another issue here: the whole question of personal requests, or direct appeals, versus institutional rules. Some professionals have been a little bit loathe to discuss the rules and regulations of an institution because of a connotation of something regimented and undemocratic. Anybody who is involved in the actual practice of residential treatment would agree that there have to be some rules that are indigenous to the institution, and I would submit that far from being a necessary evil that we must tolerate, the actual adherence to institutional rules can serve a very beneficial and therapeutic function. The new child care worker does not always have to rely on his own relationship with the child and say, "No, you may not do that, because I do not want you to do that." He doesn't always have to put it in the context of *me* and *you*. He can say, "This is a rule that applies to all the children, not just to you."

Trieschman: One of the ironies is that we talk a great deal about the importance of the relationship between the child care worker and the child; yet we sometimes put so many requirements on that relationship that we make it ineffectual. It is a little like taking too many problems to the United Nations: the international quality of the organization is destroyed by separation into individuals. The use of direct appeal with a child is a very helpful treatment variable and one that should be controlled. There are times when it would be undesirable to burden a barely growing relationship between a child and an adult, with the adult having to represent his own "book" of rules. It would be nice for him to be able to say "our setting requires you to do this, and this is a rule that all boys must follow."

Whittaker: We also get into difficulty sometimes by assuming that a relationship remains a somewhat static phenomena. It is, rather, an ever-changing variable, and for any number of reasons, an extremely positive relationship with a child might deteriorate in a matter of minutes during a particularly stressful time.

Trieschman: One obvious example of this is a young boy who happens to have a very strong relationship with a female counselor. In the course of a group activity with other boys, the game deteriorates and the counselor calls it to a halt. This is a very poor time for her to call on her personal relationship with a boy. The last thing he may want to do is to reveal the highly positive nature of this relationship in front of all the other boys. The last thing he wants to be seen as at that particular moment may be as the counselor's personal friend. It would be much better at that point to use some other appeal. Making all the rules of the institution into personal appeals actually prevents one from being able to use the relationship variable in a therapeutic fashion.

Whittaker: Fritz Redl has outlined in detail the variables that one would be wise to examine before trying to manage a particular behavior. One of the most crucial is the particular state of a relationship with the child at a specific point.

Punishment

Whittaker: Do you think it's more fruitful not to raise the question of "punishment" versus "permissiveness" but rather to talk about what form of punishment is contemplated in an institution?

Trieschman: Yes, it's more important to look at the form that the punishment takes, who administers it, how it is handled in the context of the milieu. The only real danger is to think that punishment is what controls kids and permissiveness is what gets them well. This means that every time we punish a child, we know we're doing it for expediency and control, and we wait breathlessly for the moment when we can permit in order to make him well. I think a reasonable human being requires both a sound ego and a sound super-ego. The ego is what modulates our behavior, makes it appropriate to our needs and to reality, produces our satisfactions and our competence; the super-ego is more often a "Thou shall and thou shall not" kind of thing. I think our only real requirement is that we make sure the super-ego kinds of processes work in conjunction with the ego.

Whittaker: Both kinds of responses are necessary for a correct job in child rearing. Parents certainly use a combination of the two.

Trieschman: Clarity of communication may be the more important thing to talk about. That is, the clarity of the message to the child may be more important than either punitiveness or permissiveness. There are times when a prolonged discussion about a particular naughty act is more uncomfortable for the child than a clear message of what was wrong with it and what the consequences of it were. In talking to children who have very fragmented egos, one of the sure things is that there isn't very much ego to talk to. If we structure our conversation with the child in such a way that we're saying, "Tell me what you think about it and what ought to happen next," we may put him into a most uncomfortable situation because we're asking him to negotiate when he doesn't have much with which to negotiate. One of the things that is false about many of the discussions of punishment is the notion that in punishing a child any real understanding of why he behaved the way he did is lost. That's not necessarily true. We only have to reflect on our own backgrounds or experiences with children in residential treatment to know that after a punishment, after a clear message that something was wrong, and after the consequences of it, a child sometimes does develop insights about why he did something or why something shouldn't be done. Insight and punishment aren't mutually exclusive processes.

Loyalties

Trieschman: The child thinks of himself both as "Johnny Walker Home" and "Johnny Smith," and he has loyalties and sets of expectations on his behavior that are somewhat different for the two groups. On many occasions he has to consider them together. For example, when a child care worker helps him read a letter from home or write a letter to home, there are many opportunities for commenting on differences or similarities between his identity as "Johnny Walker Home" and his identity as "Johnny Smith."

Whittaker: I've noticed that often children who are new to a residential treatment center exhibit a certain amount of surprise, puzzlement, and perhaps even some anger that the child care worker knows of some of the intimate details in his family life, not only the fact that he has a brother and a sister, where he lives and where he went to school, but also the fact that there were some problems in his family and these were some of the reasons he came into treatment.

Trieschman: Nowhere can the discomfort of split loyalties and responsibilities be more readily seen than when both child care worker and parents are present with the child on a visiting day. The child bumps himself and both the child care worker and the parents take a step backward instead of a step forward, each expecting the other to do something. It becomes a kind of an Alphonse and Gaskin situation when two people's concerns for the child meet. The thing that we have to be clear about is that within the residential treatment center, the child's directions and care are the responsibility of the child care worker. This does not exclude parents when they come to visit; it actually helps them to visit more comfortably. They know that while they're having coffee or visiting and talking to the teacher the child's safety is the responsibility of the staff of the treatment center. They know that the child-rearing functions are not suddenly turned over to the parents just because they happen to be visiting. However, I think it should also be clear that when the child care worker provides transportation to the child's home, the child care worker is not in charge of saying, "You ought to do this, or that." He doesn't control that environment.

Whittaker: We are spelling out the limits of responsibility both for the child's sake as well as for the parent's and the child care worker's.

Trieschman: That's right, we are being clear with the child about the beginnings and ends of these responsibilities and being clear with him that we understand his two identities (and I'm using the word identity rather loosely) and that he does care about two places, his home and the place where he lives. You acknowledge that it's even possible for him to like the two places or to be angry at the two places or to like one and be angry at the other. If we were not to make that clear, we might participate so completely in transference phenomena that it would be very hard to use them therapeutically. Unless it was clear to him that his parents and our staff were not identical, that there are two places and two sets of people who have been important in this child's life and continue to be important at different times, we could never talk to him about a distortion.

Whittaker: How true that this is a real issue with children! How often we've seen children who have gone home for vacation and have told parents how terrible the life in the residential treatment center is and how much they wish they were back at home, how they can't stand any of the staff and are having a terrible time; and then they have returned to the institution and said exactly the same thing substituting the word "home" for the word "institution!"

Trieschman: That's right. They will bad-mouth us to their families and bad-mouth their families to us. It's as though the child gets caught moving between two armies, and he has to pretend to be loyal to one when he's on one side and loyal to the other when he is in their camp.

Whittaker: As you point out, the child tends to view the question of loyalty in an either/or fashion—loyalty to family precludes loyalty to treatment center and vice-versa. It is necessary to legitimate to the child the fact that for the period he is in treatment he is a functioning member of two groups and will indeed have loyalties to both and will at times feel closer to one than the other.

Trieschman: If we are expecting this kind of thinking on the part of the child we have to make these explanations to our child care workers so that they do not feel themselves as competing parents or feel that any discussion they have with the child about home puts them in danger of criticizing the child or ask the child not to tell things at home about what happens at the residential center. The counselors must feel clearly that there are these two loyalties, these two identities, and that the child participates in both of them. Yet there are times when we really have to be urging one or another of the loyalties on them.

Whittaker: Could you give an example?

Trieschman: Yes, I think of the child who's getting ready to leave the residential treatment center. We have to have him beginning to think in terms of "Johnny Smith" who's going to live with the Smith family, rather than as "Johnny Walker Home."

Whittaker: At the same time, he may prefer to think of himself as remaining in the institution and not deal with separation.

Trieschman: However, at a point when a child is uncovering past traumatic experiences with his family, perhaps through acting them out with the staff, it is somewhat self-defeating to choose to translate all this into things that really happen at home and force him at that point to visit at home and deal with those issues in the home setting. At that time it is wise to help him see himself almost exclusively as "Johnny Walker Home" so that he can work out the problems in a somewhat more benign circumstance than the first time he faced them. Why buy into all the other troubles by forcing him to deal with both loyalties at the same time?

Whittaker: It's often a problem for the therapist or the caseworker to explain to the parents that visiting, at least in the beginning, should be on a somewhat irregular basis depending upon the progress of the child.

Trieschman: It is indeed a problem, and the parents often have another version of this same issue when they ask questions such as, "What time do you put him to bed? I want to put him to bed at the same time." "If you allow him to curse at you without washing his mouth out with soap, do I have to do that at home?" Parents try to erase the differences between home and residences, to make it all one thing. We should discourage that process.

Whittaker: In other words, they literally try to "solve" their problems with the treatment center's solutions.

Trieschman: They try to make some concrete consistencies between the home and residential treatment center. From the beginning everybody has to deal with the fact that this is another living situation for the child; that in itself will promote some discomfort on the part of the parents and the child. The discomfort is part of what gives us a base for treatment of the child. We can make no other contract with parents; home visits, vacations, and eventual separation are all going to be related to the child's progress in treatment as well as to the state of the family's treatment. Any other guaranteed amount of time is bound to work against us.

The Child Care Worker as "Therapist"

Whittaker: The child care worker in the residential treatment center often has an in-depth understanding of children's behavior and psychopathology, and the question frequently arises in the supervisory sessions as to how much they should apply this knowledge when the children raise direct questions.

Trieschman: Exactly how much depth of understanding, or interpretation to get into in the life space troubles a great many child care workers. Sometimes we suffer from the delusion that interpretation is a technique of control and if the child says something that we understand in terms of his background and his problem, what we should immediately say is, for example, "You only say that because you have trouble getting along with your mother," and that will end his problems. We all recognize that's naive and comes off as a hostile comment and has very little to do with behavior control. The problem for the child care worker is sometimes posed as a choice. Let me give an example. A child care worker is outside with a child. The child anxiously looks to the sky and asks, "Is that a hurricane cloud?" The child care worker has been at the staff meetings and knows that this child is very anxious and feels the world is coming apart around him, the danger comes from all possible sources, and his annihilation is imminent. The mounting fear and anxiety often drive him to a spiral of activity that is disruptive to the environment. The child care worker wants to know if he should say at that point, "No, that's not a hurricane cloud. I know you're worried about something, and I know you're afraid something terrible is going to happen, and you feel that way often." He wants to get into a kind of in-depth therapeutic involvement with the child, when what the child asked about was a cloud in the sky. Alternatively, the counselor can say, "No, it's not a hurricane cloud. Hurricane clouds look black," filling him with reality reassurance and thus hoping to allay the anxiety.

Whichever way the child care worker is advised, he begins to see that neither one of the alternatives is very effective. The child who is given repeated reality reassurances will ask a new version of the anxiety question —about locusts, or weeds, or dead trees falling. The child who is given only an in-depth understanding of his reasons for asking the question will express it again in a new set of concerns about the world and go away with insufficient information about the clouds and weather. We must help child care workers, perhaps even help ourselves, to understand how we can weave into our conversations with children some reality information and reassurance as well as some communications with the child of his anxiety. The weave has to take a particular form; an anxious child needs to *do something* with his own anxiety. We can get him participating in the search for knowledge about weather: reading weather reports in the newspaper or learning about different cloud formations or perhaps building a small weather station. We're giving him some activity other than antisocial acting out, as a means of dealing with his anxiety because he's not always going to have us around to reassure him about every possible event. We overlook a very restorative function of the milieu if we don't attempt to blend reality reassurances and reality information and connect them in the child's mind with a means for him to allay his own anxiety the next time.

Trieschman: What about the child care worker waiting to get the word on "what it all means" before doing anything about a situation?

Whittaker: We therapists probably should share a certain amount of responsibility for this attitude. For example, the therapist who gives an order to a child care worker to inform him immediately when a child misbehaves tends to disenable or emasculate the child care worker in the eyes of the child. The children are very perceptive of the organization in terms of where the power lies. If they think they're not going to get results from the child care worker, or if they feel in any way that he is not going to be powerful enough to protect them or control them or act in their best interest, they are going to push the system in whatever way they can until they deal with the person who *is* in charge, who *does* have the power. We have to tell our beginning child care workers that action is generally better than inaction. We are all going to make mistakes, but it is far better to act on the situation, if it is going to require some sort of intervention, rather than to wait for the counsel of the "experts."

Trieschman: Inaction *is* a kind of action that is quite clear to the children.

Whittaker: Yes, inaction is a denial that something is going on. If Johnny is standing on the furniture and the counselor is simply ignoring it, Johnny will escalate to something a little more potent until he catches someone's eye.

Trieschman: When something important is happening and something should be done about it, by all means some action should be taken, but taken quietly—the implication being that a response does not necessarily have to be something terribly dramatic.

Whittaker: The child care worker has to be sure that the administrator or the therapist will support the decision he makes or his uncertainty will work to the detriment of all patients involved. There will be occasions when the therapist or administrator might disagree so strongly with a particular course of action taken by a child care worker that he deems it advisable to change the course of action. But this can be done in such a way —involving both child care worker and the child, perhaps discussing it with the child care worker first—that it does not appear as the administrator undercutting the child care worker. We cannot present an absolutely consistent image to the child at all times. There is some educative value in any situation; the child can learn that all adults do not always act in the same way in the same situation.

I may have given the impression that every decision of the child care worker is subject to change, depending upon the view of the therapist or the administrator, but this is far from the case. Obviously, every institution has a body of rules and general precedents. For example, in most institutions physical agression between children or between a child and an adult simply is not allowed. Physical aggression on another person will be stopped in *all* cases.

Trieschman: Another false implication is that every decision needs a lengthy explanation and an insightful understanding before one can expect a child to follow a direction. This is more trouble than it's worth, and it's a terribly painful experience for children to have people requiring that everything be done on the basis of complete understanding. It's just too much to understand. There are some things that are done simply because that's the way it is; later, perhaps, the child can understand why these things aren't allowed and may even participate in making some of the rules. For example, children learn some of the function of rules in playing games and in being able to play a particular kind of a game that they like. They see the function of rules is not something imposed by some cruel tyranny, but is a functional necessity between people in order to do something.

Interpreting Behavior

Whittaker: You raise an interesting point here that reminds me of another problem we sometimes encounter. You raised the whole notion that each behavioral incident, or misbehavior of a child does not require a lengthy verbal working through of the issue. Sometimes a simple command itself may be all that is required. This raises the question of translating rather directly and literally terms from traditional fifty-minute hour psychotherapy into the therapeutic milieu, for example, calling every irritation the child causes us "countertransference."

Trieschman: Sometimes our explanations of children's motivations become overextended in the minds of the child care worker in the life space. I can think of one particular episode that I've seen occur many times, especially with new counselors. The new counselor comes into a room where two children are fighting; the fighting stops with the counselor's appearance and he spends a kind of desperate half hour trying to round up both children to have long conversations with them about what promoted the fight. He feels a failure if he is unable to do it. This somehow implies that children who are normal would not have a fight and that there is something so terribly abnormal about children having a fight that it requires delving into all the motivations of both parties. Usually the incident is over when the child care worker represents by his voice and appearance the rules of the institution—we don't hack each other up!

Whittaker: A problem can arise in a system that has good communication when a child's particular difficulty in a certain area becomes common knowledge to the entire child care staff. Do you think it might be a good rule now and then for the therapist or the administrator not only to pass on to the child care worker his view of *what* would be appropriate to say, but also some notions about *who* should say it and *when?*

Trieschman: Some things are important to have repeated to the child for a number of days and a number of times. To drop a situation that is particularly noxious for the whole environment prematurely gives the child the wrong picture of what's valuable to him and valuable to us. However, for most situations and most pieces of behavior, it's important to have some direction as to who should mention it and in what context they should mention it.

Whittaker: We've been concentrating a little bit too much on the negative aspects of this; that is, working the child over too much for a particular piece of noxious behavior. Over-enthusing with a child about a forthcoming pleasant event can also boomerang. I'm reminded of the child care staff who discussed at the staff meeting the importance of Christmas and Christmas vacation and so overworked the issue with the children that they packed their bags and were ready to go home by Thanksgiving—with three weeks left until vacation!

Trieschman: Too much excitement, too much depression, too much criticism can be produced by the repetition of messages again and again. Another problem, again in systems with good communication, is that the staff gets together and makes a very good generalization about some of the behavior they've observed among the kids in the cottage for the past week; they see it as much related to the fact that there an open house is scheduled and the children are worried about being put between their "Johnny Smith" self and their "Johnny Walker Home" self. So everything gets processed in terms of this one variable. Having an idea about what a pattern of behavior is connected to or what the mood of the group is, can sometimes be used too universally by the staff so that everything that happens, from a dropped knife at the dinner table to a misspelled word in school to trouble in falling asleep at night to a fuss with another child, is responded to as if it were a direct product of the upcoming open house.

Updating the Treatment Plan

Whittaker: It is important for the therapist or the person with the overall responsibility for the treatment of the child to make sure constantly that the treatment plan is kept up to date for the child care workers.

Trieschman: Some of our capacity to understand what a child is working on can backfire if we don't revise the plan often enough. If we don't have regular communication about the progress of the child in treatment, we can be thinking and behaving as if he is still a needy hungry child who just wants some more individual attention, nourishment, and special snacks from the people in the environment. In fact he is feeling comfortable enough in his environment and now wants something expected of him and is able to do something more, and yet we continue to see all his behavior in terms of "neediness" rather than in terms of his desire to take on new tasks.

Whittaker: Some of us still harbor the old misconception that the child comes to the residential treatment center with a Santa Claus bag full of problems and when he's worked on these he is "ready to leave."

Trieschman: If it were only true that a child came with a specified illness, that we understood it, could name it and apply the right medicine, then send him home, it would be a much simpler world. In reality, children come to us off the track of growth and development, stuck in some ways and with some particular symptomatic ways of maintaining their illness and being fixated in some way. Our reward for treating that illness, however, is often that the child grows and develops sufficiently to take on the next problem of growth and development that may be an extension of his self beyond; he goes from, "Will I get fed and can I trust anybody" to "How could I work together with a friend to do something?" "How could I go out to school?" "How could I be a leader of the group?" "How could I take on a new subject in school?" When he comes up against a new problem, he's never quite sure that it will be solved; he may show us again some of his old hangups, some of his old symptomatology, some of his old problems. That can be discouraging for the child because he feels that he really hasn't gotten any better or that he has gotten worse. The successes of his past accomplishments are set awash by the new problem.

Whittaker: It's certainly an embarrassment to the child care worker to feel his efforts have failed; he must have done something wrong; Johnny's not cured after all, he's worse than when he started!

Trieschman: When the child's own discouragement is matched by the staff's discouragement, the child's willingness to take on the new task is diminished. There will always be new tasks because we're working with children who are growing and for whom the world has increasing expectations in terms of school accomplishments, self-control, and behavior. They're always going to be taking on new problems. One has to see this, and it's especially important that this knowledge be carried into the life space because that's where the symptom exacerbations of the old problems are going to return. The people in the life space, the child care workers, must understand that though the child may be experiencing some of his old issues and old behaviors, they can help the child understand that he's working on the right new problem.

Whittaker: Don't you think, too, that it's the function of the director, the therapist, or the person in charge of the overall treatment to keep a "weather eye" on the "horizon" and watch for situations that are going to occur in the child's immediate future that might signal a regression to some earlier behavior? Under ideal circumstances he can prepare the child care staff and they can prepare the child for the problem that he is about to face.

Trieschman: I agree with that so much that I tend to think of it as almost the key element of communication. The psychotherapist must inform the child care worker when the child has gone on to a new area of development or has given up an old symptom, an old way, an old habit that he has relied on but is not yet sure of his new more mature way of doing things. It is especially important for the psychotherapist to forewarn, if he can, or at least explain very quickly when it appears to the child care staff that though they still need to control the return of the old behavior and deal with it within the context of the rules and traditions of the institution, they need to help the child to see this as a worthwhile struggle, that perhaps he could even struggle with the problem a better way this time around. Otherwise, I think we have the possibility that the child care staff will respond to the return of the old behavior or old symptom exactly as they did the first time, and it will appear punitive to the child and he'll decide that the new struggle isn't worth anything. He may completely give up attempting to master the new task.

Whittaker: The general lesson we learn as administrator-therapists is that we cannot simply enjoy the luxury of reconstructing developmental task behavior. We must always be looking ahead and trying to predict some of the problems a particular child in treatment will face and make sure that the child care staff is aware of our hunches.

Trieschman: Some of our successes with youngsters in psychotherapy will appear in the life space as nasty side effects. It's as though the medicine we give has troublesome side effects. It's a problem that has a parallel in individual treatment: when a child becomes less withdrawn, he may be more angry and assertive than his family is prepared for. It is often not smooth and easy to live with, a "new way" of trying things which is characteristic of growth and development in children. No parent would decide to limit a child's walking because it was going to cause a problem, but in the process of taking his first tumbling steps in a new direction a child does not walk very steadily and he leans on things, tips things over, and knocks down furniture. Fortunately we can't persuade children not to walk because walking has so much intrinsic pleasure for them, but trying new developmental tasks often produces rough edges in the child's general behavior and level of anxiety. Thus, the long-term view of what a child in residence is going to be like is extremely important for all to know to avoid creating discouragement every time there is a regression. The goal of the milieu is not to take in children who are very troublesome and expect they will be less troublesome the second day and even less troublesome the third day and by the 365th day they will be 365 units less troublesome. It's very possible that they may be less troublesome for the first two weeks than they will be for the second two weeks, and we may have a very good period in which a great deal of growth and development is going on, but when a new task is taken on we may see the return of troublesome behavior and difficulties. It's not a smooth descending course from intake to discharge but more a period of "ups and downs" and the therapist–administrator must make it one of his primary tasks to look at the troublesome periods, to find if they are, in fact, genuine regressions or failures of treatment or if they are, in fact, discomfort and trouble over progress.

Program Activities

Trieschman: We must consider the importance of activities in a therapeutic milieu. Activities are the stock and trade of the child care worker and the medium in which he builds his relationship with the children. Play activities and programs are called by some the primary meeting ground between the child and adult in the milieu. Obviously they are going to have a great deal of importance in all the interactions that go on between the adults and children. Programs and activities are *not* time killers; they are not for keeping children busy until they get to therapy; they're not for tiring them out so they won't show us their nasty symptoms; they're not muscle-building, or educational games. They are the real substance of the most meaningful interaction between children and adults in the therapeutic milieu.

Whittaker: Redl and Wineman made the point, which we re-emphasized in our earlier work,[1] that activities really should be looked upon as *full-fledged therapeutic tools* and not simply time fillers or diversions.

Trieschman: Once that is clearly established, the subject of activities becomes an important area to discuss. How to select from the whole range of possible activities: group activities, individual activities, "bouncy ones," "quiet ones," and individual versus team games. How to select activities for the mood of the group, the time of the year, the time of the day, the kind of ego-functioning available to the children for whom the activity is being planned—these are all important facets of the subject. Games and activities are also mediational processes for a particular child with a special problem. The child who is smaller than his peers and for whom a great deal of his fantasy about his own anger and his own fear have been attached to his body image and his sense of smallness and inadequacy can derive real therapeutic benefits in finding that in some games small size is a great advantage. The child who learns to play fancy hand games (perhaps finger puppets or cat's cradle games) often finds that they are both more socially acceptable and a more comfortable outlet for the energy that he had previously spent in manneristic motions and movements. Thinking about activities for individual children is valuable.

Whittaker: For years, social group workers have been talking about the therapeutic use of activities and the subtleties of using activities therapeutically with individual children. Unfortunately, they have been talking mostly to each other, and the impact of social group work has been rather limited. Until recently the use of activities as a clinical modality has been considered to be an ancillary form of treatment rather than something that is expected to have a lasting effect upon the child.

Trieschman: To use a game effectively requires more than knowing how to play, some diagnostic skills and clinical judgement about situations and children and events are also necessary.

Whittaker: Almost 20 years ago Erikson reminded us that activities or games or play for children represent a step forward into a new world, for the adult recreation or play or activity represents a respite from the work-a-day world. A child's world is *really* a world of play; therefore, if we are to intervene in that world effectively, we must know something about the activities that are meaningful to him. Then we will be able to work in this medium.

1. See: "Program Activities: Their Selection and Use In A Therapeutic Milieu" in A. E. Trieschman, J. K. Whittaker, L. K. Brendtro, *The Other 23 Hours: Child Care Work in a Therapeutic Milieu.* Chicago, Aldine Publishing Co., 1969.

Trieschman: In some ways the view of play that's been brought to the therapeutic milieu has often been the useful view that in part points out the importance of play in understanding the child's thoughts. What kind of house the child draws, his kind of doll-house play, the way he runs the toy cars around the blocks are diagnostically important because they tell us something about what he's thinking and feeling; play is his way of communicating. There is no doubt that this is an extremely helpful means of understanding "where the child is at," so to speak. It's a short-sighted view of play, however, when it is extended to the total living situation. We can end up viewing all the play activities of children as helpful diagnostic hints about what is going on in their affect life and in their fantasy life. We can say, "Gee he's building a house and the house has no windows and so it's important for us to note this child's sense of either being enclosed or wishing to be enclosed." But this view of play robs us of our opportunity to help play become a trial solution for the child, an attempted way out of an emotional bind. The child who tells a fantasy story or plays a game about the burial of an animal is not only revealing to us that he's worried about a death in the family; he is also taking some remedial action. He is, in fact, trying to find new ways to think about it and to deal with it. If we remember the significance that play has in helping us understand what's going on in a child's mind, we can begin to see that play activity can be a form of remedial action that allows for growth and is not only a time filler or a diagnostic tool.

Privacy

Trieschman: "What about the importance of privacy?" is a frequent question. It's a legitimate question to ask when talking about group situations for troubled children who have difficulty living together, going to school together, and playing together. Sometimes the debate about privacy including avoidance of publicity in residential treatment does take on a civil liberties quality, but I prefer to think of it in terms of acquiring skills needed to be fully human, one of which is a capacity to deal with solitude. We should view "being alone" as a desirable state for some kinds of activities.

Whittaker: Too often we've overemphasized the inability of the youngsters to deal with other people and have tended to underemphasize their ability to be alone with themselves, to handle solitude. So, we may spend a great deal of time teaching children to be with others and spend precious little time teaching them to be by themselves.

Trieschman: Solitude is a necessary condition for some kinds of activities, whether it's reminiscing or practicing school work or thinking through a problem. It's a condition one has to be able to endure. Character-disordered children are more frightened of solitude than of being with other children, because they thrive on the world of stimuli around them and the manipulation of it. We do little to teach a child how to view solitude as a necessary asset.

Whittaker: Much of the child's day in a residential treatment center is spent in the company of others. He sleeps and eats with other children, attends school in a group situation, and his play usually involves other youngsters; in addition, there are usually a number of helpful adults around—the child care staff, the therapist, the administrator, maintenance people. A child in a residential treatment center *seeking* privacy is confronted with a rather difficult task.

Trieschman: Because all this "groupiness" exists in the residence, we do very little to teach the youngster how to use privacy, how to deal with solitude. Privacy is usually punishment. A child has been disruptive and put in his room, something has gone wrong and we've put a child on the couch away from other people. We have to be very careful that this isn't actually creating problems rather than solving them. I am not saying that taking a child away from a group ("antiseptic bouncing" is what Redl has called it) is not a good technique. But we also have to help children to find productive uses of being alone so that being alone does not become the equivalent of "I'm bad, no good, punished, inadequate." At times when it would be easier for us to deal with children one at a time—for example, first thing on waking up in the morning—we can help children to use their time alone productively and interestingly; we can teach them games to play alone; we can provide them the materials to write something or make something. We must provide quiet niches or places within the physical spaces in our building or on our campus that a child himself can choose to use when he would like to be out of the group. Sometimes a child misbehaves in a group situation because he doesn't know any other way to change the state of affairs. None of us are always pleased to be in a crowd, and we have the freedom and capacity to choose to be alone. We can help children to learn to choose that alternative.

Whittaker: Often children, especially new children, question the child care worker about the practice of keeping records. "Why are you writing down what we've done?" "Are you only writing down the bad things?" "Who is going to see this?" They may comment on the record keeping as an invasion of privacy.

Trieschman: We make no secret of our recording, we need think up no devious explanations of why we do it. Our reasons for doing it are to communicate to each other about the children with whom we're concerned and whom we're helping, and this is a perfectly good reason to give to children. It must be clear that this is *not* a demerit record only; it's also a merit record.

Whittaker: We're noting the positives as well as the negatives.

Trieschman: Yes, but it's not a report card in which we balance out positive and negative, either. It's a way in which we communicate with each other. I have heard of places where older children were actually allowed to write their own comments on what they did for the evening. This is not a bad thing to do.

Whittaker: What a child brings back with him from the outside, perhaps from a trip to the store, or from his public school class or from a visit to home often causes a problem within the area of privacy. He will return with a closed parcel or a shopping bag and will announce to the group in general, "I've got something from home and it's mine and it's private and it's none of your business."

Trieschman: Well, it's a touchy problem; for some children a good deal of *who they are* is in their possessions, which represent extensions of themselves. The child who *needs* to hide or make mysterious what is his is telling us something. He's saying that he needs more privacy than he's been able to have, and we must take that as a clue and provide for him in a constructive way. His very statement is baiting us; he's saying, "This is mine and nobody can touch it." This means a terrible invitation to the other kids to try to find out what it is, to the staff to feel that it contains some dramatic mystery that may prove very troublesome if they don't find out about what it is. Although such a situation bears looking into, interpreting it as an issue of privacy; a child's need to have something of his own can cause more trouble for the child. He begins to buy himself friends with that bag, which turns out to have candy in it, and makes half-enemies and half-friends, causing him more difficulty.

Whittaker: Privacy also becomes an issue when people other than the child care staff—for example, visitors who come to see how the program is run—enter the milieu. Often we have noticed a dramatic effect upon the children when we announce that a visitor is coming, often marked by periods of what I would call "instant regression" and a tremendous tendency to show the "bad" aspects of the self. The children suddenly seem to feel very much exposed and threatened.

Trieschman: A profound announcement about visitors, making a very dramatic thing about their coming may communicate to the children a certain amount of anxiety on our part about how we are going to look to the visitor, whether it's a board person or a professional colleague.

Whittaker: In the beginning we often made the mistake of "overexplaining" who the visitors were and why they were there, when actually many of the visitors were coming to see a specific individual or consult with the staff and would have no contact with the children. There is also a wide range of people who arrive daily and could be placed under the heading of visitors: milkmen, electricians, and service people. One must look at the kinds of contacts the visitors are actually going to have with the children, and he must somewhat modify the introduction with this in mind.

Trieschman: Yes, I remember very vividly my early days in residential treatment, when I felt that I not only had to explain *who* each visitor was, but to state carefully that he was a friend of mine. I was probably saying, "Please don't be threatened by the visitor;" then I would try to diminish the threat by saying he was a friend of mine, and I'm a friendly person so he would be friendly to the boys! A much more sensible, realistic, but still protective way to introduce the visitor is to explain the limits of his visit, the limits of his role and function on campus. ("He came to see the secretary about repairing the typewriter.") The limitations contain more realistic safety and diminution of threat than any long-winded explanation to the child that tends to raise his anxiety. What to tell the children about visitors must be seriously considered especially in a residential treatment facility that has a training or demonstration program, with occasions to have visitors who want to come to see the program. The general rule at Walker Home has been that it is a place that people like to come to visit for a variety of reasons. The Walker Home is still for the boys who are living there, and we don't take visitors to some places, such as the boys' bedrooms, without their permission. There are ways to have visitors without the child feeling that the place is no longer his place to live and play and work on problems.

Whittaker: One of the most effective techniques is to have children assist in the tour of the property.

Trieschman: This must be optional to the child because some children love to be guides and other children really don't like to have any contact with visitors.

Whittaker: In one sense, too, success breeds problems in this area. A well-known and successful treatment program will precipitate requests to visit the facility from various professional groups, board members, and students. It helps to have one person responsible for scheduling so that three groups do not arrive on the Monday morning after a weekend when the kids have all been visiting home!

Living Space

Trieschman: In thinking about the desired spaces for a residential treatment center, one must have ways of separating a certain amount of administrative traffic from the actual life space of the children so that the children's living room is not the same place where a salesman would stand to wait to see the bookkeeper. This is a problem that more than one center has experienced in the process of growing and changing from a building that was never intended for residential treatment to a residential treatment center. It is also necessary to have reasonable ways for people to observe processes without having to stand in the classroom or game room. A kind of openness would be desirable because child care staff are going to be working with groups of children, and having everything off a series of hallways, around corners, down corridors, or upstairs creates a difficult space to supervise. I do not mean "supervise" only in the sense that the children can be watched all the time (though obviously being able to see adults around will offer some assistance to their control functions of the ego) but also so that adults are accessible visually to a child who wants something. Although openness for supervisability and accessibility to people in the environment is desirable, too much openness would allow an upset in one activity to spread automatically to the entire environment, "instant contagion." There's undoubtedly more than one design or architectural solution to the problem of having *openness and accessibility* as well as *separation* of areas. If we want the children in our care to learn about group living and also about dealing with solitude, we must have both kinds of spaces available. We must have places where groups of children can comfortably get together, play group games, have discussions; and we also have to have spaces where children can be comfortably alone.

Readings

Introduction

What follows is a series of selected readings in the area of residential treatment organized under the several headings: What is Milieu Therapy? Individual Treatment in a Therapeutic Milieu, Group Treatment in a Therapeutic Milieu, The Nature of Cottage Life and Strategies for Therapeutic Interventions, Staffing and Personnel in a Therapeutic Milieu, The Place of Activities in a Therapeutic Milieu, and Working with Families. These areas are of key importance to the field of residential treatment but are clearly not exhaustive.

We were constantly torn between the desire to be inclusive and the realities of the space limitation imposed upon us by publication requirements. Consequently, areas of great importance to residential treatment, for example the school program, are left virtually untouched. In some cases, as with behavioral modification, we felt that other collections had already adequately covered such areas, in others we can only hope that further volumes will be compiled.

At times we included articles because of their seminal influence on the field; clearly, the works of Bettelheim and Redl on the nature of milieu therapy would fit this category. At other times, we sought articles that would have a special interest for those involved in the day-to-day work of caring for children in a therapeutic milieu; Appelberg's article on the care of the physically ill child in a residential treatment center and Churchill's article on prestructuring group content provide examples of this latter type. Other papers were chosen because of their utility in staff training and others because of the particular view they present of the therapeutic milieu; Garland and Kolodny's article on scapegoating and Polsky's paper on delinquent subcultures would be examples of the former and the latter.

After a certain point, space (or the lack thereof) became the only important variable, and we were forced to leave out many papers of considerable merit. This section of the book is meant to be read according to interest, and it is our hope that having sampled the fare, the reader will return for a more complete helping.

PART ONE
WHAT IS MILIEU THERAPY?

1.   Introduction to New Staff

GUSTAV JONSSON

To you who are a newcomer to the Children's Village, welcome! This welcome comes from the adults in the village, not from the children. For most of our children you are a very suspect person. From them you will meet with open scorn and concealed suspicion. This greeting will probably meet you: "Who are you, you old bitch?" Or, "Who is that bloody bastard?"

And that is the way it is. You are an old bitch or a bloody bastard. These children have their reasons for saying so, for that is the experience they have had of adults, and you are an adult. In the Children's Village we have only emotionally disturbed children, who have suffered in their earlier surroundings, due to the treatment they had from adults. That is why they came here. The Children's Village is not the place for normal children but, as it is called in official language, a home for neurotic and emotionally disturbed children.

That the children have suffered does not mean that they all have had a poor, overcrowded home, that they have had drunkards as fathers and negligent mothers. There are also children in the village coming from socially acceptable homes, but in all cases their emotional life has been disturbed because they have not received the security which they need. This is not said as an accusation against parents or others who have taken care

Reprinted with permission of the author in personal communication to the editors.

of them. It is not always so easy to have to do with children, not even when they are one's own.

There Are No Evil Children

From the first moment in the Children's Village you will have to understand that unhappy children are not usually romantically pale with sorrowful faces and shy, quiet manners. This is false romanticism. In the Children's Village you are in the world of reality. Here you find unhappy children who express their longing for understanding and tenderness in a language which is natural to them: swearing and pestering and using foul language, kicking and punching and stealing, playing truant, bad table manners, sex talk, smoking and boasting.

There is a "true story," psychologically true, about Mr. Average Swede. On his way home from a drinking party one beautiful spring night he passes a park in Stockholm where the cherry trees are in full bloom. Mr. Swede's heart is filled with joy and emotion in the presence of the Beauty of Nature. He grasps a lovely spray of blossoms exclaiming: "Are you blooming. . ." and then becoming embarrassed by his own emotions, he continues the sentence as a true Swede: "Are you blooming, you bloody cherry tree?" Remember that story sometime when you meet a child in the village who greets you: "Hello, you old bitch!"

You will have to understand from the beginning that expressions of sympathy and desire for contact in the Children's Village may take unusual forms both in words and actions. "I like you, will you be my friend?" might very well be expressed by curses and a blow in your stomach. The question is if this method of expression is not often a guarantee for the genuineness of the emotion.

Anyway, you will have to understand that it does not do to dismiss these children as evil or foul-mouthed. The first commandment in the Children's Village thus reads: "There are no evil children."

In the Children's Village you will find not only aggressive, noisy, and destructive children, but also shy, anxious children. These I do not need to say much about. You will like them in any case. But the longer you stay here the more clearly you will see the truth in our basic principle: that the difference between an abandoned, weeping boy and an impertinent, swearing blackguard is only on the surface.

Are the children allowed to do as they like? Do we not bother about the children swearing? Do we think it is desirable that they let off steam by swearing, fighting, stealing, and breaking windows? Should children be allowed to do as they like?

No, and again no!

Let me once and for all underline this sentence: *In the Children's Village the children are not allowed to do as they like*. I know that it will not help much to say this, because for the next thousand years of the existence of the Village it will be the popular opinion, anyway outside the Village, that in it there is a crazy doctor and other blue-eyed idiots who believe that children must do as they want if they are to be happy.

The thing is that the children simply do not know what they want. Typical for neurotic children is that they are dominated by conflicting impulses, both to do and not to do a single act. This rule might apply to all of us, because the real motive behind our behavior in important matters is very often determined by subconscious factors hidden from ourselves. That this deep truth is concealed from so many of us is due mainly to our well-developed ability to rationalize, to find a motive after the act has been done. What really determines our behavior is often emotion and not reason. Because the children do not know what they want, or both want and do not want a thing, it is clear that they often get into a serious dilemma if we let them continue. They will develop guilt feelings for what they have done, and try to get away from these feelings by continuing their behavior; and then the vicious circle is completed. To let off steam in a psychological sense does not mean to act in a way that was earlier forbidden. The emotion that follows the act is psychologically the main point. If that emotion is fear, the child's condition will be worse if he "acts out." The theory that children shall be allowed to do what they want is a simplification to the point of absurdity. As a popular notion it is crazy. It has never been postulated by any of the prophets of so-called "free education." It has been invented by the slanderers of the Children's Village, and we decline it with thanks!

The Chinaman's Fatal Mistake

Once upon a time there was a boy in the Children's Village who became annoyed at the many foreign visitors who walked around in the Village to have a look at us. He reacted by writing a satire. It dealt with a Chinaman visiting the Village who only understood Chinese, and thus he was subject to a little misunderstanding. He thought that the children were the staff and the adults were patients. In his report on his travels he described very colorfully how the staff, by all possible means, tried to arouse the patients from their apathy and get them to be active. The patients went around in their kitchens, cooking and cleaning. The staff poured syrup in their hair, threw eggs in their ears, smothered their pancakes with pepper, and emptied the garbage can into their soup. But the patients only continued in their morbid apathy.

We might learn something from this story. It illustrates a rule discovered in other institutions where an attempt has been made to treat neurotic children according to psychoanalytic principles. The rule says that passivity from the adults is wrong, because the children experience this passivity as *apathy* and *lack of interest* in them. Everybody knows that the most infernal method of making people helplessly enraged is to keep cool, calm, and collected when they swear and rave. In Sweden it is known as the *"wife-tormenting method."*

No Laissez-Faire System

It is thus no use standing looking at the children when they are breaking windows and tearing down curtains. There are some dangerous people who have read a little modern psychology and got the idea that one should not intervene. *This is not psychology, it is quackery.*

No Saint's Halo

The quack treatment will result in giving the child guilt feelings, and provoke his anxiety through your going around like a saint, patient and submissive. Such a saintly attitude might be ennobled to a therapeutic attitude if account were also taken of the feelings aroused in the child, perhaps to speak to him about his feelings, explain, understand, and thereby have a calming and reassuring effect on the child. But this needs good insight in analytic therapy and cannot be practiced in a small house with many children where each of them needs different treatment. To act the saint in everyday life is, in psychological terminology, to have a masochistic attitude and testifies mainly to a neurosis in oneself.

No Martyr Halo Either

In child guidance work a certain kind of mother is sometimes met with, the so-called martyr-mother. It is she who says to her child: "How can you behave like that to your mother who is so kind to you and has given up so much for your sake." There is a male variant, too, the martyr-father, who sacrifices everything so that his son may enjoy what he desired in vain out of life. These parents are themselves neurotic and their parental love is unsound. In the Children's Village this sort of thing does not fit in.

We do not expect thanks from the children. You win nothing demanding gratitude. Should gratitude be of any value it must come spontaneously, and not be forced. As I said before, these children as a rule have no reason to feel gratitude toward adults, considering the way we have arranged conditions in our society for them.

No Detailed Advice

Now what shall a poor inexperienced girl do with these difficult children? What is to be done when the children do not eat, do not want to go to bed, smash windows, steal, play truant, kick and scream? That is what people ask in the papers, after lectures, in letters, and so on. You too. But from us you will get no answer. We cannot answer that question. And that is of fundamental importance. One shall not be able to answer that question.

There is no patent advice for every particular situation. Children are so unlike. One child rejects food for one motive and another does it for quite another reason. It would then be wrong to treat them both according to the same prescription. It is the same with the window breaker and the child who is cruel to animals, the thief, or any of the other types we welcome to the Children's Villlage.

You will be forced to try to understand every child and his particular problems before you can handle him correctly. That is not learned in one day, and it is not meant to be. You must, however, grasp from the beginning that it is necessary to know a great deal about a child's earlier life to be able to understand him. Then you will see the truth in the French proverb: to understand is to forgive.

It is intended that you shall gain this knowledge about the children as individuals by attending the evening conferences and house and school meetings which are held regularly each day or every other day. There you will have a chance to discuss what you should have done when Tom did so and so or Bill behaved in some other way. Such questions can possibly be answered or at least discussed.

Learn to Know Yourself

It is not only the children who are crazy in their own way. Even we adults are different. We too all have our particular craziness. When you work with children in a place like the Children's Village you will discover that both the sweetness and the horror of this job are that no one gets off scot free. Whether you want it or not, an upheaval occurs in the depth of your soul. We all have our inhibitions and our complexes (mikos), and when we observe children who, unpunished, can do what we ourselves once wanted to do, but were not allowed to, it will provoke a very special agitation inside us. When we see a boy openly smoking it will awaken old memories about how we wanted to smoke as children but dared not. Still worse is to experience children who spoil food, dirty themselves all over, use exhibitionist sexual language, or do something else connected with past desires and impulses within us which we, normally enough, have learned to control.

You will also find that there are certain children you cannot stand and others you will love very much. Observe that your colleagues feel sympathy or antipathy for quite other children. Even this is connected with impulses and needs within ourselves. By observing your own reactions and contemplating them you increase your self-knowledge and acquire living psychological knolwedge beyond books and gray theories.

Debutant Illness

Many small emotional waves may become a great storm. There is usually a delay, an incubation period of a few months, before the symptoms appear. Then you will get one of two variants, an extrovert or an introvert type.

Those who get the introvert form will say something like this: I will not do, I am not fit for this sort of work. Tiredness and sleeplessness and attacks of weeping are among the symptoms.

Those who get the extrovert form will say something like this: The ideas of the Children's Village and this foolish doctor are mad, it cannot go on like this. There must be some order. No human being can stand this.

In the first case, the criticism and agitation are directed against one's own ego, in the second case one's feeling of insufficiency is projected onto the surroundings.

This is not of course the basis of all criticism of oneself and the ideas of the Children's Village. There are good reasons for criticizing both yourself and the Village; but you must find your way to a realistic criticism, not a feigned criticism.

For obvious reasons the treatment of debutant sickness will not be dealt with here. It calls for individual sessions with someone either within or outside the village who understands psychotherapeutic methods.

What I want to say is that one shall not immediately condemn either oneself or the Village as inadequate. That is why I mention the illness. It is an occupational disease in the Village and similar institutions.

Be Yourself

Thus to do a good job in the Village one must learn to know the children and to know oneself. Then everything goes of itself. One cannot give general advice on how to stop a boy breaking windows or what to do with a girl who is continually stealing. In these cases everyone has to find his own melody. If you want to ask advice, you certainly may do so. But do not try to run away from the strain of feeling your way and thinking out your problems yourself. For some it is natural to show his feelings openly and directly to the children. For others a quieter manner may be more natural. We reckon that there is a Happy, a Quiet, a Shy, and perhaps a Crazy among us in the Village.

To Feel Lice on Your Own Skin

For those who want to learn mental child care the Children's Village has something to give which cannot be read in books. That is why we consider it important that the students should have at least one month practical work in a house. Nobody knows what lice mean without having felt them on his own skin, and nobody knows what problem children mean before having felt them.

This is what happens. One comes to the village, has read a little about modern child psychology, listened to lectures, participated in study groups, and so on. That is all very well. But there is one important lesson remaining. You wake up one morning feeling bad. Your head aches, you are tired, want to cry. The discomfort is creeping under your skin. The children are rowdy. You do something which is contrary to everything you have read in your books or heard at lectures. You lose your temper, scold a child or grumble at everything, burst into tears, or do something which you later consider absolutely wrong. In the evening or the next day, perhaps a moment later, comes the morbid paleness of reflection.

This experience is precious. Then one knows something more and something very important on how a mother and father of a problem child may feel, or his teachers or someone else who lives in daily close contact with such children. For everyone who will be working in social guidance clinics, visiting homes as a social worker, and so on, it is necessary to know how it feels for those one tries to advise. All this is well-meant advice on showing more patience or more tenderness and affection toward the children seems rather meaningless and even cynical if one cannot at the same time give the mother or father or teacher strength to follow the advice.

One might add that nobody really knows what enuresis means who has not had to make the bed of a bed wetter, or what encopresis is who has not had the job of washing soiled pants. Anyway, one learns to understand the mothers better.

Do Not Scold the Mothers

Much of the contact with the parents goes over the telephone. They often ring up the house parents, mostly to complain or criticize, seldom to thank or praise. It is psychologically instructive that these complaints very often come from parents who have themselves been criticized for neglecting their children or have been considered unfit to take care of them. It is only human to try and cancel out this criticism by criticizing others who now have the care of their children. That is why their criticism sometimes is unreasonable and out of proportion. You will have to take it calmly. It is part of our job to be criticized and slandered.

Our good neighbor, the director of the Hammagarden reformatory school, once played "red Indians and Whites" with his boys. In the course of the game the boys captured their director, bound him to a tree, and danced their war dances around him. Next week the rumor went around

that at Hammargarden the director ties the boys to the trees in the forest
and whips them. The director's comments on this rumor was the only
correct one: "Well we have our job and our salary so that this sort of
thing may be said about us."

Do not, then, take it as a personal insult, and become bitter, when unjust
accusations are directed at you by the relatives of the children or others.
There is a good rule for answering complaints on the telephone. In simple
language: let people bark until they have finished. In psychological terminology: let them discharge their emotions. One shall not contradict, not
discuss, just keep silent and take it.

When Lightning Strikes

It sometimes happens that lightning strikes. Houses may be set on fire,
animals be burned to death, all kinds of accidents may occur. It is very
unfortunate, and we certainly try to avoid the lightning as far as it is possible. But nobody is personally angry with the lightning. It is an impersonal, elemental force.

Within human nature there are forces which one cannot always control.
Now and then outbreaks of this type will occur in the houses of the Children's Village. It must be so. It takes a long time to heal wounds brought
about in the children throughout many years. So during this period there
will have to be explosive storms now and then.

The well-trained member of the staff knows this and acquires the ability
to forget and go on. It is no use collecting reproaches against the children
for later use. You will be worse off, the children recharging for new explo-
sions. Forget it and go on.

Physical Punishment is Forbidden

One thing is so obvious that it really does not need to be mentioned. That
is that one shall use no kind of physical punishment. It is formally forbidden by the Social Board in all children's homes in Sweden, but more important is that physical punishment is, and always will be, a wrong method of
bringing up children. As physical punishment we naturally include boxing
the ears, pulling hair, and so on. The greatest disadvantage of this method
is that one gets the children against oneself, and creates a wrong atmosphere around oneself.

Climate Therapy

The most important task for the staff in the Children's Village is just to
create the right atmosphere within the institution. We consider that the
atmosphere which surrounds the children is the main factor in helping

them. To this atmosphere belong first and foremost tolerance and under-standing of the children. This sounds maybe a little vague and general, so I will try to illustrate it with a few practical everyday examples.

The Road to the Children's Heart is Through the Belly

A kindness which is to have any value has to be shown through action, and not only in words. This goes for children even more than for adults. All children will become attached to those persons who look after their daily needs. Those who buy their clothes, tie their shoe laces, wash their faces, and so on. And those who cook their food.

There are also deep-rooted psychological explanations for the fact that everything concerned with food and drink means a great deal to children. (In psychological language it is called satisfaction of basic oral needs.)

For the neurotic child, food certainly plays an even more important role than for other children. I do mention especially this about food because I know that psychologically oriented people sometimes acquire a scornful and mocking attitude to everything connected with food, clothing, and material matters generally. This contempt for what the children eat and wear has no foundation in modern psychology. On the contrary, old-fashioned, honorable, and respectable care of children and deep psychology are in agreement here.

To Care for the Children

Children are very receptive to the atmosphere in their surroundings. In the usual home, with usual sensible parents, the children comprehend that one cares for them, feels anxious about them, is fond of them, etc. This we also try to realize in the houses in the Children's Village.

In practice this means that one "wonders." One wonders where the children are just now, if they have enough clothes on, so that they may not catch cold. One wonders if somebody will be meeting them at the bus station when they go home on a week end, and so on. All these small signs of interest together build a fund of security in the children's daily life. One of the tasks of the house parents in the Children's Village is to try to build up this secure background. The material care works hand in hand with the mental care.

Frontiers Which Should Not Be There

In old-fashioned institutions, both for children and adults, there was an invisible frontier. On one side were the interns, on the other the staff. It was obvious from the clothing which side of the frontier a person belonged. The interns had blue-striped cotton clothes, the staff wore yellow buttons on their coats.

Many of the children who come to the Children's Village carry this frontier within them. Adults belong to the enemy side. The enemy is overwhelming and cannot be openly defeated. Instead one has to outwit him.

If these children are to become socially well adapted, as we say, two alternative methods may be chosen. One can keep strictly to discipline and orderliness, and make the child yield and follow prescriptions. This method leads unquestionably to more order and method within the institution and will make the work easier for the staff. It may certainly also give results with the children in the form of punctuality, work, hygiene, and so on. But the question is, what will happen in the long run? Do the results persist? This method may often prove to be a "Dobeln" medicine, curing today, but making things seven times worse tomorrow.

The Children's Village therefore rejects this method. We try to concentrate directly on the emotional situation within the child. We want them to get rid of the feeling of an enemy frontier between adults and children. Many people agree with all this in principle and in theory. In practice, however, there is likely to be disagreement. So let us go back to everyday life again.

Smoking forbidden? Let us choose an example which usually gives offense. Most of the boys coming to the Children's Village are smokers. We have a full set of habitual smokers, cigaret-stump suckers, specialists in deep inhalation, and so on. We certainly want to check their smoking. But by what method? We believe that prohibition is not the way. Then they would smoke on the sly. The staff would have a full-time job supervising, and what would we do when a sinner was caught? We try to counteract tobacco smoking not through sign boards and prohibitions, nor by punishment. We test our way along positive lands, for instance, by letting the Village Parliament (elected representatives among children and staff) or the Village Assembly (everyone in the Village who can walk and talk) discuss and establish rules for smoking, etc.

Washing ears and brushing teeth. Obviously we want the children to learn hygienic habits also, like washing themselves and brushing their teeth. And we have nothing against good table manners. But if we want the children to acquire good habits, we must get them to wash their hands and brush their teeth without hate and defiance in their hearts. In other words, one cannot attack the child with hygienic arguments. Then one may meet with a repulse. This may involve not only table manners and tooth brushing but may also mean a persistence of the basic oppositional attitude which brought the child to us.

Anatomically it may sound crazy, but if we want the children to brush their teeth and wash their ears, we will have to go via their hearts. Not before they approve of their house parents will tooth brushing and ear washing be of lasting value.

About Hens and Other Things

In every good poultry yard there is a pecking law. Every hen knows precisely which hens she can peck at and which she must avoid. Every good military regiment has an order of precedence. Each man knows who is of higher rank, who shall command and who will have to obey. In the Children's Village there is no order of precedence. This is because an order of precedence very often turns into a pecking law. Lowest on the scale will be the children, pecked at by everybody.

Direct your criticism upward, willingly to the Medical Superintendent or some other central figure in the Village. The ability to bark at the chief we consider belonging to the more useful of human virtues. We prefer the hedgehogs with their thorns pointing upward and the soft surface downward, rather than the scrubbing brush, smooth on top and with its spines pointing down.

To Belong Together

On festive occasions, annual celebrations, etc., speeches are often made on Solidarity and the Common Good. At the Children's Village we are not very interested in serious speeches on these occasions. Solidarity we want in everyday language. One such everyday expression is to "tell the others." The teacher tells the house parents when a boy has a day off from school. The house parents tell the teacher when a child is ill and cannot come to school. Those who enter a house to put something straight with a child ought to tell the house parents in passing what it is about. The students tell the house parents when they take a child to town or to a cinema. We all break this rule of telling the others sometimes. But that is no reason for rejecting it.

In addition, one shall respect other people's jobs. You should not arrange to meet a child at mealtimes. You should not go out for a walk with him when he should be at school. The house parents should send their children to school on time. From evening entertainment the children should be sent home when it is bedtime.

The Small Tricks of Coexistence

Those who have for years had to deal with mentally sensitive people, children or adults, have gradually learned small tricks to reduce friction between themselves and the environment. Most of them depend on one's own personality, but some of them can be taught to others. Let me take a few examples to be used in case of need in the Children's Village.

An angry neighbor enters. He has had something stolen, and starts complaining as soon as he comes in the door. You rise, offer him your hand: "May I introduce myself . . . please come in and sit down." In 90 per cent of the cases you will succeed in having your neighbor introducing himself, and afterward the atmosphere will be far more comfortable for you. That Swede has not been born who does not feel solemn just after an introduction. That is at least one good thing with our Swedish solemnity and conventionalism. To greet people and give your name is a good custom which we commend to all newcomers. But the important thing is not to "introduce oneself to the boss;" it is more important that you introduce yourself to people who have nothing to do with the employment of staff (as maids in the staff dining room, the cleaners, and all the others whom you will meet on your job). We have found it most practical to do without greeting ceremonies, titles and surnames, etc. But sometimes even such things may have a certain psychological effect, as when occasional visitors come to the houses. Usually the doctor or someone else accompanies the people who want to have a look at us. It is then of some significance that the house parents consider themselves hosts, and show visitors around in their house. The idea with this is not to make a good impression on the visitors, but for the children in the cottage it will feel more like their own home if the house parents or the children themselves say "hello," and "please come inside." If possible, one shall also ask the children if one can have a look at their rooms. It seems more like an institution if the Medical Superintendent shows visitors around than if the house parents act as host.

There is another good, old trick for winning the hearts of the parents when they ring or visit. When the old King Oscar II traveled around in Sweden opening railway stations and bridges, he took with him his Master of the Royal Household, who noted down in a book the small conversations which His Majesty had with private people. Next time the King came to the place he looked in his book and could say: "Well my dear Mr. Johansson, how is Stella's backache now?" From then on the people there spoke with admiration of their popular monarch who was able to remember that the stationmaster's wife was called Stella and that she suffered from lumbago, although it was many years ago he had visited the station.

In the same way as the late Oscar II, a house father and mother can ask the parents when they ring if little sister still has her bad cold or if they had a nice time during their holiday in Tomelilla with Aunt Mary.

Morning Spirits and Bicycle Thefts

In the Village we have many children who steal. They steal money, bicycles, and so on. Why? The question may seem simple. It is obvious that everyone wants money and bicycles. If you ask the children directly, you will receive such a rational motivation. They have learned to answer sensibly from their countless interviews with the police or other persons in authority. The first time the answer was perhaps less learned and more primitive: "Why did you steal the bike?" "I don't know." You ought to understand the deep wisdom and honesty contained in this "I don't know." Indeed, we know much less than we realize about the motives of our own actions. I have said this before, but it needs repeating. It is very important, especially concerning children who steal. That they are not ruled by their reason may be deduced from the fact that the children steal and steal and steal without gaining anything, beyond all reason.

But why do our children steal? Obviously for many different reasons. Every theft, like every other human action, is a result of many different factors. But there is one essential thing. Deeply rooted and frequent stealing is connected with emotional conflcts within the children. The stealing has an emotional background and is not the result of rational considerations. We all know how we feel when we wake up "on the wrong side." We feel bad and do not know why. But we show it by closing the door unnecessarily hard, kicking small stones on the pavement, bumping into people on the tram. Why? One has not rationally decided to do so in order to give vent to one's bad temper. No, it just happens with the door and the stones and the elbows. If someone asked why we do so, we would consider the question silly and answer: "I don't know"—like the bicycle thief.

He too is under pressure from an inner emotional mood. He knows very well that one shall not steal, just as we all know of our own bad-tempered mornings that one shall not slam doors or push in the trams. But it seems to make things easier for us to do it although it is wrong or perhaps, more correctly, just because of that. And perhaps it is just because the cycle thief has been told so many times that theft is a sin that he cannot keep his fingers off the bicycle.

It is silly to think that we can extract any deep truth by asking the children why they steal. And it is of no advantage for their treatment to hold long discussions with the children. If we want to find the basic motive behind this stealing, we must concentrate on their emotional condition. Chronic stealing and chronic asociality both spring from an emotional background. The primary motives are subconscious. Those must be brought out into the light if the thief is to be cured.

Punishment Does Not Pay

Since we see the problem of children stealing in this way, it is obvious that we do not believe that anything is to be gained by punishment. On the contrary, by punishing children we risk losing their confidence and preserving the inner defiance against all adults—the frontier which I said should not exist.

That does not mean that there will be no consequences at all when the children do something wrong. Even if the thief escapes the negative moral judgment, he will have to take the social consequences: most simply by returning the stolen goods to the owner, who will have to be satisfied and grateful for that.

The older children may sometimes be in a position to pay back the full value of the stolen or damaged goods. Often this is impossible, especially for the younger children. Compensation will then be more symbolic. The children then repay a small part of what they have stolen or damaged.

By and large, we have found that this system with economic compensation but without moral condemnation functions well, especially as it does not leave the children feeling bitter.

Beware of Thieves

Many of us living in the Village have been robbed by our friends. At first one is irritated, perhaps angry. Later one gets used to it and learns to leave one's valuables in the safe in the office instead of in one's room or pockets. This is a little troublesome, but it is worth it. For many this has been a dearly bought experience, in a literal sense. Here I offer it to the newcomer free.

The children are especially inclined to steal from newcomers, not only because all newcomers are so easily taken in. It is rather that the children feel insecure and anxious in the presence of new faces. It is as if they want to see if the new friendship will stand the strain of a theft. Often they are disappointed because some of the staff have left the Village, and take their revenge on those taking their place. That is why it is especially at the beginning of your stay that you risk being robbed by your friends.

One Keeps Silent in the Children's Village

Every newcomer will have to sign a promise of secrecy. This you must keep, and keep near to your heart, figuratively speaking. All social workers must keep this promise in mind so that it acts as an automatic barrier. Mention no names when telling relatives and friends about the Village. Remember that in a bus and elsewhere, the mention of the Children's Village causes people to cock up their ears. One thing you will have to go through. If you are at a party, sitting quietly round a tea table or at a dull dinner, and someone asks what you are doing now, and you answer, "the Children's Village," your fate is sealed for the evening. You will be surrounded not only by sharp ears, but inquisitive tongues and skeptical eyes. You will have to fight for your life the rest of the evening. In this, your hour of visitation, we count on your loyalty. Remember the rule from all really good restaurants: if you like it, tell others; if there is something you do not like, tell us. We are used to criticism, and are prepared to meet an attack— but preferably from the front.

If you are starting work in a house and it is winter and cold, consult our common friend Arne, he will teach you how to manage the central heating. And our common mother, the superintendent of the stores, knows a lot about the art of cooking, polishing floors, and other daily tasks. In the Children's Village we wish to practice practical psychology, so do not forget the practical aspect of the job.

September 20, 1961

Welcome,
GUSTAV

2.   The Concept of a "Therapeutic Milieu"

FRITZ REDL

Speculations about the therapeutic value of the "milieu" in which our patients live are neither as new nor as revolutionary as the enthusiasts, as well as the detractors of "milieu therapy" occasionally want them to appear. If I may risk shocking you so early in the game, the most extreme degree of "holy respect" for the tremendous impact that even the "little things" in an environment can have is represented in the original description of the conditions for a Freudian psychoanalytic hour. The ritual of interaction between patient and therapist is certainly sharply circumscribed. Even items such as horizontality of body posture and geographical placement of the analyst's chair are considered important conditions. Of course, the "basic rule" must be strictly adhered to, there should be no noises from the analyst's children coming through from the next room, one would worry whether patients might meet each other on the way out or in. The idea that months of solid work even by the greatest genius of transference manipulation might be endangered if doctor and patient should happen to meet at the Austrian equivalent of a cocktail party, instead of in their usual office terrain, is certainly impressive evidence for the great

Reprinted with the permission of American Orthopsychiatric Association from the *American Journal of Orthopsychiatry,* Vol. 29, No. 4 (October 1959).

impact classical psychoanalysis has ascribed to factors such as time, space, and other "external givens."

If you now want to argue with me by reminding me that all this is true only for the duration of the 50-minute hour, and that other "milieu" factors in the patient's wider circle of life have not been deemed as relevant, then I might concede that point. But even so, I would like to remind you that we have always had a holy respect for two sets of "milieu" factors, at least in child analysis: we have always lived under the terror that the parents or teachers of our child patients might do things to them which would be so traumatic that we could, of course, not analyze them while all this was going on; and we would insist we couldn't touch a case unless we could get the child out of the terrain of parental sex life and into a bed of his own, or unless the parents stopped some of the more extreme forms of punitive suppressiveness at once. These are only two of the illustrations we could think of. You will find a much more impressive list of "milieu variables," which certainly need to be influenced by the therapist, in Anna Freud's classic, *Introduction to the Technique of Child Analysis,* though not under that heading, of course.

The other case in point of my argument that even classical psychoanalysis has not neglected concern with "milieu" influences as much as it is supposed to have, relates to our evaluation of failure and success. At least in our informal appraisals I have time and again observed how easily we ascribe the breakdown of a child analysis to the "negative factors in the youngster's environment," and I have found in myself an inclination to do the same with the other fellow's successes. If my colleague seems to have presented an unusual piece of therapeutic "breakthrough," I find the temptation strong to look for the good luck he had with all the supportive factors that were present in his case and which, to my narcissism, seem to explain his success much better than the technical argument he put forth.

Now, seriously, if we secretly allow "milieu particles" to weigh so strongly that they can make and break even the most skillfully developed emotional therapy bridges between patient and doctor, hadn't we better look into this some more?

The fortunate fact that the answer to this question has, historically, been an enthusiastic "yes," however, has started us off in another problem-direction. Since more and more of us got impressed by more and more "factors" which in some way or other could be subsumed under the "milieu" term, the word has assumed such a variety of connotations that scientific communication has been overstimulated, but at the same time blocked in its development toward precision.

Since avoiding the traps of early concept confusion is an important prelude to a more rigid examination of meanings and their appropriate scope, we might allow ourselves the luxury of at least a short list of "dangers we ought to watch out for from now on," provided we keep it telegram-style, so as not to take too much attention from the major theme. Since time and space for argument is dear, I shall be presumptuous enough to confront you simply with my personal conclusions, and offer them as warning posts, without further apology.

Traps for the Milieu Concept

1. The cry for *the* therapeutic milieu as a general slogan is futile and in this wide formulation the term doesn't mean a thing. No milieu is "good" or "bad" in itself—it all depends. And it depends on more factors than I want to list, though some of them will turn up as we go along.

2. It won't do to use our own philosophical, ethical, political convictions, or our taste buds, in order to find out what really has or has not "therapeutic effect." Even the most respectable clinical discussions around this theme drift all too easily into A's trying to convince B that his setup is too "autocratic," or that what he called "democratic" group management isn't really good for those youngsters. Whether a ward should have rules, how many and which, must not lead to an argument between those who like rules and those who don't; I have seen many a scientific discussion end up in the same personal taste-bud battle that one otherwise finds acceptable only when people talk about religions or brands of cars.

3. Even a concept of "total milieu therapy" does not imply that all aspects of a given milieu are equally relevant in all moments in clinical life. All games, for instance, have some kind of "social structure" and as part of that, some kind of "pecking order" which determines the power position of the players for the duration of the game. Whether the specific pecking order of the game I let them play today had anything to do with the fact that it blew up in my face after five minutes is a question that can be answered only in empirical terms. I know of cases where the pecking order was clearly it; I have to look no further. I know of others where it was of no *clinical* relevance at the time. The boys blew up because they got too scared playing hide-and-seek with flashlights in the dark. In short, the scientific establishment of a given milieu aspect as a theoretically valid and important one does not substitute for the need for a diagnosis on the spot. It alone can differentiate between potential milieu impacts and actual ones in each case.

4. The idea of the "modern" and therefore social-science-conscious psychiatrist that he has to sell out to the sociologist if he wants to have his "ward milieu" studied properly is the bunk. Of course, any thoughtful appraisal of a hospital milieu will contain many variables which the mother discipline of a given psychiatrist may never have dreamed about. On the other hand, the thing that counts is not only the description of a variable, but the assessment of the potential impact on the treatment process of a given group of patients. That is basically a *clinical* matter, and it remains

the clinician's task. The discipline that merges social science with clinical criteria in a balanced way still has to be invented. There is no short cut to it either by psychiatry's stealing particles of social science concepts or by selling out to the social scientist's domain.

5. The frequently voiced expectation that the discovery of what "milieu" one needs would automatically make it easy to produce that style of milieu in a given place is downright naïve. An instrumentology for the creation of "ward atmosphere," of "clinically correct policies of behavorial intervention," etc., has yet to be created, and it will cost blood and sweat to get it. The idea that all it takes to have a "good treatment milieu" is for a milieu-convinced ward boss to make his nurses feel comfortable with him, and to hold a few gripe sessions between patients and staff, is a daydream, the simplicity of which we can no longer afford.

"Therapeutic"—In Which Respect?

The worst trap that explorers of the milieu idea sometimes seem to be goaded into is the ubiquitous use of the term "therapeutic," if it is coupled as an adjective, with "milieu" as a noun. I have described the seven most common meanings squeezed into this word in scientific writings and scientific discussions elsewhere,[1] but I must at least point at this possible confusion before we go on. Whenever people demand that a really good "therapeutic milieu" have this or that quality to it, they may refer to any one— or a combination of—the following issues:

1. Therapeutic—meaning: *don't put poison in their soup.*
    Example—Demand for absence of crude forms of punishment in a place that calls itself a "residential treatment center."
2. Therapeutic—meaning: *you still have to feed them,* even though that has little to do directly with a specific operation you are planning to perform.
    Example—Youngsters need an activity program, so if you keep them for a while you'd better see that they get it, even if your specific theory of psychiatry thinks nothing of the direct implication of play life and activity diet in terms of therapy as such.
3. Therapeutic—meaning: *developmental phase appropriateness and cultural background awareness.*
    Example—It would not be therapeutic to keep adolescents in an infantilizing "little boy and girl" atmosphere; or: a fine lady fussing over a little boy's hair grooming might convey "warmth" to a neglected middle-class child, but would sim-

1. "The Meaning of 'Therapeutic Milieu,' " in *Symposium on Preventive and Social Psychiatry, 15–17 April 1957,* Walter Reed Army Institute of Research (Washington, D.C.: U.S. Government Printing Office, 1958).

ply be viewed as a hostile pest by a young toughie from the other side of the tracks.

4. Therapeutic—meaning: *clinically elastic.*

Example—The fact that rules and regulations were too rigid to fit particular disturbance patterns or needs of patients, I have heard referred to as "untherapeutic," and with all due respect to numbers and group psychology, there is a point where the inability to make exceptions becomes "untherapeutic" too.

5. Therapeutic—meaning: *encompassing fringe-area treatment goals.*

Example—Johnny is here for treatment of his kleptomania. His therapist works hard on that in individual therapy. Johnny also has a severe deficiency in school learning, and is clumsy in his play life with contemporaries. Even while the therapist is not yet in a position to pull any of these factors in, some other aspect of the milieu to which Johnny is exposed must give him experiences in this direction. Or else, the place is not "therapeutic enough" for him.

6. Therapeutic—in terms of *"the milieu and I."*

Example—Some types of cases with deficient superego formation can be lured into identification with value issues only through the detour of an identification with the group code within which they live. For those cases the "therapist" is only one of the therapeutic agents. The "institutional atmosphere" that makes the child want to identify with what it stands for is another, *on equal rights.* In this case, this part of the "milieu" is expected to become a direct partner in treatment of the specific disturbance for which the child was brought in.

7. Therapeutic—in terms of *re-education for life.*

Example—Especially for larger institutions the demand is often made that the institutions should not only provide people who treat the patient, but that they should also have features in them which come as close to "real life outside" as is possible, or else they wouldn't be "therapeutic enough." Thus, all those features that would seem to be needed for a very sick person are considered as rather countertherapeutic and bad, though unfortunately still necessary, while all semblance to open community life is considered a therapeutic ingredient in its own right. How far one and the same institution can cater to illness and at the same time lure into normality is then often a case for debate.

Enough of this dissection of an adjective. I hope I am understood correctly: Any one of these meanings of the term "therapeutic" is a justified issue in its own right. Any one of them may, in a given case, assume priority importance or may fade out in relevance to the zero point. All I am trying to convey is the importance of remembering who is talking about what

—and about which patients—when we use the term in a scientific free-for-all. So far I haven't been too impressed with our ability to do so.

By the way, even in all those seven cases the term "therapeutic" may still be used in a double frame of reference: (a) Was it therapeutic for a given patient—if so, how do you know? (b) Is this expected to be potentially "therapeutic"—meaning beneficial for the treatment goal—from what I know about the basic nature of the issue under debate? These two frames of reference need to be kept asunder too.

A "Milieu"—What's in It?

Obviously I am not going to use the term in the nearly global meaning which its theft from the French language originally insinuated. For practical reasons, I am going to talk here only of one sort of milieu concept: of a "milieu" artificially created for the purpose of the treatment of a group of youngsters. Within this confine you can make it somewhat wider if you want, and think of the "Children's Psychiatric Unit" on the fourth, eighth, or ninth floor of a large hospital, or you may hold before your eyes, while I am speaking, a small residential treatment home for children that is not part of a large unit. Of course, I know that the similarity of what I am talking about to other types of setups may be quite great, but I can't cover them all. Hence, anything else you hold before your eyes while I talk, you do strictly at your own risk.

So, here we are on the doorstep of that treatment home or at the keyhole of that hospital ward. And now you ask me: If you could plan things the way you wanted to, which are the most important "items" in your milieu that will sooner or later become terribly relevant for better or for worse? The choice is hard, and only such a tough proposition gets me over the guilt feeling for oversimplifying and listing items out of context.

1. *The social structure.* This is some term, and I have yet to see the psychiatrist that isn't stunned for a moment at its momentum—many would run and hire a sociologist on the spot. Being short on time, I have no choice, but let me hurry and add: this term in itself is as extendible and collapsible as a balloon. It doesn't mean much without specifications. So, let me just list a few of the things I have in mind:

a) A hospital ward is more like a *harem society than a family,* no matter how motherly or fatherly the particular nurses and doctors may feel toward their youngsters. The place I run at the moment is purposely shaped as much as possible after the model of an American camp, which is the only pattern I could find which children would be familiar with, where a lot of adults walk through children's lives in older brother and parentlike roles without pretending it to be an equivalent to family life.

b) The *role distribution* of the adult figures can be of terrific importance for the amount of clarity with which children perceive what it is all about.

Outspokenly or not, sooner or later they must become clear about just who can or cannot be expected to decide what; otherwise, how would one know when one is getting the run-around?

c) The *pecking order* of any outfit does not long remain a secret to an open door neighborhood-wise toughie, no matter how dumb he may be otherwise. He also smells the outspoken "pecking order" among the adults who take care of him, no matter how carefully disguised it may be under professional role titles or Civil Service Classification codes.

d) The *communication network* of any given institution is an integral part of its "social structure." Just who can be approached about listening to what, is quite a task to learn; and to figure out the real communication lines that are open and those which are secretly clogged in the adult communication network is usually an unsoluble task except for the suspicious outside researcher.

I mentioned only four illustrations of all the things I want included under "social structure." There are many more, and I have no quarrel with the rich inventory many social scientists have invented for this. The quarrel I have goes all against oversimplification, and if you tell me social structure is only what goes into a power line drawing or a sociogram, or that social structure is the only important variable in "milieu" that psychiatrists have neglected in the past, then you have me in a mood to fight. By the way, if I list "social structure" as one of the important milieu variables, I'd better add in a hurry: A mere listing or description of the social structure extant on a given ward is of no interest to me at all if it doesn't go further than that. From a clinical angle, the excitement begins *after* the sociologist tells me what social structure I have before me. Then I really want to know: What does it do to my therapeutic goals? What does it imply for my choice in techniques? In which phase of the therapy of my children is it an asset, and in which other phase does it turn into a serious block? To use just one example for the clinical question to be added to the social scientist's answer: The kind of ward I run—harem society style—makes individual attachments of child to worker difficult to achieve; on the other hand, it pleasantly dilutes too excited libidinous attachment-needs into more harmless distribution over a larger number of live props. Question: Is that good or bad, and for whom during what phase of their treatment?

2. *The value system that oozes out of our pores.* Some people subsume that under social structure. I think I have reasons to want a separate place for it here, but let's not waste time on the question why. The fact is, the youngsters not only respond to what we say or put in mimeographed writing; they smell our value-feelings even when we don't notice our own body odor any more. I am not sure how, and I can't wait until I find out. But I do need to find out which value items are there to smell. Does the arrangement of my furniture call me a liar while I make a speech about how much

at home I want them to feel, or does that gleam in a counselor's eye tell the child: "You are still wanted," even though he means it if he says he won't let you cut up the tablecloth? By the way, in some value studies I have missed one angle many times: the *clinical convictions* of what is professionally correct handling, which sometimes even questionnaire-clumsy workers on a low salary level may develop, and which become a motivating source for their behavior in its own right, besides their own personal moral convictions or their power drives.

3. *Routines, rituals, and behavioral regulations.* The sequence of events and the conditions under which people undergo certain repetitive maneuvers in their life space can have a strong impact on whether they can keep themselves under control, or whether their impulse-control balance breaks down. Since Bruno Bettelheim's classic description of the events inside a child while he seems engaged in the process of getting up or getting himself to sleep, no more words should have to be said about this. And yet, many "therapeutic milieu" discussions still waste their time on arguments between those who like regularity and those who think the existence of a rule makes life an unimaginative drudge. All groups also have a certain "ritual" by which a member gets back into the graces of the group if he has sinned, and others which the group has to go through when an individual has deviated. Which of those ceremonial rites are going on among my boys, thinly disguised behind squabbles and fights, and which of them do adult staff people indulge in, under the even thinner disguise of a discussion on punishment and on the setting of limits? Again—the mere discovery of phenomena fitting into this category is not what I am after. We are still far from having good research data on the *clinical relevance* of whatever specific practice may be in vogue in a specific place.

4. *The impact of the group process.* We had better pause after pronouncing this weighty phrase—it is about as heavy and full of dodges as the phrase "social structure," as previously pointed out. And since this one milieu aspect might well keep us here for a week, let me sink as low as simple word-listing at this point. Items that I think should go somewhere under this name: overall group atmosphere, processes like scapegoating, mascot-cultivation, subclique formation, group psychological role suction,[2] experiences of exposure to group psychological intoxication, dependency on contagion clusters, leadership tensions, etc. Whatever you have learned from social psychology, group psychology and group dynamics had better be written in right here. The point of all this: These phenomena are *not* just interesting things that happen among patients or staff, to be viewed with a clinical grin, a sociological hurrah, or with the curiosity stare of an anthropological slumming party. These processes are forces to which my

2. Some more detailed description of this appears in *Group Processes: Transactions of the Fourth (1957) Conference,* Bertram Schaffner, Ed. (New York: Josiah Macy, Jr. Foundation, 1959).

child patient is exposed, as real as the oedipus complex of his therapist, the food he eats and the toys he plays with. The forces producing such impacts may be hard to see, or even to make visible through x-ray tricks. They are there and as much of his "surroundings" as the unbreakable room in which he screams off his tantrum.

5. *The trait clusters that other people whirl around within a five-yard stretch.* I first wanted to call this item "the other people as persons," but I know this would only call forth a long harangue about feelings, attitudes— Isn't it people anyway, who make up a group? From bitter discussion experience, I am trying to duck these questions by this somewhat off-the-beat phrase. What I have in mind is this: My youngsters live as part of a group, true enough. But they are also individuals. And Bobby who shares a room with John is within striking distance of whatever personal peculiarities John may happen to throw at others. In short, we expect some children to show "shock" at certain colors on a Rorschach card. We expect children to be lured into excited creativity at the mere vision of some fascinating project outline or plane model seductively placed before their eyes. Well, the boy with whom Bobby shares his room is worse than a Rorschach or a plane model. Not only does his presence and the visualization of his personality do something to Bobby, for John not only *has* character traits and neurotic syndromes; he swings them around his body like a wet bathing towel, and it is going to hit whoever gets in its path, innocent or not. In short, personality traits remain psychological entities for the psychologist who watches them in the youngsters. They are *real things that hit and scratch* if you get in their way, for the roommates and all the people on the ward.

We have learned to respect the impact of certain extremes in pathologies upon each other, but we are still far from inspecting our milieus carefully enough for what they contain in "trait clusters" that children swing around their heads within a five-yard range. Let me add: not all traits and syndromes are "swung;" some stay put and can only be seen or smelled, so they become visible or a nuisance only to the one who shares the same room. Also; we are far from knowing what this all amounts to clinically. For the question of just what "milieu ingredients" my ward contains, in terms of existent trait clusters of the people who live in it, is still far removed from the question of just which *should* coexist with each other, and which others should be carefully kept asunder.

6. *The staff, their attitudes and feelings—but please let's not call it all transference."* This one I can be short about, for clinicians all know about it; sociologists will grant it to you, though they may question how heavily it counts. In fact, the attitudes and feelings of staff have been drummed up for so long now as "the" most important aspect of a milieu, often even as the only important one, that I am not afraid this item will be forgotten. No argument needed, it is self-evident. Only two issues I would like to battle

around: One, while attitudes and feelings are very important indeed, they are not always all that counts, and sometimes other milieu items may gang up on them so much they may obliterate their impact. My other battle cry: Attitudes and feelings of staff are manifold, and spring from many different sources. Let's limit the term "transference" to those for which it was originally invented. If Nurse's Aide A gets too hostile to Bob because he bit him too hard, let's not throw all of that into the same terminological pot. By the way, if I grant "attitudes and feelings of staff" a place on my list of "powerful milieu ingredients," I mean the attitudes and feelings that really fill the place, that are lived—not those that are only mentioned in research interviews and on questionnaires.

7. *Behavior received.* I tried many other terms, but it won't work. There just isn't one that fits. In a sentence I would say: what people really *do* to each other counts as much as how they feel. This forces me into a two-hour argument in which I have to justify why it isn't unpsychiatric to say such a thing. For, isn't it the underlying feelings that "really" count? That depends on which side of the fence your "really" is. The very fact that you use such a term already means you know there is another side to it, only you don't want to take it as seriously as yours. In short, there are situations where the "underlying feeling" with which the adult punishes a child counts so much that the rather silly form of punishment that was chosen is negligible. But I could quote you hundreds of other examples where this is not the case. No matter what wonderful motive—if you expose child A to an isolation with more panic in it than he can stand, the effect will be obvious. Your excuse that you "meant well and love the boy" may be as futile as that of the mother who would give the child an overdose of arsenic, not knowing its effect.

This item of *behaviors received in a day's time* by each child should make a really interesting line to assess. We would have to look about at "behaviors received" from other boys as well as from staff, and see what the implications of those behaviors received are, even after deducting from them the mitigating influences of "attitudes that really were aiming at the opposite." The same, by the way, should also be taken into consideration for staff to be hired. I have run into people who really love "crazy youngsters" and are quite willing to sacrifice a lot. Only they simply cannot stand more than half a pound of spittle in their face a day, professional attitude or no.

In order to make such an assessment, the clinician would of course be interested especially in the *forms* that are being used by staff for intervention—limit-setting—expression of acceptance and love, etc. The totality of prevalence of certain forms of "behavior received" is not a negligible characteristic of the milieu in which a child patient has to live.

8. *Activity structure and nature of constituent performances.* Part of the impact a hospital or treatment home has on a child lies in the things he is allowed or requested *to do*. Any given activity that is halfway shapeful

enough to be described has a certain amount of structure to it—some games, for instance, have a body of rules; demand the splitting up into two opposing sides or staying in a circle; and have certain assessments of roles for the players, at least for the duration. At the same time, they make youngsters "do certain things" while the game lasts. Paul Gump introduced the term "constituent performances" into our Detroit Game Study, and referred by this term to the performances required within the course of a game as basic. Thus, running and tagging are constituent performances of a tag game, guessing word meanings is a constituent performance in many a charade, etc. We have plenty of evidence by now that—other things being equal—the very exposure of children to a given game, with its structure and demand for certain constituent performances, may have terrific clinical impact on the events at least of that day. Wherever we miscalculate the overwhelming effect which the seductive aspect of certain games may have (flashlight hide-and-seek in the dark just before bedtime) we may ask for trouble, while many a seemingly risky game can safely be played if enough ego-supportive controls are built right into it (the safety zone to which you can withdraw without having to admit you get tired or scared, etc.). In short, while I would hardly relegate the total treatment job of severely disturbed children in a mental hospital ward to that factor alone, I certainly would want to figure on it as seriously as I would calculate the mental hygiene aspects of other factors more traditionally envisioned as being of clinical concern. What I say here about games goes for many other activities patients engage in—arts and crafts, woodwork, outings, overnight trips, cookouts, discussion groups, musical evenings, etc. Which of these things takes place, where, with which feeling tone, and with what structural and activity ingredients is as characteristic of a given "milieu" as the staff that is hired.

9. *Space, equipment, time and props.* What an assortment of names, but I know as yet of no collective noun that would cover them all equally well. Since I have made such a fuss about this for years, I may try to be shorter about it than seems reasonable. Remember what a bunch of boys do when running through a viaduct with an echo effect? Remember what may happen to a small group who are supposed to discuss plans for their next Scout meeting, who have to hold this discussion unexpectedly, in a huge gym with lots of stuff around, instead of in their usual clubroom? Remember what will happen to a baseball that is put on the table prematurely while they are still supposed to sit quietly and listen, and remember what happens to many a well-intended moral lecture to a group of sloppy campers, if you timed it so badly that the swimming bell started ringing before you had finished? Do I still have to prove why I think that what an outfit does with arrangements of time expectations and time distribution, what prop-exposure the youngsters are expected to stand or avoid, what space arrangements are like, and what equipment does to the goals you have set for yourself, should be listed along with the important "properties" of a place

where clinical work with children takes place? So far I have found that in hospitals this item tends to be left out of milieu discussions by psychiatrists and sociologists alike; only the nurses and attendants have learned by bitter experience that it may pay to lend an ear to it.

10. *The seepage from the world outside.* One of the hardest "milieu aspects" to assess in a short visit to any institution is the amount of "impact from the larger universe and the surrounding world" that actually seeps through its walls and finds its way into the lives of the patients. No outfit is airtight, no matter how many keys and taboos are in use. In our own little children's ward-world, for instance, there are the following "seepage ingredients from the world outside" that are as much a part of our "milieu," as it hits the boys, as anything else: Adult visitors and the "past case history" flavor they leave behind. Child visitors and the "sociological body odor" of the old neighborhood, or the new one which they exude. Excursions which we arrange, old haunts from prehospital days, which we happen to drive through unintentionally on our way to our destination. Plenty of purposely pulled-in outside world through movies, television, pictures, and stories we may tell them. And, of course, school is a full-view window hopefully opened wide for many vistas to be seen through it—if we only could get our children to look.

There is the "hospital impact" of the large building that hits them whenever they leave the ward floor in transit, the physically sick patients they meet on the elevator who stir the question up again in their own mind: "Why am I here?" There are the stories other boys tell, the staff tells, the imputed secrets we may be hiding from them whenever we seem eager to divert attention to something else. As soon as the children move into the open cottage, the word "seepage" isn't quite as correct any more. Suffice it to say: the type and amount of "outside world" particles that are allowed in or even eagerly pulled in constitute a most important part of the lives of the captive population of an institutional setting, and want to be given attention to in an appraisal of what a given "milieu" holds.

11. *The system of umpiring services and traffic regulations between environment and child.* Those among you who have a sharp nose for methodological speculations may want to object and insist that I am jumping category dimensions in tagging on this item and the next one on my list. I don't want to quarrel about this now. For even though you may be right, it is too late today to start a new chapter, so please let me get away with tagging on these two items here. In some ways they still belong, for whether there are any umpiring services built into an institution, and what they are like, is certainly an important "milieu property" in my estimation.

What I have in mind here has been described in more detail in a previous paper.[3] In short, it runs somewhat like this: Some "milieu impacts" hit

3. *Strategy and Techniques of the Life Space Interview,* Am. J. Orthopsychiatry, 29: 1–19, 1959.

the children directly; nobody needs to interpret or translate. Others hit the child all right, but to have their proper impact someone has to do some explaining. It makes a great difference whether a child who is running away unhappy, after a cruel razzing received from a thoughtless group, is left to deal with this all by himself; or whether the institution provides interpretational or first-aid services for the muddled feelings at the time. Some of our children, for instance, might translate such an experience, which was not intended by the institution, into additional resentment against the world. With sympathy in the predicament offered by a friendly adult who tags along and comforts, this same experience may well be decontaminated or even turned into the opposite.

A similar item is the one I had in mind in using the phrase "traffic regulations." Much give-and-take can follow naturally among the inhabitants of a given place. Depending on the amount of their disturbance, though, some social interactions which normal life leaves to the children's own resources require traffic supervision by an adult. I would like to know whether a given milieu has foreseen this and can guarantee the provision of some help in the bartering custom among the youngsters, or whether that new youngster will be mercilessly exposed to the wildest blackmail with no help from anyone, the moment he enters the doors to my ward. In short, it is like asking what medical first-aid facilities are in a town before one moves into it. Whether this belongs to the concept of what makes up a "town," or whether it should be listed under a separate heading I leave for a later chance to thrash out. All I want to point at now is that the nature of and existence or nonexistence of umpiring services and social traffic regulations is as "real" a property of a setup as its walls, kitchen equipment and clinical beliefs.

12. *The thermostat for the regulation of clinical resilience.* If it is cold in an old cabin somewhere in the midst of "primitive nature," the trouble is obvious: either there isn't any fire going, or something is wrong with the stove and the whole heating system, so it doesn't give off enough heat. If I freeze in a building artificially equipped with all the modern conveniences, such a conclusion might be off the beam. The trouble may simply be that the thermostat isn't working right. This, like the previous item, is a property of a given milieu rather than a "milieu ingredient" in the stricter sense of the word. However, it is of such utmost clinical relevance that it has to go in here somewhere. In fact, I have hardly ever participated in a discussion on the milieu concept without having this item come up somehow or other.

The term under which it is more often referred to is actually that of "flexibility," which most milieu therapy enthusiasts praise as "good" while the bad men in the picture are the ones that think "rigidity" is a virtue. I have more reasons to be tired of this either/or issue than I can list in the remaining time. It seems to me that the "resilience" concept fits better what most of us have so long tried to shoot at with the flexibility label. A milieu certainly needs to be sensitive to the changing needs of the patients during different phases of the treatment process. It needs to "tighten up" —lower the behavioral ceiling when impulse-panic looms on the horizon; and it may have to lift it when self-imposed internal pressures mount. Also, it needs to limit spontaneity and autonomy of the individual patient in early phases of intensive disorder and rampant pathology; it needs to throw in a challenge toward autonomy and even the risking of mistakes, when the patient goes through the later phases of recovery. Especially when severely disturbed children are in the process of going through an intensive phase of "improvement," the resilience of a milieu to make way for its implications is as important as its ability to "shrink back" during a regressive phase.

Just How Does the Milieu Do It?

Listing these twelve variables of important milieu aspects which can be differentiated as explorable issues in their own right is only part of the story. I hold no brief for this list, and I am well aware of its methodological complications and deficiencies. The major value of listing them at all lies in the insistence that *there are so many of them* and that they *can be separately studied and explored.* This should at least help us to secure ourselves against falling in love with any one of them to the exclusion of the others, and of forcing any discipline that wants to tackle the job, whether it be psychiatry, sociology or what not, to look beyond its traditional scope and directly into the face of uncompromisingly multifaceted facts.

Since the major sense in all this milieu noise is primarily the impact of these variables on the treatment process of the children we are trying to cure, the question of the clinical assessment of the relevance of each of these items is next on the docket of urgent jobs. This one we shall have to skip for today, but time may allow us to point at the other question leading into the most important core of the problem: If we assume that any one of these milieu ingredients, or whatever you want to call them, may have positive or negative impacts on our therapeutic work—how do they do it? Just what goes on when we claim that any one of those milieu givens "did something to our youngsters?" This gets us into one of the most noteworthy gaps in all our theory of personality, and frankly, I don't think even our most up-to-date models are quite up to it. True enough, we have learned a few things about just how pathology is influenced in the process of a specific form of psychiatric interview, and we know a little about influence of human over human, here or there. We are not so well off when we come to the impact of more abstract sounding entities, such as "group structure." We have even more trouble to figure out just how space, time and props are supposed to do their job, whenever we claim that they have the power to throw an otherwise well-planned therapeutic experience out of gear.

One phase of this problem sounds familiar—when psychiatry first began to take the impact of "culture" seriously, we were confronted with a similar puzzler: Just where, within the individual, is what going on at the moment when we say a "cultural" factor had some influence on a given behavior of a person?

This problem is far from solved. I think it might help, though, to introduce a thought that might lead to greater specificity in observation and ultimately to more "usable" forms of data collection. Frankly, I have never seen the "milieu" at work. My children are never hit by "the milieu" as such. It always hits them in a specific form and at a given time and place. I think the researchers who play with the concept of a "setting" have a technical advantage over us in this field. Of course, the setting alone doesn't interest me either. For what it all hinges on is just what *experience* a given setting produces or makes possible within my child patient and what this child patient does with it.

Rather than study the "milieu" per se, and then the "reactions of the children," how about making it a four-step plan? Let's keep the "milieu" as the over-all concept on the fringe; its basic ingredients come close to my youngsters only insofar as they are contained in a given setting. For example, my children on the ward can be found engaged in getting up, eating a meal or snacks; they can be found roaming around the playroom, or in a station wagon, with all their overnight gear, on the way to their camping site. They can be found in their arts and crafts room, or schoolroom, engaged in very specific activities. Enough of illustrations—the point is, in all those settings the whole assortment of milieu aspects hits them in very *specific forms:* There is an outspoken behavioral expectation floating through that arts and crafts room at any time. There are spatial characteristics, tools, and props. There is the potential reaction of the other child or adult, the feeling tone of the group toward the whole situation as such; there is the impact of people's goal values and attitudes as well as that of the behavior of the child's neighbor who clobbers him right now with his newly made viking sword. In short: *I may be able to isolate observations of milieu ingredients as they "hit" the child in a specific setting during a specific activity.* On such a narrowed-down level of observation, I may also be able to trace the actual *experience* which such a concrete situation in a given setting produced in the child; and if I know what the child *did with the experience,* it may make sense, since I have both ends of the line before me. The youngster's reaction to his experience—the nature of the ingredients of the "setting" on both ends of the line, plus plenty of good hunches on the child's experience while exposed to its impact.

It seems to me that much more work needs to be done with the concept of "setting" so as to make it clinically more meaningful, and that sharper observational techniques, capable of catching "implied milieu impact" as well as "child's coping with" the experience produced by the setting, need to be developed. This, however, leads into a theme to be discussed in other sessions of our Annual Meeting.

One more word before closing. It is time that we take Erik Erikson's warning more seriously than we have done so far—and I mention him as symbolizing a point of view that many of us have been increasingly impressed by. If I may try to say what I think he would warn us about after all this discussion of "milieu impacts" on therapy of children, it would run somewhat like this: Why are you still talking most of the time as though "milieu" or "enrivonment" were some sort of rigid structure, and the individuals were good for nothing but to "react" to it?

How does some of that "environment" you talk about come into being, after all? Couldn't we reverse the story just as well, and ask: "What do your child patients do to their milieu?"—not only: "What does the milieu do to them?" Mine, by the way, are doing plenty to it, and I have little doubt but that many of the items which we describe as though they were fixtures on the environmental scene are actually products of the attitudes and actions of the very people who, after they have produced them, are also exposed to their impact in turn.

I, for one, would want to exclaim loudly what I didn't dare whisper too much at the start of my paper, or I would have scared you off too soon. I would like to find out not only what milieu is and how it operates, but also how we can describe it, how we influence it, and by what actions of all involved it is, in turn, created or molded. At the moment I am convinced of only one thing for sure—we all have quite a way to go to achieve either of those tasks.

3. A Therapeutic Milieu

BRUNO BETTELHEIM
EMMY SYLVESTER

This paper describes the treatment of emotionally disturbed children in an institutional setting. The clinical material on which this discussion is based concerns a syndrome developed in non-therapeutic institutions which may be called "psychological institutionalism." For the purpose of

Reprinted with the permission of American Orthopsychiatric Association from the *American Journal of Orthopsychiatry*, Vol. 18, No. 2 (April, 1948), pp. 191–206.

showing how these children are rehabilitated at the Orthogenic School, two cases will be presented in full.

Psychological institutionalism may be regarded as a deficiency disease in the emotional sense. Absense of meaningful continuous interpersonal relationships leads to impoverishment of the personality. The results of this process are observed in children who have lived in institutional settings for prolonged periods of time, but it is not limited to them. It also occurs in children who are exposed to a succession of foster homes or to disorganized family settings.

Non-institutional living *per se* will therefore not cure or avoid institutionalism. Neither can psychotherapeutic measures be effective which neglect the core of the disturbance. Only measures arising from benign interpersonal relationships among adults and children can combat the impoverishment of the personalities of children who suffer from emotional institutionalism. Since behavior disorders in the common sense do not necessarily form part of the clinical picture, the factors which cause impoverishment of personality are only rarely subjected to psychiatric study. Understanding these factors furnishes leads to the construction of a therapeutic milieu.

A frame of reference that consists of depersonalized rules and regulations may lead the child to become an automaton in his passive adjustment to the institution. There is no need for independent decisions because the child's physical existence is well protected and his activities arranged for him. Compliance with stereotyped rules rather than assertive action constitutes adequate adjustment, but does not allow for spontaneity. Reality testing is not extended to variegated life conditions. Complete determination by external rules prevents the development of inner controls. Emotional conflicts cannot be utilized toward personality growth because they are not intrapsychic conflicts, but only occasional clashes between instinctual tendencies and impersonal external rules. The cause of these serious deviations in personality development—the absence of interpersonal relationships—is also responsible for their remaining unrecognized. The child lives in emotional isolation and physical distance from the adult. Even in instances where the child lives in proximity of touch and experience with adults, such closeness does not serve the purpose of personality growth if the significant characteristics of the normal child–adult relationship are not maintained. Frequent change in the personalities and absence of proper and consistent dosage of the adult's distance from and closeness to the child, turn into shadowy acquaintance what should be intimate relationships. This "not knowing" the adult deprives the child of images of integration.

In a therapeutic milieu, on the contrary, the child's development toward increasing mastery must be facilitated. Training in skills and achievements, specialized programs and activities, are of peripheral importance only.

They are therapeutically justified solely if they originate from the central issue of the therapeutic milieu. A therapeutic milieu is characterized by its inner cohesiveness which alone permits the child to develop a consistent frame of reference. This cohesiveness is experienced by the child as he becomes part of a well defined hierarchy of meaningful interpersonal relationships. Emphasis on spontaneity and flexibility—not to be misconstrued as license or chaos—makes questions of schedule or routine subservient to the relevance of highly individualized and spontaneous interpersonal relationships. Such conditions permit the emergence and development of the psychological instances, the internalization of controls, and the eventual integration of the child's personality. It may be assumed that these milieu factors which determine the children's rehabilitation in the therapeutic milieu, have validity for the institutional care of children in general.

The personality defects which result from the absence of these factors in an institutional setting are clearly demonstrated by a control group of six- to eight-year-old children who were not considered disturbed by their environment. The reason for the psychiatric study was a "purely administrative one"—they had reached the age limit of the residential institution in which they had spent the greater part of their lives. They arrived at the clinic in groups and presented themselves as physically well developed, neat and well-groomed youngsters. Their behavior in the waiting room was rather striking: they seemed to have an unusual amount of group spirit and had completely accepted their respective positions in the group as leaders, followers, protectors, or proteges.

This apparent social maturity was in marked contrast to their behavior in the individual contact with the psychiatrist, in whose office many were excessively shy whereas others became aggressively demanding. These forms of behavior were fixed. Lack of the flexible adaptability which even disturbed children show during the course of a psychiatric interview, characterized these children. The shy ones remained shy throughout the interview. Others were unable to modify their demands which appeared in two different and mutually exclusive varieties. They took the form of "toy hunger" in the children who had interest in toy material only, and of "touch hunger" in those whose need was exclusively for physical contact. The children who were not overwhelmed by rigid shyness entered conversation readily, and it was possible to get a picture of their subjective world.

In spite of psychometrically good intelligence, all conception of coherence of time, space, and person was lacking. Their lives were oriented to washing, dressing, eating, and resting, experienced as pleasurable and unpleasurable purely in terms of their own bodies, and only loosely connected with the adults responsible for their care. Hardly any of the children referred to the staff by name. Some were able to distinguish individual staff members according to the functions of physical routine they supervised. For many children, there existed one exception in this nameless world: the nurse in charge of the sickroom. This seems significant, since she was the only person who, temporarily at least, was in full charge of all the needs of the child.

The automaton-like rigidity of these children, their egocentric preoccupation with functions of their own body, their inability to master a one-to-one contact with an adult, are indications of a serious lag in personality integration.

The deviation in personality development shown by these children allows important conclusions. It demonstrates the dangers of rearing in a setting where a number of adults take care of isolated functions of the child rather than of the whole child, and stresses the necessity of giving each child the opportunity for a continuous central relationship to one adult in the institution.

Upon admission to the School, the children, whose personality development in the therapeutic milieu will be presented, showed striking similarities to this control group. While the severe psychopathology of the patients will become obvious in the description of their gradual rehabilitation, it should be kept in mind that none of the children in the control group were considered in any way abnormal by those who managed the institutional environment in which they lived.

The following case material demonstrates the slow and gradual emergency of personality structure in two children who showed all the characteristics of emotional institutionalism when they were admitted to the School. Here, the simple activities such as eating, bathing, and going to bed, which had also been provided in the non-therapeutic institution, are carried out within meaningful interpersonal relationships. Thus they become essential therapeutic tools for personality rehabilitation.

Case 1[1]

A ten-year-old boy of superior intelligence had lived in various institutions since his birth. His adjustment demanded psychiatric attention only when self-destructive tendencies of long standing culminated in a suicidal attempt. His life had been characterized by scarcity and tenuousness of personal ties. During the process of rehabilitation, it became obvious that his self-destructive act was more a desperate than a pathological effort to break through his isolation. This he revealed in a situation which was characteristic for him in the beginning of treatment at the School. An explosion of rage had followed his awkward and ineffectual attempt to get close to other children by provoking their aggression. It was then that he said, "I

1. Credit for most of the direct work in the rehabilitation of this boy is due to Miss Gayle Shulenberger and Mrs. Marianne Wasson.

went up on the Empire State Building and jumped off. After that everybody was my friend."

Although he had always lived in proximity to others, he had never experienced the structural hierarchy which differentiates children from adults and thus permits their interaction. He neither knew how to react to adults nor how to get along with children. For him, adults were those who were bigger than he, individuals who by virtue of greater strength and size enforced rules, inflicted punishment and prevented children from "bothering them."

One counselor devoted herself particularly to him. Though he was for a long time unable to reciprocate the offered relationship, he immediately utilized the additional comfort which the contacts with the counselor offered. Toward the end of the first month, he expressed his first appreciation of her devotion when he snuggled against her and said, "I am a laughing hyena." He could express happiness only by coloring his incorporate tendencies with primitive feeling tones of joy. It took another month before he was able to ask any personal questions of her, the person whom he knew best. Once, when he had assured himself of his hold on his special counselor who had let him cling to her arm, he asked her where she lived. Although it was clear to all other children that the counselor's room was three doors from their dormitory, his deep isolation had to lift before he could envisage her as a living, personal entity.

This breaking through of his isolation was apparently meaningful to him and he feared its return because his ability to maintain contact was still very tenuous. The arrival of a new boy in the dormitory became an immediate threat to him. However, he found means of reassuring himself; he asked his counselor to come over to his bed and asked to kiss her good night for the first time. He then told her a story which he called a "joke:" Two people had started to go somewhere but soon found themselves back in the same place from which they had started. His insecurity and fear that the newcomer would set him back with his counselor to where he had started showed that he still lacked faith in the reliability of human ties which he had just learned to appreciate.

He became more aloof for several days, but then realized that his fears of abandonment were not justified. This gave him the courage to display regressive behavior for the first time. Though prompted by the threat of a newcomer, this regression was actually progress, since he experimented actively with his ability to cope with vicissitudes in human contacts. Only with his counselor did he begin to act like a small child. In baby talk he called her his mother, saying, "My mamma washes my hands for me. She gets me clean socks." He asked her to help him dress and to spoon-feed him. He was permitted to experience this primitive child–adult relationship. Two months later, baby talk and desire for spoon-feeding were given up spontaneously and new aspects appeared in his relationship with his favorite counselor. Formerly he could maintain contact with her only as his expectations of immediate and tangible gratification were fulfilled. Now the relationship to her became time-structured. His helplessness, the primitivity and urgency of his needs made him desire the permanency of her support. While walking close to her he said, "I am going to hang on to your arm for the rest of my life." It took a whole year for him to develop a feeling of closeness to two adults, his counselor and his teacher. With the rest of the staff, he got along without conflict since he recognized that they served useful functions.

The relative freedom in the therapeutic milieu remained unacceptable to this boy so long as he lacked inner control and the ability for self-regulation. For many months after entering, he complained that the School was not strict enough. Everyone, including himself, was being too spoiled. He praised the disciplinarian spirit of the orphanage from which he had come. In this way, he expressed the fear of his own as yet unintegrated impulses, which at the School were no longer controlled completely by outside rules.

In his eating habits, he experimented with gratification and control of primitive impulses. In addition, through these eating habits he tested the attitudes of the significant figures of his new environment toward his needs.

The boy, who had been well fed and of normal weight upon admission to the Orthogenic School, began to overeat, to suck his thumb, and complain that the staff tried to starve him. Gratification of primitive needs alone gave him a sense of security and means of emotional expression. In eating he also found compensation for the barrenness of his existence, which had to remain limited so long as he could not avail himself of the opportunities for satisfaction offered in the therapeutic milieu. He either insisted that the adults force him to eat, or he ate incessantly. Awareness of his lack of inner control and judgment made it necessary for him to have his devouring tendencies constantly permitted and regulated by others.

He had to check up on the food supplies in the kitchen and store rooms to make sure that he could expect continued gratification. This evidence had to be tangible. When he noticed that the milk supply was lower than usual, his doubts could not be dispelled by verbal assurance; he had to wait around until the milk was delivered.

After he had overcome his starvation fear, he became secure enough to regress once more, and actually recapitulated to the feeding of an infant. He had the courage to discover a baby bottle with nipple which had been on the kitchen shelf since his arrival, and said, "What about that bottle?" When asked, "What about it?" he answered, "I thought I might put some milk in it." He was not prevented from doing it; he used the nipple, then discarded it, but persisted for several days in drinking out of the bottle. Then he began to suck milk out of bottles through straws and for a long time carried a milk bottle around in school and on the playground.

For nearly a year his incorporative needs had been met unconditionally in quantity and form of gratification, before he showed spontaneous attempts to control his gluttony. He began to show some discrimination with regard to food, then he refused second servings, often of dishes he liked best. With self-imposed limitations, his wish for adult control of his eating disappeared. He had begun to have mastery over his primitive desires.

Certainty of unconditional gratification by others and his trust in his ability to master his impulses had to be firmly established before he showed awareness of the needs of others, which is essential in establishing any true interpersonal relationship. Such awareness first centered around eating, the function of such great importance to him. He began to arrange tea parties in which he himself prepared and served all the food. He showed great concern that everybody should have enough to eat. These parties were at first limited to his favorite counselor, the person who for a long time had satisfied all his desires. Then he stopped grabbing food from the plates of the other children and gradually included them in his parties.

Since there had never been any pressure on his table manners, the spontaneous changes in this area are significant indications of his inner changes. His greed, his noisy smacking and sucking, gave way to the eating habits of a normal child. Thumb sucking was relinquished for the socially more acceptable chewing of gum. Personality changes paralleled this process of arriving at mastery of primitive needs through their unconditional gratification. While initially his time was spent mostly in daydreaming, he gradually began to participate in active sports, learned to swim and play baseball and showed great pleasure in these achievements.

After two months at the School, his artistic ability spontaneously came to light. His first artistic productions had a bizarre quality and were mainly elaborations of death and cemeteries. While he had up to then continuously disturbed the classroom by hyperactivity, noisiness, and frequent temper tantrums, he now began to isolate himself in painting when the pressure became too great. This temporary and self-chosen isolation was permitted. It made his classroom experience more acceptable to him and to the others. The topic of his drawings changed; while he still needed occasional retreat from the classroom situation, he no longer drew cemeteries but maintained some contact with the class by elaborating on the topics of the moment by painting farmers in the field, Indians, and animals in an aquarium.

His painting lost none of its imaginative and creative qualities. He derived much personal prestige when the principal asked him for one of his paintings for his office; and on the next day he offered paintings to others, indicating that he had accepted the status they were ready to give him. He began to show interest in his clothes and accepted his counselor's suggestion to select them personally. In the store, he showed fear of this personal responsibility which had been delegated to him, but immediately utilized the experience of being respected as an individual. During this shopping expedition he talked about his fears for the first time and told his counselor that he often asked her to sit on his bed at night because he worried about death at that time.

Gratification of primitive needs had made possible the emergence of sublimation. He was permitted to use his artistic talent to master the classroom situation. He received prestige and praise for his painting. These freed his intellectual abilities, and in ten months he made academic progress equivalent to fourteen months.

The inability to connect present action, past experience, and future expectation led to many instances of confused and explosive behavior because regular repetition of routine at the orphanage had made the boy's life an "empty" continuum. In the absence of meaningful experiences, his existence had not been structured into past, present, and future.

Maturation as a historical process can proceed only if the child's life experience is structured in the dimension of time. Although in the therapeutic milieu children are not overwhelmed with too many activities, still the boy complained that there was too much to do. Holidays are made enjoyable in a casual way, to avoid over-excitement. Instead, small everyday activities are made carriers of interpersonal relationships. Although he did not yet know what made one day different from another and was still unable to react to the events that structure everyday life, he responded to the major event of Easter. He accepted the present and took part in the egg hunt. He was cautious and not too enthusiastic, but for the first time expressed concern about a future event: he wondered about Christmas and asked whether it would be possible for him to participate in its celebration and what it would be like. He could already envisage an event in the future but was able to tolerate it only on the assumption that it would be similar to the experience in the present which he could accept. He wanted to be sure it would not necessitate new adjustments.

Hallowe'en he enjoyed tremendously. He now took the sources of pleasure in his existence for granted. On Thanksgiving Day he complained that while living in the orphanage, he had had no fun on holidays. He was now able to appraise his present life in terms of his past, and said "This is my first real Thanksgiving." He went on to complain that at the orphanage the children "never did anything." They just had a meal like any other day. Then he reminisced about Hallowe'en. His story was rather jumbled but he had begun to see his life in the therapeutic milieu as a sequence of meaningful and variegated events which he had the courage to face. He looked forward to Christmas as a new "different" holiday. Structuralization of his existence into present, future, and past was taking shape.

In the service of mastery of the new situation, all mechanisms that had proven their adequacy were activated. New clothes had begun to give him security through prestige. Accordingly, on Christmas morning, he was the only boy who took great care to dress in his best outfit. His tolerance at seeing others receive gratification and the ability to postpone his own gratifications, were recent acquisitions. His behavior was in line with them. He went to the fireplace where the stockings were hanging, and instead of grabbing his presents, he insisted on telling the other children about what he found in his stocking and admiring what they found in theirs. Then he very slowly repacked all the presents in his stocking. It seemed to the adults that he had not noticed a sled and some other presents and they pointed these out to him. He replied harshly and ran out of the room, muttering to himself, "This is enough. I cannot stand more of this." Later, in the afternoon, he unpacked some of his toys and started to play with them.

In a previous step of his rehabilitation, unconditional gratification of his seemingly boundless needs had been therapeutically indicated. This permitted recapitulation and gratification of infantile expectations and established the basis for personality growth. Once he had learned that food is always made available and that presents do not disappear, he could make a further step. His new capacity to permit himself gratification was a new achievement. It represented ego growth even if guilt about receiving it may have prompted him to postpone gratification.

Therapeutic response from the adult had to be in line with the status of his ego development. Because he was not forced to deal with his gifts according to conventional adult expectations of gratitude, he was really able to enjoy the gifts—in his own time. Thus the adults' respect for the patient's self-set limitations again represented unconditional recognition of his autonomous tendencies. Through such attitudes of the adult, the boy derived a sense of personal integrity from incidents in his everyday life. This modified his conception of himself and established self-esteem. He became able to face the "bad" past and also developed trust in a benign and manageable future, while he took his present existence for granted.[2] Two successive dreams which he spontaneously related to his counselor illustrate this.

In the first dream, he was king of the universe, Superman. He had a million dollars and ruled everyone. In the second dream, he went to visit the orphanage. He was in the pool (where the older children had thrown him into the water and never given him a chance to learn to swim). He showed them how well we was able to swim and dive. All the children sat around the pool and admired him and liked him very much.

The first dream shows how he attempted to compensate for his lack of personal status in the orphanage by ideas of omnipotence. In the second dream, his recently acquired real achievements, swimming and diving, give him prestige among those with whom he used to have none. Thus the

2. It should be mentioned that in children whose past experiences have been less malignant, the same process leads to the emergence in memory of the positive factors in their past lives.

new strength permitted him a more assuring perspective on past and future. While the past had been bad, a similar situation would not again find
him helpless.

He learned to see his past in a light which no longer overwhelmed him.
Trust in his ability to master situations which once had overpowered him
made his outlook of the future realistic and therefore more optimistic. A
similar change occurred in his daydreams: instead of being a great dictator and Superman, he now daydreamed about becoming a street car con-
ductor after having lived in a nice foster home for quite a while.

During the year of his stay at the School, the boy made significant steps
in personality growth. Environmental attitudes which made such development possible were to him personified in the first counselor who had gratified his dependent needs, permitted him defensive activity, and mediated
between him and the outside world whenever he needed such help. As he
experienced the implications of interpersonal relationships in his contacts
with her, his total human environment began to take on shape and
structure.

When he came to the School, all he knew about people was that there
are small children, and big children who tell the small ones what to do.
Human interaction was a matter of domination through strength or material possessions. For a long time, contact with other children consisted in
forceful attempts to take their toys. This behavior was dented when, on St.
Valentine's Day, he unexpectedly received valentines from some of the
other children. He was happy that he should have made friends. Gradually, he became able to share his toys occasionally, and there was a lessening of the inner struggle which first arose with such performance.

He was surprised that he had found a new *modus vivendi* with other
children and searched for an explanation of their kindness. He came to the
conclusion that "the children here act right because the grownups treat
them right." This was his first recognition of a benign hierarchy of human
interrelations. Such awareness was possible only because he had experienced it explicitly in his contacts with the counselor.

Since he was no longer isolated, the slowness and blocking disappeared
which had been equivalents for depressive reactions. The desire and abi-
ity to communicate gave new meaning to his artist creations; he discovered spontaneously that personal ties were the source of his new strength.
He told the psychiatrist that he had much more energy now and explained,
"Before, I thought that I could get energy and strength from food only;
now I know that I get energy from other children, counselors, baseball,
swimming, and drawing, that is, if I make a picture for somebody."

In a later interview, about one year after admission to the School, he expressed his contentment in a fictitious telephone conversation. As the chairman of the board of directors, he called the School's principal to check up
and offer help. He asked, "What do you need for your children? Candy,

paper, paint, crayons, nothing? They know you have all they need? That is good. Good bye."

He became eager to understand the relationships of grownups to one another, since he now knew what adults have to offer children and what children may mean to each other. Their relationships were no longer empty or overwhelming and threatening, and he could therefore accept them. He stated with great pride that he now knew what grownups were— they "act like ladies and gentlemen. They go to college, they care for children, they like children. I will be a grownup too someday, but not for a long time." He had acquired a well defined reference frame and can be expected to proceed further in growth.

Case 2[3]

This case, like the first, is also characterized by a child's desperate effort to cope with an unbearable reality. The outward signs of this struggle for mastery were hyperactivity, destructiveness and stealing, severe inhibition of intellectual functioning, and extreme suspiciousness. These symptoms appeared first when Mary was six years old. She had been transferred to a foster home from the nursery where she had lived after her parents had deserted her at the age of three. While at the nursery, she had not presented any manifest problems, but in the foster homes her behavior became progressively more difficult and led to many changes in homes until she came to the Orthogenic School at the age of nine. Her disturbed actions were only the surface ripples of her megalomaniac fantasies, evidence of the unavoidable clashes between external demands which she could not fulfill, and her magic world to which she could no longer successfully retreat.

Psychiatric study before admission to the School showed that she was quite detached from the many adults and children with whom she had lived. She was utterly confused about their identity. Physiological activities like eating and sleeping were not gratifying experiences, but duties imposed by rules or the wishes of others. She hardly knew what playing meant. She said, "Where I live, there is a doll buggy, but I must not touch it." She explained, "Once I was a baby, but I was never wheeled in a buggy."

When asked where she lived, she answered, "In a place where you get clean clothes after playing. Then you take a nap and eat sometimes." She was unable to name any of the children or adults in the orphanage. When asked whether she had a friend, she said, "They tell me that John is my friend." When asked who took care of her, she replied, "A nurse, that is a lady, any lady."

---

3. Credit for most of the direct work in rehabilitating this girl is due to Miss Marjorie Jewell and Miss Joan Little.

A large segment of her life was spent in autistic fantasy. She said that she was a good girl because she did not bother anybody. Nothing bothered her either since she, and everything around her, was magic. She only had to open her window, say goodbye to the children, then she could fly to God who was nice always.

A few days after admission Mary said she liked the School. "It is like in the nursery before, but it is better, because it is all in one. The school is just here and not five blocks away." Through simplification in denial of any difference, distance, or discrepancy between the constituents of her outside world, she reduced her new environment to manageable proportion. In the foster homes she had had to protect herself from being overwhelmed by the multitude of external events, since the empty existence of her early years had not equipped her to deal with them adequately. But the autistic mechanisms which she applied did not help her to master the presistent demands of reality; when she attempted to withdraw more deeply, her inadequacy only increased and anxiety resulted. Her confusion which led to constant misinterpretations and contaminations seemed to reduce her intellectual functioning to a near feebleminded level.

In the School her need to avoid anxiety determined the nature of her initial adjustment. This need was met as her spontaneous methods of mastery remained unchallenged by external pressure. At that stage, the existence of actual sources of satisfaction and stimulation in the therapeutic milieu was of value for her only because she was not forced to combat external pressure. Still, the presence of such factors was essential from the beginning for her rehabilitation. They had to be available when she was ready to take advantage of them. Opportunity for stimulation and gratification distinguished the therapeutic milieu from the barrenness of nursery life which had led to impoverishment of her personality, while freedom from the pressure which had made her foster home experiences so deleterious, precluded necessity for further confusion and withdrawal.

Since she could not, *a priori,* expect conditions in the external world to be different from her past experiences, she had to apply her old mechanisms of mastery in the new environment. Her courage to explore reality had first been severely curtailed by lack of stimulation in the orphanage, and later by her experiences in foster homes. Protective withdrawal into a world of all-powerful magic was therefore maintained at the School until she developed sufficient confidence in herself and trust in others gradually to modify her defenses.

Mary had not learned to live without magic protection, and now met benign, relatively powerful figures. In proportion to the abject degree of her helplessness, she needed protective figures of such strength as could only be furnished by endowing them with magic powers. Under the aegis of these figures, she could venture forth to test reality with greater comfort and security. Thus, in a way, she tried to establish magic contact with what seemed to her the most important figures in her new environment, the principal and the psychiatrist. In order to be able to retain them as "magic" figures, all realistic contact with them had to be avoided, and they had to be both depersonalized and unified. To do so was also in line with her past efforts to organize her world by recognizing persons only as carriers of useful or dangerous functions. This tendency she demonstrated by depriving the two figures, the principal, and the psychiatrist, of the only personal characteristics of which she was aware, their names. She contaminated them into "Dr. Bettelster." Whenever she used this contamination, it designated both of them in the magic and protective functions she assigned to them. She refused to recognize them as persons and avoided personal contact. Because she rebuffed their efforts, contact was discontinued.

She began to approach the principal about one of his functions with which she had become familiar—his role as mediator. She established a routine of complaining to him, remaining aloof at the same time. She did this in line with her magic expectations, and not in terms of a realistic interpretation of his function. She invariably expected him to take her side, protect her, and punish the others. The fact that she received protection only when she needed it, and that other children were not reprimanded just because she complained about them, did not change her conviction of his role as her special protector. When other children expressed fear about events which were beyond control, she reassured them with the statement, "It cannot happen here because of Dr. Bettelster." Gradually, after she had established personalized contacts with her favorite counselor, she separated the psychiatrist from the principal, still adhering to the conviction of their inherent identity: she then called the one Dr. Bester and the other Dr. Vester. Much later, after she had finally found true security in the relationship to her counselor, it became possible for her to divest them of some of their presumed magic characteristics, to accept them tentatively as real, and recognize them as two different persons with different names.

Under the magic protection of the most powerful figures that she had created for herself, she was able to explore segments of reality and to approach a relationship with her counselor. In the meantime, the other children had to remain anonymous and unreal because to acknowledge their presence would have interfered with her need to claim her counselor for herself.

Gratification of her most urgent needs became the basis for her human contacts. For many months she over-ate, staying in the dining room after the others had left and scavenging for food in spite of the large helpings she had already eaten. After each meal, she wrapped food in a napkin to take with her for fear she might be hungry before the next meal. Whenever a course was put on the table, she jumped up excitedly and looked at her counselor for reassurance that she would get more food. Frequently she ate directly from the plate without utensils in order to finish in time for a third and fourth helping. No limitations were put on her needs. After a month she required fewer helpings of food. Now her eating habits did not reflect greed but became distinctly babyish. She sucked her food and occasionally spat it out. Then she started to carry a small jar with her in which she kept a ration of candy. Her eating habits changed only after she had formed individualized relations to her counselor and to some of the children.

She did not tolerate any closeness and had to be permitted to "float around" in the School for some time. Out of the confused anonymity of her existence, familiarity with carriers of useful functions emerged slowly.

Children remained anonymous to her much longer than adults. A friend was a child who was "bigger and can beat you up; you go to her bed." But she was hardly able to distinguish one child from another. To her, they were nameless and existed only if tangibly present. She spoke of them as "that girl," and the only way she called to them was "Hey, yóu."

On a walk with a counselor, two of the other children ran ahead and were out of sight for a few minutes. When the rest of the group caught up with them, she said without any sign of being perturbed, "Oh there they are. I thought they were dead."

When she began to individualize the children, it was in terms of their attitudes toward the counselor to whom she had become very attached. She consistently expressed her dislike for some children who called this counselor names. In her first attempts to make friends, she adopted toward other children those attitudes which she expected from her counselor in fantasy, and had to be restrained from giving away all of her possessions. Her tendency to concede to any demand made by other children was inappropriate and had to be modified. .

Confusion had been the outcome of her attempts to orient herself toward people around her. Similar disorientation showed her helplessness in other areas. Since she had lived in many parts of the city without sufficient awareness of reality ever to find her way about, she was utterly lost in the neighborhood of the School. She showed pseudologic attitudes when she claimed to know every person and every building, in attempting to compensate for her overwhelming ignorance by such confabulation about persons and places. She claimed to recognize acquaintances and insisted that she had lived on that or the other street. Isolated actual recollections appeared later and then in connection with functions and activities she had begun to master at the School.

Conventional concepts of time meant nothing to her and she manipulated time purely in terms of her own needs and tensions. On July 10th, she recalled that her birthday had been on "June two and three" (June 23rd). This meant to her that her next birthday would be "in two or three days." Whenever she acquired any valid and usable knowledge, she used it compulsively to orient herself. When she was already sufficiently settled at the School to wish to remain, reassurance that she could stay as long as she wanted was insufficient. She had to orient herself by applying the terms of the seasons she had just learned about in class, and asked repeatedly: "Will I be here in the summer? Will I be here in the winter?" repeating the seasons many times. In this way, she sifted her new knowledge in terms of its value for the reassurance she needed. Facts were accepted and retained only after she had tested their usefulness for her immediate needs.

When she first began to experience activities and events in the external world as more gratifying than complete immersion in fantasy, she could not stand the tension of any delay in the succession of external occurrences. If she wanted to buy something, she could not accept the fact that stores were closed in the evening. She could not stand any moment without activity and continuously asked: "What are we going to do now?" Before an answer could be given, she had already wandered to some other subject and she was unable to comprehend what was said to her.

The same pressure appeared in her manner of talking. While she had been quiet and uncommunicative when she first came to the School, with turning to reality, her speech became rapid and explosive. She deleted syllables and ran words together, so that her talk was difficult to understand. Of this, she was initially unaware. Then she became frustrated about her inability to express herself. Her sentences became even less comprehensible as she now interspersed them with recurring exclamations of disgust. She finally realized this when she stopped herself in the middle of a sentence, looked apologetically at the counselor and said, "I can't even speak the English language. I can never say what I want to."

A process of gradual organization started in and around her daily contacts with her special counselor. At first her counselor was a nameless one of many. Her appreciation was unspecific as to source and form of gratification. She said, "I like them, they are good to you." A few weeks later, she dimly recalled her counselor's name; but she still could describe her life at the School only in a stereotyped enumeration of activities which were related solely to herself, such as eating, bathing, going to bed. She mentioned other children only in terms of their interference or noninterference with these activities.

After a month, contacts with the counselor centered around such simple activities as Mary initiated herself. She demanded to be carried, to be cuddled and fed. When she saw the counselor after a short absence, she shouted, "I love you," hugged her and playfully bit her. Her attitude then did not yet express the interpersonal relationship of a nine-year-old, but was the possessive clinging of an infant.

After about six months, her haunted, sober expression occasionally gave way to real smiling at her counselor. In these moments, she seemed to be in contact, her voice was natural, she finished her sentences and could be reached by the counselor's reply.

It was then, in her contacts with the counselor that she energetically and actively went about the task of getting order into her immediate world. Temporarily her activities assumed a compulsive character. She was first concerned with the order of things around her and started her new activity around eating situations. She cleaned her candy box repeatedly, stacked candy bars according to color and size, counted them and said spontaneously, "This is fun." Then she cleaned her shelves vigorously, arranged and rearranged her toys and wanted her clothes laid out exactly and neatly for the next morning. Her bed had to be perfect and she liked to sweep the floor around it and even underneath. It was as if orderliness in objects related to her had to precede inner order.

Her counselor made some comment about the amount of cleaning she did and she replied that she liked to clean, and added, "Then when I grow up," and stopped. When asked to go on, she said, "Well, it was silly and I know it is not true, but I thought that I would have all my cleaning-up done by the time I grow up." Thus she experimented with her ability to comprehend and master the objects around her in their relation to each other and to herself. In this experimentation with external order, she achieved mastery over one sector of the outside world. As she became able to internalize this achievement, she made her first steps in integration.

It should be kept in mind that her activity emerged spontaneously within the setting of her contacts with the counselor in which, within a reference frame of predictable and maintained interest, she had already experienced not only order, but also unconditional gratification.

Conclusions

The aim of any psychotherapeutic procedure is to help the patient toward adequate mastery over inner and outer forces.

The importance which milieu factors have for causing emotional disturbances in childhood is well established. It is also realized that manipulation of milieu factors can be used toward the rehabilitation of emotionally disturbed children.

In direct psychotherapy of children, recognition is given to the fact that shaping the individual's biological needs in the earliest years is of decisive importance for later personality structure as well as for prognostic considerations. When distorted growth processes can be recapitulated within the benign setting of the psychotherapeutic relationship, symptoms become unnecessary, personality structure changes, growth phenomena appear, and psychotherapy can be considered successful.

Similarly, emotionally disturbed children can be helped through living in a milieu which is aware of the factors that promote restoration of function growth, and new integration. The two children described improved in the particular therapeutic milieu because there insight was translated into uninterrupted action extending over twenty-four hours a day. The children showed improvement because they lived in an environment which, from the start, provided them with a stable frame of reference. While the adults maintained the interpersonal hierarchy in all their dealings with the children, their actions always remained spontaneous within the indications set by the psychological reality of the individual child. This was the spirit in which every child received such gratification as his instinctual and defensive needs dictated at any given moment.

The use of the continuously maintained one-to-one relationship within a therapeutic milieu as one of the many aspects of milieu-psychotherapy is stressed.

4. Changing Delinquent Subcultures: A Social-Psychological Approach

HOWARD W. POLSKY

In increasing numbers, psychologists, anthropologists, and sociologists are turning their attention to the interpersonal dynamics of juvenile delinquent groups.[1] One important source for investigation has been the training schools and residential treatment centers.[2] We have come to realize after considerable trial and error that it is no easy matter to intervene effectively in the delinquent subcultures established by aggressive adolescents. This paper is a contribution to an understanding of delinquent social structures and the bearing this has upon group intervention and individual rehabilita-

Reprinted with the permission of the National Association of Social Workers from *Social Work,* Vol. 4, No. 3 (October, 1959), pp. 3–15.
1. This sociological tradition in America goes back at least to 1930–1931 with the publication of Clifford R. Shaw's *The Jack Roller* and *The Natural History of a Delinquent* (Chicago: University of Chicago Press, 1930 and 1931). Recent cross-cultural work in this vein can be found in Herbert Bloch and Arthur Niedenhoffer, *The Gang: A Study in Adolescent Behavior* (New York: Philosophical Library, 1958).
2. See for example Richard D. Trent, *An Exploratory Study of the Inmate Social Organization,* Vol. 5 of Warwick Child Welfare Services Project, 1954–1957, Bettina Warburg, ed. (New York: State Board of Social Welfare, 1957, mimeographed.)

tion. Our fundamental source is an intensive participant-observation analysis over the period of a year in a cottage containing the oldest, toughest, and most delinquent boys in a residential treatment center.[3]

The sociologist attempts to find the mainsprings for human behavior within the matrix of interpersonal relationships in which the individual functions. He tries to determine the significant people in the delinquent's life and how they are influencing him. To be sure, the press of the environment—the external frame of reference—has as its counterpoint the indivdiual's internal reference structure. We must evaluate the pathology inherent in the psychic structure, lest we overestimate the extent to which group norms influence individuals. This must be carefully assessed in any intervention program. Our primary focus in this paper, however, is to delineate some of the social and cultural forces that shape delinquent group life and individual "careers" within it.

The theory of delinquency as a subculture has left many gaps in the analysis of its organizational character. We know little about how delinquent boys interrelate between antisocial outbreaks. What are the normative interpersonal relationships in a delinquent subculture which periodically spill over in the form of aggression against society?

An organized delinquent peer group is not merely the sum of hostile projections of disturbed boys who are externalizing intrapsychic conflicts. A large variety of diagnostic types can be found to "fit" the alternative roles the delinquent culture assigns its recruits. An important need today is a better understanding of the *system of norms and statuses* which delinquent groups create and the interpersonal soil in which antisocial acts, values, and personalities are nurtured.[4] "Economic" principles appear to operate not only in the individual, but in the group as well; delinquents are able to articulate a highly stylized social and cultural organization to which all its members must contribute and respond—often at great personal risk and deterioration.

Thus far sociologists have tended to concentrate their fire on the accommodation patterns by way of which the leaders and activists in the delinquent gangs gain recognition by adults in the community.[5] But this is akin to describing American society only by analyzing its international rela-

---

3. Howard W. Polsky and Martin Kohn, *Progress Report: Analysis of the Peer Group in a Residential Treatment Center* (Hawthorne, N. Y.: Hawthorne Cedar Knolls School, 1957, mimeographed); "Participant-observation in a Delinquent Subculture," *American Journal of Orthopsychiatry,* Vol. 29, No. 4 (October 1959).

4. Albert K. Cohen, "The Study of Social Disorganization and Deviant Behavior," in Robert K. Merton, Leonard Broom, and Leonard S. Cottrell, eds., *Sociology Today* (New York: Basic Books, 1959).

5. For an excellent summary and analysis of new developments in this approach see Richard A. Cloward, "Illegitimate Means, Anomie, and Deviant Behavior," *American Sociological Review,* Vol. 24, No. 2 (April 1959).

tions. We need more empirical studies of delinquency as a social system, emphasizing the sources of strain and anomie generated by "internal" social and cultural normative processes. As long as this approach is lacking, we shall have a distorted concept of the emergence and maintenance of delinquent groups as viable organizations.

For example, we analyzed a runaway which culminated in the theft of an auto in a town near the institution. Two boys, an introverted isolate and a rebellious scapegoated newcomer, combined forces to escape from *both* their peer group and adult authorities. The significant precipitating cause was the rejection of both boys by the cottage peer group. The sources of stress within the peer group on this microscopic level can be multiplied many times.

In our analysis we shall stress the "internal" systemic aspects of delinquency, which means that our focus will be upon the normative interpersonal relationships and processes within the group, and the values upon which they are based.[6] At a minimum four questions must be posed: (1) What is a delinquent subculture? (2) To what do we want to change it? (3) How can we change it? (4) How can we evaluate culture and individual change?

The Aggressive Society

Every social system consists of ideal or expected patterns of action and statuses and is stratified so that power, prestige, and income are differentially distributed among its members. The recruitment for positions and their consolidation vary with the character of the group and its stage of crystallization. The criteria which distinguish the superior and inferior strata depend upon the core norms of the group. The rigidity of the delinquent social structure is formed by underlying sanctions of brute force and manipulation which are used by the top clique boys and filter down through the entire social order. The boys in Cottage 6 believed that no other boy had a right to enter their cottage, but if they suspected someone else of taking something from their cottage, they felt they had the unqualified right to ransack other cottages.

Within the cottages, there are several variants of a stratified social structure based on toughness, "brains," deviant activities, and status-deflating, rigidly controlling interpersonal processes. In some groups the tough boys —the "power," "big men," or "take"—maintain absolute hegemony and

6. Our analysis of the social structure of the delinquent group has been observed by others who have described juvenile gangs. See William Poster, "T'was a Dark Night in Brownsville," *Commentary*, Vol. 9, No. 5 (May 1950); Dale Kramer and Madeline Karr, *Teen-age Gangs* (New York: Henry Holt & Co., 1953); Stacy V. Jones, "The Cougars—Life with a Brooklyn Gang," *Harper's Magazine* (November 1954), pp. 35–43; Harrison E. Salisbury, *The Shook-up Generation* (New York: Harper & Brothers, 1958).

assign the "con-artists" subsidiary positions. In other groups, the gamblers and con-artists unite with the tough leaders and maintain a pressing rule over the "punks" or "bush-boys"—the weak and less able boys. In any case, muscles, brains, and deviant activities are united in one form or another to insure a flow of psychic and material services upward to the boys in the upper half of the status hierarchy. Brute force maintains the rigid pecking order and is exemplified in violence, manipulation, exploitation, "ranking," and scapegoating. These processes occur not only between delinquent groups, but are the essential dynamic of social control *within* the delinquent groups.[7]

The paradigm in Figure 4.1 was vividly corroborated by a perceptive cottage leader and has been verified by detailed independent observation:

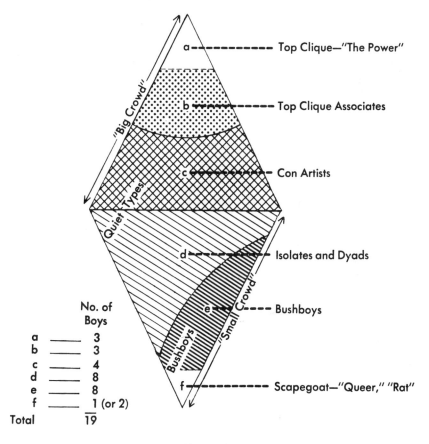

Figure 4.1

7. Delinquent interpersonal processes are discussed in detail in Howard W. Polsky, *Cottage 6: A Study of Delinquency as a Social System* (New York: Russell Sage, 1962).

Q: Well, who ran the cottage when you first came into 7?

A: Hank Shade, Frankie Gorman, Spiffy Weiner. You see, a cottage is never actually run by one guy. One guy has brains, the other guy has muscles, but always four or five, or three guys are the power in the group. They might not be the roughest guys, these three together, but they are the power of the group. What they want to do mostly is what the group does, and a lot of smart guys don't actually want to become the leader, they want to be the guy in back, they want to become the *power* of the group. And then the cottage guys clique up, you know, they fall into certain groups where they hang together and they stay together. And these groups, you know, are your power.

Q: Well, when did you become a power in 7? I know you did. It was one of the reasons they changed you. Right?

A: Well, that's true. But I came about power in a different way than a lot of other kids. I like to gamble and I'm good at it, and through the fact that you can win, well, then you have money. That automatically makes the group have to come to you at one point or another.

Q: That's right.

A: Guys are going AWOL, they got to come to you to get money. So what they try to do is when you get money and they're looking out for themselves, they try to get you to like them. And in order to get you to like them, when you make a suggestion they follow it, because there is no reason to antagonize the hand that's feeding you. So that's how I came into power. Guys owed me money, so guys were afraid to get me mad because they'd have to pay. I had my own strong-arm boys that were willing to collect for me. . . .

Q: Like who?

A: Like Foster, and Simon, like myself. You see, I mean I wasn't . . . the whole point is that I never had to use them. I'd collect my own debts, but yet everybody knew that these guys would help me collect my debts if it ever came to something like that, and it never did.

Q: Well then, were you the three guys who were sort of the top guys up there?

A: Yes.[8]

We have found in several cottages a diamond-shaped social system which persists over time as old leaders leave and middle- and low-status boys rise in the hierarchy.[9] Delinquent status positions are useful in predicting the boys' interrelationships in the cottage. This is why we view their behavior as a social system. Every stratum combines a cluster of privileges and duties. The translation of each clique's norms into concrete action is the function of the diverse roles in the cottage.

The top clique is the "power"; within it boys of inferior status were ranked and exploited by the tougher boys; the former attempted to take over the cottage when the toughs left. Below the top clique are the "con-

8. Howard W. Polsky, *A Treatment Center Alumnus' Own Story* (Hawthorne, N. Y.: Hawthorne Cedar Knolls School, 1958, mimeographed.)

9. Howard W. Polsky, *Continuity and Change in a Delinquent Sub-Culture* (Hawthorne, N. Y.: Hawthorne Cedar Knolls School, 1959, mimeographed.)

artists," who are not afraid to fight, but more typically employed their manipulative abilities and skill at deviant activities to exploit boys further down in the hierarchy. The "quiet types"—or "regular guys"—have abandoned gross delinquent activities, but are not typed "punks"; several are regarded as mentally or socially retarded by the older boys and have a long history of foster home and institutional placement. The bottom stratum consists of "bushboys" or "punks," the targets of the boys above; they carry out the menial tasks in the cottage, are looked upon as "dirt" or "sneaks," not to be trusted, and frequently singled out for violence and ranking. At the very bottom are the scapegoats—the "queers"—who are the focal targets for the entire cottage; some break down under the pressure and run from the institution; others compulsively ingratiate themselves with higher-status boys or accept the minimum duties required at this station and, biding their time and using violence and ranking upon boys arriving after them, eventually climb up the status hierarchy.

Social distance between the cliques within a cottage is quite large. The cliques are ranked and each person recognizes to which one he belongs, and its relationship to the others. Clique members share common activities and outlooks. They reinforce each other in opposing "out-cliques" and exert social control throughout the group.

The statuses are unusually "frozen." A new boy coming into the cottage must identify with the lowest stratum. He is put into the "punk bedroom" and undergoes a period of severe manipulation and testing. This includes social ostracism as well as performance of menial duties for older boys. He learns how to take it and if he survives, how to dish it out too. One of the chief ways a boy can change his status is through physically challenging higher-status individuals. This frequently culminates in a fight or "standoff." The outcomes of these fights are burned into the boys' memories and can drastically change one's status and horizons in the cottage.

The delinquent social system is essentially inequalitarian. Individual boys become alerted, sensitized, and preoccupied with power relationships; it is to each according to his status, from each according to his status. This colors the most incidental interactions. I have observed unbelievable anxiety in the simplest request for milk on the part of a low-status member who was addressing a high-status boy. It is our feeling that this authoritarian type of social structure organizes and controls the major portion of the boys' lives, inculcates delinquent norms, defends them from facing threatening problems—school, girls, jobs, community disgrace—and blocks involvement in constructive activities.

Among the boys hostility is so pervasive that after a while it becomes the automatic response and is displaced readily upon any available target. The stultifying process works as follows: when violence is used against individuals within the group (and they are always around), it creates an intense need on the part of the perpetrators to rationalize their behavior. Thus

they condemn those against whom they commit violence by citing the latter's "queerness," "sneakiness," and "grubbiness." This justifies increased
violence and manipulation against them, which in turn reinforces stereo-
types. The omnipresence of the strong-weak continuum, the followers'
identification with power figures, and the lack of *alternative identifications*
exaggerate the importance of toughness. The vigilant alertness for potential "pretenders to the throne" leads to projection of hostility in situations
in which it does not actually exist.

The analysis of delinquency as a social system enables us to view the
developmental phases of the group. With each turnover in the cottage, especially when the leaders leave, a crisis is precipitated. The boys then subject
one another to a period of intensified manipulation and testing until each
recognizes where he stands in the total system. Out of this interregnum of
testing and manipulation new alliances and out-groups are formed. New
members become extremely vulnerable because of their function as targets
for the other boys to gain prestige. The punk "invites" his oppressors to
harass him. The scapegoat's fears are monitored by his tormentors as they
stimulate one another to exclude him from their midst. Thus by examining
the total social system we have a better understanding of its hierarchical
components. All the group members must learn how to orient themselves
to one another.

There is another dimension to cottage social control based upon personality factors. Within each clique there are pecking triangles which are
miniature reproductions of the larger social organization. Regardless of
the extrinsic characteristics of each clique we believe that there are intrinsic personality factors which predispose individual boys to fulfill specific
roles. Psychodynamically, a high-placed punk in Clique I has more in common with a punk in Clique IV then he does with a dominant member of his
own clique. What specific personality traits huddle together with each role
is now being explored. We want to emphasize that the complementary role
sets in each clique that fulfill the requirements of the aggressive society
can be understood fully only if we are flexible enough to shift from group
to personality variables when the analysis demands it.

Several sociologists have asserted that delinquents pursue "malicious,
negativistic, and nonutilitarian" goals.[10] However, this appears to be a
cultural bias. If one evaluates their culture according to society's value system, their actions appear nonutilitarian. Looking at the delinquent social
system from within, however, our perspective changes. The drastic restric-
tions for achieving status within a delinquent group lead to exaggerated
conformity with the group's norms. If one can gain prestige by showing
defiance against adults, this is not a negativistic activity from the point of

---

10. Albert Cohen, *Delinquent Boys: The Culture of the Gang* (Glencoe, Ill.: The
Free Press, 1955).

view of the boy who is attempting to gain recognition with his group. Thus before we conclude that a boy trying to swing from one of the trees is trying to kill himself because he cannot control repressed conflicts, we have to analyze such an act in the context of his strivings in his primary group.

Group participation shapes personality organization; the latter partially determines role incumbency. Peer interpersonal patterns are crucial for the development of the boy's attitudes and philosophy of life, his aspirations for the future, the kinds of activities in which he will excel, and the form and content of relationships he will make with adults. In short, we must challenge the delinquent subculture as well as its individual constituents.

Control Versus Change

Staff members who have to deal with these boys on a day-to-day basis learn to accommodate themselves to the delinquents' system of social control. Counselors will assign a bushboy to a "regular guy's" bedroom and thereby help him avoid extreme forms of ranking and violence. Social workers have been known to prod their charges to fight in order to change their social status. The "pro-academic" youngster is removed from an "anti-academic" cottage. Top delinquent leaders are accorded community-wide prestige; one "tough boy," a dictator who exercised rigid control over the other boys in a cottage, inadvertently was given the top award for the most improvement.[11]

In order to maintain a state of equilibrium the cottage parent "strikes a bargain" with the delinquent leadership. The latter "agrees" not to cause disturbances within the institution outside of the cottage. The price that the staff pays is "restricting" the aggression and hostility to the cottage. The unintended consequence of such compromises is reinforcement of the authoritarian social structure. Our observation of the cottage parents in the senior unit indicates that their background, their isolation from the professional staff, and the dense interaction with twenty disturbed delinquents results in a role adaptation which alienates them from the relevant structures of the treatment institution and its philosophy.

Many of the inequalities institutionalized in the peer group are reminiscent of the boys' typical family situations in which we find the incipient cause for delinquent acting-out. Many of these boys are in revolt against highly unstable, controlling, narcissistic mothers and weak, indifferent fathers with whom they are unable to identify. These parents and delinquent gang leaders have served as the chief models for the boys' superegos. The natural inequality between parents and child is further exploited in

11. We have analyzed the relationship between the cottage culture and the institution in a paper entitled *Why Delinquent Subcultures Persist—The Double Standard "Interaction" Hypothesis* (Hawthorne, N. Y.: Hawthorne Cedar Knolls Schools, 1959, mimeographed.)

the peer group so that "the whole relationship is not one of universal goodness but of arbitrary power."[12]

It is important to point out that we not only have to change the stereotyped ideology upon which the boys' social structure is based, but modify their interrelationships as well. The leadership in the delinquent group we analyzed frequently verbalized democratic and laissez-faire principles:

> Observer: Did you stay in the same bedroom with Red Leon and Stein?
> Steve: No, when I first came, I roomed with two other guys. Then I started buddying around with Red Leon and I finally moved into the end room. It was me, Red Leon, and Wolf. Then it was the big room.
> Observer: Then it was the big room? What do you mean by that?
> Steve: Well, I mean by the big room is that we were about the only guys in the cottage who were considered big around the campus—me, Red Leon, and Wolf. We were considered the biggest on the campus.
> Observer: By biggest, you mean toughest? Because you certainly weren't the tallest or heaviest.
> Steve: Well, all the guys considered us the toughest, me and Leon especially. But we never really looked for trouble. The only time we'd fight was when trouble came to us.

This vocabulary has to be challenged in concrete situations. The toughest boys claim that "they never look for trouble." Yet they are the chief controllers and perpetrators of the delinquent orientation. How does this occur? Steve Davis, the undisputed leader in the group, talked about Ricky Kahn as follows:

> Well, Rick Kahn, when he first came up, he was a bushboy. I got that slang word from the gang. They call a guy a bushboy when he does another guy's clothes for him, or runs errands for him. Another guy tells him to do that and do that, and he runs and does it. That's what we mean by bushboy. But he used to do a lot of that for me and we got along.

In other words, "getting along" with the top delinquent leader is conforming to his expectations for behaving as a bushboy. In turn, the latter internalizes the delinquent leader's image and practices the same kind of exploitation with new boys who enter the cottage after him. Thus the delinquent cycle is perpetuated.

We have discovered that these very disturbed ("maladaptive") delinquents are able to create a well-organized social structure. Critical questions in an institutional setting concern not only individual pathologies, but the ways in which they are mutually reinforced in the peer group and between it and the staff. Therefore we believe that to maximize the therapeutic influence we must go beyond the concept of accommodation with the

---

12. Eric Homburger Erickson, "Growth and Crises of the Healthy Personality," in Clyde Kluckhohn and Henry A. Murray, eds., *Personality in Nature, Society and Culture* (New York: Alfred A. Knopf, 1956), p. 209.

intact delinquent social system and think in terms of penetration and change.

The foregoing presentation has stressed the concept of group delinquency in terms of authoritarian interpersonal processes, fascistic values, and deviant activities. We want to change the boys' activities, goals, and interpersonal relationships. Gambling, liquor parties, and "kangaroo courts" are gross activities that we agree should be prohibited; what is less stressed is changing the boys' interrelationships.

Social work is committed to a democratic ideology.[13] We would like to influence delinquent groups toward democratic rather than authoritarian relationships. Each individual has a right to participate in the decision-making process. Might is not right. Activities should fulfill rather than negate human dignity and integrity. The stress upon *democratic* procedures is crucial because we know that the boys can become involved in many nondelinquent activities using authoritarian methods. (This is why spotless cottages in institutions are suspect.) The boys must be enabled to formulate realistic goals and handle frustration constructively. We would emphasize the boys' acceptance of each other even though they may differ about the criteria of acceptability. High evaluation of other human beings should be stressed, apart from their social status. Basic social rights should be so institutionalized that all have an equal chance to gain satisfaction on bases other than authoritarian. The group worker and other adults should strive to promote consensus for *democratic procedures* as the ground rules under which individual interests may be pursued.

We have found that intragroup (and outgroup) aggression and manipulation alternate with long periods of apathy, boredom, aimlessness, and depression:

> "It's boring around here. We're around all day, then stay up all night shooting the shit, just shooting the shit, and playing with *Oscar*." The guys chimed in agreement: "The trouble is, there isn't anything to do around here all day, it gets boring. In the morning we have a couple of details and work . . . imagine on our vacation [recorded during Christmas]. Spend a little time in the gym in the afternoon and then there's nothing to do until we eat and then we come back and look at television, play a little cards . . . and just sit around shooting the shit."

This is the cottage milieu which is structured by the boys' aggressive tendencies. One of the key tasks of the professional worker responsible for the cottage is motivating the boys toward goals which are realistic in terms of individual and group achievement and which are meaningful *to them*.

13. See among numerous writings Herbert Bisno, *The Philosophy of Social Work* (Washington, D.C.: Public Affairs Press, 1952); Gisela Konopka, "The Generic and the Specific in Group Work Practice in the Psychiatric Setting," *Social Work*, Vol. 1, No. 1 (January 1956), p. 72.

The Basic Institutional Change

The boys do become aware of positive values and goals in their individual casework interviews. However, the pressure encountered in the daily cottage living situation can be so overwhelming that it counteracts values which are and could be engendered in the social worker's office. The first step necessary for change is to acknowledge the existence of the delinquent subculture with all its ramifying importance for individual and group rehabilitation.

The next step is to fashion an institutional arrangement whereby we can place at the center of the cottage a professional person who works directly with the boys on a cottage level. This residential worker, together with cottage parents, caseworker, and other adults who come in contact with the boys, must begin thinking creatively about supplanting the aggressive vicious cycles in the cottage with positive relationships, activities, values, and goals. No longer satisfied to react merely to the boys' internal delinquency, we propose that they take the initiative to plan a viable cottage program which unites the group's propensities for health and all the available resources in the institution. Only by constant feedback with a professional (or professionally oriented) residential worker responsible for the boys' collective living situation do we create the possibility of continuous and cumulative development rather than having to start all over with every major turnover of boys. This resident worker is a middleman between the boys and the administration. We assume he will be primarily a social group worker, but with experience and background in working with disturbed individuals.

One way of conceptualizing our approach is by visualizing the delinquent culture as being "invaded" by the culture of the group worker. He will be resisted as he tries to maintain his standards. Increased social tension is inevitable. The boys will try to resolve the situation by making the intervener conform to their values. They may be enraged at the threat to the system that has served them. Thus we have to evaluate carefully the investment of the different strata in the cottage violence, ranking, and manipulative patterns. We must know not only each boy's role but his attitude toward it, and carefully assess his actual behavior vis-à-vis members of his own status and above and below it. The crux of the group worker's problem is focused in emphathizing with the boys' gripes, constantly challenging them to resolve their collective problems, and at the same time retaining adult standards. One cannot underestimate the amount of pressure in the form of testing and seduction to which the worker will be exposed.

We view remotivation as confronting the boys with constructive alternatives to achieve satisfactions articulated with meaningful realizable goals. As long as the conduct routines in the peer group remain unchallenged, the boys will continue to elaborate authoritarian roles via delinquent interpersonal processes. If we present the cottage with other expectations, then we introduce the element of choice and "constructive conflict" which can lead to new self-images.[14]

Assumptions Underlying Individual and Culture Change

There are two ways of looking at maladjusted adolescents. Above we have emphasized delinquency as a social system. We have to go further. We have to ask ourselves what childhood compulsions force individual boys to behave destructively and reinforce authoritarian group adaptations. We have to pinpoint the specific intrapsychic processes that lead them to fashion this way of life. We believe that an adequate social-psychological formulation must comprehend intrapersonal and interpersonal approaches— with varying degrees of emphasis on each.[15] Thus a boy who is a punk but also a paranoid may need special supports beyond revamping the group's standards and changing his role. Youngsters with severe neurotic pathology benefit substantially from a close relationship with an individual therapist or caseworker. It provides a transference experience on the basis of which neurotic delinquents can acquire insight and new identifications.

The conflicts arising out of changing peer group relationships and between the standards of the boys and the group worker will tend to heighten intrapersonality conflicts. Pressures stemming from interpersonal and intrapsychic stresses increase the possibilities of reactive deviant behavior. For extremely defensive, irrational, emotionally disturbed youngsters the group worker will have to call on his caseworker colleague. An important contribution can be made here by a combined group work and casework attack upon juvenile delinquency in the residential treatment center. Each has a unique contribution to make toward helping the disturbed delinquent; learning about each other's perspective and skills by working together with specific groups and individuals will result, we believe, in more effective treatment.

This leads us to one of the major problems which the group and "island culture" therapists have not as yet posed for themselves. How much real personality change is effected through group participation? Sociologists involved in group treatment claim that delinquents for the most part are normal boys reacting to abnormal situations. Change the culture and individuals will change by assimilating new roles and values. However, the implication here is that *basically* the character structure of these youngsters is sound. Nevertheless, a contradiction remains—when the delinquent

14. George H. Grosser, "The Role of Informal Inmate Groups in Change of Values," *Children,* Vol. 5, No. 1 (January–February 1958).

15. Talcott Parsons, "Psychoanalysis and Social Science," in Franz Alexander and Helen Ross, eds., *Twenty Years of Psychoanalysis* (New York: W. W. Norton & Co., 1953), pp. 186–215.

boy returns from a physically or psychologically removed neighborhood, should he not, according to theory, after a short period resume his delinquent way of life?

Apparently the sociologists fall into an obsolete "imitation theory" of personality. Psychological processes are oversimplified. The boys are perceived as nuts and bolts which have been pressed into a cultural mold. In order to understand the complete interplay of personality and social and cultural forces, we must incorporate into our thinking dynamic explanations of personality; the impact of the milieu upon the personality must be detailed in light of clinical experience. We shall not be able to do this until we welcome into our interdisciplinary family psychoanalytically oriented practitioners who are trained to diagnose the manifest and latent intrapsychic factors in personality structure. Once this is done we can then seek to explore how the "role expectations of the social system" become the "need dispostions of the personality."[16]

The Technique of Changing Delinquent Subcultures

The theory for changing individuals by changing the group's norms and structure can be summarized briefly:[17]

1. People are influenced to behave antisocially in much the same manner as they are conditioned to behave in socially conforming ways. The basis for change is that the individual will accept new values, perspectives, and modes of conduct if he will accept a new group as an instrument in which to achieve satisfactions. Boys "out of step" with society strongly feel their peculiarity and alienation from socially conforming peers and adults. By affording them an opportunity to express their hostility in a permissive setting, they learn that they are not as "queer" as they imagine people think them to be.

2. It is also assumed that delinquents have, in addition to a great storehouse of negative and distorted values, positive strengths. They will be manifested only if the boys have a feeling that they are not being attacked.[18] Given an opportunity to make constructive choice, they will do so if they are properly guided. Two prerequisites are freedom to make meaningful decisions (this does not mean the absence of limits) and confidence that adults are there to help them *achieve, individually and collectively*—not only to restrict them.

3. It is indispensable to this approach to have attached to the cottage a professional practitioner who would (a) be able to serve as a socially

16. Talcott Parsons, *The Social System* (Glencoe, Ill.: The Free Press, 1951).

17. Kurt Lewin, "Conduct, Knowledge and the Acceptance of New Values," in *Resolving Social Conflicts* (New York: Harper & Brothers, 1948).

18. Gordon W. Allport, "A Psychological Approach to the Study of Love and Hate," in P. A. Sorokin, ed., *Explorations in Altruistic Love and Behavior* (Boston: Beacon Press, 1950).

ideal model in his transactions with the boys and (b) be able to use himself as a link to the administration and community to enable boys to release pent-up emotions by affording them constructive outlets for resolving problems which emerge in the institution and which come out of their group interaction.

4. It is assumed that with continued positive interaction and successes in resolving problems, the group can become a positive instrument which the boys want to utilize in order to achieve further satisfactions and rewards. Prestige is allotted to group members not because of antisocial behavior, but according to the contribution made toward the achievement of collective goals which rise out of the boys' interaction in the group. Prestige is added to a boy's stature as he fashions a role which helps the others achieve recognition and group goals. Conversely, individuals who obstruct the group's goals are pressured to conform. Authority begins to inhere in the consensus of the group, which now has a more positive orbit and is gaining a more constructive self-image.

5. In addition to these social dynamics within the group, its relation to outside groups and individuals is critical. Part of the group worker's job is protecting the boys from delinquent-prone adults. He must help his charges graduate from the group if consistent improvement is demonstrated; a feeling of direction is helpful, and the knowledge that the others have been instrumental in helping him to gain the maturity he needed to strike out on his own.

6. The extremely disturbed youngster in the cottage will need special support at every phase of the group intervention; this can be given only partially by the resident worker in the cottage situation. The one-to-one social worker-client relationship appears to be the ideal setting for the youngster to "explode" or reveal privatissima which are disabling him from satisfactory interpersonal relationships. In his special setting the psychiatric caseworker may be able to give the kind of support the extremely disturbed youngster needs in order to survive in the cottage without disrupting the group.

It is important to conceive of the total therapeutic approach to the boys and evaluate its steps in relation to the sum process. The over-all goal is to move the boys to a level of collaboration in which they feel free to (1) raise all kinds of questions—concerning family, sex, peer group, work, school, recreation; (2) become accustomed to having the group, or cliques, including the intervener, discuss these issues constructively; and (3) develop an action program in which they can carry out the decisions they reach as a result of democratic discussion. Only when these criteria are met can the group become a constructive source of authority, new roles develop, and socially acceptable values form the norms of the group's activity.[19]

19. Lewin, *op. cit.*

One Step Backward, Two Steps Forward

Dynamically, the attempt to change delinquent subcultures is similar to the process of Western colonialism, which sometimes leads to native movements that rally the most reactionary elements to ward off all change.[20] This is sparked by the invested leadership. Our intentions, materially or spiritually, are not exploitative, but can be so defined by delinquents.

The presentation of new rewards and tasks to the boys is the opening tactic. The first step is to convince the boys that by cooperating they can undertake new activities which they cannot engage in now. If the boys accept new ways of relating on a superficial level as *conditions* to receiving concrete rewards, we may ultimately move toward a point where they will co-operate without such "bribes." If they can be persuaded to conform to new values and conduct on utilitarian terms, we might then explore how these changes can be incorporated permanently into superego structures. We believe that this "superficial" manipulation is an important intermediate step for delinquents from actively *opposing* to *internalizing* new norms of conduct.

Psychodynamically, there are important gains for each member if he can overcome his initial resistance. The aggressive leader rests uneasily with his power because of its tenuous foundation; the manipulator constantly seeks opportunities for exploitation, not only because of satisfactions he gains, but because of his own fear of being a sucker; the bushboy must develop a whole strategy of distasteful ingratiating tactics in order to survive. A permissive peer group environment would free those boys to expend their psychic energy in ego-strengthening pursuits rather than in futile efforts to dispel anxiety through delinquency.

We feel that if the group worker "sticks" to the boys during this rough period of mutual adjustment and active opposition, they will come to realize gradually that he is there not to "do them in" or to assume the role of the unconditional giver, but to help them. We need much more experience in learning how to work through "group transferences," with specification of the important group and individual variables in the process.[21]

Measuring Culture Change

Any evaluative program for gauging change in a group in a natural setting offers tremendous problems for those who are sticklers for reliability and validity. The fact is, we have little systematic knowledge of successful in-

20. A. Irving Hallowell, "Sociopsychological Aspects of Acculturation," in Ralph Linton, ed., *The Science of Man in the World Crisis* (New York: Columbia University Press, 1950).

21. Harold Esterson, Martin Kohn, and R. Magnus, *Countertransference in a Clinical Group* (Hawthorne, N. Y.: Hawthorne Cedar Knolls School, 1957, mimeographed.)

tervention in a delinquent group as an ongoing social system. Although there have been more than seventy years of experimentation with these strategies, little work has been done to date to validate their therapeutic influence. Empirical experiments are sorely lacking in the field.

The measurement of change from a delinquent social structure to a less delinquent one involves focusing upon the boys' interactions, the group norms and roles, and the extent of involvement in nondeviant activities. Each one of these realms of group process can be defined in operational terms. In our studies we have focused primarily on peer group interactional processes as a basic criterion of change.[22] In any culture, norms, activities, and interactions are all interrelated and the researcher can select one or several key variables to evaluate change as a function of intervention.

The process of intervention is dynamic and dialectical; it includes not only stages of peer group development but, concurrently, stages of acceptance of the adult—the purveyor of socially acceptable norms. Once he is accepted, he must be cautious about the issues he can raise with the group. At first he may take up general issues. Only later when the group begins to crystallize and gains a positive identity will it feel secure enough to explore individual or group problems of a more threatening nature. Regression and rebellion may occur at any stage and will have a different meaning each time.

Methodologically, the next steps in research in group treatment can be summarized as follows:

1. Measurements of group processes so that we can objectively state: *Group X has moved so far from a negative hostile aggressive orbit to a positive one.*[23] We have begun to approach this problem in our utilization of Bales's interaction instrument to determine the extent of delinquent processes in one group of extremely aggressive boys.[24]

2. Measurement of individuals' attitudes toward peers, adults, themselves, school, work, and so on.

3. Measurement of the role performances of group members.[25] (This is revealed by Bales's instrument.)

4. Finally we must try to quantify the highly qualitative dynamic clinical diagnoses of psychiatric practitioners; this must be done before and

22. Howard W. Polsky and Martin Kohn, *A Pilot Study of Delinquent Group Processes* (Hawthorne, N. Y.: Hawthorne Cedar Knolls School). Paper read at American Sociological Society Meeting, Seattle, Wash., August 1958. (mimeographed.)

23. Harold L. Raush, Allen T. Dittman, and Thaddeus J. Taylor, "The Interpersonal Behavior of Children in Residential Treatment," *Journal of Abnormal and Social Psychology,* Vol. 58, No. 1 (January 1959).

24. Robert F. Bales, *Interaction Process Analysis* (Cambridge, Mass.: Addison-Wesley Press, 1950).

25. Norman A. Polansky, Robert B. White, and Stuart C. Miller, "Determinants of the Role-image of the Patient in a Psychiatric Hospital," in Milton Greenblatt, Daniel J. Levinson, and Richard H. Williams, eds., *The Patient and the Mental Hospital* (Glencoe, Ill.: The Free Press, 1957).

after group treatment, so that we can determine whether members have changed fundamentally—internalized nondelinquent outlook and conduct —or are merely superficially adapting to a new behavioral setting.

When these four methodological prerequisites have been fulfilled adequately, we shall be in a much better position to shed some light on the effectiveness of group treatment for fundamental personality reorganization, and *how* new role and value assumptions become part of and change group members' basic character structures.

In the foregoing we have tried to conceptualize delinquency as a peer group authoritarian social system with terrifying internal conflicts as well as anticommunity outbreaks. We have outlined the difficulties of introducing a group worker amidst the boys in their daily lives. We have anticipated the boys' resistances and how best to overcome them by *not controlling* but *changing* their culture. This cannot be done by remote control; our best professionals with maximum support of the institution have to learn how to create truly therapeutic day-to-day cottage living situations. Speculation is now momentarily suspended and the larger complexities of experimentation begin. In this way theory and practice never cease building upon each other.

5.   Developing a Unified Theory of Residential Treatment

JAMES K. WHITTAKER

Introduction

Despite the success of Fritz Redl and David Wineman's classic, *The Aggressive Child,*[1] relatively few articles have appeared in the clinical literature describing the application of the "life space interview" and "behavior management" techniques developed by the authors at Pioneer House in Detroit in the late 1940s. The method consists of a series of interview strategies and behavior management techniques which are used to deal with

Reprinted from *Mental Hygiene,* Vol. 54, No. 1 (January, 1970).
1. Originally published as separate volumes: *Children Who Hate* (1951) and *Controls From Within* (1952).

the problems and "issues" that develop between a child and his physical and social environment; the primary locus of treatment rests not in individual psychotherapy, but in the child's own natural life milieu. The use of this model of intervention in a residential treatment center assumes that the persons closest to the child for the longest periods of time (the child care workers) will have the major impact on his pathology and thus should bear the major responsibility for his treatment. Thus, the child care worker becomes the life space therapist. All of the human and physical resources of the residential treatment center are ordered in such a way as to produce a truly therapeutic environment which is both the primary means of treatment, as well as the context within which it takes place.

Yet the life space model of treatment has not been put into practice on any large scale; this is true in regards to the application of specific techniques, as well as in the development of treatment centers on the model of Pioneer House.

Factors in Lack of Utilization

I would suggest at least three probable reasons for this:

1. Despite Redl's great skill at classification, his terminology is sometimes "fuzzy." Terms such as: "hypodermic affection," "antiseptic bouncing," and "reality rub-in" are too folksy for the more scientifically minded mental health professional to accept. Coming as it did, at a time when the behavioral sciences were placing a great deal of emphasis on precision, quantification and simplicity in theory building, Redl's rich and sometimes "overripe" terminology was too much to take. Similarly, his frequent medical and technological analogs—"neglect edema in the land of plenty" and "new tool salesmanship"—to cite but two, frequently stagger the imagination. A close reading beyond the titles reveals that most of Redl's concepts are quite well defined and are usually accompanied by one or more examples of the phenomena he is describing. What seems important is that one accept or reject the life space interview strategy on the basis of its utility, rather than on its labels.

2. A second major factor in the rather limited use of the life space model of treatment has to do with the connotations of an overly "permissive" environment which the book and some articles have conveyed to a portion of readers. This is due in part to the type of children Redl chose to treat. Aggressive and acting out, many of these children were well on their way to becoming sociologically trained delinquents: clearly not the type of youngster usually dealt with in an open setting. Though Redl himself views "permissiveness" as possible only within certain boundaries[2] and has writ-

2. Fritz Redl, "The Concept of Punishment," in N. Long, W. Morse and R. Newman, Eds., *Conflict in the Classroom* (Belmont, Calif.: Wadsworth, 1965), pp. 345–51.

ten in detail of the false dichotomy between "permissiveness" and punishment—as well as on the value of rules, structure and routines—many have
understood "permissiveness" to be a synonym for license. The most unfortunate aspect of this viewpoint is that it often rejects the entire model
because of a criticism of what is perceived to be the underlying philosophy. This appears inconsistent, since one need not accept the model in its
entirety. This is the problem with the way in which current models of treatment are used in residential settings; typically, the treatment of choice
most commonly used in an institution marks the treatment center as "that
type" of program, to the exclusion of other modalities. What is needed, is
an overall theoretical framework for milieu treatment that has room for
life space treatment techniques, as well as those of traditional psychotherapy and some of the newer innovations in the clinical application of sociobehavioral learning theories.[3]

3. A third and perhaps most plausible explanation why relatively few
applications of the life space model of treatment have been made, has to
do with the structure within which institutional facilities for emotionally
disturbed children have traditionally been established in this country. It
is fair to say that many, if not most, residential facilities are organized
more around the needs of the professional groups who run them than
around the needs of the children they purport to serve. Thus, we have a
"medical model" of residential treatment which is usually just an extension
of the psychiatric team from child guidance. In this system child care
workers are used to care for and often live with the children, but their
function is not usually seen as much as "treatment," as it is to provide a
safe, benign and hygienic environment for the child between psychotherapy sessions. A variation on the medical model is the "social work" model
of residential treatment. Here the same kind of role rigidity is maintained
despite a shift in the status hiearchy. Typically, psychiatric social workers are responsible for the treatment of the children—usually office interviews—though they may make use of psychiatric and psychological consultants. In recent years the elevation of so many specialties to professional
status has in some ways served to the detriment rather than to the benefit
of the children in care. For example, in the course of a single week's time
the disturbed child might be expected to see his psychotherapist, group
therapist, family caseworker, occupational therapist, recreational therapist,
music therapist—and so on. The implicit assumption, of course, is that each
specialist brings his particular knowledge and skill to bear on the child's
problem in such a way as to produce a single, lasting treatment effect. The
difficulty is that children usually do not come to treatment with such neatly
encapsulated and "well defined" problems. In addition, such a model pro-

---

3. For theoretical eclecticism within an overall framework see Albert E. Trieschman, James K. Whittaker, Larry K. Brendtro, *The Other 23 Hours: Child Care Work
in a Therapeutic Milieu* (Chicago, Aldine, 1969).

vides little flexibility in that what is actually accomplished has more to do with the particular area of competence of the specialist than with the needs of the individual child.

The life space model of treatment eschews such specific role definitions and adopts a far more generic approach. It is a model of treatment developed from the problems posed by the children in care and not from the needs of any single professional group. Herein probably lies a major source of the reason why the model has been adopted so infrequently: it wreaks havoc with the traditional notions of "who does what" in a residential treatment center. In addition, the life space model contains a built-in threat to the therapist used to working only in the sanctity of his office and within the context of the 50-minute hour. Dealing with problems in the life space is akin to working in a fish bowl: both successes and failures are clearly visible to all. It has been the experience of this writer, however, that nothing serves to strengthen the relationship between child care worker and therapist more than the sight of the professional groping to find a way to manage a child with whom the child care worker has been having difficulty for an entire morning. Children also seem to perceive that adults really do work together and there are many fewer attempts to play one staff member off against another.

Summary

From its beginnings, residential treatment has been operating on a patchwork of theoretical remnants borrowed from child guidance practice, traditional psychotherapy, social group work and special education. The actual practices and standards of evaluation for residential treatment have had more to do with the needs and requirements of the mental health professionals than with the needs of the children such settings were designed to serve. Most so-called "therapeutic milieus" (and who would admit to having anything else?), pay lip service to the value of life space therapy, while still placing primary responsibility for treatment in the 50-minute hour. It would seem time that those professionals interested and involved in residential treatment begin to develop models of intervention that would eventuate in a unified theory base for residential therapy. I would suggest the following criteria for this theoretical framework:

1. That it be developed from the needs and requirements of the children in care and not from the needs of any professional group.

2. That we ask, "What needs to be done in a truly therapeutic milieu?" rather than start with a preconceived notion of what persons are eligible to perform certain tasks.

3. That this theoretical framework be broad enough to incorporate current and future innovations and not be limited to a single point of view. It is clear by now that the models of residential treatment that will survive

will be those that are self consciously eclectic and flexible enough to adopt new strategies and techniques as they are developed.

The urgency of this task of theory building is paramount. New methods of treating emotionally disturbed children are being developed in other areas—particularly in the community mental health movement—and it is imperative for those who believe that residential treatment still serves a vital purpose in the total mental health picture to specify just what that purpose is.

RECOMMENDED READING

Dittman, Allen T. and Howard L. Kitchener, "Life Space Interviewing and Individual Play Therapy: A Comparison of Techniques," *American Journal of Orthopsychiatry,* 29:1 (January, 1959).

Long, Nicholas J. and Newman, Ruth G., "Managing Surface Behavior of Children in School," in N. Long, W. Morse, and R. Newman, *Conflict in The Classroom,* Belmont, Calif., Wadsworth, 1965.

Morse, William C. and Edna R. Small, "Group Life Space Interviewing in a Therapeutic Camp," *American Journal of Orthopsychiatry,* 29:1 (January, 1959).

Morse, William and David Wineman, "Group Interviewing in a Camp for Disturbed Boys," *The Journal of Social Issues,* 13:1, 1957.

Newman, Ruth G., Fritz Redl, and Howard L. Kitchener, *Technical Assistance in a Public School System.* School Research Program, P.H.S. Project OM-525, Washington School of Psychiatry, 5410 Connecticut Ave. NW, Washington, D. C., 1962.

Redl, Fritz, "Strategy and Techniques of the Life Space Interview," *American Journal of Orthopsychiatry,* 29:1 (January, 1959).

Redl, Fritz and David Wineman, *The Aggressive Child,* Glencoe, Ill., The Free Press, 1957. This is a one volume edition containing in their entirety Children Who Hate: The Disorganization and Breakdown of Behavior Controls (1951) and Controls From Within: Techniques For the Treatment of the Aggressive Child (1952).

Trieschman, Albert E., James K. Whittaker, and Lawrence K. Brendtro, *The Other 23 Hours: Child Care Work in a Therapeutic Milieu.* Chicago: Aldine Publishing Co., 1969.

Whittaker, James K., "Training Child Care Staff: Pitfalls and Promises," unpublished paper, 1969.

Wineman, David, "The Life-Space Interview," *Social Work,* 4:1 (January, 1959).

PART TWO

INDIVIDUAL TREATMENT
IN A THERAPEUTIC MILIEU

6. Helping Children Learn to Deal with Sadness

ALBERT E. TRIESCHMAN
BERNARD LEVINE

Introduction

"I am going to raise hell if I can't find my model airplane." The child's threat of an upset often mobilizes adults to think exclusively about aggression and acting out. The child's sadness and sense of loss are easily overlooked in our eagerness to "get things under control." Yet we all know the "children who hate" often are children who have suffered many significant losses—so many losses or so chronically suffered that they are "cried-out," unwilling or unable to deal with any more sadness. We help them improve their competence to deal with anger when perhaps we should focus on developing their competence to deal with loss.

In our work with hyperagressive children at Walker, we have been forced to think about ways we could help children learn to deal with loss and sadness, while we were coping with their acting out.

Our commitment to the therapeutic milieu and to effective child care work within that milieu pushed us toward thinking in terms of teaching about sadness in the circumstances of daily living.

Prepared for presentation at the Annual Meeting of the American Orthopsychiatric Association, March 1971. Reprinted with permission of the authors.

Opportunities for Teaching about Sadness

Some events have the clear ring of loss phenomena, and we rarely over-look them as opportunities to talk to a child about being sad. The "home-sickness" of new arrivals on our campus, the discharge or graduation of a child's close friend, the death of a pet, the leaving of a favorite staff mem-ber, the death of a parent—these "big-league" events call out for the con-sideration of a child's loss-bearing capacities even if the behavior we see is primarily angry and disruptive. Though we may not always have a very clear idea about how our interventions can help the child except through ventilation of feeling, we at least focus on the sadness. Quite the opposite of "missed opportunities" to deal with sadness, we sometimes overplay minor events. There is a temptation to connect "little-league" events that include a minor loss to reminders of the major life shattering losses. In caricature we say, "It is sad when your model airplane is missing; there are even important people in your life you are missing." It is often wise to re-sist this temptation. Even when we succeed in making the connection be-tween the minor and the major loss, we have converted an easier-to-bear loss into a more difficult loss before we help the child work on mastery. It is as if we were to begin teaching addition with five place numbers.

Some of the small losses that present worthwhile opportunities—in and of themselves—to help children develop loss bearing, include broken or missing toys, no mail, the box top offer that doesn't come, losing a game, difficulty in mastering a skill. Much of what we can do to help a child deal with sadness applies equally to loss of possessions (extensions of the self) and to loss of self esteem.

Some events of the day have a capacity to call on children to deal with loss. The anger displayed at the loss of fun and diversion when a game, activity, or a trip comes to an end is sometimes a protest over the difficulty of dealing with the loss. Staff attention to the teaching of loss-bearing ca-pacities at such times not only helps extend the emotional competence of children, but also helps keep behavior within reasonable limits.

Bedtime for some children represents the loss of exciting external di-version; for others it operates as a strong reminder of other bedtimes and other homes and the attendant losses. The darkness reduces the attachment to the day and chases the attention of the child to thoughts about himself and his body—and it is often in that arena that there is much sense of loss.

Mealtime may also be a time particularly loaded with associations of missing parents, via favorite foods not on the table.

As we pay attention to the loss-bearing implications of ordinary daily events we become attuned to the susceptibilities of particular youngsters and to our particular opportunities to help children learn to deal with sad-ness in the life space.

Developmental Precedents

When the infant discovers his mother is someone separate from himself and important to him, he is at once heir to the problem of coping with her comings and goings. The creation of a human bond to a particular care-taker, to a need satisfier, in the second half of the first year of life is the original attachment known to be so vital to later emotional health and maturity. At the same time, the child usually develops a sense of constancy that his mother still exists despite her absence from his sight or sound. The infant's early practice in dealing with this separation experience is well known as the anticipatory anxiety or crying when put in the crib to nap. The signal of this impending brief separation and temporary loss mobilizes the child to protest the experience actively and ventilate his feeling. Some-times after, his babbling and play recreates some interesting sights and sounds originally present in the play with his mother.

With the onset of active mobility in the second half of the first year, the child risks putting his mother out of sight by means of his own creeping, crawling, and then walking. The tension-creating and tension-reducing function of games in managing little doses of affect may have one of its roots in the peek-a-boo game so popular at just the time in development, the time when comings and goings of the child's mother are multiplied by his own capacity to put himself apart from her.

As a child then increases his sense of autonomy in the second year he faces the challenge and opportunity for mastering other losses and dealing with the effects appropriate to them. The experiences of the toddler with both language and more advanced ambulation confront him both with the opportunities for omnipotent thought and with the shortcomings inherent in his omnipotent pose. Uttering the demand, "Cookie," for example, does not always make it appear. Stairs easy to climb up are not always so easy to come down. Yet the child is also learning techniques to cope with the erosions of his omnipotence, not only through denial but through games of making things not only appear but remain in one place. Active games of collecting, hoarding and holding on, creation of rituals and compulsions all buttress the loss of the feeling that "it's all mine whenever I want it." In the experience of toilet training, learning to bear anxiety concerning the loss of body parts as well as body contents is a further incentive for the development of early coping techniques for dealing with sadness and loss.

Often as early as the second year the necessity of giving up mother as an exclusive caretaker may occasion a loss as, for example, precipitated by the birth of a sibling or the addition of mother surrogates—grandmother, teacher, or babysitter. The child is faced with the loss of his exclusive diadic relationship with mother. The appearance of partial restitutions of these losses in the form of transitional object development is well known.

Blankets, teddy bears, dolls constitute the earliest form of partial restitutional phenomena available for a child to use at later times when important relationships are lost, comprised, diluted, or temporarily absent.[1]

Later changes in relationships provide smaller or larger opportunities to do a little or a lot of "grief work" in childhood. A child must face the loss of the idea that "everyone is just like me" when he becomes aware of sexual differentiations. He must give up his mother as the exclusive object of his sexual and romantic wishes. He must face the partial loss of the special, exclusive, intimate family appreciation of him when he becomes "one among many" to his teachers at school. Finally, perhaps the most painful occasion of loss and sadness—and in the minds of some of the really first experience of "grief work" in life—occurs when a child gives up the view of his parents as ideal infallible people and sees them as imperfect, unfit to identify with completely and invests much of his energy in peer values and relationships.

This sequence of loss-bearing opportunities suggests the possibility of creating a hypothetical model of capacities to deal with loss and sadness layered one on another, none given up or rendered inappropriate, but each added to the previous one as perhaps a new and more complex competence, hopefully all available to a mature fully human being.

Models of Affect Functions

In helping children develop competence to deal with loss, we invariably utilize one or more of the functions of any affective state in promoting our teaching, whether it is to foster ventilation, alternate discharge, communicative functions, or signal functions. In Freud's first formulation of the role of affects, they were seen as quantities equivalent to psychic energy. Catharsis or ventilation of affect fit in as a concept within the framework of the hydraulic model of "communicating vessels." We supply this model implicitly when we think of helping a child manage sadness by draining away or discharging something dammed up.

To encourage a child to ventilate his feelings of sadness directly is a useful teaching device. One might say to a child, "*One* of the things you can do first when you're feeling sad like this is to cry. It's all right. The tears won't last forever; you'll be able to stop." One might suggest a private place to an older child, too embarrassed to cry openly in the company of peers. However, one also has an opportunity at times to point out another child's appropriate use of tears and possibly to promote a vicarious participation (though flight, disruption by contagious spread of unmanageable affect, or denial are possible consequences as well). In noting children's

1. The superficially paradoxical sight of stuffed animals on the beds of tough but sad delinquent or predelinquent children is a common one to those familiar with residential treatment settings.

reactions to the death of a president,[2] the authors comment on how unbearable it would be if a child could not quickly get over the acute portion of a painful loss. Counting on what Wolfenstein calls the "short sadness span" of children, one can reassure the child that he will be able to stop crying.

An equally useful device is to help a child develop the capacity to *repress* or *suppress* sadness, to "forget about it." Though crying is of major therapeutic importance, there are times that for the benefit of helping a child repair his life and proceed to grow, crying must stop. In residential treatment of acting out children having to promote appropriate affect *expression* may be more common a task, but for learning skills and participation in scholastic affairs to take place the task of "putting the sadness in the back of his mind" has to be given to the child.

A later view of affect function proposed by Freud was that of a safety valve, an alternate discharge of energy when discharge through action was not possible. When acting out behavior—a familiar experience to people in residential treatment—is discouraged or blocked, one can often anticipate a massive reaction of sadness beneath the fury and rage of a child. The child who has desperately used action and acting out to blunt or avoid feelings of sadness will go to great lengths to flee the impending emergence of sadness. After many repetitions of the pattern of sadness-arousal, acting out, interruption of acting out, tantrum, and sadness expression, one might be able to "talk a child through" to the last stage, thus short-circuiting the acting out and tantrum behaviors in order to get to the underlying affect sooner. (For example, one might say something like, "Every time you start knocking over furniture like that we stop you, you fight, we hold you, you cry, and get sad. Maybe we don't have to go through all that this time?")

Freud made a third forumlation of the function of affects. In this view they served not so much as safety valves but as ego functions in the service of providing signals to a person. Thus a person's feelings let him know what is happening inside him and what is going on around him. One might view the anticipatory crying of an infant when its mother *starts* to leave as serving one of the earliest signal functions; or perhaps even earlier, the anticipatory excitement and cessation of crying when the child sees the bottle coming or even hears mother's voice from the kitchen. Signal functions therefore give a warning, a preview of things to come.

In working with ego defective, acting out, or character disordered children one is often faced initially with a child who either is quite deficient on employment of signal functions or who avoids signals like a plague. We see many children for whom signal function is more like the threat of signal misfunction. The signal may go off and the child feels he has no skills

---

2. Martha Wolfenstein and Gilbert Kliman, eds., *Children and the Death of a President* (Garden City, N. Y.: Doubleday & Co., Inc., 1966).

to cope with the internal state aroused. It must seem like a fire station that has an alarm system but no fire engines to put out the fire. A child with inadequate affect-coping mechanisms, to avoid becoming disorganized by the signal might seek to avoid it and flee from it; but often he does become disorganized by it.

Teaching signal functions can be an enormously important therapeutic activity in residential treatment. Naming emotional states for many children is the first active step taken toward the development of emotional awareness. One can develop a "primer of affects" and may, in some instances, even influence the character of the emotional state partly by the name given to it. Unless the process stops at naming and the state is reified (for example, "emotionally disturbed," "pathological liar") the language of feelings can be used to teach and remind children of their feelings and the possible ways of behaving when "sad" (or "happy," or "confused," or "excited," or "frightened," or "irritated," or "disappointed").

One can also teach a child that when he names feelings and can talk about them, he can know them himself and then tell others how he feels. They in turn can anticipate how he might act or what they might do in order to help. The child can learn that the signal can lead to a constructive communicative function. One attempts to help a child move out somewhat from the egocentric position that convinces him that either everyone feels the same as he, or if he feels it, everyone should know it without any necessity of his communicating.

To enhance the awareness of feelings the techniques of roleplaying, improvisation, and acting can be used with children who can comfortably move back and forth between pretend and real situations. When a child is nearly able to emerge sufficiently from his egocentricity to take another's point of view, this next stage in the development of emotional awareness might be attained somewhat more readily by the use of role-playing techniques.

Another teaching device in the service of heightening the awareness of feelings is the instructive use that residential treatment center staffs make of their own affective states. When we feel disappointment, experience loss, or lonely for a good friend, and then model and share this emotional experience with children, our example is subject to imitation. Unless the experience is an unusually intense one such as the reactions of adults to catastrophic events or tragedies, children can imitate small segments of our own management of sadness. When we ourselves can ventilate, bear the affects and keep working, use a little humor to partially deny, the children can use the opportunity to be observant pupils.

When we exploit small segments of reality to teach about dealing with sadness, whether we assume we are preparing children for dealing with major losses or not, we are making use of the innumerable opportunities that occur daily, such as the end of a pleasant game, the loss of a favorite counselor until tomorrow, the broken toy, no mail. At these times it is also possible to use the technique of encouraging partial replacements for losses, reattachments to things that give pleasure (a new friend) or of allowing and guiding a temporary period of detachment, that is transitory withdrawal (anticipating the consequences that withdrawal brings with it such as the threat of abandonment, being forgotten, the equation with punitive exclusion) for the child who does not know how to use solitude and has a tremendous investment in warding off sadness by being constantly in the thick of things, a prior learning experience might need to be the stepwise development of the capacity to be alone (and find that there is a "constancy of people" who still accept him on return). In residential treatment these small segments of reality occur from wakeup through the daytime hours of programmed and unstructured activities until bedtime.

The people closest to the child in his naturally occurring circumstances —child care workers, teachers and house parents—as well as therapists can participate repeatedly in the teaching of capacities to know sadness and learn to bear it.

Summary

We have considered some of the life space opportunities for helping children learn to deal with sadness and some formulations about the child's natural development of loss-bearing capacities. We used this knowledge to suggest styles of interventions that can be used by adults helping children learn to master experiences of loss. It is important to note that we have *not* focused on pathological depression or distortions of the mourning process. Indeed these occur—and with frequency among disturbed children—but the necessity of developing the competence to master loss is a human necessity, not *just* a "cure" to a mental "illness." We think that our techniques help adults make an alliance with that part of the child struggling against his difficulties. We see this alliance as more productive when it is predicated on teaching emotional competence than when it is narrowly conceived as "curing mental illness." Hopefully, our notions help the adults who encounter the child in 23 hours outside therapy to be constructive agents of change in the child's life.

7. The Role of Psychotherapy in Residential Treatment

Edward D. Greenwood

In talking about the role of psychotherapy in a residential school, I believe the approach should be made in three steps: 1) to classify the various institutions which I include under the heading of residential centers; 2) to state the factors which make psychotherapy in guidance clinics somewhat different from that employed in residential centers; and 3) to state the relationship between psychotherapy and the total program. The latter section includes integration of therapy into total group living and the limitations that are present in doing psychotherapy in residential centers.

Now let me list quickly the varieties of institutions doing residential treatment. There are wards in general hospitals affiliated with medical schools; sections or units within a state hospital system; private schools, begun as centers for retarded children, which have gradually expanded to include emotionally disturbed children. Some residential centers were originally organized as agency institutions for neglected children and then increased their functions to include psychiatric treatment for disturbed children.

The types of children and age range vary in each institution. Those centers dependent on funds from agencies emphasize clinical service and may provide some training and a little research as well. Those centers lucky enough to obtain special grants or funds and which are part of a large training program tend to emphasize research and training. They also have the advantage of being more selective in the type of child admitted and have a greater staff-to-patient ratio.

Although I have skimmed over the highlights of the variegated groups providing residential treatment, it must be obvious that programs will be different among the various types of institutions; and the philosophy toward treatment will also be distinctive. Yet there are some fundamentals which apply to all.

Reprinted with the permission of American Orthopsychiatric Association from the *American Journal of Orthopsychiatry*, Vol. 25, No. 4 (October 1955), pp. 692–99.

Before I talk about these fundamentals, I should like to clarify differences between child guidance clinics and residential centers. For the largest number of children who are in need of treatment, the well-organized child guidance clinic can provide the necessary service. However, there are some children whose illnesses are so overwhelming that they require a total alteration of their daily living program. The comparisons I shall make apply to these disturbed children who need to be removed from their homes.

When a child goes to a guidance clinic, his living conditions continue as they were in the past. He still goes to the same school, lives in the same neighborhood, continues contacts with his siblings and parents. On the other hand, when he enters a residential school he is confronted with an extremely different living experience. He meets new adults and children with whom he will play, work and fight. The adults do not react to his outbursts, his sarcastic remarks, his negativism or his physical complaints the way his parents did. The degree of participation in the group activities will depend upon the extent of his ego disturbance. If he is so sick that he cannot enter group living, he is permitted to remain on the periphery as an on-looker. As he is able to move closer to the group he is encouraged to do so.

The child in treatment in a guidance clinic still has to share things with siblings, if he has any; and frequently the disturbance in these relationships is as strong as his parental struggles. In a residential center there are quasi siblings or sibling surrogates who depend on the same adults that he does, but have different natural parents. The struggles or difficulties with these quasi siblings are not usually as intense as those he has had at home. If he is an only child, he may be involved for the first time with intimate peer relationships. Again, the adults handle the problems which arise differently from the method he has been accustomed to at home.

In the guidance clinic, while in treatment he continues in the same school; in the residential center he goes to a school which is conducted and supervised by the center or to a public school where there is cooperation on the part of the principal and teachers to help him. The attempts to provide a healthier atmosphere for learning are also an obvious difference.

The child's play life when he is going to a guidance clinic is still organized around the old atmosphere of the home and the school. His needs for recreational outlets may be ignored, or he may be forced into activities beyond his capacity to benefit from them. When he is in a residential center, there is a large variety of activities planned primarily to meet the needs of children.

Some of the most frequent difficulties between the child and parent are encountered in the daily routines. When a child is at home, such things as eating, sleeping, bathing and dressing can, and many times do, become the primary sources of trouble. In a residential center these daily chores are handled by the staff according to a planned program which is modified periodically as the child progresses. This is an essential part of the child's therapy. I suggest as reference reading the very excellent and perceptive study of the management of these routines in Bruno Bettelheim's book *Love Is Not Enough.*

The intake policy of a child guidance clinic is usually limited by the degree of parent participation and the availability of staff time. In a residential center, in addition to the stated intake policy, there is the added problem of admitting a new child into the setting without disrupting the group already in residence. At times this means a slower rate of admission, not because there is a shortage of staff time, but the children in the residence are not ready to admit "the stranger."

Let us now consider the differences in psychotherapy as used in the treatment center and in the child guidance clinic. When a child comes to the guidance clinic, his parents are more or less intimately involved in the treatment program and either have counseling or psychotherapy with a case worker or another staff member. Many children who enter a residential center have had some psychotherapy in a guidance clinic or with a private psychotherapist; and either because of the emergence of behavior patterns which endanger the children or because the parents' personal problems are of such magnitude that they cannot cope with these children, the children are removed from the home.

The atmosphere for psychotherapy of a child in a clinic or with a private practicing therapist is somewhat different from that in a residential center. In a clinic the child-therapist relationship is established in the environ of an office or playroom which is separated from the rest of his living environment. He sees the therapist in this setting and rarely sees him in any other situation. The child may or may not be aware of the other children who are in therapy with the same therapist.

In a residential center the psychotherapy is part of the social atmosphere and of the total treatment program. The children in residence have discussions about the relative merits of the therapist or therapists. These discussions occur at mealtimes or during bull sessions which take place frequently. When a new child arrives in the setting, an orientation course is organized by the other children; so before long he has some impressions as to the characteristics and abilities of all the staff, including the psychotherapists. The child knows that various staff members make either verbal or written reports on his behavior. Whether the therapist uses this material or not, the child is fully aware that the therapist knows about it.

One technique which has broad application in a residential school is the use of one staff member, or one group of staff, against the others. Although we see this phenomenon in other settings, it is more damaging in a residential setting. The destructive way this can be used by children to avoid utilizing either the environment or the psychotherapist can be attested to by those who have been exposed to such experiences.

In a guidance clinic the *modus operandi* is the use of psychotherapy. The psychotherapist has the stellar role. The child-therapist relationship is the crux of the plan. In a residential center he becomes a member of a larger team, but his role is not the only one of significance in the treatment of the child. We occasionally see psychotherapists who give lip service to the value of milieu therapy but still feel they are a cut above the other staff and that fundamentally the only therapy is the psychotherapeutic sessions with the child. Now in a residential center we are required to provide 24-hour service to all the children every day of the week. This means that the planning of the environmental program must provide treatment and protection for all the children. The psychotherapist must recognize this fact and avoid developing blind spots that lead him to believe that his sessions are the only therapeutic adjunct.

One of the most difficult areas in residential work is the amount of "acting out" a particular institution can tolerate. Since there are numerous types of behavior which come into the category of acting out, I shall limit my comments to the behavior which may be destructive to the child or to the children and adults around him. If the children are not in formal psychotherapy, different methods are used in handling this type of behavior. If children in psychotherapy continue repetitiously to act out, there is some serious question as to what is really happening in the environment. This poses a tantalizing and emotionally laden question. Can we justify keeping any child who is continuously destructive and disturbing to the other children in the unit? This query frequently causes problems between the psychotherapist and those responsible for the group living. The tendency is for those working with the reality problems of the child to recommend removal, while the psychotherapist takes the point of view that this is a necessary unfolding of the child's hostile feelings and should be tolerated by the environment. In the role of administrator I would answer the question in the following way. If there is no place in the setting to provide security and isolation for the child, then he should be sent to a place which does provide this type of protection. It is unsound to injure or unnecessarily disturb 15 or more other children in order to provide treatment for one child.

There are occasions when we see a withdrawn child who is in psychotherapy begin to act out. This is an obviously desirable change; but if it then becomes a repetitious pattern, we may begin to wonder whether the psychotherapy is effective. The entire question of acting out needs to be reviewed from the following points of view. Does it have to appear in daily living experience continuously, or can it be primarily limited to the therapy sessions? If it cannot be so limited, is it a sign that we have underestimated the degree and type of resistance which the child has toward getting well? This one area causes more staff disturbance than almost any other.

It is conceivable to me that classical child analysis is the treatment of choice. However, from the practical point of view this would be impossible at the present time for most residential centers. 1) There are not enough trained child analysts; 2) the length of time necessary for treatment makes it impractical for many institutions to undertake the process; and 3) the cost may be so high that a large number of parents or agencies could not afford it. Then, from a theoretical point of view, I wonder what percentage of children sent to residential schools are suitable candidates for classical child analysis. Can analysis be used with the impulse-ridden child with such poor ego functioning that he cannot stand the least amount of frustration, or with the child with a borderline ego formation or with a minimal amount of superego formation?

Some children with uncontrollable id impulses and very weak egos may not be suitable for any kind of individual psychotherapy, even if it were available, but could benefit greatly from a therapeutic milieu. In some instances, as some of these children develop more controls, plans for psychotherapy may eventually be considered. This also could apply to certain types of severely withdrawn and autistic children.

Since treatment for children is more of a re-educative process than it is for adults, we must fully utilize the most valuable and essential contributions which those responsible for group living and all its ramifications make to the child. Some children make a satisfactory adjustment to the institutional setting with little or no assistance from formal psychotherapy, and gradually are able to return to their homes or enter foster homes. We have not attempted to modify the child's basic character structure. Nonetheless, there are certain changes within his ego which make it possible for him to return home. They can be considered a very satisfactory outcome of the treatment program. By this statement I am saying that for a goodly number of treatment centers, such limited treatment goals or objectives may be all that can be offered. Some of our colleagues may tend to look askance on such a limited objective, yet there is no incontrovertible evidence that children who have had psychotherapy oriented to the mere removal of symptoms have more relapses later in life than those treated by more intensive psychotherapeutic methods aimed at changing the character structure. A few centers having a small number of children do place emphasis on research and training and do devote time to a modification of the basic character structure. It would be of value to have a follow-up study on the results obtained by these centers.

Whether psychotherapy is done by a social worker, psychologist, educator or psychiatrist is less important than the type of training and experience he has had. The particular discipline is also less important than the actual experience in a residential setting. Special training, including supervision in child psychotherapy, is essential. Just a desire to work with children or extensive training in adult psychotherapy and even in adult psychoanalysis does not really prepare one for the field of child psychotherapy. This point is often difficult for some therapists to accept.

Another factor which is more important than the particular discipline of the therapists is the question of whether one is a full-time or part-time staff member. There are aspects of identification with an organization which are enhanced by full-time assignments. The staff relationships and interplay can be better understood and incorporated into the over-all planning if the therapist is an integral part of the setting. Areas of tension and friction can be recognized more readily and handled before they become obstacles to progress when the therapist is a member of the team.

Anna Freud makes a statement which is of vital significance. In *The Psychoanalytical Treatment of Children* she says: "Where a child's analysis *cannot* be organically grafted onto the rest of its life, but is intruded like a disturbing foreign body into its other relationships, more conflicts for the child may be created than can be resolved by the treatment." I believe this principle applies regardless of whether the child is in inpatient or outpatient analysis or in any other form of individual psychotherapy.

Frequently, because of limited funds and a dearth of available psychotherapists, it may be necessary to obtain the services of a part-time psychotherapist. However, part-time staff are really outsiders or strangers who may have little opportunity to become an integrated part of the staff. All too frequently the relationships to the children and to the supervising case worker may be the therapist's only contacts with the institution. If he has little or no interest or orientation in the group living phenomenon, there may ensue real difficulties in the treatment process.

We also recognize that a percentage of the therapists in many centers are trainees who are supervised by a more experienced therapist. The supervisor, as well as the trainee, must know the climate and atmosphere in which the therapy is being done. This material needs to be used and related, and related repeatedly, to the basic child-therapist struggles. When errors or weaknesses in technique occur, as from time to time they must, it is most helpful for the trainee and the rest of the personnel if these are explained as errors rather than as shortcomings of the environmental staff.

An example might make this point a little clearer. A young, capable psychotherapist knew that his aggressive, hostile young patient had a very sharp knife hidden in his room. It was found one evening by the recreation worker and turned in to the office. At first the psychotherapist adamantly defended his stand of not revealing such material and, in addition, was annoyed with the recreation worker who found the knife. Some time later he was able to recognize his countertransference struggle, but even then was unable to face the recreation worker and admit the error in technique.

In the training of a psychotherapist, I believe an area of valuable observations and study is omitted; that is, an opportunity to work in the residential center as a residential or group worker. This type of assignment should be made for a long enough period to absorb the climate of the milieu program.

An additional factor is that the trainee in psychotherapy needs constantly to remember that group workers are the parental surrogates who are not in opposition to him but are interested in supporting his efforts.

We seem at times to underestimate the importance of our reactions to children of different cultural backgrounds as well as different cultural interests. This at times becomes an obstacle to psychotherapy. Maurice Friend makes the following statement in the book *Social Science and Psychotherapy for Children:*

> What is needed by the child therapist is the capacity for inner freedom, so that alien customs are not transposed into fixed images, as so frequently happens in dealing with anything alien to self. A lack of this capacity plays a great role among the phenomena of countertransference. If the therapist is not sufficiently aware of his personal reactions to different cultural upbringings, he will react as he would non-therapeutically to something alien and threatening; that is, by repression, by fearfulness, by excessive effort to change, or by a flight reaction expressed in such defeatist terms as "one cannot do anything with such parents," or "with such schoolteachers." The child therapist, of all persons, must resolve early narcissistic problems of his own development.

Supervision is an intrinsic part of all types of professional work. The first requirement for an experienced psychotherapist who takes on the responsibility for supervision should be a real identification with the residential center. He must be convinced that psychotherapy is part and not the only therapy available, and should not need to develop a clique to further his own objectives. The supervisor should utilize the information from all areas of the residential center; he should look for the healthy as well as the unhealthy aspects of a child's ego. In addition he should help diminish the aura of mysticism and magic around psychotherapy which is so frequently felt by the rest of the staff.

Effective psychotherapeutic supervision is geared to teaching a technique. However, from time to time anxiety becomes so great in the supervisee that there is a tendency to offer therapeutic help instead of supervision for the child's treatment process, a fact which tends to defeat the purpose of supervision. Suitable supervision fosters growth and development of the qualities and attributes of the supervisee rather than imitation and emulation of the supervisor.

Psychotherapy contains basic principles which are used by each psychotherapist in ways which express his orientation, training and personality. If his training and orientation include some experience in a residential treatment center, he modifies and adapts his techniques to the needs of children in a therapeutically oriented setting.

I have presented some comments on the group which makes up the residential center and then pointed up the differences in the role of psychotherapy in clinics and in residential centers. I hope it is evident that the aims and goals of psychotherapy must be related to the total treatment program.

8. Some Aspects of Psychotherapy in a Residential Treatment Center

RICHARD D. BRODIE

It is the thesis of this paper that individual psychotherapy in a residential setting differs sufficiently from out-patient psychotherapy to justify an effort to outline some dimensions of the problem. The problems the child brings into therapy, especially in the early phases, are determined not only by his psychopathology but also by specific conflicts which are aroused by his removal from the home and by the nature of his peer group. The therapist's relationship with the patient shifts from the more traditional office-centered neutral role to that of a more active participant in the child's daily life. Certain functions normally performed by parents such as visiting the schoolteacher, accompanying a frightened child to a medical exam, attending Boy Scout functions, etc., are more or less regularly done by the child's therapist. Informal contacts outside the office, frequent conferences with residence personnel and participation in decisions about numerous aspects of the patient's life become a part of the therapist's activity to a degree which cannot happen in outpatient therapy. Finally, the therapist gears his efforts initially toward encouraging the patient to interact with his milieu which is intended to be therapeutic and growth fostering and which is much more predictable than the environment of an outpatient about which we usually know very little.

While these variations make the psychotherapy a more complex process to understand, particularly in sorting out transference reactions from the

Reprinted with permission of American Orthopsychiatric Association from the *American Journal of Orthopsychiatry,* Vol. 36, No. 4 (October, 1966), pp. 712–19.

child's reaction to one as a real person, they also permit a more effective and comprehensive effort toward the final goal which is defined here, as it was by Bettleheim, as "the mastery over inner and outer forces."[3]

The degree to which the therapist involves himself in the child's daily life varies according to the child's involvement with the milieu. Four phases of attitudes and behavior are postulated. They represent the stages of evolution of the child's relationship to the residential treatment center. The major foci of this paper are on the second and third of the following phases: (1) A "honeymoon period" characterized by total compliance to the perceived demands of the residence, (2) a period of intense rejection, (3) a period of (ambivalent) dependence, and (4) a period of increasing independence during which the child becomes involved in preparing to return to the community.

In the first phase, which is often of very short duration, the child's behavior is scrupulously conforming. This appears to be accomplished by inhibition of impulses based on an externalized superego which is perceived as unduly severe. This perception may be due to the child's having experienced placement as a drastic form of punishment.[15]

The second phase is characterized by the active or passive rejection of the residence sometimes alternated with excessive demands impossible of fulfillment. Derogation of the residence, its personnel and practices are paramount and, to the degree the child is able, he joins with his peers in establishing the validity of his notions regarding the negative or ineffectual efforts of the staff. In many ways, this phenomenon resembles the early phase of group therapy[19] when, after an initial period of breast beating and attention to the task at hand, the group bands together against the leader. In so doing, they avoid recognition of their dependency upon the adults. By banding together for the purpose of expressing hostility, they achieve a degree of closeness without experiencing the anxiety which is aroused by the tender feelings associated with closeness.

Whether the child in an inpatient setting manifests his rejection by running away, withdrawal, depression or aggression against the environment, he appears to be expressing two facets of his concern. First is his denial of his feelings of abdication by his parents, frequently expressed as recurring strong wishes to go home, combined with the expression of varied ingenious notions as to how the residence staff or the therapists were to blame for the child being in "this lousy place." Second is his profound mistrust of establishing another relationship in which he is dependent and therefore vulnerable.

The principal differences in conducting psychotherapy occur during phase two, and the main body of this text will be devoted to that phase.

Larry, an 11-year-old borderline psychotic boy, had been in the residence for a year when I began to see him. He had spent a good part of the previous year requesting to go home and refusing to participate actively in the residential program including therapy. In school, he did no work other than silent reading. He was negatively regarded by most of the residence personnel. When I entered his room, not without trepidation, to introduce myself to him on the day the residence opened, he turned his back and refused to speak with me. I left a slip of paper on his desk which contained his therapy schedule and informed him of this, to which he replied that he would have no therapy.

When he arrived the next day, bolstered by a decision he and some of his peers had made to "get $5.00 models out of their therapists," he launched into a tirade about my cheapness, the lack of supplies in my office, which was accompanied by swearing, spitting on the floor and threats to destroy me as he thought he had his previous therapist. Over the next several weeks there evolved a sequence of behavior and thought, which focused on the negatives of his environment as contrasted with the fancied positives of his home, and finally culminated in the notion that I was the cause of his being in the residence and therefore the proper object for his intense rage. When I commented that I must indeed be very powerful since at the time of his entrance I knew neither him nor anything about the residence, he grinned and conceded that perhaps there were a few people around who were not totally bad. This signaled a beginning shift in Larry from total rejection to ambivalent dependency characterized by splitting residence personnel into good and bad. He was still a year away from being able to focus his rage and feelings of abandonment onto his parents. Only when he became somewhat secure in the residence could he evaluate the destructive aspects of his own home.

The transition into phase three occurs gradually and evokes a variety of countertransference problems. Although it is generally agreed that the child's relationship to his therapist is less intense than that of an adult,[8,9,17] due to his natural dependence on his parents, the entrance of a child into a residence, which is often located far from his home, alters the usual paradigm in therapy and places the child in a position where he needs to find a central object for his dependency. It is not surprising that the therapist becomes invested with this role. The intense ambivalent expression of the child's most primitive needs places a considerable amount of stress on the therapist's energy and on his capacity to manage anxiety and anger without interfering with the therapeutic process.[2,13] It also provides him with more therapeutic leverage than is possible in outpatient treatment.

A part of the general problem of dealing with intensified dependency demands is the therapist's real function in the life of the child[11] and especially his possession of both power and information. Although administrator-therapist splits[23] exist in principle, they frequently are inseparable in practice. To expect the patient to be unaware of this is naive and destructive of the patient's trust. In fact, the taking over by the therapist of certain administrative functions seems to be indicated in some cases, particularly those in which anxiety is avoided by marked behavioral constriction which is difficult to alter by verbal interchange. These children, probably originally phobic, have substituted behavioral avoidance accompanied by experiential dislike and apathy. They resemble some of the children described in the literature of school probia[13] whose original panic and dread gives way over time to marked ego constriction and blunting of affect.

> One such patient is David, who compared to most of the boys, was a model of decorum and stability. He rarely became upset, was nearly always on the "honor list" and was involved only superficially with the staff and most patients. He did a minimum of school work, and avoided most physical activity, such as basketball and Scout overnights. In the first month of treatment with me, he indicated that he had "slid by" his previous year of therapy and intended to do the same with me. All of his avoidance of interaction was well rationalized by derogation of both the residence and such "kid stuff" as basketball and Boy Scouts. I told him that I did not know him well enough to be certain of what anxieties he was covering up by avoiding these activities, but that we would find out during the year as his participation in Boy Scouts and basketball was to become a mandatory part of his treatment. In disbelief, he told me that these programs were optional and that anyway he went home every three weeks, and his mother would brook no interference with these plans. I told him that the director of the residence* and I had agreed that the plan I outlined would be best for his treatment and that I would deal with his mother if this became necessary. In the ensuing year, David's fear of injury and related inability to become aggressive in other than a passive way, were demonstrated again and again on the basketball court. Parts of many of our therapy hours were spent in the gym playing basketball, which turned out to be an excellent vehicle for eliciting and dealing with fears of hurting me and himself. My assumption of an active fatherly role enhanced the development of a strong, albeit ambivalent, dependency relationship, and led David to a discussion of feelings of vulnerability, and inadequacy in an affectively meaningful context.

By assuming a parental role, the therapist further complicates the technical problems involved in using information obtained outside the therapy hour with the child in a constructive manner. Even in outpatient therapy, the use of information obtained from parents and teachers and others is a controversial issue.[9] Weiss[24] recently stated that in child analysis no outside information need be obtained or used. His arguments do not appear to be valid for residential treatment, especially when the communicative patterns of the residential therapist are aimed at increasing trust and enhancing learning.

The importance of communication in the etiology and treatment of childhood disorders has been stressed by Reusch,[21] Goldfarb[16] and Anthony[1] among others. All of the children in the Manville School suffer from

---

*Dr. Robert A. Young whose assistance with the cases described here and whose help in clarifying issues in residential treatment is gratefully appreciated.

learning disorders whatever their primary diagnosis. The presence of family secrets,[22] and more recently the existence of a pattern of secrecy in communication[20] has been found to be a significant factor in the mothers of children with learning disorders. For the therapist to be secretive and withholding with the patient may reproduce and perpetuate certain crucial aspects of the environment in which the patient's difficulties originated and place undue strain on the relationship to the detriment of the mutual respect necessary for successful therapy. For all patients communication or lack of communication has a special meaning correlating to some degree with social class and with parental use of language.[4,7] In a residence, it is further complicated by the abundance of information which is available to the therapist. The use of the information with the patient can have an accusatory or feeding quality dependent on the patient's history. When the patient has experienced much secrecy, withholding and behind-the-back maneuvers by his parents, an open approach is indicated.

David's parents had been in severe marital discord for years. Very little communication occurred between each other or between them and the children. While proper social decorum in the form of an armed truce existed, David was bewildered by the absence of explanations from his parents. Early memories revolved around being told not to see or hear what was going on. His placement in the residence had been sudden, and the reasons for it obscure to him. In treatment he was eager for information about what the counsellors knew and said about him, what teachers said, what was in the counsellor's notes, and how and what had led me to say or do a certain thing. Each question was answered fully and directly and led to an increase in trust and in material relative to his own life. His curiosity, long inhibited, became alive again, and he engaged in long discussions with certain counsellors and teachers. His hunger for information began to encompass things of a more objective and less personal nature. In short, one major aspect of his learning problem, that related to the acquisition of knowledge, became accessible to the milieu.

Larry, on the other hand, had been barraged by stimuli which his young mind had lacked the capacity to assimilate. In his first 18 months, he witnessed from his crib, frequent sexual behavior on the part of his natural mother, culminating in her running off with another man. From then, through his sixth year, he witnessed frequent arguments, was alternately indulged and punished and slept with his father, who was in a profound depression over the loss of his wife. When his father remarried, his new stepmother, an ambulatory paranoid schizophrenic, engaged in a three-year running battle with him, aimed at proving that he was crazy so that she could feel that she was not. When he entered the residence, his experience with the receipt of environmental stimuli in general and words in particular had been largely in an ego-assaultive context. He showed no interest in the notes for more than a year, and would tolerate no communication from me of information obtained from counsellors (phase 2). In his second year of treatment with me he allowed me to comment on what he said to me, but did not want me to

tell him about the observations of the residence staff (entering phase 3). In
his third year, he eagerly sought information from the counsellor's notes
(phase 3).

David avoided peer relations just as he avoided interaction with other
aspects of his environment.

In therapy, David's references to peers were disparaging, and he held himself aloof from them. Historically, he had experienced no close peer relationships. In his family, which was characterized by aloofness, his guarded relationship with his parents was reflected in his lack of closeness with his two
younger sisters whom he regarded as the personification of ego-alien primitive
impulses. In line with the therapeutic program outline with David (above), his
disparaging contempt of peers and aloofness from them was challenged by
me, the defensive character of his behavior and his underlying loneliness were
emphasized. The constant challenge by me in the context of our fairly close
relationship set him to increased involvement with his peers, which provided
more material for therapy and (to his surprise), provided gratification for him.

The advantage of treating a patient in a residence is clear both in terms
of the pressure one can put on the patient once a therapeutic alliance is
established and in terms of the feed-back available from the therapeutic
milieu.

Prior to the pressure in treatment David had rarely presented difficulties
to the child-care staff.

After he had been in residence for a little over one year, the counselor's
monthly notes read as follows:

> David still seems to be the same quiet, cooperative boy of the past months
> . . . he often seems uninterested in or unaware of activities going on about
> him." Later in the year the following description was recorded, "For the last
> few weeks, he has spent very little time in his room. Tommy has been the
> object of scapegoating, led by David. Recently David has been in an argu-
> mentative mood. He has continued to set the group against the counsellors.
> He himself has been revolting against the rules and the attitudes of the coun-
> sellors." At the end of a year, the counsellor's summary noted: "Until March,
> 1963, David was obeying rules without incident, but since March he has re-
> belled against the rules and has had a difficult time accepting any explanations.
> David's peer group has increased during the year. Some of the changes noted
> from one year ago are that David appears to use scapegoating of others less,
> does more acting out against counsellors and has more and closer ties with
> his peers.

Peer Group Acceptance

When the child begins to use mastery of school material and Boy Scout
achievements as a source of peer group acceptance, the therapist has a
golden opportunity to enter the picture and enhance the emergence of
socially rewarding autonomous ego functions as well as to improve peer

group acceptance. While it may be argued that such aspects of the child's development should be handled by others so that the therapy should not be contaminated, it is often the case that the child must test out his approach to learning in the relative comfort of the therapy hour. As Ekstein[14] pointed out, learning to love precedes loving to learn, and learning in a love relationship precedes learning in a neutral relationship.

> Larry's maneuvers around math were extremely phobic. He floundered upon presentation of the simplest addition problem and refused to take the annual achievement test in arithmetic. Given the WISC by a female staff psychologist with a small scar on her leg, he reacted to the arithmetic subtest by asking her what happened to her leg, and then fleeing the office. For two years he was terrified of engaging himself in arithmetic. In his third year of residential treatment, he arrived carrying an arithmetic book and asking me for help. When I set up a problem for him, he headed out the door, announcing that I was a mental nut. I called him back and told him that calling his therapist a mental nut had become a religion with him. He returned to his seat and confronted the problem. Several weeks of calling himself stupid, referring to his sister's good arithmetic skills, the cost of his residential treatment, and his parents' financial difficulties ensued. The comfortable therapeutic relationship was used to encourage skills in their nascent phase. After these few sessions, I rarely saw Larry in the context of math tutoring. His teacher reported erratic work, but steady progress in math. His peers ceased teasing him about his stupidity in math.

Sibling Rivalry

The occurrence of sibling rivalry is a common characteristic of both adult and child therapy.

> A college student with achievement difficulties is seen in the same office as the children who are patients of the author. Following an hour with a child patient in which there was arithmetic material scattered on my desk, the adult patient arrived for his next appointment with his college statistics book and demanded tutoring. On another occasion, the same patient, after viewing a plastic model built by an outpatient, spent his whole weekend compulsively building models.

Sibling rivalry in a residence is more intense due to the physical closeness of the patients and their constant contact with each other. The patients of the same therapist compete for him, and all of the patients compete among themselves as to who has the best therapist.

Severely traumatic experiences with siblings emerge with striking clarity in a residence, and are acted out with the other patients.

> When Larry was in his third year of residence, a new patient was assigned to me. Larry regressed dramatically and, shortly thereafter, as he was leaving

on an afternoon trip, he spied me sitting outside the clinic with two social workers. Repetitively, at the top of his voice, he yelled, "You already have a wife; why are you f———ing around with them." For several weeks he acted out his terror at my taking on a new patient while at the same time he denied it in therapy. The blending, in his mind, of his father's remarriage, with my taking on another patient, was condensed in his expletives toward me and his subsequent behavior in the residence.

Scapegoating

Probably the most difficult and heartrending problem of residential therapy is that of scapegoating. The closeness of the peer group situation, the terror of the children, their intense sadomasochistic fixations and a history of having been the scapegoat in the family, all contribute to the difficulty. These pathologic phenomena are superimposed on the developmental phenomenon of scapegoating, which occurs in late latency and adolescence.[6] In addition, the scapegoating and sibling rivalry which occur among the staff also contribute to the complexities of the problem.[13]

The therapist in a residential setting is likely to encounter both the scapegoat and the scapegoater. While the group issue of scapegoating must be handled by the child-care counselors, teachers and administrative personnel, the feelings and masochistically provocative behavior of the patient need to be handled in therapy. The general aim is to increase the thickness of the patient's skin while maintaining some balance between avoiding overprotection and standing idly by while your patient is destroyed. The overprotective therapist not only irritates the child-care staff but also, by infantilization increases the negative stereotyping and scapegoating of the patient. The therapist who remains aloof leaves his patient unprotected. The therapist's task with the patient is to explore the reasons in the patient which provoke the scapegoating and to enhance his development in the direction of peer group respect.

Larry was both a scapegoat and a scapegoater from the time he entered the residence. Isolated from his peers he attempted to provoke attacks on other children in order to circumvent attacks on himself. Therapeutic endeavors began to diminish his scapegoating, which had all of the characteristics of an identification with the aggressor even to the point where this sensitive Jewish boy glorified Nazis and drew the swastika everywhere. However, he remained without positive peer relations. Toward the end of his second year in the residence, Larry was invited to spend the weekend with Mike, a quiet but fairly popular boy on his floor. Suddenly Mike withdrew his invitation. Consultation with Mike's therapist, who is a close friend of the author's, revealed that an older and bigger boy had devalued Mike by constantly saying that if Mike brought Larry home, Mike would be the laughing stock of the residence. Mike's therapist was reluctant to push Mike. I did not want to see Larry's defensive hostility heightened by the rejection of friendly overtures. We decided to see if we could help the two boys work it out. Two joint meetings were held. In the first session, the boys joined together in an attack on the residence and their therapists. In the beginning of the second joint interview, Mike and Larry competed with each other to see who had the worst home and the most miserable siblings. Finally, Mike stated that he feared Larry's devaluation of his home in the residence, while Larry was anxious about his bed-wetting. The boys agreed to tell Mike's parents about Larry's bed-wetting, and Larry agreed not to devaluate Mike's home. The weekend was pleasant for the boys, and they both achieved an increment in peer group esteem and self-esteem.

Psychotherapy and Milieu Therapy

Lourie[18] has described residential treatment as follows:

> We would define residential treatment as therapeutically directed institutional or group care for emotionally disturbed children in which all possible ways of helping—casework, education, recreation, planned group life, and psychotherapy—are utilized and integrated into a clinically oriented and directed treatment plan for the individual child. It is not merely the removal of the child to benign environment where he is available for psychotherapeutic interviews. The essence of residential treatment lies in the milieu—in the complement of adult-child relationships and experiences which can be clinically manipulated and controlled in the interests of therapy.

The integration of psychotherapy and milieu therapy is most important during the time the child is actively rejecting the residence, in order to facilitate positive views toward the child and avoid the calcification of negative stereotyping.

> In my first year of working with Larry, I observed that he was generally negatively regarded by residence personnel. He had been in the residence for one year and in treatment camp for two years when I began to work with him. The head teacher upon inquiry informed me that he did nothing in school. Counsellors regarded him as an extremely difficult boy who caused constant frustration by his ambivalent response to all things offered. In the early phases of Larry's treatment, the therapist's role in the residence was aimed at dissipating the stereotype[10] and thus encouraging a benign and even benevolent attitude toward Larry.

In the third phase, the manipulations of the environment are less crucial. Here the conjoint therapeutic efforts of the therapist and other residence personnel are geared more toward the patients' unaddressed difficulties, i.e., less toward pervasive problems and more toward identifiable specific conflicts.

In the fourth phase the milieu is accepted as representative of the outside world and therefore nontherapeutic or at least nonidiosyncratically adaptive.

In his last year in residence, David complained incessantly about the rules. Although I could have ameliorated their effect on him, I refrained. Finally, he asked me what I thought of his being kept off the honor list for having taken only one shower in the last week rather than two. I told him that I thought that it was ridiculous for a residential treatment center for sick boys, but that it was not an unusual rule for a boarding school. He replied that he was in a residential treatment center and therefore he was not going to take a shower. I replied that this seemed reasonable to me if that was the way he saw himself, but that he would have to decide whether or not he felt ten minutes of avoiding a shower was worth a week's restriction.

On another occasion he was given a room restriction for a very minor offense by a counsellor. He asked me what I thought of it. I replied that I thought it was unfair but I could not understand the stress which the counsellor was under at the time. He asked me to rectify the error. I said that I probably could, but that it would be at his expense since it would be hard for the counselling staff not to react on him for my interference with their efforts. He chose to serve the restriction.

In his most recent follow-up interview, David told me that his after-school employer sometimes landed on him, according to his mood, about various things in the store, but that David could see that he had troubles with his wife and daughter, and that things blew over the next day.

Summary

Some aspects of psychotherapy in a residential setting have been presented. Intensification of peer group difficulties and dependency conflicts are described as they emerge in the various phases of milieu therapy which are postulated. Alterations in therapeutic strategy are discussed relative to the therapist's greater responsibility for the patient's overall life, the increased amount of information available to him, and the potential for integrating psychotherapy and milieu therapy.

REFERENCES

1. Anthony, E. J. 1964. Communicating therapeutically with the child. *J. Amer. Acad. Child Psychiat.* 3(1): 106–126.
2. Bettelheim, B. 1955. *Truants from Life.* The Free Press, Glencoe, Illinois.
3. ———. 1950. *Love Is Not Enough.* The Free Press, Glencoe, Illinois.
4. Bernstein, B. 1964. Social class, speech systems and psychotherapy. *The Brit. J. Sociol.* 15(1): 54–64.
5. Bibring, E. 1954. Psychoanalysis and the dynamic psychotherapies. *J. Amer. Psychoanal. Associat.* 2: 745–770.

6. Blos, P. 1962. *Adolescence, A Psychoanalytic Interpretation.* The Free Press, Glencoe, Illinois.
7. Brodie, R. D., and M. R. Winterbottom. 1964. Some observations on the learning environment of children growing up in the south end of Boston. *Project Literacy Report.* 3: 17–22.
8. Brody, S. 1964. Aims and methods in child psychotherapy. *J. Amer. Acad. Child Psychiat.* 3(3): 385–411.
9. Buzbaum, E. 1954. *Technique of Child Therapy. The Psychoanalytic Study of the Child.* 16: 251–274. International Universities Press: New York.
10. Caplan, G. 1963. Types of Mental Health Consultation. *Amer. J. Orthopsychiat.* 33(3): 470–481.
11. Cohen, R. L. 1964. The influence of child guidance practices on children's in-patient units. *J. Amer. Acad. Child Psychiat.* 3(1): 151–161.
12. Coolidge, J. C., R. Brodie and B. Feeney. 1964. A ten year follow-up study of sixty-six school phobic children. *Amer. J. Orthopsychiat.* 34(4): 675–684.
13. Ekstein, R., J. Wallerstein and A. Mandelbaum. 1959. Counter-transference problems in the residential treatment of children: treatment failure in a child with a symbiotic psychosis. *The Psychoanalytic Study of the Child.* 14: 186–218. International Universities Press, New York.
14. Ekstein, R. 1964. From learning to love to loving to learn. *Bulletin of the Reiss-Davis Clinic.* 1(3): 1–21.
15. Ginandes, S. 1964. Children who are sent away. *J. Amer. Acad. Child Psychiat.* 3(1): 68–88.
16. Goldfarb, W., D. Sibulkin, M. Behrens and M. E. Jahoda. 1958. Parental perplexity and childhood confusion. In *New Frontiers in Child Guidance.* Aaron H. Esman, ed. International Universities Press, New York, Pp. 157–170.
17. Kramer, S., and C. Settlage. 1962. Concepts and techniques of child analysis. *J. Amer. Acad. Child Psychiat.* 1(4): 509–536.
18. Lourie, N. V., and R. Schulman. 1952. The role of the residential staff in residential treatment. *Amer. J. Orthopsychiat.* 22(4): 798–809.
19. Mann, J. 1955. Some theoretic concepts of the group process. *Internat. J. Group Psychother.* 12(1): 3–13.
20. NIMH Progress Report. 1964. Symbolic Processes in Learning Inhibition. Grant No. MH 60335–03: 18–41.
21. Reusch, J. 1952. The therapeutic process from the point of view of communication theory. *Amer. J. Orthopsychiat.* 22(3): 690–700.
22. Staver, N. 1953. The child's learning difficulty as related to the emotional problem of the mother. *Amer. J. Orthopsychiat.* 23(1): 131–141.
23. Stanton, A. E., and M. Schwarz. 1954. *The Mental Hospital.* Basic Books, Inc., New York.
24. Weiss, S. 1964. Parameters in child analysis. *J. Amer. Psychoanal. Assoc.* 12(3): 587–599.

9.   The Concept of "Parental Force"

Milford E. Barnes, Jr.

To the best of my knowledge, the term "parental force" was first used by
Robinson in 1950.[1] He used it then to refer to the parent-like role played
by a foster agency during any period of psychiatric treatment of a child in
the custody of such an agency, and to refer to the need of a child for the
agency to fulfill such a role. As Robinson used the term, it would roughly
connote a responsible, conscientious, and emotionally involved legal guardian. It is a convenient term for this role of a foster agency, but certainly not
an essential term. What is essential is the role itself, whatever it may be
called.

The Need for Parental Force

We are all aware of the tremendous importance of the child-parent relationship in the emotional development of a child. The original studies of
Anna Freud, Burlingham, Lowry, Goldfarb, Spitz, Bowlby, and others[2] on
the severe results of institutionalization and maternal deprivation upon
children sounded the knell for the old "orphanages" of the past. These
studies led to the present emphasis upon adoption and placement in foster
family homes. Freud, of course, had emphasized the importance of the
evolution and satisfactory resolution of the "family romance" as the *sine
qua non* for the emotional development of a child, and certainly many

Reprinted with permission of Child Welfare League of America, Inc., from *Child
Welfare,* Vol. 46, No. 2 (February, 1967), pp. 89–94.
1. J. Franklin Robinson, "Arranging Resident Psychiatric Treatment with Foster
Children," *Quarterly Journal of Child Behavior,* II (1950), 176–184.
2. Anna Freud and Dorothy Burlingham, *Infants Without Families* (New York:
International Universities Press, 1944); Lawson G. Lowry, "Psychological Privation
in Infancy and Subsequent Adjustment," *American Journal of Orthopsychiatry,* X
(1940), No. 3, 576–585; William Goldfarb, "Psychological Privation in Infancy and
Subsequent Adjustment," *American Journal of Orthopsychiatry,* XV (1945), No. 2,
247–255; and John Bowlby, *Maternal Care and Mental Health* (Geneva: World
Health Organization, 1952).

contemporary studies have reinforced this emphasis.[3] As an oversimplification, one might say, "No Oedipal evolution and resolution, no growth." If there are no defined and enduring parent figures present in the child's life in relation to which the child can first develop and then resolve his feelings, he will either fail to develop the capacity for attachments, develop fragmentary ones, or evolve the attachments with fantasy figures. Where no consistent and enduring parent figures exist, treatment is at best difficult and in many instances impossible.

A recent volume of the *Journal of the American Academy of Child Psychiatry* is devoted to a symposium on the treatment of the child without a family, and the general tenor is certainly far from optimistic.[4] The need of a child for adequate parenting takes precedence by far over any other, and when it is not met, to at least a minimal degree, it presents both the child and the potential therapist with a difficult, often insoluble, practical and theoretical problem.

Anna Freud sums up this dilemma beautifully in *The Psycho-analytic Treatment of Children; Technical Lectures and Essays*.[5] Here she clearly states her conviction that a child cannot form a true transference neurosis with a therapist, first, because "its original objects, the parents, are still real and present as love-objects—not only in fantasy as with the adult neurotic" and, second, because "the behavior of the children's analyst . . . is not such as to produce a transference that can be well interpreted." As therapists treating an adult, "We remain impersonal and shadowy, a blank page on which the patient can inscribe his transference fantasies. . . . But the children's analyst must be anything but a shadow . . . he is a person of interest to the child. . . . The educational implications . . . result in the child knowing very well just what seems to the analyst desirable or undesirable, and what he sanctions or disapproves of."

She goes on to point out that it might be possible in a residential treatment center to develop a true transference neurosis and treat it, "But when we come to consider the termination of the child's analysis, we shall see how many obejctions there are . . . what gives us any assurance that after we have secured a successful resolution of the transference the child will of itself find its way to the right objects? It returns home at a time when it has become a stranger there and its further guidance is . . . entrusted to the very persons from whom we have forcibly detached it."

3. Peter Neubauer, "The One-Parent Child," Psychoanalytic Study of the Child, XV (1960), 286–309; Anna Freud, "Adolescence," *Psychoanalytic Study of the Child,* XIII (1958), 255–278; and Peter Blos, "Preoedipal Factors in the Etiology of Female Delinquency," *Psychoanalytic Study of the Child.* XII (1957), 229–249.
4. Augusta Alpert, *et al.,* "Children Without Families," *Journal of the American Academy of Child Psychiatry,* IV (1965), 163–278.
5. Anna Freud, *The Psycho-analytic Treatment of Children; Technical Lectures and Essays* (London: Imago, 1946), pp. 34 ff.

Freud is, of course, talking about children who are living in families, but what she says is fully as applicable, if not more so, to children without families.

A child is a growing and developing being, and his emotional growth must occur in relationship to meaningful people in his life. It does not and cannot occur in the absence of feelings. However "healthy" a child may be at any given time in his life he still has further development to make the most that treatment can do for any child is to bring him "up to date" in his ability to relate to another person. It cannot make him prematurely adult, nor would this be desirable if it were possible. Such progressive development can only be brought about by means of a continuing growth-fostering relationship with some meaningful person.

Two of the most important elements of such a relationship are endurance through time and common experiences, both tribulations and pleasures.

The true objective of psychotherapy with a child is not the establishment of a permanent psychological structure, but the bringing of a child into an appropriate growth-fostering relationship with the emotional environment constituted by the important people in his life. This relationship is a two-way proposition. Not only must the child care for the persons who supervise him, but the adults who supervise the child must care for and understand him, must be able to understand the nuances of his communications and must sense his needs. It is quite ridiculous to assume that this kind of relationship can be established without preparation on the part of the child and the adults involved. It can come only from at least a certain minimum of shared experiences over at least a certain minimum period of time.

Parental Force in Treatment of Children

It is an all-too-common practice to refer a child for either outpatient or residential treatment, with little or no consideration being given to the child's primary need for adequate guardianship and protection. All too often, especially with inpatient care, the conscious or unconscious assumption is that the community is getting rid of the "bad" child, the hospital or training school will henceforth be his parent, and the community will have nothing to do with the situation until the child has become "good." This assumption is theoretically wrong, practically impossible, and morally inhumane. These children *always* return to the community sooner or later, and they cannot be "gotten rid of."

We have already explored some of the theoretical problems; there are, indeed, many more. From the point of view of humanity it is certainly cruel to ask a child to undergo as painful and as frightening an experience as psychotherapy without anyone to visit him, comfort him, or plan with him. If the child does truly improve, his defenses will be lowered, and he will be able to care more and hence will be more vulnerable to hurt.

For whom shall he care, then, when he is ready and able to do so? For what can he hope except to get out of the hospital, training school, or residential setting, as the case may be, and into a "nice foster home"— ephemeral as that idea might be. If we continue this kind of practice, we should do it humanely. We should arrange that the institutions involved truly "adopt" the child, and we should furnish them with adequate means and staff to do a good job of the adoption—including the means to support the child through college if that seems indicated. Surely the wards of a comparatively rich state should not be treated like poor stepchildren if the guardianship is taken seriously.

This is one mode of providing psychiatric treatment of children without parents. It can work, but not unless it is clearly recognized that negligent state guardianship is no better than negligent parental guardianship, and that the state must make due preparations to see that the proper care is provided for its wards. In this situation, the state, or some branch thereof, would be undertaking to furnish the necessary "parental force."

Another alternative is to accept a child's primary need for adequate and consistent parenting, and plan for this *before* seeking any kind of treatment, and this is the sort of thing suggested by Robinson.[6] According to this view, a duly appointed child-caring agency is conceived of as the permanent guardian of the child, obligated to see the child through all vicissitudes. The agency should seek the kind of help it needs from any available source, but in so doing, it continues to be responsible for the child and for the proper guardianship of the child. If residential treatment is indicated, the agency should choose the place, just as a natural parent would. The agency should have a definite and limited purpose, usually that of bringing about a suitable growth-fostering relationship between the agency worker and the child.

To this end, the agency worker should be an active participant in the treatment process, visiting the child, seeking better understanding and communication with him, encouraging him, planning with him for his future, and guarding him against any abuse or poor practices, even to the point of removing him from a treatment center if it does not seem to be doing its job well. If one mode of treatment does not seem to be working, the agency, as a responsible guardian, should seek another mode just as a natural parent would. Even if admission to a correctional institution becomes necessary, the agency should seek to support the child while he is there and to care for him on his release.

In these ways the agency can provide a reliable and lasting guardianship, with the child both struggling and submitting as he grows; this kind

6. Robinson, *op. cit.*

of support is possible even if there is a change of workers. A foundation of common experience is built up, and a solid relationship develops on the basis of these memories, both happy and unhappy.

Where such a parental force is active, a therapist is freed from carrying any of the parental role and can provide treatment more effectively. A hospitalization can be seen in its true light as an interlude in the child's life, and not as a permanent state. Because the agency carries the continuing responsibility, it can provide continuity in planning for the child and it becomes possible to set up sequences of therapeutic experiences instead of desperate last stands. It becomes possible never to despair, even with the most difficult cases.

Finally, it becomes possible to cope with the dilemma described by Freud by maintaining a continuity of the child-agency relationship during residential treatment, so that when a child is prepared to leave the hospital he will continue under the guardianship of people who have shared in his experiences during his stay in the hospital, who have a meaningful relationship with him and are prepared to receive him. They are not strangers, but are partners in a job done together. The agency and the child have suffered and triumphed together.

A Case Study

HISTORY AND BACKGROUND

There are now several agencies in Iowa that could offer excellent examples of the success of such procedures. Our space permits only one example:

A 7-year-old boy from an extremely neglectful and injurious home was admitted to the Children's Unit of the Independence Mental Health Institute. He had absolutely no parental backing, and in spite of all efforts none was obtained for him during his stay there.

He showed no improvement over a period of three years, and was finally discharged and sent home because of the hopelessness of the situation and because of his failure to show any improvement. Shortly after his return home it became apparent to the local community that the situation was impossible, and the county sought treatment for the boy at the Beloit Lutheran Home at Ames, an open residential treatment center.

It was immediately obvious to the staff there that no treatment would be effective without the support of a strong parental force. The Iowa Children's Home Society of Des Moines agreed to undertake this responsibility and, after assuming it, requested that the boy be admitted to Beloit for the express purpose of beginning to bring the boy into a meaningful relationship with his worker. At the time of admission it was clearly recognized by everyone concerned that the boy was so intensely anxious and so fearful of his own dependent feelings that his initial stay in an open setting might well be quite brief, and that he would almost certainly require either a closed hospital setting or a training school admission. Nevertheless, it was felt that even a brief experience in this open setting would be of value in initiating the child-worker relationship, beginning the process of emotionally detaching the boy from his totally negligent mother, defining the problems, and setting the stage for a more adequate use of any closed setting by the boy.

This estimate of the situation proved accurate. The boy could be maintained at Beloit only three months, after which it was necessary to seek his admission to the Boys' Training School at Eldora, Iowa. It also became quite apparent that the more the lad was tempted to care for and invest in his worker, the greater became his panic and the worse his behavior. It became clear that the misbehavior was a defense against closeness and positive feelings.

The worker maintained his contacts with the boy during his stay in the Training School, and the relationship steadily improved to the point where it was felt that the boy was ready for another try at treatment. Accordingly, he was readmitted to Beloit. Again, however, when the boy's defenses lowered, his anxiety increased to such a degree that the open setting did not provide sufficient security, and after three months he returned to the Training School.

This time, however, his return was more constructive. He knew much more about himslf, had fairly well accepted the enduring support of his worker, and was able to utilize the second Training School experience much more effectively than the first. He was steadily becoming less anxious, less constricted, and less shallow emotionally. After three months he returned to Beloit for another treatment experience. He was quite successful in maintaining himself, and he made such major strides emotionally that plans were beginning to be made for a foster home placement.

At this point the boy's fearfulness rose again and he became more self-depreciatory. Many aspects of depression appeared, and he ultimately had to force another self-punitive return to the Training School. This time, however, the self-depreciation was expressed relative to the worker. The boy felt he did not deserve to be liked or cared for. He was suffering because of the depth of his feelings, and was not simply "pushing the panic button." His misbehavior had a different quality in that he avoided violence and injury to other persons and even to the property of others. He did steal things, but not out of hate as before. Instead, the thefts were a demonstration of his own worthlessness. Certainly he was still trying to defend himself against caring, but with a great deal more ego.

DISCUSSION

We do not yet know what the next step will be, but it is our expectation that he will go from the Training School into some form of placement. Probably further treatment should be done on an outpatient basis if it is done at all, and very possibly it will not be necessary. The boy's relationship with his worker has been fairly well cemented by now. Both have made successes, and both have made mistakes and have misjudged each other. By now they have formed a meaningful bond that, if not nearly ideal and still subject to distortion, is, we believe, most supportive to this boy's ego.

It has taken four years of hard work by many people in four different agencies, but a child for whom the only possible prognosis seemed to be life-long incarceration is now likely to become a self-supporting—if far from ideal—adult. There is a definite possibility that his growth will continue until he reaches a quite adequate adjustment. Prolonged incarceration, once a virtual certainty, is now unlikely.

If this case turns out as well as we hope, the success cannot be claimed by any one of the participating agencies. Each played its limited role, and their activities were mutually interdependent and mutually supportive. The thread of a consistent, durable, faithful guardianship tied the various experiences together, with the bond being strengthened by each experience.

A case could have been selected with a temporarily "happy ending." This case has been deliberately chosen because the ending is still in doubt. No one should be misled as to the difficulty and tenuousness of treating a child who has been subjected to years of rejection and neglect. No one can really feel satisfied with any arbitrary ending point. The real test of the treatment will be the overall adult adaptation of the person involved, and not his situation at any given age.

It is noteworthy in this case, as in a great number of similar cases, that no progress of any kind occurred until a consistent parental force was introduced into the picture. It is a matter for deep regret that such a force could not have been obtained when the boy was seven rather than when he was ten and had built up strong defenses backed by the experience of more than three years of being thwarted and disappointed whenever he dared to hope for human contact.

It should be clear that this relatively brief presentation does not adequately portray the complexities and difficulties that an agency must deal with in undertaking the role of parental force with a seriously disturbed child. Great skill and professional dedication as well as warmth, patience, and courage are needed in the workers and the agencies attempting this role. Those agencies that have been involved in this kind of work have evolved many practices and routines as their experience has progressed, and it is to be hoped that they will be willing to publish and discuss elements of their techniques as these become clearly defined. There are pitfalls in the selection of cases, as well as in the initial preparation, in the relationships with the child, in relationships with a parent, who remains peripheral over a long interval, in the relationships with treatment and correctional services, and so on. All of these problems need more work, but they are best described by those actively involved in the work.

Summary

In summary, let me put forward the following propositions:

(1) A child grows emotionally by virtue of the evolution of his relationship to the meaningful people in his life. These people are ordinarily his parents, but the parents may be essentially absent.

(2) In the case of a child without a family, proper guardianship comes ahead of treatment. Parents are more important to a child than doctors, and treatment cannot be effective unless proper guardianship is established first.

(3) The establishment of the conscientious guardianship of a child, which Robinson has called the establishment of a parental force, gives meaning to the treatment and facilitates it in many ways.

(4) The presence of an enduring parental force permits flexibility in treatment plans and a long-term approach to the child's problems.

(5) A conscientious guardian is needed by any child, and particularly by those who have experienced the loss of a parent or guardian. The task of providing one is theoretically sound, pragmatically successful, and morally merciful and humane. The last quality alone would justify the effort involved.

(6) The role of conscientious guardian or parental force is a difficult one, requiring great skill and maturity. It needs much investigation as to improvements in procedure, and it is expensive and time-consuming, but it is justified by its successes and by comparison with the incomparably more expensive problems that occur so frequently in the absence of an effective parental force.

10. Some Aspects of Residential Casework with Children

SELMA FRAIBERG

The place of the caseworker in a children's institution has broadened in recent years so that we can almost speak of a new field of specialization in social work. In an earlier period the caseworker's function within the institution was largely confined to intake, interviews with relatives, and liaison work between the institution and other agencies. More recently caseworkers with training in child guidance have joined the staffs of residential treatment homes and in-patient psychiatric services as thera-

Reprinted with permission of *Social Casework,* Vol. 37, No. 4 (April, 1956), pp. 159–67.

pists, sometimes working directly with child patients, sometimes as members of the psychiatric team working with the patients' parents. Although residential therapy by the caseworker is, in itself, a fascinating topic for discussion, I should like to deal here with another aspect of institutional casework bordering at times on therapy but actually having a domain of its own in social service.

The casework of which I speak differs from therapy in its goals and its methods. It is not directed primarily toward bringing about fundamental character changes; it is directed toward helping the child with his everyday problems of adjustment. In the many institutions where therapy is not offered, or is limited to a few children, the caseworker must handle many of the daily crises of institutional life. At such times the caseworker is not a therapist but a counselor. His methods are not those of therapy but those of casework; he utilizes the interview to help a client find a solution to an immediate and pressing conflict.

In many ways this type of casework is more difficult than the practice of psychotherapy, for in psychotherapy we usually have all the advantages of intimate knowledge of a patient at a time of crisis in his life. We have the steady and continuing relationship of therapy within which we can explore the meaning of an event and assist the patient in finding solutions. But as caseworker-counselors, as members of an on-the-spot emergency squad, we are required to deal with crises in the lives of disturbed children even though we have very little knowledge of their inner lives. We therefore must call upon our highest faculties of diagnosis to deal with the immediate situation. *We must make use of behavioral observations and make inferences from behavior about the inner meaning of the conflict. We must be specialists in diagnosis.*

The material presented in this paper is taken from experience at a clinical camp, the University of Michigan Fresh Air Camp, where I was supervisor of the casework division for three summers in 1947, 1948, and 1949. Our camp served boys between the ages of 8 and 14 who were referred by social agencies, clinics, and courts for diagnostic study. The majority of the boys stayed one month; approximately one-third remained for two months. Almost all the boys had serious conduct disorders and a high percentage of them were delinquents. The cabin counselors were students in the undergraduate departments of psychology, sociology, social work, and education. The caseworkers were second-year social work students. In the third year of our program, a full-time graduate caseworker was added to the staff. Psychiatric consultation was available through the University Medical School. For purposes of research and teaching, counselors and caseworkers maintained detailed records of each child's behavior at camp, from which I have drawn material for this paper.

We must grant, of course, that experiences in a clinical camp for summer residence only cannot be equated with long-term institutional care.

But since many typical problems occur in both settings, some problems of institutional casework can be examined through these clinical camp experiences. The crises in a child's daily life, the use of the casework interview to examine a problem of adjustment and to bring about resolutions of a conflict, and the problems of diagnosis and interview technique will be found in nearly all residential work.

Intake

Let us begin with a description of the casework department, of the ways in which its clients are referred, and of the types of problems that come to its attention. The formal title "Casework Division" lends a sensible and conservative tone to the variety of activities that are carried on, but in reality this department is a highly unconventional social service center in a highly unconventional community. There is no door in camp with the name "Casework Division" lettered in gold. To be candid, there is no door either. Caseworkers, like other camp personnel, may be located on the dock, in the woods, on the steps of the lodge, or in the camp library.

On what basis do youngsters come to caseworkers? If we accept the client's statment of the problem, as is customary in statistical studies of intake, the data give us a cloudy picture. It is an interesting fact that not one of our clients—by his own statement—steals; but everyone else in camp steals. Almost all our clients are persecuted—"Everyone is always picking on me." Invariably the client works hard, makes his own bed, and cleans the cabin; but nobody else does. None of our clients, we are proud to say, uses bad language; but everyone else does. We have almost never had a client who started a fight; you know who did. In brief, very rarely does our client have a problem when he comes to us according to the most thorough statistical studies. Theoretically this factor should lighten the casework task.

Our clients come to us out of all the ordinary and the extraordinary experiences of camp. Most often they are brought to the caseworker for the first time by a counselor or staff member after some preliminary discussion of the reason for seeing the caseworker.

> Johnny is waiting for the caseworker on the steps of the lodge. This is a stinking old camp, and he hates everyone in it, and you can't have no pop or shows, and he wants to go home. And anyway he hasn't had a letter from his mama since he came here. . . .
>
> Bill arrives, accompanied by his counselor. He has been on a tear for several days, is wild and uncontrollable in the cabin, and cannot be reached by the counselor in any way. . . .
>
> A small urchin comes flying down the road pursued by a posse of indignant citizens. He screams the name of his caseworker, who comes out to meet the lynching party. A great noise is set up by the mob. The 8-year-old spokes-

man for the posse squeaks out a dreadful accusation: "He stole my potato chips." . . .

It's dinner time. Butch is on table duty and is serving chile. His 165-pound bulk moves lethargically between table and kitchen. Suddenly he slams the bowl of chile on the table with a curse and runs out of the dining hall. A caseworker goes after him to find out the trouble. . . .

Five members of Cabin 8 are grimly marching down to Main Lodge. They are leading one of their brethren to the caseworker. They dump two cameras and a fishing pole at her feet and all begin to talk at once. It appears that Cabin 8 has nourished a viper in its bosom. This viper has cunningly stolen and concealed these various items. The caseworker, in a searching glance at the group, is impressed by the fact that this Committee for the Abolition of Vice looks a little shifty-eyed, and the criminal looks for all the world like that goal of biblical tradition which was sent out into the wilderness for the well-known reasons. . . .

Also trouble in Cabin 9. Pete has been ousted from the group. No one will sit next to him at the table, no one will be touched by him, no one will talk to him. He has a pimple on his face and it is rumored that he has a venereal disease which will cause the teeth to rot and the hair to fall out. . . .

It is late now, bedtime. Enter George in tears. George thinks he'd better go home. Right now. He's all packed. He got a letter from home this afternoon and his dog has not been able to eat a meal since he, George, has been in camp. He'll die if George doesn't come home. The letter is produced and it says all that. Lacking a service for neurotic dogs, the caseworker promises to make a full investigation the next day.

These are some of the ways in which our clients come to us. In the majority of cases our first interview with the child takes place shortly after such a crisis. Obviously, there are both advantages and disadvantages in interviewing a child under these circumstances. The advantages lie in the immediacy of the event and the problem, the possibility of exploring feelings and behavior on the basis of a concrete and recent experience. The disadvantages derive from the fact that under the pressure of the critical event, the defenses of the client may become strengthened so that anxiety is replaced by "tough-guy" antics, persecutory feelings, or denial. In any case, it is the task of the caseworker to seek causes for the disturbed or irrational behavior, to apply his casework skills toward helping the child to understand his own behavior and to work out some reasonable adjustment to the realities of his group life.

The Meaning of the Crises

Let us examine a few of the "reasons for referral" which we have briefly cited. What goes into these crises that children bring to our doorsteps? How shall we explain the sudden yearning for home, the impulsive attacks on other kids, a mad dash out of the dining hall, a crusade against vice by a tribe of sinners?

Here is Bill, whose persistent attacks on other kids in the cabin have brought him to the caseworker. Why does Bill mercilessly beat up other kids in his cabin? And what has led up to the crisis today? For Bill, with his bag packed, announces that he is going home. At first he will not even talk to the caseworker. The caseworker points out to him that something must be bothering him inside to make him want to fight like this and now perhaps he is afraid and wants to get away from it. There is a quick denial from Bill, then he bursts out with a tirade against camp. He doesn't like this camp. "They don't beat hell out of the guys that steal. When I went to Camp B they always punished the guys for stealing." Angrily he tells about one of his cabin-mates who has been stealing and "nothing is done to him." This same boy had given Bill one of the stolen articles but Bill had not known then that it was stolen.

With less experience with delinquents, the caseworker might at this point conclude that Bill has been falsely accused of some theft and is leaving camp in indignation. Or he might feel that this is a youngster with strong moral judgments about stealing who cannot tolerate the delinquencies of his cabin-mates. But the caseworker's experience with delinquents at camp causes him to reflect at this point. He discerns, in this familiar story, the anxiety of a child who is guilty about his own stealing as well as that of others, and is now fearful of punishment. The worker permits Bill to talk on for some time about the delinquencies of other boys, then tactfully suggests that maybe Bill, too, might sometimes have taken things, and if he had been punished for doing so he may be afraid of what will happen here. Bill first denies this vehemently—then admits that he has been stealing since he was 5 years old and that he has been in the detention home so many times he can't remember the number.

And why does Bill beat up the other kids in the cabin? "Because," he explains to the caseworker, "they don't mind the counselor and somebody has to *make* them." On the face of it, this is absurd. Is this another alibi? No, this seems to have something to it. Bill seems to be saying, "Guys who steal should be beaten up." And, later, that guys who don't mind the counselor should be beaten up. In this camp the counselors, the staff people, do not beat the boys. So Bill does the beating up. But why? Why does he, personally, call upon himself to be the hatchet man, as it were?

We have seen this pattern many times in camp. The mechanism can be described this way: "I steal things. I am bad. And I don't mind the counselor. When you're bad and you get a good strapping you feel better for it. But they don't do it here. I feel funny when I've been bad and I don't get punished. Look at all those other guys, stealing, talking back to the counselor. They ought to get beat up good. That's what. But nobody does anything to them. They just talk to them. It drives me nuts. *I'll* give them what's coming to them. I'll show them you can't get away with that sort of stuff." And the fighting is on. For Bill does to the other kids what he thinks should be done to him. He attempts to get rid of his own anxiety and guilt through inflicting punishment on the other guilty ones. In this moment he behaves toward the other kids like a tyrannical parent. It is a mechanism familiar in analytical psychology, known as "identification with the aggressor." Out of fear of punishment from the adult for his own transgressions, the child identifies with authority and does to the other transgressors what he thinks should be done to him.

Our diagnostic hunch is confirmed when, in a later interview, this problem is made more accessible to us through a cabin event. Bill is plotting a "ganging up" episode against Dick, the cabin scapegoat. He has planned with other members of the cabin to "beat up on Dick." The counselor asks Bill to discuss this with the caseworker. To the caseworker's questions Bill replies that Dick never wants to stay with the group and he is always making wise-cracks about the other guys in the cabin. They are going to fix him for this. The caseworker begins to raise some questions with Bill. Aren't both of these problems that he sees in Dick also his own, Bill's, problems? Reluctantly Bill admits this is so. Then the caseworker points out to Bill that he seems to expect punishment himself for misbehavior in the group, and because he doesn't get it he feels he has to punish other guys for these things. This is something that Bill is able to see. He calms down, enters into a more serious discussion with the caseworker about his fighting, and finally relinquishes his ganging-up plot against Dick.

We are well aware that, from these brief contacts with the caseworker, Bill has not altered his character pattern. We cite this example chiefly because we can observe here a pattern of aggression and its dynamics with such clarity; we can see how complicated our task becomes when we seek the reasons for a pattern of aggression and attack which on the surface seems erratic and inexplicable. One of the chief values in these interviews with Bill may lie in the diagnostic clues to his pattern of delinquency, clues that should prove valuable to the agency that will continue its work with the boy.

Let us look at another of the crises mentioned earlier. Butch is the 11-year-old boy, who, in the midst of serving food at his table, blows up, slams a bowl of chile on the table, and storms out of the dining hall. What has happened? His counselor and his cabin-mates are as mystified as everyone else in the dining hall. It just happens, that's all—just like that. We are entirely without clues at this point. Of course, it may be that Butch has had a traumatic experience at the age of three with chile con carne, but it is unlikely. It may be that he doesn't like serving; but why? Most of the boys like to take turns serving, and march importantly up and down the dining hall to get refills at the serving counter.

The caseworker, as he follows Butch out of the dining hall, has to do some fast thinking. What does he know about Butch? Only that he weighs 165 pounds, is slow and lethargic, often depressed. He seldom participates in group activities. His only interest in camp is food. This is so well known it is a camp joke. Butch eats ravenously at all times. We know, too, that Butch came to camp directly from the detention home where he was held following a long history of truancies and the recent theft of a bicycle. But what has all this to do with a bowl of chile and a sudden rage?

The caseworker catches up with Butch. Almost immediately when Butch sees the caseworker he becomes tearful and brings forth his grief in a torrent. He doesn't want to have to serve those guys at the table. "They eat like a bunch of hogs!" He has to keep running back and forth with serving plates all the time and he hasn't been able to sit down and eat anything himself. There is great exaggeration in this last statement, of course, but Butch is really upset.

We begin to understand. For a child to whom food is all-important and all-absorbing, a terrible sacrifice is necessary to carry out the work of giving others food when he, himself, is the victim of an insatiable hunger. The caseworker understands this. He gives no sermons on good-sportsmanship and cooperation, but listens sympathetically to the child's outpouring. And as Butch pours forth his grief, he begins to relax a little. He becomes a little guilty about the whole business and volunteers that he will take care of serving duty for the rest of the day.

The caseworker chooses now to go into the matter a little more. He asks a question about the boy's feelings here at camp. Butch says all he wants is to be by himself. The caseworker asks him what he thinks about when he is alone. Butch then tells the worker that he worries all the time about returning to the detention home after leaving camp. (This is a real possibility in the event that the agency cannot find him a foster home.) Butch explains that he lives with his father, his mother is dead, and he has been cared for by his older sister. He adds, as an afterthought, that he mostly has to take care of himself. He asks the caseworker to find out "what is going to happen" when he, Butch, leaves camp. The caseworker assures him that any fellow would worry about that and that he will try to find out what the plans are for Butch and will let him know. Butch seems much relieved and returns to his cabin—after a little snack.

Now the strange scene in the dining hall begins to make sense. We have a lonely, frightened boy, deeply deprived in every sense of the word. To this child food has larger meaning than that of simple nourishment. Food is love, food is survival, food is necessary to satisfy his deepest and most fundamental cravings. But it can never satisfy them entirely and it is poor nourishment at best for this child's impoverished life. To share his scanty portion with a bunch of greedy hogs? To *feed them* when he wants fundamentally *to be fed* in the most primitive and infantile sense of the term?

Impossible. So he slams the bowl of chile on the table and marches out of the dining hall.

What shall we do about the crisis in Cabin 9? Pete has been ousted by his cabin-mates. No one will have anything to do with him. No one will even sit next to him at the table. Why? Because Pete has a pimple on his face. Our experience in cabin-scapegoating has often led us to discount such statements of the kids against their scapegoats as "Aw, we don't like the way he eats at the table; he ain't got no manners." (This, of course, comes from a cabin group where forks and knives are used only when necessary, that is, to reinforce a threat to slit somebody's throat.) But a pimple—we had never had a pimple scapegoating before. What is going on? Is it an act? Is it a camouflage for something else? The incident doesn't make sense. We have to assume that the pimple has a myth surrounding it and we begin our investigation by trying to find out "what is a pimple and what could it do?" A pimple, we learn, is something catching. You can catch something from it. A disease. How do you get a pimple? From doing something. Pete and George did something. On the overnight hike. Two weeks ago. That's how come Pete got the pimple. Now he's got the disease.

The myth now gradually unfolds. Pete and George were discovered in sex-play by two other members of the cabin two weeks ago. Arnie and Larry, who found the two, appoint themselves a two-man Committee for the Abolition of Vice in Cabin 9, highly motivated in their tasks by reasons that do not bear close scrutiny. They approach the counselor in great indignation and wrath to tell their tale. The counselor handles the situation with serious attention but with no great alarm. The boys, who expected a great scene, are disappointed and surprised that nothing more terrible has happened to the culprits than a quiet discussion. Although the story quickly makes the rounds, the counselor's dignified handling of the experience calms the group and, after a couple of days, talk about it ceases.

Then, almost two weeks later, comes the pimple. In discussion with the boys it is seen that they honestly believe that Pete has a venereal disease. They offer rich evidence from boys' lore that this is what happens if you do what Pete and George did. The counselor discusses venereal disease frankly with the boys, assures them that they have some mixed-up notions about it and that Pete's pimple has nothing to do with what happened. This discussion serves to diminish anxiety in the group.

But what of Pete? The wretched and unhappy scapegoat is seen by the caseworker. He wears his pimple like the mark of Cain; he is inwardly bound to the morbid conviction that his friends are probably right about his disease. The caseworker talks with him at length about the whole problem. He is vastly reassured to learn that his pimple is a commonplace thing, that it has nothing to do with the episode with George.

At the same time the counselor discusses the whole matter with the group, since it has by this time become a group issue. The counselor clarifies with the group their misconceptions regarding the pimple and within a few days the event has faded in significance.

Our experience has shown the importance of early handling of all such group and individual problems. Often such problems appear so ludicrous at first glance that an inexperienced counselor might dismiss them as boyish nonsense. There is a temptation, for example, to make a speech to the cabin group, to tell them that all this sounds a little nuts, to plead for everyone's working together and loving his neighbor and his counselor, and to whoop up a little group spirit. Such a device, if it works at all, is only a temporary expedient. In spite of it the myth of the pimple will grow, take on vast proportions, damaging the group and the outcast child. We know that for effective handling we must seek out the reasons for behavior and for feelings in order that we may base our handling of the events on a diagnostically clear situation.

Re-enactment of Problems

We shall turn now to the question of why we have so many problems in camp. Why should these children produce such serious problems in this setting? We know that these youngsters come from environments in which there are many factors, both in the home and in the community which combine to bring about severe behavior problems and delinquent patterns. These children tell us of brutal beatings from parents, of neglect and homelessness, of being deprived of one of their parents. But why, in this camp environment, where brutality is absent and every effort is made to understand the complicated nature of the child, should the same problems emerge, sometimes in diluted, sometimes in strengthened, form?

We may conclude that our staff is something less than saintly, which it is, of course, and that perhaps if the ideal counselor should one day be found—one of inexhaustible patience and with limitless capacity for love —then no further problems would exist in camp. We have never set out to look for such a counselor. Yet we are certain that even if we found the superman counselor, these children would still be compelled to reproduce their problems in one form or another.

How shall we explain why Bill, who has spent years perfecting his hatred for all authority—for the cops who throw him in the detention home, for the father who "beats hell" out of him—continues his stealing in this new, nonpunitive environment of camp and *complains* that here we do not beat children? How shall we explain Butch of the insatiable appetite, who receives practically unlimited quantities of food, yet behaves as if we wish to deprive him of food? At camp we see children steal from a beloved counselor. We see a child invent a fantasy in which a perfectly reasonable and gentle counselor becomes a cop or an FBI agent. We see a child who has suffered neglect and rejection for all the ten years of his life attempt to manufacture a situation in which he will again be rejected.

We observe, then, a tendency within the child to reproduce his problems in a new environment, regardless of the differences between this milieu and his familiar one, and in spite of good personnel and modern methods of child education. Perhaps this single factor has caused more disillusionment and discouragement among institutional workers than any other. How thwarting to see your gift of love to a child turned aside and rejected, to see him react at times as if you were a tyrant. Yet this phenomenon is now familiar to us and we are no longer surprised when we see it manifested. We know now that when a child is separated from his parents—the primary love objects—he tends to recreate the old environment in the new, to endow the new objects with the attributes of the old, and thus to invest these new figures with the various emotions and fantasies that belonged to the original objects.

We believe that an understanding of this factor, of transference, is basic for the equipment of the institutional worker, and that it is important to utilize this understanding in handling the daily problems that arise. If we understand the ways in which these transference reactions are manifested in the camp situation, we should be able to make valuable deductions regarding the nature of the child's symptoms and behavior problems as they are related to his own history and family relationships.

A justifiable question arises: Do we simply provide a theater in camp for the acting out of a transference neurosis? Shall we sit quietly by while this marvel develops before our eyes? It immediately becomes clear that this would be an impossible procedure even if it were desirable for some therapeutic reason. For we know that if a child were permitted to act out his impulses and symptoms in this fashion, a camp would be reduced to complete chaos. We are required by the dictates of camp management, as well as therapeutic good judgment, to establish some degree of control of behavior. However, much of our judgment regarding handling of behavior depends upon our diagnostic understanding of the child. Since we understand that the child will inevitably transfer patterns of behavior and symptoms to the new environment, it seems to us that we have here, in the factor of transference, an important and indispensable tool for diagnosis and treatment.

Much that is seemingly inexplicable in a child's behavior at camp takes on form and meaning when we examine it in the light of transference. Here is a synopsis of events in one case as reported by the counselor.

In a cabin of seriously delinquent boys an event takes place that sets off a cabin uproar. Twelve-year-old Art has done something that nobody in the group is willing to stand for. Art, a chronic bedwetter, has been surly and aggressive all day. He is particularly belligerent toward the counselor, a man, and has tried in numerous ways to provoke the counselor to anger. He has finally chosen a single incident to justify his anger against Jim, the counselor, and complains that Jim failed to waken him for a boxing match after the rest hour. Thereafter he spends the day in endless petty and provocative tactics. At bedtime Art is negativistic and temperamental, devises numerous antics to keep his cabin-mates awake, and takes joy from the counselor's unsuccessful efforts to calm either him or the group. Finally he announces that he is *not* going to sleep on a rubber sheet, that nobody can make him, that he is going to "piss all over the mattress." Apparently no one takes this threat seriously. Art then rips off the rubber sheet and puts his plan into action, gleefully urinating on his bed before the astonished eyes of the group. There is a great noise in the cabin, of course, and even Art feels that he has gone too far this time. The counselor finally calms the boys, assuring them that the matter will be gone into with Art on the following day.

What shall we do? As caseworkers in a camp we understand fully the implications of such an act for the group, and the boys' indignation at such an exhibition is in a large measure justified. We wish to handle this event with Art in such a way that there will not be a repetition of such infantile behavior. Our experience has shown that if we ignore such events any of several things may happen. One, this exhibitionistic behavior or a variation of it may recur; two, the group may become infected eventually and join in such antics; three, the group may take matters in its own hands and make a scapegoat of Art. We choose, then, to go into this matter with Art. But our approach will also have to be based on the meaning of this event to Art.

When the caseworker sees Art the following morning it is obvious that he expects extreme punishment. When the fear of punishment is dealt with, Art with some reluctance discusses the incident. He knows, he says, that he shouldn't have done it, but he did it because he was mad at Jim. This we already know but we are interested in knowing why a chronic bedwetter should choose an act of exhibitionistic urination at bedtime as a means of expressing aggression against the counselor.

The caseworker encourages Art to discuss his feelings of anger against Jim. Art tries vainly to find a reason, then concludes vaguely that he guesses he was mad at Jim because he did not waken him for the boxing match. We can be certain that this is only the apparent reason to Art but, as often happens in such situations, the basis for the hostility is lost in a maze of irrational feelings. The caseworker now asks Art if this is the way he usually gets back at people when he is mad. No, he says promptly, he usually fights them. Is this what he wanted to do with Jim? He says he would if Jim weren't so big. The caseworker asks if Art gets mad at home, too. "Sometimes," he acknowledges. Sometimes he gets mad at his mother. "How do you get back at your mother?" Art smiles. "The same way."

The caseworker suggests to Art that maybe his bedwetting and the business of last night are "kind of the same thing," that is, one way of getting even with grown-ups. He adds that this is the way very little boys get even with grown-ups and it certainly shouldn't be necessary for a boy of Art's age to do this. Some discussion follows about Art's feelings toward the counselor and the ambivalence that has been so often expressed toward him. In later interviews this is gone into more fully.

We should say that there were no further episodes of exhibitionistic urination. It is also of some incidental interest that following this particular interview Art had dry nights for almost a week. (He had always wet nightly.) There were occasional wet nights thereafter and almost always they could be tied up with revenge fantasies. We cite this with no wish to take seriously a slight symptomatic relief in the case of a boy with numerous and complex problems. However, it may be seen how valuable it can be to study such a symptom when it is acted out in transference.

In reviewing this material we see how the unconscious meaning of the symptom, enuresis, is acted out in this episode of exhibitionistic urination. Our knowledge of the dynamics of transference allows us to suppose that part of the unconscious meaning of Art's enuresis has to do with aggression against his mother. The motive for repression of these aggressive impulses and fantasies can only be fear of the consequences, of the attendant dangers of bringing forth such aggression consciously. In camp we observe how the boy's ambivalence in relation to the parental figure is transferred to the person of the counselor. At the same time, since it is less dangerous to have aggressive feelings in this new relationship, his impulses partially break through and he finally acts out the symptom in the transference to the counselor.

Along with the acting out we see the boy's provocative behavior as well as the expectation of punishment for his aggressive feelings toward the counselor and for the exhibitionistic urination. We must assume that the provocative behavior that preceded the bedtime event belongs to the same symptom picture. That is, he feels that, for having these aggressive feelings toward the counselor, "I *should* be punished," and then, "I *wish* you would punish me." In the absence of punishment Art is exposed to the full realization of his guilt feelings and, as a result, some opportunity is provided for at least a superficial investigation of this behavior. Through tying up the exhibitionistic act of urination with the symptom of enuresis, the caseworker restores to the child some measure of control of his behavior. We should point out here the differences in handling of this episode and therapeutic handling in the larger meaning of the term. If this were an institution with a year-round program and long-term treatment goals, we should have chosen to go into this entire episode in greater detail.

Conclusion

In these ways, then, and also in many others, the caseworker counsels the child who presents special problems in camp which, for one reason or another, cannot be handled within the group. We see how the caseworker's task is oriented to the structure of the camp and to the group. The caseworker's job is to help the child function in his group, to do whatever is necessary through interviews with the child, through consultations with the counselor and with other staff members, and through communication with the family and agency, in order to bring about a reasonable adjustment in camp.

PART THREE

GROUP TREATMENT
IN A THERAPEUTIC MILIEU

11. The Social Group Work Method and Residential Treatment

HENRY W. MAIER

"I would lie to my mother if I were not to tell you guys right now that she and I have a hell of a lot of trouble with each other." Carl, 15, blurted out this emotion-laden statement during the second session of his social work group. In the same week, several months after his commitment to the state's correctional institution (a residential treatment center), he was heard to announce to his cottage mother, "Gee, do you have to get permission every time you step outside this goofy place? Why don't you print P-R-I-S-O-N on the door!" After a long pause, he added, "Mrs. Kusak, may us guys have some apples? We want to play ball until supper. I have some milk, too. I'll be back by six."

In these two episodes we find expression of first a remembered relationship to a real mother and then an actual day-to-day living relationship with a cottage mother. In the first episode the individual can use the helping situation to reflect safely about his life situation. In the second one he uses the group living situation to deal directly with life questions. The former

Reprinted with permission of the National Association of Social Workers from Henry W. Maier "The Social Group Method and Residential Treatment," in *Group Work as Part of Residential Treatment,* Henry W. Maier, editor (New York: National Association of Social Workers, 1965), pp. 26–42.

involves a testing, reliving, and improving of basic life relationships within the context of a social group work situation. In the latter we note that basic life experiences are being tested and reworked within the context of an *ongoing* everyday primary life situation, namely, the cottage, which temporarily assumes the major function of family living. Both group situations —the social group work and the group living one—afford Carl opportunities to experience, to come to grips with himself, and to learn new and more effective ways to cope with his feelings and his relationships to elders and peers. In both groups, Carl works on the same personal problems, yet each group introduces different avenues for treatment. These differences are most relevant both conceptually and for practice.

This chapter focuses on two primary considerations: the practice of social group work as part of residential treatment and the difference inherent in working with clients within a social work group and in group living. "Residential treatment," "social group work," and the relationship of these two treatment methods to each other will be defined. Furthermore, group work practice questions related to the phenomena of separation, placement, privacy, and different modes of human functioning will be dealt with.

Residential Treatment

Residential treatment entails a therapeutically designed round-the-clock living-in experience, the purpose of which is care and treatment. Its clinical components are an integration of functions, structure, physical setting, and immediate social environment. Residential treatment separates the client from his natural setting—from family, peers, and community life experiences. It introduces conditions for helping the client to experience the care and treatment that may enable him to return to his natural setting and to meet his life's demands more effectively. Residential treatment involves the temporary replacement of family living with group living in a controlled environment. Three spheres of socially engineered intervention become pertinent:

1. A preventive program designed to create a physical, social, and ideological environment that will avert, or at least minimize, experiences that are beyond the client's threshold of successful mastery while simultaneously protecting the community from the client's deviant behavior and guarding the client against undue pressure from family, peer, and community association.

2. A program that will provide the client with at least the potential assurance of being able to cope successfully with the routines of everyday living.

3. A program offering a manifold treatment effort, combining specific professional functions such as social group work, casework, child care work, psychotherapy, remedial education, and medical care, so that the

totality of the residential group living experience can serve as a corrective life experience.[1]

Residential treatment, by its very essence, creates a network of groups: living, work, social work, classroom, recreation, denizen, and staff groups, and the communal group of the total institution. Other groups and group associations emerge spontaneously within this intentional community. There are friendship groups and social alliances among the denizens and among staff members, as well as friendships that cut across both strata. Each group needs to be understood and utilized within its own context, as well as in relation to the institutional community as a whole, because each variation offers a different group experience and, consequently, a potentially different avenue of treatment.

Residential treatment takes into account the complications of living and treatment. It focuses on the problems that brought the clients to the service. Furthermore, residential treatment offers opportunities for learning to cope with life situations emerging out of placement and residential living. Daily hazards of living, then, become opportunities for treatment!

The group, as an arena for trying out and living out *new experience,* becomes especially relevant in residential treatment. Residential treatment serves individuals who cannot benefit from ordinary reflective and relationship therapy, otherwise they could have been helped through some form of outpatient treatment. For these clients the essence of therapy becomes located in the series of experiences they find within the residential treatment program. For them treatment is anchored in the experiences of discovering the consequences of behavior and actual effective coping with the tasks before them. Social group work efforts become especially relevant, because in group work the worker is preoccupied with the activities of the group and with the opportunities for each group member to demonstrate to himself in the presence of others his actual competence and his questions about areas of incompetence. Group experiences can become the most vital resource for ego development.

DIFFERENT ROLES OF THE GROUP WORKER

Social group workers function in different roles in institutional settings. The multiplicity of their professional functions suggests that they need to continue to examine and define their special tasks for themselves and their colleagues. If a social group worker is called on to function as a supervisor of group living staff, training specialist, or administrator, he will undoubtedly bring to bear his specialized knowledge. His professional alignment remains social work; his professional functions, however, are those of a supervisor, teacher, or administrator, whichever is demanded of the par-

1. For more detailed analysis *see* Henry W. Maier, "Residential Treatment of Children," *Encyclopedia of Social Work* (New York: National Association of Social Workers, 1965), pp. 660–664.

ticular situation. Most important, he does not practice social group work within any of these tasks just outlined.

Essence of the Group Work Method

This monograph, however, purposely focuses entirely on the application of the social group work method, especially the differential application of the method in the service of a multiplicity of groups. In social group work practice, as in all social work intervention in general and in residential treatment specifically, the social group worker utilizes the social group work method in order to engage his clients and himself in a purposeful group experience. His objective is to enhance the social functioning of each client preventively and rehabilitatively. The social work group provides the worker with his arena of practice. By means of the group sessions the worker introduces conditions in and through the group that serve as intervening, that is, *associate,* experiences to each client's ongoing life experience in his family, peer, school, work, and/or other community life. The content and focuses of the group worker's intervening activities in any setting are based on three major considerations:

1. The nature of the clientele who, with the worker, make up the group.
2. The context in which the group experience proceeds.
3. The formulation and acceptance of treatment objectives by the worker and his clients.

In brief, social group work intervention is based on each client's personal circumstances, the circumstances of the social group work experience, and the continuous understanding about the intervening group experience as a means and context for effecting change within each client's personal life situation. The application of the social group work method involves four developmental aspects concurrently that are basic to *any* small group experience:

1. *Dependency*—a shift from dependence on a single individual to dependence on one or several persons or possibly the group as a whole.
2. *Coping arena*—the utilization of a socially safe milieu for trying out old and new relationship patterns, skills, ideas, values, and forms of behavior.
3. *Place of belonging*—having an opportunity to acquire a social membership in an identifiable social unit (and possibly locale).
4. *Reference system*—the development of a personal reference system and eventual identification with a group of individual members or the entire group. (In the case of younger or developmentally inhibited children or in the earlier stages of a group's life, the identification with one or several group members constitutes the semblance of a "reference system.")

These four facets of group membership parallel the progression of human growth and development. (1) The development of dependence on a single key person creates a developmental readiness to expand and shift such dependency to more and more individuals. (2) Satisfied dependence on one or several persons encourages the testing of new relationships, personal skills, ideas, behavior patterns, and personal experiences. The satisfaction of dependency and the experimentation with something new become closely associated with the persons involved. (3) Doing "things" within a group leads to the recognition that such experiences are distinctly associated with a particular group. Association with such a social unit merges into a sense of belonging to a societal unit. (4) Finally, when an individual identifies himself with a group, he tends to select aspects of such a group assocation as points of reference for his behavior, thinking, feelings, and belief in his association with other individuals apart from the particular group. The context of the associations with a particular group provides the individual with a reference group.[2]

RELATION TO RESIDENTIAL TREATMENT

Social group work has an affinity to residential treatment. Conceptually, the practice of social group work remains the same, whether as part of a residential treatment program or when pursued within a nonresidential service. Here, as in all social work, the client's problems, his personal situation, and his accessibility for help are the prime determinants for treatment. The fact that clients may be labeled descriptively as one thing or another, i.e., "emotionally disturbed," "delinquent," "retarded," and the service designated as "residential treatment," "inpatient," and so on, does not actually define the individuals involved or the treatment they may require. Each client must be understood and treated for his capacities and incapacities in coping with his personal complications, at a given point in time, keeping in mind that these transcend his institutional life and the critical incidents that have resulted in his institutional placement.

The group worker in his role as a member of the institutional team shares in the over-all formulation of his clients' treatment plan. This includes special considerations for his clients' group living experiences. The group worker must perceive both his clients' needs within the group and their total progression within residential treatment. He is both his group's worker and the institution's treatment agent. At the same time, other members of the team contribute to the formulation of treatment goals for the clients served by social work groups.

DIFFERENCES IN PRACTICE

Practice of the social group work method in a residential treatment service requires special attention. Foremost, placement and primary group living introduce a host of special components that are unique to residential treatment.

---

2. Henry W. Maier, *Three Theories of Child Development, The Theories of Erikson, Piaget and Sears and Their Implications for the Helping Process* (New York, Harper and Row, 1965), chap. vii.

1. In the practice of social group work generally, the worker is mindful that helping occurs in association with continued life experience at home and with peers beyond the home setting. However close the social worker's relationships to his clients may become, they remain tangential to those experienced by his clients in everyday life. In a residential treatment situation, the group worker is faced with similar factors, yet the differential circumstances in the clients' living situation introduce variations that are noteworthy and starkly influence the worker's intervening activities.

In the opening paragraphs of this chapter, we learned of Carl's struggle over sharing with his fellow group members his experience and feelings about his mother. In Carl's situation, the worker would have to be mindful that this boy's outburst, ". . . if I were not to tell you guys right now . . ." was as much an appeal for his peers' nurturing support as an attempt to come to terms with his emotional entanglement with his mother ("I would lie to my mother if I were not to tell . . ."). Clients are provided with a protected everyday living experience that allows them continued experimentation with new roles and values, while preparing them for life outside the institution. At the same time, the assurance of peer support in assisting the making of therapeutic gains adds relevance when we are cognizant of the fact that it is a matter of personal survival for an individual to live within the norms of his peers, as well as to square away previous personal entanglements for the sake of successful treatment.[3] These factors also hold true for work with street corner gangs, when the corner gang assumes the quasi-functions of primary life as well as a reference group experience in lieu of nurturing family and meaningful "other" group experiences.

2. In his group work practice within a residential treatment setting, the worker must clarify for himself which factors in his clients' behavior are related to complications that lead to placement and which are an outgrowth of the processes and circumstances of placement and institutional living. Both considerations require the worker's constant attention. A clearer diagnostic assessment of these factors will help the worker to delineate his treatment objectives.

The worker has to be especially cognizant of the many hurdles associated with institutional placement and living. It will be essential for him to study and appraise his clients' past thoroughly with the specific goal of utilizing his understanding of their living pasts to help them find ways to compensate for the past and to cope with the present while shaping a different future. The latter holds especially true for the factors associated with separation and compensation for separation.

Separation phenomena also apply to children and youth placed in residential centers. In residential treatment, separation involves the trauma of severing ties with central adults, peers, and established patterns of living,

---

3. A most stimulating study of this treatise is found in Howard W. Polsky, *Cottage Six: The Social System of Delinquent Boys in Residential Treatment* (New York: Russell Sage Foundation, 1962).

while being confronted almost simultaneously with the demand for coping with heretofore unknown and starkly new patterns of living. Each individual comprehends separation as a repetition of his past experiences, in addition to being confronted with new conditions. The combination must at times seem overwhelming to the client, and, like surgery in medicine, it involves a major psychosocial adjustment. The worker's awareness of these dynamics challenges him to conquer his preoccupation with only phenomena of separation, deprivation, and communal rejection and to include and use his recognition of the client's eventual capacity to compensate for these experiences and to cope effectively with the new reality.[4] In other words, a conceptual shift is required: not the sense of separation and rejection, but the experience of compensation for separation and rejection, becomes the vital area to be "worked out."[5]

In residential treatment the social worker has to keep in mind that groups may be formed to help clients explicitly with the complications inherent in group living, with their separation from and preparation for return to community living, with their value orientation to treatment, and with their effectiveness in coping with their group living experiences.[6]

3. The fact that institutional living tends to be analogous to "fish-bowl living" makes it necessary for the group worker to design the social group work experience as much for the opportunity to gain a sense of personal privacy as to gain a sense of successful "togetherness." In fact, the very idea of belonging voluntarily to a group involving oneself and being noticed by others for one's contributions bestows a sense of individual recognition and personal privacy to each group member.

The social work group can serve as a resource for the client to pursue and express his interests privately (to tend to his hobby or ideas) without the danger of becoming isolated. Membership in such a group can also help an individual to achieve corporate privacy—that is, the satisfaction of belonging to a group that is all the individual's own, protected against the threat of overt interference or separation from other peer groups in the institution.

4. Most important, the worker can introduce experience that might, in part, compensate for three inherent features of institutional living: anonymity, standardization, and authoritarianism. The social work group can become a vital arena for each individual to experience in the presence of

4. A vivid example of the practice application of this concept is found in Esther Appelberg's discussion of the clients' preoccupation with food. *See* "The Cottage Meeting As a Therapeutic Tool," in Henry W. Maier, ed., *Group Work as Part of Residential Treatment* (New York, National Association of Social Workers, 1965), pp. 142–154.

5. *See* Zira De Fries, Shirley Jenkins, and Ethelyn C. Williams, "Treatment of Disturbed Children in Foster Care," *American Journal of Orthopsychiatry,* Vol. 34, No. 4 (July 1964), pp. 615–624.

6. *See* chapters by Esther Appelberg (pp. 142–154), Leonard N. Brown (pp. 155–168), Howard W. Polsky (pp. 116–130), and Hyman J. Weiner (pp. 133–141) in Henry W. Maier, *Group Work as Part of Residential Treatment.*

others his own individuality and competence. Moreover, his and his group's activities can become his living laboratory for dealing with factors beyond his control. He can learn and realize that he counts, that he can influence and cope with his environment. In many ways, the social worker helps his clients to get hold of and become part of the social forces that surround them just as the settlement worker serves the constituents of the neighborhood.

Preceding paragraphs suggest that the social work practitioner in a residential treatment program needs to take into account the complications that arise out of the processes of residential treatment as well as the problems that brought the clients to this type of service. We are reminded of René Dubos' observation that all treatment—psychosocial, medical, or physical—creates sets of new realities that need attention and therapeutic considerations as much as either the conditions to be replaced or the new ones to be accomplished.[7] Therapeutic intervention builds in its own set of hazards and there is the necessity for treating these hazards as well as the ones they are to overcome. The organization of this publication recognizes this dichotomy.

A GUIDING DICHOTOMY APPLIED IN PRACTICE

As suggested, the social worker needs to take into account whether he intends to deal with (1) the complications associated with residential treatment per se or (2) the problems that brought the clients to the residential treatment service. In either event, the worker creates opportunities for learning to cope with the social situations that residential treatment offers. These "opportunities" include both specially structured situations and the crises arising spontaneously within any treatment situation.

The organization of this monograph is an attempt to highlight this conceptual division. Part II contains practice material related to helping clients with the problematic functioning that brought them to the residential treatment service. Part III focuses on social group work efforts in helping clients to meet the demands of everyday living within the institution.

This conceptual organization of treatment in residential settings can be further delineated and illustrated by the following practice material. The social group worker may want to deal with present complications as part of helping clients to cope with their immediate life situation and gain greater competence for future functioning or he may want to use an ongoing situation as a welcome source for reflecting and "working over" pervasive associated experience, feelings of the past (of the client's case history).

Illustrative of this is a minute critical incident in Carl's social work group:

7. René J. Dubos, *Mirage of Health* (Garden City, N.Y., Anchor Books, Doubleday and Company, 1961).

The boys came to the meeting quite high in spirits. Carl pulled the shades down. Jim, in passing, played with a shade, causing it to topple down. He picked it up and started to hang it back, then obviously dropped it purposely again. Carl commented that Jim was after attention. Immediately the others started to tease Jim cruelly. Jim angrily walked out of the room. The worker stated her concern over Jim's withdrawal and conveyed that she wanted Jim to know of her concern. After placing a hammer and nails on the windowsill, the worker found Jim on the front steps. He readily followed her into the meeting room, where the others were fastening the shade back into place. Jim seated himself on the windowsill and the rest of the group settled quickly for discussion in the circle of chairs placed near the window.

In this episode, the worker has at least two clinical alternatives. She can either help the group members to discern their and Jim's current feelings about this incident and their relationship to past desires for acceptance and associated failures in such endeavors, or she can attempt to focus on Jim's handling of being picked on and the others' futile attempts at trying to live effectively with each other. In either event the group worker's immediate treatment objective would be to help the group members to experience and handle frustration differently—to help them develop a more mature sense of competence.

Returning to the subsequent events in this record, we find:

The group settled quickly for discussion in a circle of chairs near the window. The worker immediately shared her puzzlement, asking, "What happened?" Jim: "I just got mad." Larry: "You can't face the truth, Jim." Others cited incidents when they had gotten mad. Some of their comments were half in jest but yet with much undercurrent feelings. Most of their remarks dealt with incidents of being picked on by others in the cottage. Jim, with his back toward the group, listened but conveyed an air of detachment. Rick started to pick on Jim again. When Rick called him a "flip-out," Jim began to defend himself. The worker suggested that she had a hunch there might have been arguments that started prior to the meeting. Jim voiced his fury: "I don't want to kiss anyone's a—. I want someone I can talk to."

The discussion shifted first from picking on others to sharing each other's sense of lonely frustration and then to sorting out and looking at the difficulties of group living. The discussion gave the members of this group an opportunity to reflect on their struggle to find a sense of identity and social position within their present life situation.

As stated, the worker could have attempted to utilize the critical incident cited as a strategic moment for dealing with accumulated feelings and perceptions of past experiences. She might have injected: "I am puzzled. Have things like this bugged Jim or any one of you before you came here?" It can be predicted, on the basis of past practice experience, that such a leading comment would have induced the boys to unpack, share, and reflect on past experience that in one way or another is still troublesome and gnawing in the present. To repeat, the worker has to discern for himself within which aspect of his clients' functioning he needs to intervene. Is he to deal with his clients' over-all life management or is he to face with them questions pertaining to their specific adaptation to stresses emanating out of residential placement and living?

THREE MODES OF INTERVENTION

The conceptual differences inherent in the professional's decision to focus on dealing with feeling (affect), understanding (cognition), or experience (behavior), a question relevant to all social work practice, is especially pivotal in group work with children and youth in residential treatment. Most children in residential treatment bring with them not only an unusually complex past, but also a diffusion of feelings, understanding, and experience that complicates all attempts to help them to cope with the demands and opportunities of everyday life. A worker must clarify for himself and tacitly convey to his clients whether he is dealing with questions primarily involving their feelings, comprehension, or behavioral experience.

To illustrate, Carl's introduction of his conflicted feelings about living up to his image of his mother suggests the possibility of group members and worker exploring together Carl's and other clients' feelings about their relationships to their mothers, their alternate strivings for dependence and independence, their inner feelings of conflict over past ties and new hopes for continued close relationships with their mothers. In such an attempt the worker could endeavor to help Carl and the others to sort out and "work through" feelings about their mothers. She would utilize the concept that as each client feels more comfortable about his relationship to his mother (and his father, in the same way), he will understand and experience her differently, which will enable him to function more competently in his everyday relationships with peers and elders.

The worker could also focus on helping Carl and the others to understand their ambivalent feelings more clearly. She would then rely on the hypothesis that finding a comprehensible explanation about one's feelings leads to a change in behavior. That is, if these clients were to comprehend their situation more clearly they would feel and experience their parental and family situations differently, and consequently they would be able to cope more realistically with their life situations.

Finally, the worker could perceive the situation as a question of providing Carl and others in the group with a different and corrective personal experience, because in experiencing their own competence in the present they could acquire the capacity to relate and to function more effectively in the group and eventually in their lives beyond the group and the institution. With Carl, the worker would have proceeded with the prediction that Carl's experiencing a different relationship to a woman through his personal association with her in discussion, sharing of food, and other well-chosen activities would enable him slowly to change his and others' basic feelings and understanding about women. In short, through joint experience he would live out and change his relationship patterns to women and consequently perceive and feel about them differently; hopefully, he would function more competently in all spheres of everyday living. If Carl's worker had been a man, then the worker would have had to utilize his relationship differently. In the latter case he would have utilized joint experience as a means to foster and strengthen Carl's identification with a man and such a man's feelings, understanding, and behavior toward women.

A stress on the *experiential* aspects of the social group work situation is especially relevant in residential treatment. Clients in residential treatment usually need to discover for themselves that they can relate to others and that they can plan or do things successfully. Above all, they need to experience that they can do things as they had anticipated and that they can anticipate accurately what they will do. Learning to do such things as making cookies in Churchill's group or a cake in DeNoon's group, enrolling in an "outside club" as in Brown's group, or completing a project in the presence and, above all, with the acknowledgment of others, spells for the client the all-important ego conquest: *I am competent.*[8] For every individual what counts is the living proof of competence, the *experienced experience* that he can create things and ideas and carve out a meaningful relationship with others.[9]

Preceding paragraphs introduced the concept that in practice the worker deals alternately either with his clients' affect, cognition, or behavioral experience. Each of these alternate dimensions of intervention requires the worker's diagnostic choice and application of his knowledge based on his understanding of each individual client's personality development and degree of personality integration, along each of these specific dimensions of human functioning.[10]

Group Living Conceptualized

In the introduction to this chapter it was maintained that the social work group and the living group furnish the clients with two distinctly different

8. *See* chapters by Sallie R. Churchill (pp. 96–115), Barbara A. DeNoon (pp. 88–95), and Leonard N. Brown (pp. 155–168) in Henry W. Maier, *Group Work as Part of Residential Treatment.* Robert W. White's material on the ego aspects of the development of a sense of competence contains some provocative hypotheses. *See* "Competence of the Psychosexual Stages of Development," in Marshall Jones, ed., *Nebraska Symposium on Maturation* (Lincoln, University of Nebraska Press, 1960), pp. 97–140.

9. Such an understanding may change the professional lore that "group work is square dancing" to an insight that square dancing in group work can serve as the client's vehicle for demonstrating to himself *and* others that he can do things and have a successful give and take, even with members of the opposite sex.

10. *See* Henry W. Maier, *Three Theories of Child Development,* chap. vi.

avenues of treatment. In fact, each involves different forms of relationship patterns, different levels of interaction, and, consequently, different methods of treatment.

Group living constitutes a *primary* life experience, replacing temporarily dislocated primary family living. Note that direct intervention through placement and temporary disruption of family living spells location—that is, placed persons—rather than dislocation, which would be displaced persons. Group living creates a new and substantially different primary relationship system for the child or youth placed in a residential treatment program. The caring person becomes the immediate caring reality for the child. A dependent relationship becomes a prerequisite for successful mastery of everyday living. The living group serves as the new primary social matrix, as a "home base" and an arena for everyday living experience with peers within the presence of adult care and within the context of a larger community (the institution and its neighborhood). Child-caring through group living serves as a systematic method for ordering essential nurturing experiences as part of the processes of daily living.

Group living furnishes the basic ingredients for ego growth and sustenance. The living group can easily be designated as the "market place of ego development." Ego development is anchored in the trusting relationship created through the provision of care. Care, here, stands for meeting physical and nurturing needs when necessary and allowing self-care when autonomous strivings must be supported. Children and youth in residential treatment can no longer depend on experiencing their own family care and sustaining their immediate primary relationships with their families. Separation denies them the most important component of care—care when needed. Group living deals with life questions and problems as they occur. It serves as the means and the context for a new primary life experience.

In Carl's situation, cited at the beginning of this chapter, he is struggling with his sense of dependency. First, he objects to care: "Gee, do you have to get permission every time you step outside this goofy place? Why don't you print P-R-I-S-O-N on the door!" In another way, he reaches for and lives out his dependency. He sets up for himself a caring situation: "Mrs. Kusak, may us guys have some apples? We want to play ball until supper." And at the end he resolves both aspects. He establishes that he can initiate self-care: "I have some milk, too." He defines his boundaries of self-care: "I'll be back by six." The latter also implies: "I shall be on my own until I return for your [the child care worker's] partial care." His message is: "I shall be gone until I return for you to feed and shelter me."

In this episode Carl is dealing directly with his ego development— with his self-management. He also, it can be assumed, is struggling with experiences, feelings, and perceptions of the past. In the group living situation he deals with both aspects: past and present in the living present. The child-caring person, i.e., the cottage mother, has to relate herself quite differently to this situation than if it had occurred in a social work group

—that is, an *associate* group experience (associate, that is, to a primary living experience).

DIFFERENCES BETWEEN GROUP WORK AND GROUP LIVING

The social work group has been described as an associate group experience, as an arena for time out from more permanent and everyday relationship commitments, because everyday care does not depend on these relationships. In a social work group the helper proceeds with the understanding: "Let's deal with it here. This is a special situation apart from your ongoing relationships." Such a tacit message is most reassuring for the client. He can feel safe.

In the group living situation it is different. A client can never be asked to step sideways and reflect freely on his primary care situation; he and the child care worker are always in it. In all his interactions with his worker the client struggles *directly* with his sense of belonging versus a fear of becoming a person without a place, his sense of dependency versus desertion, his sense of interdependence versus isolation. In group living the give and take between client and worker is the major avenue of treatment.

DIFFERENTIATIONS APPLIED TO PRACTICE

These theoretical differentiations are relevant in practice. A few examples may help. Sibling rivalry within a social work group is dealt with as an experience among peers in relationship to a key adult. The worker would introduce conditions through which group members would be able to work out rivalrous situations. During such critical incidents it is important that each can gain recognition in his own way and possibly acquire some understanding and feelings about similar situations in the past; moreover, each person involved can see that life experiences can be different from the way they were in the past.

In a group living situation sibling rivalry has to be perceived as a fact of dependency strivings for the personal attention of the child care worker. The worker needs to perceive it as a professionally challenging question: In which way can each one gain the satisfaction that he feels the worker is still *his,* even if others continue to remain within the worker's orbit of interest? The worker introduces conditions that may help each group member feel a sense of assurance (and reassurance) that he is fully with each one. Rivalry exists and is treated only as a secondary function, because it is a by-product of the desire to be close to the worker. In child care such a desire and its acknowledgment are therapeutically desirable and an essential step for developmental readiness for greater interdependence, which also changes sibling rivalrous feelings to more "normal" proportions.

A similar analysis can be made about a worker's position and attitude toward each client's group membership. In the social work group, membership is to be perceived and dealt with as a matter of choice. In many ways the client *creates* his membership with active help from other group members and the worker. The client has the choice at any time to withdraw, to have himself removed, or to be instrumental in creating a new group. In group living, membership is perceived and experienced as a matter of fact. Child care worker and client proceed with the full understanding that for the time being the living group (the cottage) is the client's home base. For the client there is no immediate alternative within the sphere of treatment. He can neither deny nor escape from group membership and dependence on a caring adult. He has to face life as it is within this group. Group membership can only be terminated either by activities that are felt and interpreted as personal failures or by therapeutically "working" his way out.

As a final illustration of these conceptual differences we can reflect on the previously cited case. It was seen that Carl and his worker have to solve their dilemma with the full understanding that both of them have to continue to depend on, and at times to be independent of, each other for the length of Carl's residential treatment. Had this episode occurred in a social work group the worker would have dealt differently with it. Difference in handling would not result from the fact that the social group worker is trained differently from the child care worker, but rather because the social work group involves a different relationship system. Conversely, the child care worker intervenes differently not because he may lack social work training, but because he works with his clients in a different context professionally. He is a different helper.[11]

The latter points challenge the contention that group workers are prepared to be group living counselors or child care supervisors, or are professionally qualified to train child care workers by virtue of their educational preparation and group work practice experience. Social workers with a specialization in group work can add much knowledge to the specialization of group living care. In fact, in the absence of a fully established professional career program in child care in this country, group workers are the closest in professional preparations. In no way, however, are they prepared for these roles per se. To repeat, group living requires a different combination of knowledge and skills, a different relationship system, and, consequently, a different method of intervention.[12]

Conclusion

The essence of social group work practice has been explored. It is seen that this essence remains constant in whatever setting the social group worker

11. The hypothesis that child care work (group living care work) constitutes a distinct and special method of social work has been advanced by the writer in a separate paper. *See* Henry W. Maier, "Child-care as a Method of Social Work," in *Training for Child-care Staff* (New York, Child Welfare League of America, 1963), pp. 62–81.

12. *Ibid.,* fn. 23, p. 70.

practices. A client's corrective relationship with worker and fellow group members results in their experiencing themselves and others differently and eventually developing sufficient ego growth to enable them to live and develop successfully without the aid of specially structured therapeutic helping systems. Other clients may have achieved or eventually may achieve a maturity of ego development that allows them to use the social develop successfully without the aid of specially structured therapeutic group work situation for looking at their behavior and perhaps changing it more basically.

It is the group worker's professional skills that move the clients—emotionally troubled, "delinquent," or socially inadequate—to respond to his efforts to help expand their ego functioning. The worker attempts neither to change nor to do away with emotional disturbance and delinquent behavior per se. Rather, he introduces social experiences that will make it easier for the client to develop beyond his ineffective coping or delinquent behavior. This emphasis builds on the understanding that the nature of commitment to residential treatment, voluntarily or upon request of authority, does not shape treatment directly. Although the variable of commitment establishes a different initial context, the treatment processes hinge on personal involvement, accurate treatment focus, and the worker's clear understanding of his clients' past and most recent life experiences in order to reshape appropriately the corrective experiences in the present.

Social group workers practicing in residential treatment need to be alert to the intrinsic factors of that treatment situation just as they are in such settings as a neighborhood center or guidance clinic. In an institution, separation, placement, group living, social isolation, and collaborative treatment are essential "work considerations" just as introduction to the agency, concern for friendships and family life beyond the group, community mores, and the group's responsibility for the agency program are questions with which each social group worker has to deal in working with a community center group. In other words, it is not residential treatment per se, but the variables of the client's situation that offer a different definition to the nature and scope of treatment.

12. The Therapeutic Ingredients in the Group Work Program In a Residential Treatment Center for Children

FRITZ REDL

In this Institute we are in a sense serving as consultants to the U.S. Public Health Service, considering how we can get group workers, train them and help to design a therapeutic setting.

Institutions need not only our suggestions regarding treatment design, but our trained persons to carry out the design. We must be concerned with how we can obtain funds for our training which is so relevant to psychiatric service. We must ask, "What does the function of the group worker in the psychiatric setting do to our training designs?"

The contribution of group work as a method in residential therapy is important. We should get over our "professional neurosis" which arises from our being a minority group. This produces the tendency to swallow everything wholesale or the tendency to overidentify with the so-called higher status groups and leave our skills behind.

We don't yell loud enough about what we know regarding design. There is a readiness to hear more than group work assumes. Group workers do not talk enough. Many medical persons don't know that group work exists and yet describe the qualifications of a group worker in what they are looking for.

This consideration is an important one and the demand for group workers in the residential treatment center is increasing and will continue to increase in the next ten to twenty years.

The questions are: How can group workers demonstrate, describe and interpret the contribution of group work to the residential setting? What does a group work program in a residential setting mean? What parts need to be directly therapeutic? What parts supportive?

Group work must be a part of the total design of the institution.

Reprinted with permission of Association Press from *Group Work in the Psychiatric Setting*, Harleigh B. Trecker, ed. (New York: Morrow, 1955) pp. 43–47.

The material presented here is a summary of Dr. Redl's remarks prepared by the editor from notes made by Rene Schwartz and Cuthbert Gifford.

The Therapeutic Ingredients

1. The group worker can provide the diagnostic assessment of group relevant data and secondary individual characteristics of high treatment relevance. Secondary characteristics are relevant personality manifestations which may or may not issue from basic pathology (as skill in manipulation of mob situations). We fail with many children, not because of basic pathology, but because of our inability to understand their secondary personality characteristics.

2. The group worker is highly important in figuring group composition—the clinician and the group worker as a team make the decisions. This is the framework within which group and individual treatment can function. Group composition is a real challenge for research and supervised field training. Treatment potential goes way up with good group hygiene.

3. *Treatment* is a multidefined term. Whenever you talk of a residential treatment center you speak not of an educational polishing process but of an "unpacking" process. This process must be related to particular phases of individual therapy. The group worker must design group life to support the individual therapy process and must also indicate to the individual therapist where the individual therapist's limits must be placed at any one time. Because of the interrelatedness of the two on the life process of the child, there must be constant cooperation between group life development and individual therapy development at any one time.

4. The group worker must take responsibility for the total hygiene of the program. He has a responsibility to protest when program is not hygienic. Every part of life in the institution must be coordinated. We get a "backwash" from units of work in a residential center that we don't encounter in outpatient work. The totality of institutional life is such that not only the hygiene of a particular part of the program but how it relates to the total program must be understood. The group worker must also support other staff to take the needed backwash.

5. Rules, regulations, routines and policies have great importance. They are just as relevant as individual therapy. Group work must contribute to the plan. The psychiatrist knows the impact for individual children but does not know the group psychological impact.

6. There is a tendency to forget that *what* you do with people is important, not only how you feel about them. It is frequently up to the group worker to see that handling remains hygienic—not only the affects on what we do on one child, but the group psychological hygiene is important as well.

7. We need to develop the use of the "life space interview" and learn to interview a child when something has stirred him, in close proximity to the event. This must be done by someone who "smells like" the others in the child's environment. The group worker needs to decide, "What will I pick up; what will I leave?" He needs to help make decisions about timing.

8. The group worker can contribute his knowledge about climate, group atmosphere, contagion pile-up, build up of we-feeling and the like.

9. The group worker has to raise his voice about the functioning of the staff group. Some administrators are sensitive to staff communication problems and relationships, others need help.

10. The group worker must assist in the role distribution and the function of the team. Not only is what you do important, but in what role you do it. We don't know the best role distribution yet; this is problematical at this point. Ward life is compared to family society and yet it is more like "harem society" and much psychotherapy is built on the fact that children go back to a family, not a "harem" structure. The group worker must find a way to fit in and avoid role confusion.

11. The group worker must understand group pathology as well as individual pathology. Group pathology may or may not be related to individual pathology. This contribution of the group worker must be pointed out when you sell group work to psychiatrists. It is close to their concerns and easier for them to understand than other issues.

12. It is the group worker's job to evaluate the group's help to a child. Sometimes the child does not need a group. The group worker must make a professional judgment as to when to withdraw the child or lower the level of group life intensity. In free life children may drop out of groups. In the residential center, they are psychologically forced into groups—it is our responsibility to determine exposure to or relief from group activity.

The following are problems which the group worker faces in the residential treatment center:

1. He must know he will run into children who will not respond—where group work won't do any good. He will be exposed to more intense degrees of helplessness and feelings of futility.

2. He will become ashamed, feel failure and feel that no one but he is to blame. Sometimes he won't know what to do and he must live with this feeling.

3. He must avoid his own minority group neurosis. He enters existing designs as a minority member—may end up fighting other people instead of rebelling against the design that is wrong.

4. He must "pre-inoculate" and protect self against internal strife of "either-or"—either group or individual treatment.

13. The Role of the Group in Residential Treatment

Gisela Konopka

I recently spent several evenings in the cottages of an institution for delinquent and some quite disturbed girls. On entering one cottage I saw the group of about 18 girls happily and noisily playing a game. Suddenly one of the girls jumped up in anger, threw up her hands with an "I quit," and ran upstairs to her room. The housemother just nodded "It's all right, let her alone;" and the game went on. There was no disturbance in the group. The youngster for whom the group's presence and mood had probably been too hard to take had her opportunity for privacy without being coaxed, punished, admonished or "talked to." It was a most healthy and helpful handling of a situation which too often leads to unnecessary conflict.

It may be surprising that I should start my discussion on the importance of the group as a treatment tool in the institutional setting with an example which shows the importance of providing privacy. I do this purposefully. It is to me the essence of good group life to provide the vital balance between association with other people and the opportunity to be alone.

Institutional life is marked by the fact that people, children or adults, are thrown into group associations which they have not chosen and which nature has not prepared for them, the latter being the "normal" group associations in most of our lives, the family and the self-chosen group.

The population in all our children's institutions is becoming a more and more difficult one, since we are placing those children who can't accept normal family relationships mostly in families. This means that the impact of the group living relationships becomes even stronger and is charged with greater tensions, more outbursts, more problem situations.

It does not suffice to add some clinical services to institutional life which offers little satisfactions, little understanding of the individual, and increases tension by great demand for conformity. We have done this in far

Reprinted with permission of American Orthopsychiatric Association from the *American Journal of Orthopsychiatry,* Vol. 25, No. 4 (October, 1955), pp. 679–84.

too many cases. By such practice we provide some relief for the child, but we also increase his feeling that half of the world is against him, that stigma is still attached to the institution, and we play into the need of the disturbed child to make some people all "bad" and others all "good" and lose sight of reality. Houseparents who have to get children to bed or get them up in the morning feel that they are made out to be the villains while the clinical staff are fairy godmothers and godfathers. This kind of relationship harms the child just as much as it makes for poor working relationships on the team. *What we ask for in a good institution is harmony between the clinical treatment and daily group life.* This should become the criterion of evaluation of every children's institution.

What are the aspects of a healthy and helpful group life? In a short paper I can only enumerate them, but I hope that in discussion we can enlarge on them or supplement them.

1. A relaxed group atmosphere. By this we do not mean "permissiveness" in the sense of letting the child do whatever he or she wants to do. We mean by this an atmosphere which allows individuals to act and feel according to their own individuality as long as they are not harming others. It also must give the child the feeling that he is not all the time under scrutiny. The creation of such a relaxed group atmosphere is the major task of the houseparent or counselor and is a highly skilled assignment. In fact to me this is the core of the specific task of the persons directly responsible for the group living situation, something unique to their function. It involves not only patience, kindness and warmth, but also an understanding of themselves to know how they react at different times, and a keen understanding of individuals as well as group behavior in order to use different methods to keep this kind of atmosphere or to be able to restore it when a crisis has temporarily destroyed it.

2. A balanced use of the group. Again this is the domain of the houseparent or counselor. It is the skill of involving the whole living group in certain activities or heightened interaction while at other times letting it fall into subgroups or individual activities while keeping compresence, or allowing individuals the freedom to remove themselves from the group and be solitary.

3. A stimulated group. I do not mean that the cottage group should be in eternal animation. I do mean the skill—and again this is the function of the houseparent or counselor—to avoid one of the great evils of institutional life—boredom. In an institution for adolescent girls a small revolt had broken out in one of the cottages. Visiting one cottage after another after this event I again was struck by the fact that the cottage closest to a similar experience was the one with the most suppressive and unimaginative housemother, where the girls sat around in the evening doing nothing. The same evening I entered another cottage, where the girls were playing all kinds of games in different subgroups, laughing, singing, teasing the

housemother for "introducing them to gambling." It was the combination of a good relationship with the housemother and her imaginative way of using the evening hours that produced the healthy group reaction.

4. A group that gives the feeling of belonging, that develops some bond. This is very difficult to achieve, because often there is great turnover in the institution, and again we must remember that these groups were not established by the choice of the members. The person working with the group must make a conscious effort to create the feeling that there can be safety and warmth in relationships. This includes the opportunity to show oneself as "good" or as "bad" as one sometimes feels one is. The need for "belonging" is one of the deepest in the human being and usually the child placed in an institution has lost this precious gift. Somewhere this must be restored. It may be in relationship to one adult, but it also is important—and even more so when we deal with adolescents—in the group life with contemporaries.

5. A significant and helpful relationship between the houseparent or counselor and each individual child. The function of the houseparent cannot be that of a housekeeper or disciplinarian. They also need not be psychiatrists. They must be able to develop a meaningful and individualized relationship with the youngsters while creating the kind of group we described in the previous four points. By "meaningful relationship" we mean a warm and sensitive relationship with deep respect for the personality of each child as well as some understanding of individual and group dynamics. Over and over again thoughtful houseparents have asked me how they can be "fair" to everybody and yet really individualize, since needs are so different and they can easily be accused of favoritism, when they simply give more affection to one child who seems to need it so badly. I can only say that in general children themselves are quite aware of differences in needs and sensitive to them, and when they begin to see that their counselor is willing to give special attention to everybody, when he really needs it, they will accept this. I am aware of the fact that this is not always so in the beginning of the relationship, since we frequently have to overcome a great amount of distrust. The fear of being treated with injustice is usually very great. Yet it was a group of rather tough 13-year-old boys who asked their counselor to come in in the evening and stay a little longer with Jim "because he is so darn unhappy at night," and one added wistfully, "You'll do the same for me some day, won't you?" There was real recognition of the need for individualized and diversified attention combined with the trust that the counselor would do this for everybody.

All this has related to the living group. It is the most essential group for the child in the institutional setting and therefore must be carried out in the most helpful way. Many will say that this is impossible with the kind of personnel we can get for our institutions. I thoroughly disagree with this defeatist attitude. We can attract to institutions—and it has been proven in several institutions in the country—better qualified and motivated personnel, if we not only raise salary standards and working conditions, but also give the houseparent and counselor the place on the team that they deserve. They must become part of the treatment process, become responsible for the group living situation and the individualization of the children in the group, and therefore must receive enough information about the children and take part in clinical staff meetings. On their part they must accept the professional role that they have to play when they work with people. In addition to this I would insist that every good children's institution should have a houseparent supervisor, whose task it is to give individual and group in-service training. This is the role of the professionally trained social group worker, who can currently and consistently support, help and teach the houseparents and counselors to keep their group life one that is most helpful to children with difficulties.

There are other group associations in the life of our children in institutions which are important to them and must be part of the whole treatment process. There are the organizational groups, which help them to become part of the administrative setup (without their taking on the role of administrator), which help them develop an identification with the setting that must replace the family in their lives, without being able to imitate the family. I mentioned the short rebellion in the girls' cottage that I had witnessed. After the destruction of the room the director of the institution and I sat for a long time with the girls and discussed with them what led to it, the problems they had. We also told them what we tried to accomplish in not emphasizing punishment and so on. In the course of this discussion one of the girls said, "We should know much more about all this. It is the first time that I feel part of this and understand what we all want to accomplish." The organizational group allows for freedom of expression around administrative questions, but its sole purpose should not be to "let off steam" or to make some rules. Its value lies in a growing identification with "a whole" as well as the forming of responsible decisions. These kinds of groups carry great potentiality for good staff-child relationships (and indirectly child-society relationships) as well as learning in interdependent decision-making and individual growth and insight. They definitely should be conducted either by the head of the institution himself (if it is a small institution) or by the professional group worker on the staff.

Because of the involuntary make-up of the living group it is essential to make room for voluntary group associations in the form of clubs inside or outside of the institution, or of special activities which one may or may not join. The richer the program of these group associations and the more related to the needs of the youngsters, the more they will be of real help to each individual. "Recreational activities" have often been used only as an adjunct to the institutional life and have been looked upon somewhat with disdain. The reason for this is that we have stereotyped "recreation" as something not very necessary, or as pure entertainment or as only sports activities. We have not seen that play means something completely different to the child than to the adult. Erik H. Erikson has said it best: "What is infantile play, then? We saw that it is not the equivalent of adult play, that it is not recreation. The playing adult steps sideward into another reality; the playing child advances forward to new stages of mastery."[1]

This means that the recreational activities are directly related to the child's reality, his need for learning, for expression, for feeling his own importance and beginning to feel part of something larger than himself. Seeing children in creative dramatics or in a simple make-believe game makes this so clear to us. The mastering of a skill can mean the difference between feeling unworthy and outside of the society of contemporaries, and the sudden realization that one can be as good as everyone else. If it is impossible for a child to master a certain skill he will need the help of the sensitive group leader to accept this and *not* feel that this makes him a wholly incapable person. These kinds of groups and activities therefore deserve the same intensive attention as the clinical treatment.

And finally we think of the small formed groups directly used for psychotherapy, the small groups in which the youngsters discuss their difficulties and strive toward better understanding and insight into them. There has been much discussion of such groups so that I shall not go into the method of conducting them. It is clear that with younger children one will use the activity group more; and with adolescents, the discussion group. Besides individual clinical treatment such groups provide special attention to those children for whom the impact of the living group is too much, or who are too hard on the living group. They have an opportunity to practice the art of human interaction in a much more protected, much less demanding group. They certainly return to their living group, but the therapy group—besides giving them an "out" at times—hopefully sustains them beyond the actual meeting time. There must be a close interchange of observations between the one responsible for the living groups and the person conducting the therapy group, so that they may be prepared for the impact that comes from the one or the other setting and can most helpfully deal with it. Not every child in an institution needs to be in such a group. The referral to such a group should be the result of staff discussion. The person in charge of such a group should be either the social group worker or the psychiatrist, depending on the setup of the agency and the experience of the professional persons involved. There definitely should be psychiatric consultation.

We must realize that in all these different group constellations we find invaluable opportunity for diagnostic observations. Verbal communication between an adult and a child helps us gain some insight into their problems

1. Erik H. Erikson, *Childhood and Society* (New York, Norton, 1950), pp. 194–195.

and behavior, but nothing is more telling than the way the children relate to contemporaries, unhampered by the unconscious alterations that the face-to-face relationship with an adult imposes on their behavior. The more understanding the observer has of individual and group behavior, the more valuable will be his diagnostic observations. Since our institutions aim more and more at treatment to help the child leave the institution, diagnosis becomes more important than ever. This means that the team of the clinical personnel and the houseparent becomes indispensable to all our institutions.

I do not want to give the impression that I am forgetting the extremely important role of individual contact and individual treatment. Because the impact of the group is so strong in institutional settings and because of the need to share beloved adults with so many, it is extremely important to give the children an opportunity for individual relationships with adults who at least for the time of their meeting with them belong to them and to them alone. Casework and individual psychiatric services are therefore indispensable. It is essential that we see the interrelationship of treatment, not each part separated, but a common effort to move toward the best help for the child.

I started out by saying that the healthy balance of group life consists in allowing people to be with others and to be alone. The healthy balance in treatment relationships consists of the opportunity of relationships in groups and in face-to-face contacts.

Only if we have genuine respect for each other's competence—the houseparent, administrator, psychiatrist, psychologist, caseworker, group worker, nurse, or anyone else needed to give our best help—can we expect children to regain trust and respect for an adult world around them.

14. Group Therapy and Casework with Ego-Disturbed Children

David Wineman

The purpose of this discussion is to sketch some of the clinical implications of group therapy for a specific type of problem children—those with what can be called severe ego-disturbances. I shall try also to show how the

Reprinted with permission of *Social Casework*, Vol. 30, No. 3 (March, 1949), pp. 110–13.

application of group therapeutic principles can eventually be dovetailed with a clinically realistic application of casework interview techniques.

In limiting group therapy to a specific clientele in this discussion, I do not imply that it cannot be used for other types of problems, just as an examination of the use of surgery in cases of stomach tumor would not imply that its usefulness was limited to stomach tumor. Similarly, the use of casework is being discussed with respect to one group only.

The Ego-Disturbed Child

The clientele in this group consists of children with severe behavior disturbances along pre-delinquent lines. They are hyperaggressive, destructive, truanting, lying, highly impulsive. They cope with all their problems through externalization rather than withdrawal. Instead of building up classical neurotic defense patterns against their aggressions—like phobias and compulsive rituals—they attempt to push their primitive impulses upon outer reality. Their symptomology is on an expressional level. The list of their symptoms is a roster of conflict patterns with societal demands rather than conflict patterns between one part of their personalities and the other. This description may serve as a rough diagnostic diagram for the behavior disturbance type in relation to which I am discussing the application of group therapy and casework therapy.

This is the kind of youngster who basically needs to be placed away from home in order for any treatment to "register." He is usually too disturbed for foster home placement but insufficiently advanced, in extremity of behavior, for the closed institution represented by the psychiatric ward or the training school for delinquents. What he really needs is a 24-hour all-year-round treatment setting with a controlled environment whose framework remains flexible enough to permit just the right amount of community-style experiences.

Pioneer House, in Detroit, was such an institution and our children (boys between the ages of 8 and 11) were just the kind described. There the children lived in a group and the life pattern of the youngsters was heavily channelized along group psychological lines. In addition to using group therapeutic devices, we tried a variety of interviewing approaches. These approaches, while differing from formal casework as it is practiced in the agency setting, still resemble casework more than they do group therapy. It is by focusing upon the relationship between these two techniques within the Pioneer House setting that I wish to define the problem. So at the outset I should like to emphasize that I am discussing a special type of group therapy and a special type of casework.

It is now necessary to present symptom structure of the Pioneer House child in sharper focus than in the crude diagram already advanced, in order to trace what therapeutic coverage was given over to the group therapeutic climate, what to casework interviewing, and the strategic connections between the two approaches.

Symptom and Treatment Specifics

Children who function in the manner described can be said to have failed in the development of ego structure. This is why they are so strongly fixated upon primitive action symptomology, since through action alone they achieve mastery over their instinctual demand systems. The outside world fights this type of expression and twists it into pathological formations which only multiply many times over the original inadequacies in their ego development. Any treatment, in order to be minimally effective with them, must provide an expressional mode which is tolerant toward their symptomology and which at the same time pulls the ego toward the acceptance of reality demands. This bivalent function of the treatment climate can be best carried out in the group setting where the activity structure is designed to parallel the ego pattern of the child, but at the same time to tease, as it were, the ego into gradually more structured functioning than would be its bent. This aspect of group therapy may be called an "ego supportive function" since it (1) recognizes the weakness of the ego through creating a flexible activity climate; (2) tries to improve the ego's integration pattern by removing conflicts between drive satisfaction and the outside world. An example may be clarifying:

With highly aggressive youngsters it is possible to use certain games that enable them to ventilate their aggression without coming into conflict with the adult. In certain catching and hitting games the rules of the game prescribe who is hit and how hard. Thus, game rules—not only in aggressive games but in peaceful games as well—function as symbols for societal rules and, if a youngster plays the game, the group—not the adult—forces him to abide by the rule. In this way the liberation of aggression under code-prescribed conditions is therapeutically progressive since the ego of the child is geared to an externalized, behavior-modifying, value system, not alone to his impulse-dominated one. In activity planning with this type of child, in general, we try to provide the child with as many recreational successes as possible.

Therapeutic recreational programming for disturbed children is thus built around the principle of suiting the activity to the need of the child. In this way activity planning becomes a kind of *life net* for the ego. It dispenses direct therapy through the provision of reality openings for expression. It gives structure to the ego by tying impulse demands closer to reality demands.

A third symptom pattern of this type of youngster is that of disturbed social relationships. The conflict configurations which have occurred in the outside world soon manifest themselves in the member-to-member dynamics of the group. Jealousy, aggression, greed, and the gamut of disturbed interpersonal conflicts are unavoidable in the living situation. The group leader can manipulate these manifestations of interpersonal pathology in terms of the individual diagnostic needs of the group members. This means that, under conditions favorable to the expression of disturbed person-to-person behavior, we can utilize the technique of objective, professionally executed, clinical handling on the firing range of the symptom itself. Previously, disturbances of this type were handled by harassed, biased, rejecting adults. It is of clinical significance, therefore, that the adult human reaction to the child's conflict mechanisms should be built on diagnostic principles, not on counteremotional drive patterns.

Group Therapy and Casework

This brings us to a consideration of just how approachable these children are to objective evaluation of their problem behavior. This is the meaty clinical issue around which we can draw up the strategic connections between group therapy and interview therapy in the small institution. From everything we have said about these children, we may easily deduce that they are, at the outset of treatment, completely insulated against any type of problem awareness. To expect the converse would be to misdiagnose the difficulty, to believe that they had already built up some part of their ego into a self-evaluative mechanism in which they could criticize their own behavior, want to change, and so on. It is a function of treatment under group conditions to use the group experience to help them *concretize* their problem awareness. They cannot be approached through interview techniques at the outset since no part of their conscious personality is free to detach itself from the rest of their behavior for purposes of self-observation. Through the effects of repetitive recreational success, ego tensions are gradually drained. Through the countless demonstrations to the child on the part of the group leader of the irrelatedness of his mechanisms, the child is slowly made aware that something in his behavior is not quite right. The draining of ego tension through activity predisposes the ego toward receptivity to educational influences aimed at building up new standards of values. Here again let us take an example to see how it works:

From the case history of Billy, 10, we know that among his other severe problems, was that of intensive and open sibling hatred with a slightly older brother. We expect to see in the group setting a simple duplication of this, but we are wrong. What we see is an overemphasized positive attachment to another group member, Donald, 11, who is one of the most admired children in the group. Billy completely surrenders himself to Donald and becomes his outspoken slave. Observing Billy's need to love Donald, we tentatively conclude from the case history that he is defending himself strongly against the brother hatred, and that he must seek to find in Donald the good brother whom he can love as a defense against his own hatred. So far, we interfere very little. Occasionally we draw his attention to the fact that he has a mind of his own and he does not have to do everything that Donald (the brother substitute) says, but it is still "his own business."

Gradually we see evidence of his aggression eating its way to the surface. In permitting himself to be dominated and brutalized by Donald, he has built up a rationale for hatred. He has enslaved himself and stimulated Donald's sadistic power drive and at this point he has converted him to the bad brother whom he can now hate. He is wary about actually focusing his aggressions against Donald, however, and instead builds up aggression outbursts against other group members which are actually displacements from his aggression against Donald. He goes further than this: he surrenders his superego to Donald, when he is really mad at Donald, he gets Donald's permission to hit other, weaker children in the group.

In this wanton brutality, for which he actually makes Donald the deciding judge, we interfere. An intensive interview is held with him in which we emphasize that we know he really would like to beat up Donald. He admits it but defends himself by saying "I won't do it because he is my boss." We say if he wants to be "silly" and make himself somebody's slave, that is his business but that does not mean he can let Donald decide what is right to do and what is wrong. If he feels like getting even with Donald, he either should hit Donald or stay away from him, because he cannot hit other kids just because for some peculiar reason he won't hit Donald. This is forbidden—and we make it very strong.

What Have We Done?

1. We have interpreted to him that he really hates Donald but does not want to admit it.

2. We have emphasized that it is "silly" to become a slave to Donald but we don't hold it against him. Stressing that it is silly, however, introduces the idea that there is something odd about it and is preparation for later interviews with him.

3. We have directly interfered in the surrender of his superego to Donald. We have now become the superego and we—not Donald—take the position of telling him what's right and wrong to do.

What Material Have We Used?

1. We can summarize for him his own group behavior, to which we can point for evidence that he willingly became Donald's slave, that we saw

him when he almost hit Donald and then asked Donald for permission to hit another boy.

2. We use the security he has in the group and with group-identified adults to facilitate interpretation acceptance.

What We Have Not Done

We have not told him that we know why he had to become Donald's slave —because he really hates his own brother and has to prove that everybody is like his distorted version of the brother, even Donald for whom he was willing to be a slave. This is material that will have to be set aside for further developments and will need more elevated self-evaluation than Billy is now capable of. In this stage of the game we stick to simple mechanism interpretation.

Repetitive occurrences of this type gradually force what we have called problem awareness onto the youngster. At a certain point problem awareness becomes usable for interview type therapy. Actually for the first several months in the Pioneer House treatment setting, interview therapy is held in abeyance except for the short range "rub in" interview where the child is brought face to face with gross unreasonableness. With increasing stabilization and the building up of new ego images of himself, interview therapy becomes more feasible and necessary.

In conclusion it is important to stress once again that this presentation has concerned itself with summarily sketching the relationship between group therapy and casework therapy in a special type of setting for disturbed children. With other types of settings the applications of both group therapy and casework therapy may differ from the impressions conveyed in this discussion.

15. Summer Camping in the Treatment of Ego-Defective Children

RALPH L. KOLODNY
SAMUEL WALDFOGEL
VIRGINIA M. BURNS

The problems involved in the social and psychological treatment of disturbed children have led practitioners in the field of mental hygiene to search constantly for new treatment methods and facilities. Group therapy and social group work have been added to individual psychotherapy, and paralleling these developments has been the growth of year-round residential treatment of various types. A relatively recent development has been the use of the summer camp for therapeutic purposes.[1] Although still modest in its scope, the trend toward summer camping as an adjunct to therapy is likely to increase.[2] Several camps in various parts of the country have been set up specifically to serve disturbed children and others with special needs. Also, some agency camps are enrolling these children in small numbers with regular campers in an attempt to further their socialization.

An early attempt to describe the therapeutic rationale of summer camping was made in a perceptive article by Hallowitz.

> If the child's behavior and needs are understood, and he meets with tolerance, warmth, and encouragement from the counselor, he will soon realize that this adult is different from his own parents. Old patterns of adjustment will no longer be necessary. New ones will come to the fore. Healthy and mature responses can be encouraged, and infantile and un-

Reprinted with permission of The National Association for Mental Health, Inc. from *Mental Hygiene*, Vol. 44, No. 3 (July, 1960), pp. 344–59.

Authors Kolodny, Waldfogel, and Burns are research supervisor, research consultant, and former camp director, respectively, for the Department of Neighborhood Clubs of the Boston Children's Service Association. The writers wish to express their gratitude to the members of the staff of Camp Bonnie Bairns for 1955 and 1956 upon whose observations this paper is based and to the Charles H. Hood Dairy Foundation and the Warren Benevolent Fund whose research grants made this study possible.

1. An interesting description of one of the first treatment camps is found in E. S. Rademacher, "Treatment of Problem Children by Means of a Long-Time Camp," *Mental Hygiene* 42(April, 1958), 385–94.

2. The nature and extent of present-day therapeutic camping is discussed in Elton E. McNeil, "The Background of Therapeutic Camping," *Journal of Social Issues*, 13(1957), No. 1.

wholesome patterns discouraged. The counselor becomes like a parent, and the child has an opportunity to relive his early, formative years in which the parent's love or denial of love is so important in his training. The child now begins to make appropriate responses and can exercise control over his asocial impulses, not through fear of punishment, but in order to please and gain the love of the parent (counselor). While at first these new patterns are created just to please someone outside himself, later they are incorporated and become part of his own demands on himself.[3]

This, of course, represents an idealized model of the therapeutic process that may occur in a camp setting and does not adequately reflect some of the technical problems involved in dealing with disturbed children. Subsequent experience in therapeutic camping has given us a clearer picture of these problems and has indicated that it is unrealistic to anticipate the achievement of such dramatic results with most disturbed children in the rather short period involved in summer camping.

The Disturbed Child's Problems as a Camper

The difficulties in work with disturbed children at camp are great. Even the relatively stable child is subjected to many unaccustomed strains in this setting. The isolation of the usual camp site and the presence of strange and unknown objects in the woods, as Redl points out, are likely to activate fantasies and stimulate fears.[4] To these tensions are added those occasioned by the requirement that the child relate closely and with a minimum of friction to a large number of peers.[5]

The disturbed child must face even more. He has to contend with the panic which separation and a new setting and people usually engender in him. He is called upon by the nature of the situation to carry out functions which demand a great deal of control; he must share an adult with many others, tolerate a number of unaccustomed routines, and weather the mistreatment which will inevitably occur at some point during interaction with any group of children. These are facts which cannot be overlooked in any discussion of the advisability of camping for disturbed children.

The Importance of Selectivity in Camp Intake

Consideration of the potentialities of camping for disturbed children must also involve some discrimination among levels of disturbance. Not all of

3. Emanuel Hallowitz, "Camping for Disturbed Children," *Mental Hygiene,* 34(July, 1950), 409.
4. Fritz Redl, "Psychopathologic Risks of Camp Life," *The Nervous Child,* 6(No. 2, 1947).
5. The highly charged atmosphere in which this must usually be accomplished is discussed in William Schwartz, "Camping and the Group Experience," *Group Work Papers* (Chicago, Group Work Section, Chicago, Ill., Chapter, National Association of Social Workers, 1958).

these youngsters respond in a similar fashion to camping, nor do all have the same ability to make use of it. Hallowitz, even while emphasizing the value of camping for disturbed children, cautions us that some of them are not ready for this experience. "Some children," he writes, "need a more controlled and repressive environment; others suffer from too close an association with members of the same sex, and still others are too disturbing to their fellows, so that while they benefit from the experience, they minimize or even destroy whatever benefits the other children might receive."[6]

As awareness of this point has increased, some treatment camps have become more selective in their intake.[7] Faced with limitations on size of staff and on numbers of counselors with appropriate backgrounds and training, they have found it wise to take as campers only those disturbed children whose egos are not greatly damaged. As Staver and her colleagues have written: "The interaction of the camp group is robust, and even a proportion of about one adult to two children is not sufficient to allow long-time individual supervision of the more disturbed child. For these reasons, we feel that children who are too disturbed to achieve any real integration with the group or to get along without virtually full-time individual supervision should not be accepted."[8]

Need for Experimentation with More Seriously Disturbed

It would be unfortunate, however, if the cautions just cited were to lead to overly rigid intake policies for camps interested in helping disturbed children or to a refusal to undertake new ventures with the more deeply disturbed among them. It is important that agencies continue to investigate the potentialities of summer camping as a medium of service and treatment, not only for those disturbed children who have displayed some tolerance for group association and whose egos are relatively intact, but also for ego-defective children whose capacity to relate in groups appears to be substantially below average.

A Camping Experience for a Group of Ego-Defective Girls—First Summer

In the summer of 1955 the Department of Neighborhood Clubs of the Boston Children's Service Association was presented with a special opportunity to study the reactions of several ego-defective children to camping.

6. Hallowitz: *op. cit.*, pp. 419–420. See also Gordon J. Aldridge, and D. Stewart MacDonald, "An Experimental Camp for Emotionally Disturbed Boys," *Journal of Child Psychiatry*, 2(1942), Sec. 3, 251.

7. See Nancy Staver, Manon McGinnis, and Robert Young, "Intake Policies and Procedures in a Therapeutic Camp," *American Journal of Orthopsychiatry*, 25(January, 1955), 148–61.

8. *Ibid.*, p. 154.

Among the clubs which had been conducted by the department during the previous winter and spring was one group composed of several teen-age girls who, at the time of their referral, had displayed a marked inability to relate to their age-peers or adults. The girls had been together for seven months prior to the summer. During that time they seemed to find satisfactions in some of the activities and the relationship with the leader and had been able to remain together as a group. Occasionally, they functioned surprisingly well as a unit. Their ways of relating were still quite primitive, however, and their behavior, by and large, continued to reflect severe impairment of ego-functioning. The department staff, while aware of the pitfalls, felt that it would be worthwhile to explore the reactions of this group to camping in order to determine whether under special circumstances—including a common group experience prior to camp and the group leader present as a camp staff member—it would not be possible for these ego-defective girls to remain at camp over an 11-day camping period and make constructive use of the experience without interfering with whatever benefits the other campers might receive.

The department's summer camping operation reflects the basic aims of our service and the approaches to group composition we employ in our year-round work. The department provides a group work service for physically handicapped and/or emotionally disturbed children who are experiencing marked difficulties in their social relationships.[9] Children are referred to the department by casework, educational, group work, medical, and psychiatric agencies. Usually they are referred individually by agencies and a group of relatively normal children is formed around each of them in his or her own neighborhood. Sometimes, however, several disturbed or handicapped children are referred together and accepted for service as a group.

At camp, as in the year-round program, we are interested in furthering the integration of disturbed or handicapped children with their "normal" peers wherever this appears to be feasible and clinically desirable. Each child attends camp with his own club, and the members of several clubs attend each camping session together. In this setting, even if his own club group is composed entirely of other handicapped or disturbed children, the handicapped or disturbed child is brought into close contact with a number of youngsters who are relatively normal and stable.

The camp itself is located 25 miles from Boston. At the time material for this paper was collected, it was conducted on a single sex basis, with about 25 children from four or five different clubs, all of the same sex, but of different ages, attending each camping session together. These camp sessions were brief, being only 11 days in duration. The physical area of the

9. The nature of the department's practice is discussed in Ralph L. Kolodny, "Research Planning and Group Work Practice," *Mental Hygiene,* 42 (January, 1958), 121–132.

camp comprised 13 acres. The staff included three regular department workers as director and supervisors and eight other counselors, all of them students in social work or related fields.[10]

The group to be studied was composed of five adolescent girls, two of whom were in the borderline or psychotic categories, and four of whom had severely damaged egos. This group had been formed on a trial basis after considerable discussion among school guidance personnel and the department's staff and psychiatric consultant.

The original member was Andrea, age 13, who had been referred by a casework agency where her mother was being seen. An only child, both of whose parents worked, Andrea had been raised by a very disturbed grandmother living in the home. When she was eight, her parents had placed her in a residential treatment center. Three years later, against the advice of the center's staff, they brought her home and enrolled her in public school where she was assigned to a special class. Here she was extremely aggressive and had to be put on a three hour a day schedule. At school, repeating the pattern she had displayed at the treatment center, she functioned as an isolate and made no friends in or out of class. Tests revealed an I.Q. of 82, although it was felt this was well below her potential. Andrea's emotional problems were complicated by a mild spastic condition.

The other members had been selected by the school guidance department from special classes. Each had at some time expressed a desire to participate in some kind of group, but because of poor or inappropriate ways of relating to others, had experienced little association with other youngsters. These other members were: Genie, 12; Grace, 13; Dolores, 13; and Janine, 16.

Genie was a seriously retarded youngster who also suffered from a hearing loss. She had been in special class since first grade and was friendly only with five and six-year-olds. She was resentful of her intellectually normal older sister. Obese, withdrawn, and slow moving, Genie frequently appeared depressed and inert.

Grace was receiving casework help at the time the group was formed. Rejected by her mother, she was oppressed by marked feelings of inadequacy. She had *petit mal* epileptic seizures. Although quite normal in her speech and outward appearance, Grace was unable to read. Physically she was quite attractive and, as the club began to function, she exhibited more maturity in social relationships than did the other members.

---

10. Since that time, the system has been changed to include both boys and girls at each session, and the acreage has been enlarged. The camping period has been extended to 18 days and the number of campers and staff has been increased. The department's camping practices are reviewed in Ralph L. Kolodny, and Virginia M. Burns, "Group Work with Disturbed and Handicapped Children in a Summer Camp," *Social Work with Groups* (New York, National Association of Social Workers, 1958).

Dolores was the most obviously "different" of all the members. Her speech and gait were infantile and in her conversation, which was often irrational, she exhibited a preoccupation with fears of death, blood, direct and physical pain. She had been seen once a week at a child guidance clinic for three months but had been taken out of treatment by her mother.

Janine had been afflicted with polio-encephalitis at the age of nine. Her speech and toilet habits were severely affected as a result, and she was left with a paralysis of the right arm. After several years of special schooling, she re-entered public school. Placed in a special class on the basis of an I.Q. of 75 she began to show signs of extreme confusion. Her disturbance became acute, and she was committed to a mental hospital where she was diagnosed as a schizophrenic. She returned to public school after discharge several months later and was now receiving casework on an out-patient basis. At her own request Janine was living with her grandmother, being unable to tolerate her brothers and sisters.

The results of our study of the behavior of these girls during the summer of 1955 have been reported in detail in an earlier publication.[11] Their first summer at camp was a stormy one for them. The stresses of the experience produced severe reactions, particularly during the first several days. A kind of group fragmentation occurred as each member became preoccupied with her own survival and paid little attention to others. Andrea sought out counselors rather than campers, but related to both primarily through bursts of hostility. She was obviously angry with her club leader, who was camp director, for not giving her enough attention. A counselor had to be with Janine constantly during the first two nights as she was very apprehensive and hallucinated, hearing bombs and sirens. Grace stayed in the kitchen most of the time, repeating the role she played in her own family and ate and worked with the kitchen staff. It was not until the third day that she felt secure enough to give up the protection of this isolated position. Dolores frequently stuffed dirt and stones in her mouth in the manner of an infant. Genie refused to eat the first meal and initially spent most of her time sitting and watching in hostile silence.

The intensity of their initial reactions diminished, however, as time went on and there was observable movement on the part of several of these youngsters toward an adaptation to camp. Andrea moved slowly in the direction of less suspicion of adults and during the last three days, especially, her belligerence decreased perceptibly. She formed a friendship with an older withdrawn girl from another club, permitted affectionate gestures by counselors, and even made affectionate overtures to them. At the end of the camp period she told her cabin counselor that, although part of her wanted to go, part of her wanted to stay. Despite her resistance and

---

11. See Ralph L. Kolodny, and Virginia M. Burns, "Specialized Camping for a Group of Disturbed Adolescent Girls," *Social Work,* 1(No. 2, April, 1956), 81–89.

withdrawal, Genie, too, was able to reach out somewhat. She became particularly friendly with two passive youngsters, age 11 and 9. Before she
left, Genie told the director that she wanted to stay at camp "forever."
Grace, toward the end, came to seek approval through her performance in
program activities and gave up acting as flunkey to several older girls, something she had done earlier. She made friends with some of the more passive
campers her own age. In contrast to her frequent expression of disappointment with activities during the year, she was able to say that she had enjoyed camp. Even Janine, after seeing her caseworker on visitors' day,
seemed to be less overwhelmed by her depressions, although she often
appeared quite unhappy. She began to go swimming daily, expressed an
interest in doing things for the camp carnival, and participated briefly in
a small dramatics group composed of three campers and a counselor.
Janine later wrote from home asking if she could some day come back to
camp as a counselor. Of all the members, Dolores gave the least evidence
of positive change in any respect. She continued throughout to eat sand
and dirt and spoke constantly of her fears of height, blood and death. She
resisted or was oblivious to routines and activities and occasionally disrupted the latter. She did, however, become less fearful of undressing in
front of others or being seen in the bathroom. She also became less confused in her attempts to distinguish among different people at camp.

Thus, for all its difficulties, and despite its brevity, there were several
indications that the camp experience was valuable to the girls. None of
them pressed for a return home; the early crisis aspect of the situation was
worked through to some extent; some positive behavior emerged as time
went on, and all of the girls expressed a desire to return.

It should also be noted that the other campers, with the exception of two
very aggressive and provocative girls, were able to tolerate the behavior
exhibited by the members of this group. Whatever tension occurred was
not expressed through the direct scapegoating of these girls but rather
through the displacement of hostility or demanding infantile behavior and
never reached an unmanageable level. Open rejection or ridicule of the
girls was extremely rare, and many campers imitated staff in their manner
of approaching or speaking to them. Occasionally, other campers would
try to involve one of these girls in an activity. In a few instances, friendships were made between them. Despite the anxieties aroused by exposure
to odd or bizarre behavior, campers seemed to feel fairly comfortable in
this setting.

The behavior these girls exhibited during the year which followed the
first camp experience was by no means consistent. It varies, of course, from
member to member. Much of it, however, appeared to indicate progress.
Andrea had her school hours extended after she indicated by her behavior
that she could tolerate this. Dolores' bizarre behavior continued, but the
school psychologist who tested her every year saw a lessening of some of her
paranoid and schizoid tendencies. Although members, individually, contin-

ued to sometimes appear hostile and depressed at meetings and to respond ineptly and inappropriately to events, they were able to function more adequately as a group. They showed themselves capable of taking greater responsibility for planning their own programs. They appeared to make some progress toward being able to talk out rather than act out some of their upset feelings. All of them came to a camp reunion in the fall and Andrea, Grace, and Dolores participated extensively in the singing and games. They spoke of camp often during the year and appeared to look forward to attending again the next summer.

Second Summer

We realized that, although these girls had profited from the experience in some respects, the gains they had made during the first summer's session were modest, and we were very much aware of the difficulties they had presented to staff. Despite this we decided to bring them to camp a second time.

There were a number of new counselors and many new campers the second summer which meant that once again these girls had to relate to quite a few unfamiliar children and adults.[12] Unlike the previous season, however, in addition to knowing the director well, they were acquainted with five other adults (two supervisors, one counselor, and the cooks). The staff, in turn contained four people who knew the girls, their problems and capacities, fairly well and who felt relatively sure that their behavior could be managed.

The behavior of these girls during the second summer indicated that our decision to take them back to camp was a sound one. While tension persisted and was sometimes severe, by and large this was distinctly a more successful session than the first. It appeared that the camp experience was now less stressful for the girls and that some accommodation had taken place. Of course, their behavior was by no means uniformly positive. Many of the maladaptive patterns seen the first summer reappeared, and their reactions were erratic. Attempts at inner control and greater amenability to involvement in camp life, however, were now more in evidence.

Andrea, who, the previous season, had immediately reacted to the stress of camp with violent outbursts of temper and verbal tirades, was initially considerably more subdued. Upon arrival at camp she could not refrain from a few hostile comments, but also asked to see the cooks whom she kissed warmly.

As the camp season progressed, she would often turn to sarcasm when her feelings became too threatening. At the same time, she could directly seek the approval and affection of counselors. It is significant that she did

12. One of two girls who had been added to the group during the year also came to camp. This was Cynthia, a very large and aggressive 13 year old who had been and continued to be very difficult to work with.

not slap at them as she sometimes had at the beginning of the first summer and instead very frequently sought to hold hands with them. While the violence of her anger was considerably diminished, she was not able to deal too adequately with her ambivalence. Sometimes, for example, she was very affectionate with her cabin counselor, but at other times she would complain that the counselor made her "sick." She could not yet trust her own feelings of affection and had to test out adults to see whether their expressions of positive feelings towards her were genuine. In contrast to the summer before, she was able to evince an interest in contacts with male counselors. She turned to them for play as eagerly as she did to female counselors and, instead of scornfully disclaiming any concern with males, spoke of the fiancee of one male counselor as "the luckiest girl in the world."

Andrea rarely complained about work assignments the second summer. She griped about extra work details but was able to appear for and carry out regular work assignments. The first summer she had begun by inveigling another youngster into taking her place at dishwashing. She did not repeat this. She did have a tendency to sometimes slip off and avoid work but, when urged by other campers, she worked quite well. She carried out all her assigned tasks and did her part regularly in cleaning the lavatory, sweeping the dormitory and the like, even when she clearly did not want to.

She was ready to participate more readily in camp program and seemed to derive more gratification from the activities despite her continued low frustration tolerance. Her preference was still for individualized activities in which she could play along with the counselor, but she derived some enjoyment from group activities such as singing and occasionally became quite enthusiastic at "sings" during evening programs. She even played the piano for a group on one occasion after volunteering when another youngster was unable to play a particular song. She had never before revealed her ability in this area. Andrea also joined the camp discussion group, which involved sharing ideas and feelings on problems of getting along with others, and was a regular member.

In the beginning, Janine continually sought contacts with counselors and invariably attempted to use these contacts solely for the purpose of discussing her feelings of depression and inadequacy. During the first few days, her communication with other campers was negligible, and although they said little about this, they did begin to stare at her as she walked about with her head down, obviously quite unhappy.

Despite her deep and persistent depression, Janine did begin to respond more positively in some respects as time went on. She became particularly interested in the camp discussion group led by the director, and as this got underway, she displayed less and less of a need to seek individual conferences with counselors.

On only one occasion did she come close to repeating the distraught behavior of her first two evenings of the summer before. This was on the seventh night of camp when she became panicky after one of her roommates, a youngster from another group, told a frightening mystery story. The director, who was called, was able to quiet her by firmness and reassurance, and Janine did not subsequently repeat this acute behavior, although she was frequently depressed.

Toward the end of the period, Janine found a source of gratification in the camp dramatics group. The previous year she had participated briefly in a small group of three campers who had talked together about dramatics, but her interest had not been sustained. The second summer she joined the new dramatics group and took a prominent part in its activities. Although frequently shaky and fearful of failure, she was willing, with support, to undertake a substantial role in the camp play. In the actual performance she acted well and received much praise from the other campers.

While Dolores' confusion and anxiety were always apparent, her conversation and behavior during the first several days indicated that she was making some kind of conscious effort to change. A number of times she said to counselors, "Last year I did strange things, but now I'm older. Last year seems like 15 years ago." Except for the first day, when she ate sand once, she did not eat dirt or anything similar for the entire period. She did not play with her food at meals, messing and blowing it about as she had frequently done a year earlier. Although she displayed the same fear of undressing in front of others as she had the first summer, she did not show any particular fear of going to the bathroom. Unlike the year before, it was not necessary to ask other campers to stand guard at the bathroom door to make sure no one would intrude upon her.

For a substantial part of the period Dolores participated better in activities than she had the year before. Although the range of programs she engaged in was still extremely narrow, she did a little individual crafts work on her own initiative and actually participated in some group activities. She enjoyed outings, for example, and joined in now, although not loudly, on singing, whenever it occurred. Although athletics frightened her, she occasionally participated in such things as relay games. There were signs of strain in her behavior during the second half of the period and, after visitors' day, when her family did not appear, she regressed perceptibly, messing more with her food at meals, squinting and staring more often and complaining that others were staring at her. Even then, however, she did not withdraw from activities to the extent that she had the first summer, and she never became disruptive as she had at that time. Surprisingly, Dolores was among those who joined the discussion group. Although her comments were at first focused solely on herself, she later was able to relate to the problems others brought up and to make suggestions for their solution.

In contrast to the summer before, Grace was able to participate in camp life without first isolating herself. At that time, it will be remembered, she had devoted the larger part of the first two days to working in the kitchen and had taken her meals there. Now she made no move to do so. On visitors' day she actually articulated this new feeling of comfort. When her mother asked her if she had been helping in the kitchen, she said this summer she didn't have to because she "had more friends" and was "having more fun."

Her feelings toward members of her own club group were marked by ambivalence, and her behavior toward them oscillated. For the most part, she was attracted to members of other club groups and even at night expressed a desire to stay in a room occupied by another club. At the same time, in some instances when derogatory remarks were made about members of her own group, she defended their reputations. Most of her contacts with her own club were after lights-out when she joined in heartily in their discussions. Initially, she sought out high status campers and became closely involved with one rather sophisticated-appearing girl with whom she was seen to engage in sexual play on one occasion. By mid-period, however, this youngster and Grace had moved apart without any outside intervention.

Genie's personal appearance continued to reflect her poor self-image, and there was no alteration in her addiction to dirty, masculine attire. She did show change in other respects, however, She participated more in activities, and while she clearly preferred to play alone with a male counselor, she was occasionally willing to play active group games when invited. Toward the end of the camping period she worked very hard at crafts for two days, making two well-constructed ring boxes, one for herself and one for another girl. After the first four days she did not resist being on time for meals and did not lag far behind the other campers as she had the year before. Although she sometimes complained about work details, she departed from her old pattern by carrying out extra tasks in order to gain attention from counselors.

The actions of some of the members of this group were, naturally, sometimes threatening to others. Campers were worried about Dolores' odd manner and conversation and occasionally expressed anger toward her over such things as her work performance during clean-up. They rarely, if ever, initiated contact with her. Janine's depressed aspect was unpleasant for them. Andrea was resented at times because of her sarcasm, and some campers felt she was being given too much attention by the director.

In general, however, the behavior of the members of this group was not intolerable to the other campers. Grace and Genie developed friendships with girls from other clubs. Occasionally, other campers were protective and supportive toward Dolores, helping her to learn a game or sympathizing with her when she was criticized. The entire cast was openly supportive of Janine and helped her to mobilize herself when she had difficulty during preparation for the camp play. It is particularly noteworthy that the other seven girls in the camp discussion group made plans with Janine, Andrea, and Dolores to have a "social" after camp and also asked if they could meet as a discussion group during the winter.

ASSESSMENT OF THE EXPERIENCE

In evaluating the overall effect of the camp experience on these girls, the emotional gains must be weighed against the amount of anxiety which the experience itself engendered. There is no doubt that it was a trying experience for them. This was particularly evident during the first year when the shock of separation from familiar surroundings and exposure to a relatively strange milieu initially produced dramatic signs of panic, withdrawal, and aggression. Because of the catastrophic intensity of their reaction, much of their behavior was characterized either by a direct expression of intolerable tensions or a protective avoidance of involvement in camp life. Socialization was, to a large extent, limited to anaclitic relationships with counselors. However, clear cut indications of recovery from this initial reaction were seen even during the brief period of their first stay. It seemed highly significant that all had strong reactions to leaving camp and expressed the wish to return the following summer.

Improvements in adaptation to camp were noted during the second summer despite the persistence of disturbed and inappropriate behavior. These girls were able to make wider use of program activities. Disruptive behavior on their part decreased. Their need for individual attention from counselors diminished, and they appeared better able to tolerate limits on their demands for this attention. Although they still had relatively little contact with other campers, three of them were willing and, in some ways, eager to be with other campers in the discussion group. Here, they were able to share the discussion leader with other youngsters, to wait their turn in conversation, and to reveal their personal feelings despite their fantasies of what this might mean in terms of exposure of problems and rejection. All of them, in varying degrees, appeared to have improved in their ability to control impulses, and for long periods they clearly exercised restraint in acting our their feelings. During the second summer, while they still showed the effects of dislocation, they responded to the demands of camp life with less distress and seemed able to derive more pleasure from the experience.

These girls were able to maintain themselves in the camp situation and improve in their responses to it, because the staff was able to tolerate and manage the acute and distressing reactions they displayed. As a result, while they did precipitate crises, the consequences of these crises were never disastrous, and the outcomes were sometimes emotionally beneficial.

THE MANAGEMENT OF CRISES

For any child there are points of stress in a camp experience which are capable of disrupting his defenses against anxiety and producing disturbances in behavior. These disturbances, however, are usually neither too severe nor frequent and can ordinarily be handled with sympathetic reassurance by counselors who are accustomed to dealing with such minor emotional upsets. Ego-defective children, however, because of their extreme vulnerability, may react catastrophically to the same stresses and precipitate management crises. Since these children have such limited capacity for sublimation, relatively little use can be made of program activities in draining off their anxiety, and this results in extraordinary demands on the counselors. These demands are not only in terms of their time and energy but also in the burden of anxiety that is imposed on them. Counselors must be equipped and willing to face the extreme reactions which accompany ego collapse, including panic, severe depression-extreme regression, and even temporary loss of reality testing. Because of the extreme pressure to which counselors are subjected, it is essential that they be given a realistic appraisal of the kinds of problems they will face and then be provided with the necessary emotional supports by senior staff.

It is possible to reduce the frequency of acute reactions by buffering the ego-defective child from severe psychological shocks through the flexible use of staff and program and alertness to emotional danger signals. Regardless of the amount of planning that goes into the organization of the program, however, it is impossible to eliminate all psychological hazards. The aim of the staff, therefore, should be to reduce the traumatic impact of crises and, through proper management, use them to provide corrective emotional experiences for the child.

Crises can be anticipated around those events in camp life which characteristically increase anxiety such as initial exposure to the setting, being subjected to new routines, the introduction to unfamiliar food, being required to sleep in strange surroundings, and the like. Because of the severe pathological behavior of such youngsters, however, it can be expected that they will overreact to even the minor tensions of camp life.

The examples which follow illustrate the extreme loss of ego-control that can occur in such children as well as their capacity for recovery when given sustained support by someone who is sensitive to their needs:

Paranoid reaction as an outgrowth of religious sensitivity. During the second camp session, Andrea, who is Jewish, complained from time to time that Jewish campers were being discriminated against. Extremely ambivalent toward her own Jewishness and very much concerned with exposure and difference as these related to all aspects of her life, she began to see anti-Semitism all about her. When the other three Jewish campers did not support her contention, she became more upset. This came to a climax on

Friday evening when she became preoccupied about the fact that there was no Jewish service. The following day, Andrea went to the director, who provided her with an opportunity to ventilate her resentments. The intensity of her feelings increased as she talked, and she went on to point out ordinary comments and exchanges of glances on the part of others as being evidences of prejudice; she also bitterly attacked the camp's non-denominational services as discriminatory. She remained adamant in response to the director's unruffled acceptance of her hostility and willingness to make adjustments, maintaining that the administration as well as the other campers were hostile toward Jews. Instead of continuing to deal with this rationally, the director responded to Andrea's feelings of isolation and her fear of surrendering her identity. As a result the fury of Andrea's tirade diminished, and she broke into tears. The director put her arm around her, and Andrea allowed herself to be comforted. The next morning, Andrea went to the non-sectarian service. A Jewish counselor had been delegated to help in planning the service, and the program was arranged with Andrea's complaints in mind. Andrea sat through the entire service, and her only comment on leaving was, "There wasn't anything wrong in that. It couldn't hurt anybody." She was tranquil for the rest of the morning, and there was no recurrence of this particular problem.

Loss of ego-control accompanied by hallucinations. Janine, who had previously been hospitalized with a diagnosis of schizophrenia, managed to control her anxiety during the first day of camp by adopting a facade of maturity. She came prepared with 10 packages of cigarettes and, cigarette in hand, she affected an urbane manner. On the surface this was so successful that one of the children mistook her for a counselor. The staff was also deceived by her apparent poise, and on the very first night, underestimating her fear of exposure and need for anonymity, ill-advisedly attempted to include her in informal dramatics. This proved too threatening, and Janine fled from the room and remained outside, smoking incessantly, until the activity was over. As bedtime approached, her anxiety increased. She was unable to sleep and sat immobile on her bed. She seemed so tense that the director, who had come into the dormitory, decided to take her out for a walk. She asked Janine if she were homesick and wanted to go home, to which she replied, "I don't know where I want to go." She could only talk about how frightened she was, and the director suggested that she might be afraid that she would break down again. Janine was taken aback at the fact that the director had known she had been hospitalized, and she wanted to know if the other campers were also disturbed. Clenching her hands repeatedly, she began to talk about being a failure, saying that no one liked her or understood her. She said she had no friends so she made them up. She talked about hating her family and, running throughout the rest of the discourse was the theme of hating doctors, because they left her constantly, and liking social workers, because social workers listened to her and helped. She described with intense anguish her fear of being abandoned. The director encouraged her to ventilate her feelings and made it plain that she and staff understood how Janine felt and could accept her behavior. She reassured her they would not punish her by sending her away from camp. Janine's agitation gradually subsided, and the director was then able to take her back to the cabin where she went to bed.

On the second day, Janine woke up appearing to feel pretty well. She participated in crafts and was able to make some conversation with children at the table although there were periods of depression during the day when she appeared not to hear what was being said to her. That night there was a costume dance, an activity which Janine again found distressing. She did not appear in costume and seemed extremely sad. She said that she was tricked into coming to camp and refused to participate in the activity. Counselors would come over to her to talk with her from time to time, but she would sit blankly as if she did not seem to hear them. Tears started to stream down her face, but outside of this, she exhibited very little affect. By the end of the evening, she was sitting next to her cabin counselor, crying. At bedtime, some of the others in her sleeping quarters tried to console her. She banged her head on the bed and became incoherent and, unlike the night before, did not respond to the director when she came in. She hallucinated, hearing bombs and seeing bad men coming to get her. The director, who was alarmed over the severity of Janine's reaction, called the assistant director and, in Janine's presence, mentioned something about perhaps telephoning the doctor. Janine became even more upset at this and pleaded with her not to call the doctor. She kept asking for her own cabin counselor and did not want the assistant director, a man, around. The director and counselor then sat with Janine. They told her they were not planning to have her hospitalized but wanted to talk with the doctor in order to help her. During this time she kept hallucinating, hearing trains, sirens, and rain drops. She kept saying, "They don't understand," and, "I'm bad." Janine then indicated that she wanted to go to bed and did so without further ado as long as her counselor stayed with her. She woke up the next day apparently feeling pretty well, although she was concerned that the director would tell her family what she had done. The next day the director called the hospital and conferred with Janine's caseworker. The caseworker agreed with a policy of firm, gentle control and support rather than exploration during such episodes as a basis for handling Janine, without depriving her of the opportunity to ventilate feelings. Janine settled down after this and did not repeat this behavior for the remainder of the period.

Depressive reaction associated with departure. Leave-taking at any camp is accompanied by a rise in tension; tears among girls at these times are not unusual. With deeply disturbed children, however, reactions are likely to be even more extreme. Counselors have to be able to accept without panic or counter-hostility the angry and contradictory behavior that is exhibited. The last morning of camp, for example, Andrea began by helping to make other beds, as well as her own at the counselor's request. Later, however, she refused to carry out her clean-up assignment, which was to sweep the room, and demanded that the counselor do this. She then asked for help with her packing. The counselor responded to this but when she had some difficulty with the lock on Andrea's trunk, this precipitated one of the child's loudest outbursts. She swore at the counselor, saying her mother had had no difficulty with the trunk, and that the counselor was no good. She was very close to tears at this point and left the room. Later in the morning when the campers were let off at the agency in town, the counselor saw her again. With her mother standing nearby, she embraced the counselor and, as she had done the previous evening, said, "Half of me wants to stay and half of me wants to go."

Janine's feelings of rage at being abandoned began to erupt again as the time for departure approached. On the last day she became openly hostile toward her cabin counselor with whom she had established a good relationship. She would ignore remarks addressed to her in an attempt to hurt the counselor's feelings. She threatened to call the counselor names when it was time to leave camp. At the same time her emotional withdrawal became progressively greater. By evening, she was quite depressed and began to cry, got out of bed and asked for the director. She said she did not want to go home where she would be pulled from all sides and where only her social worker would understand her. Nevertheless, she fell into a sound sleep when the counselor sat with her. She delayed her packing the next morning but managed to control herself until she reached the city. Here, however, she broke down and began to sob. She did not respond to the counselor's questions and continued to cry as she entered the car that was to take her home. Shortly afterwards, she wrote to two counselors saying she had been so happy at camp that she wanted to come back as a junior counselor.

Conclusion

Not all disturbed children can be helped by a summer camping experience, even when the camp in question is operated specifically for the purpose of serving children with emotional problems. No matter how well a camp is staffed and organized from a therapeutic standpoint, many youngsters with severe ego-defects may find the demands of camp life intolerable. If the anxiety produced by the experience is too great, it will prevent them from developing any sustained relationships with staff, thereby nullifying the beneficial effects of the program. Furthermore, the amount of individual attention that may require may be so great it will disrupt the operation of the camp and seriously interfere with the activities of fellow campers.

On the other hand, as our findings indicate, if enough caution is exercised in the choice of the children and careful thought is given to their management it is possible, contrary to what has been a commonly held opinion, to integrate even quite seriously disturbed children into selected camping programs. The conditions which we regard as essential to accomplish this task are summarized below:

A. *Adequate preparation*

Since the initial reaction of deeply disturbed children to being separated from a familiar environment is likely to be so severe, it is important to take measures to reduce its intensity. With the girls we have described it was felt that their previous association in a group and the presence in camp of their leader contributed substantially to their ability to tolerate the camp experience. Where these conditions cannot be duplicated, other forms of preparation must be improvised for facilitating the transition from home to camp. These might include pre-season camp visits for the child, a chance to meet his counselor and other personnel, an opportunity to ventilate his anxieties to his worker or therapist, and the presence of a familiar figure on the trip to camp and the period immediately following arrival.

B. *Heterogeneity in camp population*

There was a considerable range in the emotional status of the children at our camp. Approximately one-half were free from any serious emotional disturbance. The remainder had emotional problems of various types, but these were less incapacitating than the severe ego disorders of the girls we studied. The nucleus of stable campers was regarded as a distinct asset. Without such children, programming would have been extremely difficult, and demands on counselors would have been correspondingly greater. By their capacity for participation, they served as models for identification for other campers and provided counselors with gratifications which made it easier for them to tolerate the anxieties and frustrations engendered by the more disturbed individuals. However, had there not also been moderately disturbed campers present, the psychological gulf between the normal and seriously disturbed children might have been too great to bridge. The fact that the latter were able to observe that other campers also had difficulties reduced their sense of alienation.

C. *Flexibility in programming*

Because of the need severely disturbed children have for protective withdrawal, they must be allowed to determine the extent to which they will participate in the camp program. They should be encouraged to engage in camp activities, but demands on them should be kept at a minimum. Materials should be available with which they can work or play individually when they are unable to remain in group activities. Regulations at our camp permitted these youngsters to roam about the grounds but within prescribed boundaries. In this connection, of course, a proportionately large staff was a vital necessity so that when one of these girls wandered off, a counselor was on hand to keep her in view, accompany, or work with her. One source of support for these girls may have been in the basic organization of camp activities. During both summers, but particularly during the second, cabin units were not emphasized. Campers were not required to remain with their own cabin-mates for activities. While such a requirement might have made for superficial cohesion, it would have forced members into a consistently close relationship for which they were not ready and would have placed an overwhelming burden on their cabin counselor. If confronted with a persistent demand for cooperative performance as a unit, they might have become upset over their inadequacies in this regard. Instead, although encouraged to come together for some activities, they were each free to move in and out of groups at play as they wished, without being pressured to remain with each other. This kept their responsibility for one another down to a reasonable minimum. It also enabled staff members to share substantially with this group's cabin counselor in the major tasks involved in working with these girls.

D. *Unrestricted opportunity for personal contact with staff members*

Because of their fear of peer relationships and their feelings of isolation, children with such limited resources make heavy demands on staff members. They should be permitted to seek out counselors individually for emotional support. The staff must be prepared to accept a high degree of "adult-directed" activity and recognize that these children cannot be pressed into more extensive peer contacts until these can be tolerated emotionally. At the same time, staff members, as they respond to the needs of these children for individual attention, should encourage them to reestablish contact with other campers so that relationships do not become centered exclusively on the exploration of problems on a one-to-one basis. With the girls we have described, to have done otherwise would have played into their pathological tendencies and isolated them further from the central activities of the camp. Our counselors had to be alert to opportunities of all types in bringing these girls individually back into relationships with other youngsters. For example, the discussion group which three of them joined originated in an interview between the director and

Janine. As Janine recited her problems, the director pointed out that some of these were shared by other campers who were going through a similar stage of development. She asked Janine whether she would be interested in a discussion group where she and the others could talk over their problems together, and Janine responded to this eagerly. The positive results of this have been described.

E. *Professionally trained personnel*

It would not be feasible to admit children with such severe ego defects to an overnight camp unless a fairly large proportion of the staff was experienced in working with emotionally disturbed children. Our own staff included a number of trained social workers with experience of this kind. At that, it took all the understanding, patience, and skill they could command, and at times their own anxiety was all they could tolerate. Among the staff members who returned the second summer, it was the universal feeling that things were easier the second time around. Part of this was because of the improvement in the girls, but there was also the very important advantage of a previous summer's experience, which points up the value of specific camp experience as well as the more general social work background. In addition to having trained personnel on the camp staff, it is essential that psychiatric consultation be available. This is not only vital to the welfare and safety of the children, but also provides necessary reassurance for the staff.

It is important to reiterate that a camp experience should not be regarded as a cure for underlying pathological deviation. If carefully designed, however, it may provide youngsters who have severe ego impairment with the kinds of concrete experiences that will enable them to better manage their impulses and to react with less discomfort and confusion to the requirements of living with others. This seems to us to be especially important in the light of the scarcity of community resources available to such children. Many agencies confronted with seriously disturbed children could consider camping as one way of helping them. They will undoubtedly need to improvise in terms of their own situation, but they should be encouraged by our results to explore this possibility.

PART FOUR
THE NATURE OF COTTAGE LIFE AND STRATEGIES FOR THERAPEUTIC INTERVENTION

16. Physical Illness in the Residential Treatment Center

ESTHER APPELBERG

Residential treatment centers for children may vary in their theoretical frameworks of reference and in their practices. Some emphasize the therapeutic hour; others emphasize the therapeutic milieu. They all agree, however, that the use of the structured environment is basic to the residential treatment of children. Such agreement is the obvious justification for separating the child from his home and placing him in the residential setting.

Lack of Available Information

In surveying the literature on the subject of residential treatment, however, one is struck with the absence of references to physical illness, its possible meaning, and its treatment in the therapeutic milieu. The nurse is hardly mentioned at all. Even more puzzling is the omission of any reference to physical health or illness or to the nurse in the literature directed toward the education of the child care worker. The exceptions to this advocate that the child care staff should have training that will help them to understand health problems and that "children who are ill should be cared for in surroundings that are familiar to them, so long as this is medically and

Reprinted with the permission of Child Welfare League of America, Inc., from *Child Welfare,* Vol. 45, No. 8 (October, 1966), pp. 451–56.

socially desirable."[1] Although one can find discussions about everyday life, one will seek in vain for consideration of the meaning of a child's physical complaints and illness or the role of the child care worker in handling these important everyday problems.

Many of us who are concerned with child welfare have become so pre-occupied with the emotional problems of the child that we have forgotten or overlooked the importance of the physical body in the lives of our children.[2] We have overlooked physical health or illness as a part of normal development or as the continuation of previous attempts to cope with stress. We have failed to perceive illness as possibly reflecting new symptoms that enable children in treatment to cope with or defend against new stress. Thus, in residential treatment, instead of unifying the psyche and the soma and treating the child as a whole, as one person, we have continually kept these two apart as if the twain never shall meet.

One exception occurs in the writings of Bettelheim. He discusses how the appearance and disappearance of physical symptoms in emotionally disturbed children represent stages in the integrative process of the readjustment of severely disturbed children in the Sonia Shankman Orthogenic School. Some children are able to give up these symptoms; others acquire physical symptoms as a new and more integrated way of dealing with old and new stress.[3] In the story of "Harry, a Delinquent Boy," Bettelheim presents the case of one boy in the Orthogenic School and the role that somatic symptoms play in his illness and in his recovery.[4] Although he gives some attention to the role of the nurse, one wishes that he had discussed her role more fully. Equally neglected is the place of the "sickroom" in this therapeutic milieu.

In 1949, Anna Freud pointed out that if a child is removed from his home and placed in an environment where the adults are not involved in the neurotic struggle, the child's symptoms would disappear for some time until newer, meaningful adults were involved by the child in the neurosis.[5] Bettelheim, too, points out how a majority of the children lost most of their physical symptoms after being in his school for a year and how some of

1. *CWLA Standards for Services of Child Welfare Institutions* (New York, Child Welfare League of America, 1964), p. 52. *See also* Morris Fritz Mayer, *A Guide for Child-care Workers* (New York, Child Welfare League of America, 1958), pp. 85–88.

2. In her presentation to the Citizens' Committee for Children, Anna Freud addressed herself to this preoccupation and elaborated on the reasons for this before an audience of lawyers, educators, and pediatricians. *See* Anna Freud, *Psychoanalytic Knowledge of the Child and Its Application to Children's Services,* mimeographed (New York, Citizens' Committee for Children, 1964).

3. Bruno Bettelheim and Emmy Sylvester, "Physical Symptoms in Emotionally Disturbed Children," in *Psychoanalytic Study of the Child,* III/IV (New York, International Universities Press, 1949), pp. 353–391.

4. Bruno Bettelheim, *Truants from Life* (New York, The Free Press, 1955), pp. 389–471.

5. Anna Freud, *Psycho-Analytical Treatment of Children* (London, Imago Publishing Co., 1946).

these symptoms appeared only in connection with home visits or visits of these children's parents.[6] He discusses why these children needed these symptoms and why they were able to let go of them in the course of treatment, but he does not discuss the symptoms that might result from the new neurotic involvement with caretaking people to which Anna Freud refers. He also fails to examine how helping persons could influence these physical symptoms and their underlying causes through more conscious use of the whole treatment staff within the therapeutic milieu.

Writers who discuss the concept of transference to parental figures in residential treatment offer illustrations that deal with behavior problems only and neglect the soma. For example, in an excellent discussion of psychotherapy in residential treatment, Krug discusses the function of the child care worker who carries out many of the usual parental functions and says that "because of the intimate living experience having to do with eating, toileting, sleeping, playing and learning, children will look upon these [child care] workers as parent figures."[7] And in her third principle of psychotherapy, Krug states:

> . . . within the security of the therapeutic relationship, the child's emotional development is recapitulated in a new, corrective manner for meeting his needs for both dependency and growth . . . but children with greater disturbances in ego function and with marked pregenital fixations require repetitive demonstrations of their acceptance through important daily experiences especially those having to do with bodily functions . . . through the daily experiences residential workers have many opportunities to demonstrate to the child these concrete evidences of acceptance. As a result these children sometimes develop their first meaningful relationships in residence rather than in individual therapy.[8]

Yet, no mention is made of the parental functions of the child care worker when physical sickness affects the children, nor is any attention given to the integration of this concern in the design of the therapeutic milieu.

Although some residential treatment centers are making every effort to keep the mildly sick or injured child in the cottage, others send the child —even with a minor illness—to the infirmary or sickroom.[9] If we really be-

6. Bettelheim, *op. cit.*, p. 378.
7. Othilda Krug, "The Applications of Child Psychotherapy in Residential Treatment," *American Journal of Psychiatry*, CVIII (1952), 695.
8. *Ibid.*, p. 696.
9. From personal communications and observations, we know that in most residential centers, removal of the child for even minor illness is standard practice; written information on this subject is not clear. In a recent study [Lydia F. Hylton, *The Residential Treatment Center: Children, Programs, and Costs* (New York, Child Welfare League of America, 1964)], only 1 center out of 21 centers reported that it had a sickroom available in every cottage; another reported that it had such a room in every new cottage. Some centers reported having infirmaries or sickrooms either as separate buildings or as part of one cottage. Other centers did not have such facilities at all. Although this study gives us a picture of the medical staff and the medical facilities on

lieve this principle of psychotherapy, how can we justify removing the physically ill child from the cottage and relieving—or depriving—the child care worker of any responsibility? Do we not undermine our efforts to give the child the much needed acceptance, warmth, and familiarity in the stress and tension of physical illness and, in fact, contradict ourselves by failing to provide concrete evidences of acceptance? Do we not instead *provide* an experience of rejection by not placing responsibility for physical care of the sick child on the cottage staff?

The Child and the Infirmary

The rationale for the cottage system is known. Yet, what happens to the child who complains that he does not feel well? He is usually sent to the infirmary, where his temperature is taken and where he is kept during school, for the day, overnight, or for a few days. Babcock has pointed to the adult patient's fear of abandonment, a fear that the adult is not aware of, since it relates to the fear of abandonment that he experienced in his childhood.[10] For the child in placement—who is experiencing abandonment by his parents who deserted him—abandonment is not an infantile fear, as in the case of the hospitalized adult, but a very real one. By again removing him from the parental figure, i.e., the cottage worker, we repeat his original trauma—this at a time when "he has a great need for reassurance by people who 'belong' to him and also by persons unrelated to him but upon whom he is economically, physically, and emotionally dependent."[11] Thus, at a time when he needs his substitute parent most urgently, he is removed from him and from the cottage life that is supposed to give him some semblance of living in a home and is the basis of the therapeutic design of residential treatment.

This separation from the cottage takes place at a time when the hurt might be part of a normal childhood illness, an attention-getting device, or an avoidance of dealing with the everyday stresses that are part of emotional maturing. Even though we might recognize these underlying dynamics in the child's behavior and might talk about his need to regress, we continue to deal with them from the point of view of administrative expediency. Somehow if the body is involved, the child no longer belongs in the cottage, but in the infirmary. We do not ask ourselves how removal from the cottage influences the child's psyche at a time when he needs more in-

the grounds and those used off grounds, we do not know how these centers treat the child when he falls sick. Is he kept in the cottage, or is he sent to the sickroom, to the infirmary, or to a community facility? At what point does the medical staff play what part in contributing to the treatment of the child?

10. Charlotte G. Babcock, "Inner Stress in Illness and Disability," in Howard J. Parad and Roger R. Miller, Eds., *Ego-Oriented Casework: Problems and Perspectives* (New York, Family Service Association of America, 1963), p. 57.

11. *Ibid.*

tensive bodily care, or how his physical illness affects his "psychology" and self-image.

NURSE-CHILD RELATIONSHIP

In the infirmary, the child might then look at the nurse who devotes herself to him as a positive parental figure, whereas the cottage counselor who deserted and rejected him becomes even more invested with negative feelings.[12] Having found the good parent in the nurse, he is now in a conflict situation—unwilling to get better and to leave the infirmary to return to the bad parent in the cottage. He does not want to move out of his regression and leave the security of the bed.

Many nurses are very sensitive to the child's psychological and physical needs, but we know little about what goes on between the nurse and the child, especially in terms of how much understanding and consideration she gives to the child's psychological needs while dealing with his physical needs. All we hear is that children "love" or "hate" to go to the infirmary, but this, of course, tells us nothing.

It is apparent that we know very little about the role of the nurse, how she fits into the treatment center, and how the child perceives her. In two studies, attempts were made to determine whom, among the adults in residential treatment centers, the child considered his confidant.[13] Caseworkers and cottage counselors were named most often, and teachers and administrative staff received some mention, but the nurse was not mentioned once by the children.[14]

ISOLATION OF THE CHILD

We have also failed to take into consideration the way in which the infirmary isolates the child from his peers and how it affects the child. If he is rejected by his peers, a physically ill child may lie in the infirmary for days without being visited by his cottage group. Sometimes the cottage counselor cannot find the time for a visit to the infirmary. Thus, confinement in

12. Children in placement often received very inadequate care by their parents at times of illness.

13. Arthur Blum and Norman A. Polansky, "Effect of Staff Role on Children's Verbal Accessibility," *Social Work*, VI (1961), pp. 29–37; and Esther Appelberg, *Verbal Accessibility of Adolescents. A Comparison of Adolescents Living in a Treatment Institution and Adolescents Living in the Community with their Parents*, unpublished doctoral dissertation (Cleveland, Ohio, School of Applied Social Sciences, Western Reserve University, 1961).

14. One has to recognize that in this kind of popularity polling, the discrepancy is more apparent than real, since the odds of choosing an adult confidant from the cottage staff as against the nurse were higher. But the omission is still worth some thought, because most children had frequent contact with the nurse either as outpatients or as patients while they were hospitalized in the infirmary.

the infirmary may be perceived by the child as another rejection by his peers and the parent substitute. This may, in turn, increase his negative transference.[15] Physical complaints may be used as part of the struggle with the caretaking adults or with the child's peers. Having been allowed in the infirmary to regress and to revert to behavior inappropriate for his age, he is now unwilling to give up these secondary gains. He becomes involved in a new struggle with his peers and the child care workers who are not willing to tolerate this and want him to give up his now inappropriate behavior and demands. The illness may even be prolonged to continue the struggle.

All these speculations and many others will persist in plaguing us so long as we continue to remove sick children from the cottage, thereby surrendering an opportunity to learn about transference and somatic symptoms in residential treatment.

Why We Are Neglecting the Problem

There are various reasons why we ignore the nurse and fail to give professional consideration to appropriate use of the infirmary. For one thing, there is a lack of understanding that childhood illnesses are part of normal growth and represent something every mother has to cope with in bringing up her children. Furthermore, there is fear that the child care worker might not know how to handle physical illness and that other children might be contaminated. And there are questions of administrative expediency as well as questions of cost.

Consideration should be given to Hartmann's concept of illness and its relationship to reality adaptation so that we may understand how taking care of these inevitable occurrences in growth belongs to cottage life as part of the child's experience in growing up.[16] Moreover, many child care workers have taken care of the physical illnesses of their own children and have done it well.[17] And in the residential treatment center, some child care workers occasionally relieve the nurse. If they can relieve the nurse in the infirmary and if they can take care of their own children, why can they not care for the sick child in the cottage? With respect to contamination of other children, by the time the disease is diagnosed as contagious, the sick

15. For further explanation of the concept of transference toward the personnel in a treatment center, *see* Esther Appelberg, "The Cottage Meeting as a Therapeutic Tool," in Henry W. Maier, Ed., *Group Work as Part of Residential Treatment* (New York, National Association of Social Workers, 1965), pp. 142–154.

16. *See* Heinz Hartmann, *Essays on Ego Psychology* (New York, International Universities Press, 1964), p. 6.

17. Hylton, *op. cit.*, pp. 72–75. Eleven out of 21 centers did not have nurses on their staff. We might, therefore, rightly assume that sick children are not necessarily cared for by nurses, but by the cottage worker performing nursing tasks in the infirmary or in the sickroom.

child's peers in the cottage or in the school have usually already been exposed. Foster parents are asked to take care of the foster child who has a cold or the measles, even though there are other children in the home. Why should the same not apply to the child in residence?

The arguments for maintaining present arrangements because of administrative expediency and cost are not supportable, because administrative expediency is no justification for poor practice. A therapeutic milieu must start with an administration built not on expediency, but on sound mental health principles.

The National Center for Health Statistics has not collected financial statistics about medical treatment of children in residential centers nor about children living at home who are treated in outpatient clinics.[18] Therefore, we do not know whether there would necessarily be increased cost in operating a residential center for children if physically ill children were cared for in the cottage. In any case, the American Association for Children's Residential Treatment Centers is endeavoring to change the Hill-Burton Act so that Federal funds will be available for changes such as those advocated here. And the Children's Bureau is working on initiating a study on the housing situation in child care institutions in order to change Section 703 of Public Law 88443 (1964) so that funds may be included for building 24-hour children's institutions.

Such excellent efforts are directed to financing, but the changes indicated here are not only a question of money. Attitudes are also important, and no real changes will occur so long as the prevailing attitude is one that holds that the primary deficiencies of the centers' medical programs are "unsatisfactory infirmary facilities, lack of medical followup, and insufficient medical staff."[19]

Certainly, keeping the sick child in the cottage is a complicated matter. For example, the question of contagion cannot be ignored, and there are times when the child has to be removed for this reason. Some child care workers might experience new stresses with this additional responsibility, or they might experience a countertransference in regard to bodily illness.[20] The problem of work schedules could be affected, since the needs of the physically ill child might not coincide with regular duty hours. Arrangements for overtime pay or substitute coverage might have to be worked out. Although somewhat less desirable, substitute coverage would keep the child in his own bed, in his own cottage, and with his own peers.

18. Personal correspondence to the author from E. E. Bryant, Chief, Institutional Population Survey Branch, Division of Health Records Statistics. In the same letter, Mr. Bryant points out that his office plans to do so.

19. Hylton, *op. cit.*, p. 207.

20. Emma N. Plank and Carla Horwood, "Leg Amputation in a Four-Year-Old: Reactions of the Child, Her Family, and the Staff," in *Psychoanalytic Study of the Child,* XVI (New York, International Universities Press, 1961), 405–422.

Benefits of Care Rendered in the Cottage

Since the cottage is, in effect, the child's home, even the most rejected child will feel less rejected in his own room than if he is transferred to the infirmary. In his room, he continues to see his roommates; he keeps in touch with his cottage peers who come to look for their friends and who sometimes stop to ask him how he is or to talk with him. Staying in the cottage also gives the peer group and the adults in charge of the peer group an opportunity to be of some influence upon the sick child. This opportunity is apparently forgotten in our consideration of the practical function of the therapeutic milieu.[21] But, it should not be underestimated when we talk about the influence of the peer group.

In addition, keeping the child in his cottage prevents a child in placement from developing a distorted picture of how one takes care of a sick member of the family or the group. He will recognize that sickness does not inevitably mean being sent away from home, nor does it necessarily mean that at a time of great need, those closest to him will abandon him to strangers. Furthermore, the "healthy child" in the cottage will not be plagued by fears that he, too, will be abandoned should he come down with a cold. Being free of this fear will be helpful in enabling the child to involve himself in a positive relationship with the caretaking person.

The care the sick child needs and gets in the cottage will satisfy some basic needs common to all human beings, especially a sick child. Our providing this care will yield greater understanding and insight into the dynamics of somatic illness, and it might teach us how to deal with children more helpfully. We might learn how to encourage children to give up physical symptoms more quickly, and we might find new avenues of dealing with the sick child. Lodging responsibility for the sick child in the cottage will also intensify relationships with nurses and pediatricians, thus making them an integral part of the treatment plan.

Concluding Comments

There is no question but that rethinking and restudy might involve new administrative problems and, perhaps, additional expenditures. Today we are building new residential treatment centers and reviewing and rebuilding old ones. Some centers continue in the old, comfortable ways; infirmaries, which are costly buildings, are part and parcel of their new residential plants. It is time to raise the question of whether we want to take a new look and find a better way of dealing with old problems. Infirmaries and other community medical facilities certainly are needed for particular

21. The importance of the cottage milieu in residential treatment has been studied by Howard W. Polsky, *Cottage Six* (New York, Russell Sage Foundation, 1962).

children who require isolation because of suicidal or other destructive tendencies, or for certain illnesses that require highly specialized care. But the majority of somatic complaints and illnesses can be looked after in the cottage. This can be done by having additional coverage, providing special sickrooms in each cottage, and including the nurse and an understanding of her role in the training of the child care worker. Staff development programs should include the discussion of childhood diseases and the administering of first aid. The new arrangement for retaining sick children in the cottage can be facilitated by more systematically including nurses and pediatricians in the theoretical and practical framework of the residential center.[22]

The change we advocate here is a change in arrangements and procedures.[23] In a therapeutic milieu, however, arrangements and procedures have significant dynamic consequences. Surely this change can have profound implications for some troubled children. It should, therefore, be carefully considered.

22. For these and other suggestions, see *CWLA Standards for Services of Child Welfare Institutions.*
23. Those interested in this problem might care to consult the literature that deals with pediatric hospitalization of psychiatric treatment or the literature about pediatric wards. See, for example, Paul C. Laybourne and Herbert C. Miller, "Pediatric Hospitalization of Psychiatric Patients: Diagnostic and Therapeutic Implications," *American Journal of Orthopsychiatry*, XXXII (1962), 596–603; and Emma N. Plank, *Working with Children in Hospitals* (Cleveland, Ohio, The Press of Western Reserve University, 1962).

17. Observations on the Loss of a Housemother

JULES SCHRAGER

The person who is assigned the responsibility of giving the child day-by-day care in a children's institution is a key factor in his care and treatment. Whether he is called houseparent, child care worker, or counselor, his

Reprinted with the permission of *Social Casework*, Vol. 37, No. 3 (March, 1956), pp. 120–26.

function is the same—to serve as parent surrogate. In the process of discharging this responsibility this person comes to represent in the child's mind all the attributes, both positive and negative, with which he has vested the concept "parent." It is within this relationship of the child with a parent or parent surrogate that his character develops.

The capacity of a child to develop physically, as well as emotionally, is connected with his ability to form these primary object relationships.[1] Although it is true that the younger child depends on these relationships to a greater degree than does the older one, all children continue to require mothering until a sufficient degree of autonomy has been attained so that each one can survive as a separate biological and social entity. The nature and quality of the nurturing influences in the child's daily life will determine in great part his social achievement, his adaptation to reality, his mastery over his instinctual impulses, and his ultimate independence.

The purpose of this paper is to examine the effects, on both the children and the staff in a children's institution, of the termination of employment of a housemother. It is hoped that, through clarification of the by-products of such a routine incident, agencies will be encouraged to examine their own experiences in this connection in the hope that the number of such traumatic episodes may be reduced. Second, this paper has the equally important objective of pointing up the need for developing better methods of dealing with separation anxiety in the particular setting of the treatment institution.

Theoretical Considerations

The literature of child psychiatry is rich with information and observation concerning the effects on the child of the loss of primary object relationships. Children who have been variously described as "autistic" by Kanner,[2] "atypical" by Rank, and "schizophrenic" by Mahler, are the products of distorted or emotionally empty relationships between parent and child. Whatever the nature of the particular distortion, it seems apparent that those attributes of mothering care so essential to the totally dependent child's survival and growth have been significantly reduced or totally absent. Where deprivation in the area of mothering has been part of the child's earliest experiences, his disturbance is greater. Cases such as those reported by Spitz[3] reveal the devastating effects of such early traumata. At

1. Margaret S. Mahler, M.D., "On Child Psychosis and Schizophrenia; Autistic and Symbiotic Infantile Psychoses," in *The Psychoanalytic Study of the Child*, Vol. VII, (New York, International Universities Press, 1952), pp. 286–305.

2. Leo Kanner, M.D., "Problems of Nosology and Psychodynamics of Early Infantile Autism," *American Journal of Orthopsychiatry*, Vol. XIX, No. 3 (1949), pp. 416–426.

3. Rene A. Spitz, M.D., and Katherine M. Wolf, "Anaclitic Depression," in *The Psychoanalytic Study of the Child*, Vol. II, (New York, International Universities Press, 1947), pp. 313–342.

all levels of the child's development, the absence or loss (permanently or temporarily) of significant parental figures creates disturbance in the child which, if left untreated, can permanently scar his developing personality and can cause him great difficulty subsequently in forming meaningful relationships.[4]

In observing children who come into placement, one is struck always by the number of times they have been exposed to separation experiences in connection with the parents' attempts at finding help for themselves and the children. Whether the experience is short and the anxiety transitory, as in the case of the child who leaves his mother to enter the strange play-room of the child guidance clinic, or more extensive, as in the parents' un-successful attempts at temporary private placement, the anxiety of the child is clear. He fears the loss of the person who has cared for him (how-ever inadequate this care may have been), and dreads finding himself in a situation in which no one will fill the void caused by separation.

Whether the mother's difficulty in meeting the child's needs lies in an inhibition of motherliness which is a carry-over from her own disappoint-ing childhood relationships, or whether the parents are extremely imma-ture individuals, narcissistic and without capacity for deep emotional rela-tionship, the child has already suffered intense feelings of deprivation. Placement away from his own home represents society's attempt to provide optimal conditions for the resumption of his physical and emotional growth.

Group placement is usually indicated when the problems have been of such a kind that they have produced in the child symptoms that are so dis-turbing to himself and others as to make it difficult for him to live in a fam-ily. Whatever the nature of the group, whether it is the highly organized and therapeutically conditioned residential treatment setting or whether it is the more typical (and more available) congregate setting of a chil-dren's institution, the specific needs of the individual child constitute the basis on which choice of a placement setting will be determined.

The group setting can offer a great deal to seriously deprived children. These positive values have been defined elsewhere.[5] The fact that the group offers a source of support for the fragile ego of the troubled child has been documented. It has also been noted that controls that are lacking in the child's character structure can be "built into" the institutional frame-work. That the total institution can be perceived by the child as an all-powerful symbolic parent, organized to meet his needs, has been reported.

4. John Bowlby, M.D., *Maternal Care and Mental Health,* Monograph No. 2 (Geneva, World Health Organization, 1951).

5. Bruno Bettelheim, *Love Is Not Enough* (Glencoe, Ill., The Free Press), 1950; Herschel Alt and Hyman Grossbard, "Professional Issues in the Institutional Treat-ment of Delinquent Children," *American Journal of Orthopsychiatry,* Vol. XVIX, No. 2 (1949) 279–294; Joseph H. Reid and Helen R. Hagan, *Residential Treatment of Emotionally Disturbed Children* (New York, Child Welfare League of America, 1952).

Much of the time of administrative and supervisory personnel goes into structuring the institution's characteristics in such a way that they may be exploited for the benefit of the child in care. It is perhaps easy to forget that these parental qualities are perceived by the child as available to him through *individual persons* who take on for him the significance of parent surrogates. When such identifications take place and are carefully nurtured, the institution has a most powerful tool available for the rehabilitation of the child.[6] When, however, these attachments are allowed to develop only to be interrupted precipitously, the institution is perpetuating the cycle of loss-restitution-loss which, as we have seen, is most detrimental to the growing child.

The Institutional Setting

The following material has been gathered from the records of staff members and from notes of staff meetings in a small institution for disturbed children. These excerpts illustrate how the children reacted to the loss of a "mothering" person, the housemother, and what the effects were on both professional and non-professional staff members. Although the situations described here are those of a specific setting, I believe that similar occurrences take place in most child-caring institutions.

In this particular setting, thirteen children between the ages of seven and thirteen live together with four adults. They occupy an old residence that has been "done over" to meet the requirements of a children's institution. The circumstances surrounding the material to be discussed were as follows: A month before the actual date of separation, the children were told that the housemother was going to leave. This information was shared with the children by the unit supervisor at small group meetings. The children were told that the housemother was leaving because she was not satisfied with her present position. She wanted to be closer to her home, but had made no plans for taking another job. The housemother, however, had had difficulty in accepting supervision, had been unable to resolve her troubled feelings in this connection, and had discussed her dissatisfaction with the children. In the group meetings the children were given an opportunity to ask questions, to vent their feelings, and to express their concerns about future plans. They were assured that there would always be enough adults available to provide good care and a plan for staff coverage was explained.

Although the general tenor of the meetings was somewhat depressed, the children were able to express some of their anxiety and seemed finally to accept the fact that they would be adequately provided for after the house-

6. Norman Lourie and Rena Schulman, "Role of Residential Staff in Residential Treatment," *American Journal of Orthopsychiatry,* Vol. XXII, No. 4 (1952), pp. 798–808.

mother's departure. The children who were more sophisticated about life in an institution and who had previously experienced the loss of a housemother dealt with the impending separation in more realistic terms than those who were new to the setting. For all, however, there was clearly a "choosing of sides." The children wanted to know the nature of the difficulty between the housemother and the supervisor, although this had not been mentioned in presenting her intention to leave. By reacting in this way the children recast the situation in terms which were comprehensible to them and which referred to the past and to earlier situations of a like nature. To them it appeared, "Mother and father cannot get along together any more; they are going to separate and as a consequence we are in danger of not being cared for." On another level, however, they took it to mean that *they* had been "terribly bad," and that it was their badness that had resulted in the rupture of the "parents' " relationship. They then became tremendously guilty and tried to cope with their intense feelings in characteristic ways as will be observed in the examples that follow.

First Observations

Anna Freud has observed that "regression occurs while the child is passing through the no-man's-land of affection, that is, during the time that the old [love] object has been given up and before the new one has been found." The following excerpts from the institution's records offer some indication of the quality of disturbance that may occur when children experience a separation of this kind. First, how did the children express their troubled feelings in their relationships with child care staff?

(1) Twice today the children complained about the food. The complaints began with S (the youngest in the group) and were shortly picked up by the others. They could not be specific in their complaints, but all said that the food "just didn't taste right." I couldn't find anything wrong with the food and pointed this out. Later they complained that "there wasn't enough," although I observed that several of those who complained had left food on their dishes.

(2) Several times tonight the children asked if I were to be on duty the rest of the evening. They all knew that this is my night in since this part of the schedule had not been changed. When I reassured them, they wanted to know who else would be there and I told them. This did not reassure them and they asked me the same question in different forms several times before bedtime. I asked why they were so worried since they know that there is always someone on duty and available to them. They rejected the reassurance, saying, "Many times no one is around."

(3) Since this was Saturday and the children were to get their allowances, I got the key and the cash box from the housemother. The children asked many times if they were to get their allowances today (even though this is standard procedure). Despite assurances they continued to ask. Some felt

that "no one would remember to get the key," others that they "wouldn't get the right amount."

(4) F wandered off grounds today and we couldn't find him anywhere. He took off on his bike and didn't reappear until mid-afternoon. When he returned he was very dirty, had fallen off his bike and skinned his knee. When he was asked why he hadn't told anyone where he was going, he replied, "No one was around to tell."

(5) S and F were very upset this afternoon. They fought each other and other children. When they were separated they struggled with the worker, kicking and screaming.

It can be seen that the children were responding to the impending loss of the parent substitute in a *total* fashion. Despite the fact that the reality described to them was one in which continued care was planned and in which complete coverage had been assured, it apparently appeared to them that the *loss of one significant person* meant the removal of *all* protection and security. In (1) the complaints about food, which previously had been quite satisfactory, lead one to assume that the palatability of the food (and for food we can readily substitute any of the attributes of a usually loving and protective environment) is related to the person who provides it. The loss of the loved person produces the fantasy that the food "tastes different," and again that "there might not be enough."

When bedtime approaches, many of the fears, more manageable during the waking hours, impinge on the child's consciousness with renewed vigor. In (2) we see how the child's awareness of this causes emergence of the fear that no one will be present to help him in that period when he feels most vulnerable and in need of added protection. Despite conscious awareness of the fact that staff members will be on duty to care for him, he fantasizes that he will be abandoned to cope with his overwhelming anxiety alone and unaided.

Routines, which usually serve to provide a sense of order and which offer opportunity for planned achievement, seem in danger of being disrupted when the mothering person is absent. Money allowances, which provide the ego with an opportunity for autonomous functioning and for a degree of personal choice, seem in danger of being withheld when the "giving" person is not physically present. In (3) the children were wondering if the available person really cared and, more basically, if anyone else could be as giving.

Protective controls, which are thoughtfully built into the treatment milieu, are embodied for the child in the person of the child care worker. These controls are felt by the child as providing protection from threatening influences in the environment at large as well as from his own self-destructive impulses. In the course of the child's life in the treatment setting he struggles against these controls and attempts to establish their boundaries. His security in the environment rests on the effective functioning of these benign limits. When these controls are threatened, as in the situation described here, the child is impelled to "act out" his anxiety, driven by an inner impulse to ascertain for himself the degree of protection which remains. In (4) and (5) we see how the children try to find out how safe they really are; whether anyone really cares about what happens to them; and whether anyone remains who is strong enough to protect them against external and internal influences with which they cannot cope alone.

Reactions of Child Care Staff

The structure of a child care institution is often much like that of a family. To some extent this may be true because the unit has been designed in this fashion. Recognition is given to the fact that even in the institutional setting children need a spectrum of possible relationships available to them— relationships with siblings, with parent figures, and so on. Although it is possible for such roles to be *assigned,* one often observes that the characteristics of these roles are *taken* on by individuals because of their own character structures and are expressive of the needs they are satisfying by choosing employment in the institutional setting. Thus it happens that individuals who are assigned responsibilities that mark them as parent surrogates frequently operate as if they were older children in the "family" constellation, thereby acting out what they feel their position to be. In the context of the present problem of the loss of a parent figure, identifications may become blurred and roles may be reversed as each member of the staff attempts to sort out his own feelings and cope with them.

In the setting from which this material was drawn, the housemother is a figure of central importance in the living situation. Surrounding her and discharging the roles of "big brother" and "big sister" are young men and women who are called counselors. They have a basic responsibility as child care staff members which is colored by the fact that leisure-time supervision constitutes their specific function. Whenever the balance of their responsibilities is tipped toward "care" and away from "play," tensions arise which can be understood only in terms of their own identifications with parent figures projected onto the stage of the institutional group living experience. The following excerpts are taken from supervisory notes made during the period of crisis arising from the housemother's departure.

(1) C, a young woman who has had long association with the program, had responsibility for coverage of the group from dinnertime through bedtime. She complained that the housemother often did not come on duty during the going-to-bed period, thus requiring C to remain for a longer time than her schedule called for, since this was a difficult time for the children. Her wish was that she could come on duty earlier and leave earlier.

(2) Snack time is part of the daily routine. Customarily snacks are provided after school and again before bedtime. W, a young male worker, thought

that the children "get too much food during the snacks." He felt that they should be limited in the amount they might take and was critical of the "lack of structure."

(3) M discussed the fact that one of the children had asked her why the housemother was leaving. She had answered matter-of-factly that the housemother had "had difficulty in handling the job." Shortly afterward the same child had vomited. In a rather disgusted way, M complained that she had had to clean up his clothes and the mess.

A common plaint can be observed to run through all the excerpts above —one that can be roughly stated as follows: "Mother and father [housemother and supervisor] have decided to end their relationship; mother is leaving home and *we* are left to handle *her* responsibilities." In (1) the worker is saying she doesn't want to have to struggle with the children's problems when *she* [the housemother] should be on duty. That is *her* responsibility and the worker wants to leave before it has to be faced. In (2) the worker criticizes the supervisor since basic policies, such as those governing the provision of snacks, are made by the clinical-supervisory-administrative personnel. Food-giving, and especially the availability of sweets and snacks, requires careful planning if it is to fulfill the requirements of a therapeutic intent. Perhaps the worker is also saying that he cannot be comfortable in providing this kind of "tax-free love,"[7] a term used by Redl and Wineman to connote unconditional acceptance and love in its myriad forms. The basic resentment, however, seems to be concerned with the fact that the worker has been placed *by the supervisor* in the position of being the giving, that is, the mothering, person. He resents this and protects himself against its implication by identifying with the housemother and criticizing the supervisor for "lack of structure." It is frequently observed that disturbed children respond somatically to a wide variety of upsetting stimuli. Differences in body posture, variations in skin color, and upsets of the gastrointestinal function are frequently connected with changes in the external environment and can be thought of as responses to these changes. In (3) the worker seems to be saying, first, that the housemother is not able to do a good job, that is, to be a good mother. On the other hand, placed in the position of the mothering person, the worker is angry that she has had to "clean up the mess" and to care for the child when he expressed his guilt, hostility, and anxiety by vomiting.

Involvement of the Therapist

Thus far we have discussed the behavioral by-products of separation as they are expressed by the children and the child care staff. Within the pat-

7. Fritz Redl and David Wineman, *Controls from Within* (Glencoe, Ill., The Free Press, 1952).

tern of life in a treatment milieu, another figure looms significantly—that of the therapist. Within the therapy hour and in the isolated setting of the office-playroom, he offers to the troubled child a corrective emotional experience with an adult. To the therapist, the child brings his own unique way of relating as this has been shaped by his life experience. The therapist points his effort toward helping the child to surrender those patterns of behavior which are archaic and self-defeating, while he helps also to develop newer, more satisfying ways of coping with life experiences. The raw material for the therapeutic process is drawn from the child's storehouse of past experiences, as well as from his present life.[8]

By definition, the therapist is a part of the total therapeutic influence that is being brought to bear on the child. Because he has to be free to deal with the unconscious, irrational components of the child's personality, he is kept free of involvement in the daily life of the child. To the extent that communication between child care staff and therapist flows freely, the therapist will have an adequate grasp of the experiences to which the child is being exposed in the environment and will be prepared to deal with this kind of material when it is brought to him by the child. This communication can be planned and organized in a variety of ways, some of which have been dealt with elsewhere.[9] What cannot be planned or predicted is the quality of the therapist's response to the exigencies of life in the institutional environment. On this level, the therapist relies on his objective appraisal of the dynamics of the child's personality, and his intuitive understanding of the ways in which the particular child functions. Interacting with these are strong, unconscious feelings and attitudes which stem from unresolved situations in his own life and which can be seen reflected in his relationship with the child in treatment.

In terms of the subject matter of this paper, it will be seen that the therapist cannot remain aloof from or untouched by the psychosocial processes that are inherent in the group living situation.

(1) In a staff meeting A, the therapist, said that he had observed his patient, F, running across the heavily traffic-laden street that separates the residence from the clinic, on the way to his therapy hour. F is an impulse-ridden child. The therapist asked, "Don't they [child care staff] know that he cannot be trusted to do this alone? Why isn't there anyone around to accompany him to the clinic?"

(2) L wondered why her patient, C, was removed from the dining room. She stated that C had told her that he "had not done anything" but had been made to take his dinner alone in his room. She asked, "Are the staff having trouble controlling the children?"

8. Jules Schrager, "Child Care Staff Recording in a Treatment Institution," *Social Casework*, Vol. XXXVI, No. 2 (1955), pp. 74–81.
9. *Ibid.*

(3) D commented that his patient had been extremely upset during the
last few treatment hours. He wondered "what was going on" in the residence
and thought that if he knew more about it perhaps he'd be able to be more
helpful in the treatment hour.

It can be assumed that these situations were presented by the child and
were handled by the therapist as any other productions of the patient
would be, that is, as phenomena connected with the total process of therapy within the specific framework of the therapist-child relationship. What
was brought to the staff meeting was the residual feeling that the therapist
carried within himself. These feelings are less related to the desired course
of therapy than they are to unconscious identification with the child and
his feelings. In (1) the therapist was properly concerned with whether
anyone could protect his patient from his own impulsivity. On the other
hand, there was the tacit inference that no one was really interested in
seeing that the child was protected. In (2) the therapist feared that in the
absence of the housemother the children were at the mercy of punitive
persons who treated them unjustly. Further, she feared that, with the
housemother gone, the interests of the group would take precedence over
those of her patient. She feared that arbitrary demands for conformity
would be made of the child irrespective of clinically determined considerations. In (3) the therapist was implying that the disturbed behavior was
primarily connected with the disruption of the institutional family. He displaced onto the group setting responsibility for pathology which had its
genesis in the earlier experience of the child and which was reflected in the
current situation.

Conclusions

In summary, then, this paper has been an attempt to point to some of the
by-products of the separation of a key person from the child care staff of
a children's institution. The attempts of children, child care staff, and professional personnel to deal with their own feelings and anxieties at separation have been explored. It has been possible to observe the enormous impact on the operation of the therapeutic milieu produced by a change in
personnel.

Unfortunately, one of the significant facts about the institutional em-
ployee is his employment mobility. There has been evidence of great fluidity in the staffs of institutions serving children. The structure of the institution appears as a relatively unstable amalgam, prone to disruption from
influences within the group as well as within the individual.

In order to enlarge the effectiveness of the institutional setting, at least
two things need urgent consideration. First, techniques need to be devised
for handling the anxieties of the various staff groups, taking into account

the intricate nature of the intra-staff and child-staff relationships.[10] Efforts at dealing with this problem in connection with similar situations in the maintenance of foster homes[11] and in relation to adoptive placement[12] have been in evidence for some time. Similar work[13] needs to be done in connection with the problem of the children's institution.

Second, the importance of the child care staff member needs to be affirmed. It is not sufficient to say that the child care worker represents an essential element in the treatment team. His real significance needs to be reflected in the conditions of employment to which he is exposed. It behooves each institution to examine its employment practices in an attempt to make the child care job more appealing to persons who are professionally trained. Moreover, the value of the child care staff becomes greater as the institution invests in increased in-service training and professional supervision. In short, efforts should be made to ensure greater continuity of employment of those persons who function as significant parent surrogates in order that the recurrence of the damaging effects of separation may be prevented.

10. Alfred H. Stanton and Morris S. Schwartz, *The Mental Hospital* (New York, Basic Books, 1954); Herschel Alt, "Responsibilities and Qualifications of the Child Care Worker," *American Journal of Orthopsychiatry,* Vol. XXIII, No. 4 (1953), pp. 670–675.

11. Draza Kline and Helen M. Overstreet, "Maintaining Foster Homes Through Casework Skills," *Social Service Review,* Vol. XXII, No. 3 (1948), pp. 324–333.

12. Margaret W. Gerard, M.D., and Rita Dukette, "Techniques of Preventing Separation Trauma in Child Placement," *American Journal of Orthopsychiatry,* Vol. XXIV, No. 1 (1954), pp. 111–127.

13. Margaret W. Gerard, M.D., and Helen Mary Overstreet, "Technical Modification in the Treatment of a Schizoid Boy within a Treatment Institution," *American Journal of Orthopsychiatry,* Vol. XXIII, No. 1 (1953), pp. 171–185.

18. Characteristics and Resolution of Scapegoating

James A. Garland
Ralph L. Kolodny

No single phenomenon occasions more distress to the outside observer than the act of scapegoating. Frequently violent in its undertones, if not in actual form, it violates every ethical tenet to which our society officially subscribes. As part of that society, the group worker confronted with scapegoating in the midst of interaction often finds himself caught up in a welter of primitive feelings, punitive and pitying, and assailed by morbid reflections on the unfairness of fate which leaves one weak and others strong. It is probably safe to say that few other events in group life are as evocative of intense feelings on the part of participants, including the worker, and as provocative of group crises. Attempts to deal with the scapegoating, whether as a single event or as a pattern, are likely to leave the worker feeling about as inept as he will ever feel as a practitioner. Try as he will, he may find it very difficult to get beyond, "But that's not fair. Give the guy a chance." Nothing upsets that nice balance between moral indignation and clinical dispassion which we as social workers seek to achieve in our approach to problems more than a clear-cut act of scapegoating. Compounding our difficulties is the fact that scapegoating is also one of the most ubiquitous of the phenomena we encounter. Even a cursory reading of group work records, particularly those dealing with children and youth, turns up incident after incident in which there is the expression of observable negative feeling, unwarranted in its intensity and implicitly having group sanction, on the part of several members toward another member over a considerable period of time.[1] When the study committee of which

Reprinted with the permission of Columbia University Press from *Social Work Practice, 1967*, pp. 198–218. Copyright © 1967 National Conference on Social Welfare.

The ideas presented here were developed over a two-year period by the staff and students of the Department of Neighborhood Clubs, Boston Children's Service Association.

1. "Overview of Proceedings of the Seminar in Group Movement" (Boston, Boston University School of Social Work, 1962, mimeographed).

the authors were members several years ago asked for representative illus-trations of scapegoating, we were inundated with examples. From a camp for socially disadvantaged youngsters, for instance, came one group work-er's observations that in the six groups of eight to ten year olds in her unit she rarely saw a group in which there was no scapegoating behavior. From a Jewish Center day camp came instance after instance of vigorous at-tempts to drive out the one variously labeled by his peers as "babyish," "slow," "dumb," "messy," or "odd." Reports of the behavior of YMCA ado-lescent groups were similar, and even the interaction of groups of physi-cally debilitated children in a special hospital group work program was reported as being far from free of this behavior.

Because of its very universality, however, scapegoating and the several forms its aftermath takes may have become accepted as inevitable. The lay attitude is often, as one agency board member put it, that "everyone's ex-perienced it; one learns to live with it." The professional point of view is frequently that as a symptom of individual maladjustment and of shifts in the structure of interpersonal transactions within the group, scapegoating cannot be dealt with directly. Its reduction depends almost exclusively on other events, as, for example, changes in group structure, alterations in self-image on the part of scapegoaters in the course of group development, reduction of tension and, therefore, of aggression, as a new group situation becomes defined and familiar. The behavior itself is frequently seen as something to be diverted or cut off in the interest of "protection" or by-passed in order to work at those issues which underlie it.

Unfortunately, however, the group worker who is involved in mental health efforts in the community that entail the introduction or reintroduc-tion of the emotionally disturbed into the normal society of their peers is placed in a serious dilemma if only these two devices are available to him. His "protection" may be seen as favoritism, a matter over which members, with their sibling-like concerns, are already highly aroused, and in re-sponse to which they may leave the group. On the other hand, bypassing the attack may cause the already emotionally fragile scapegoat to flee the group permanently.

As a matter of fact, all group workers are faced with the same dilemma. None of us is really comfortable with the rationalizations which sometimes accompany the departure of members who have been scapegoated: "He really wasn't suitable for this group." "He isn't ready for a group experi-ence." The management of scapegoating is an issue of moment for every segment of the group work fraternity.

For the group worker whose particular concern is the social adaptation of the emotionally disturbed, however, all of this takes on particular ur-gency. He feels as do many psychiatrists that "the cure or adaptation of the mentally disturbed can only be accomplished in society . . . and a success-

222   *James A. Garland and Ralph L. Kolodny*

ful stay in society is the only real test of any real therapeutic endeavor."[2] He is concerned, like Peck, with bringing group work services to people like the young former patient with "the slightly 'schizy' personality . . . aiding him to rejoin a world to which he has never quite belonged."[3] But he also knows firsthand how difficult this is to achieve and the role that scapegoating plays in frustrating his designs.

Such a worker often ransacks the literature for help. Turning to social psychological formulations on scapegoating he finds Allport's notions concerning ethnic prejudices as a displacement arising out of a chain of frustration leading to aggression, suggestive of the genesis of "prejudice" toward those who are emotionally "different" in his own groups.[4] His thinking is illuminated by Allport's view of the scapegoat as a living ink blot upon whom are projected the repressed feelings of those who attack him and by Allport's comments on the masochistic elements in the scapegoat's personality.[5] In Bell and Vogel's observations of scapegoating in the small group that is the family, he finds a good deal that reminds him of what he encounters in his own age groups.[6] His understanding is deepened by their suggestion that the deviant within the group may perform a "valuable" function by channeling group tensions and by providing a basis for solidarity.[7] Their description of how disturbed parents support, usually implicitly, the persistence of the scapegoat's deviant behavior even while they are criticizing and punishing it leads him to examine whether group members act in similar fashion. In addition, he is prompted by their material to consider whether those who become group scapegoats have already been inducted into this role in their own families.

It would be rather too much, however, for the group worker to expect of theoretical material which explores the social and psychological roots of scapegoating that it blueprint for him the techniques for its management. He will find, for instance, one of the most extensive and insightful compendia of experimental research dealing with behaviors related to scapegoating in Berkowitz's volume on aggression.[8] If he anticipates finding clearcut treatment formulations, he will be disappointed. Most of the examples

2. A. Querido, quoted in John and Elaine Cumming, *Ego and Milieu* (New York, Atherton Press, 1956), p. 203.

3. Harris Peck, "A Group Process Approach to Mental Health Issues," in *The Mental Health Role of Settlement and Community Centers* (Swampscott Massachusetts Conference, 1963), p. 24.

4. Gordon Allport, *The Nature of Prejudice* (Cambridge, Mass., Addison-Wesley Publishing Co., 1954), pp. 343–92.

5. *Ibid.*

6. Ezra F. Vogel and Norman W. Bell, "The Emotionally Disturbed Child as the Family Scapegoat," in Bell and Vogel, eds., *A Modern Introduction to the Family* (New York, Free Press of Glencoe, 1960), pp. 382–97.

7. *Ibid.*, p. 382.

8. Leonard Berkowitz, *Aggression: a Social Psychological Analysis* (New York, McGraw-Hill, 1962).

presented are of ethnic-racial scapegoating, and the treatment proposals which emerge deal mostly with intergroup rather than intragroup relations. Even suggestions regarding management of the scapegoating of a minority by a majority group, however, might be transposed into intragroup action by the worker were it not for the fact that such suggestions are so hedged about with qualifications and so broadly stated as to render them less than helpful for practice. The last two paragraphs, for example, of Berkowitz's chapters, which deal with "displacement reactions" and "conflict condition," read as follows:

> Theoretically, the best way to decrease the likelihood of intragroup conflict is to lessen the occurrence of frustrations and to eliminate the gains that might be accrued through attacking other groups. From a more practical point of view, however, the wisest course is probably to try to block the generalization of frustration-created aggressive tendencies to more or less innocent groups. A number of procedures might be employed in pursuing such an aim. The easiest is to spread communications advocating peace and harmony. However, such communications would encounter a great deal of resistance if they aroused dissonance, i.e., if they opposed action to which the audience was heavily committed. Messages that attempt to persuade through creating fear are generally ineffective, perhaps because such communications are also dissonance provoking.
>
> Minimizing the perception of group differences might also lessen intergroup conflict, but research findings suggest that such hostility can be significantly reduced by demonstrating that the groups are interdependent if they are to cope with a common threat. Inability to overcome these threats heightens the intergroup conflict, however, if it is possible for each group to blame the other for failure. Equal status contacts between groups also lower intergroup enmity, particularly if informal social relationships are involved, but strong unfavorable attitudes toward the other group existing prior to the contact can prevent the development of friendships and may even increase the hostility by giving rise to perceived frustrations.[9]

More to the point, perhaps, when the practitioner narrows his search to material dealing with the actual handling of scapegoating by his colleagues he finds himself in even more difficult straits. Scapegoating per se is discussed only briefly in the group psychotherapy literature, and one finds the worker being cautioned that his attempt to do something about it may be largely a product of his own countertransference.[10] In the social group work literature, only rarely does one encounter a description of a worker soberly discussing a pattern of scapegoating behavior with a group. Perhaps one exception is to be found in Wineman's presentation on life-space inter-

9. *Ibid.*, pp. 194–95.
10. Leslie Rosenthal, "Countertransference in Activity Group Therapy," *International Journal of Group Psychotherapy*, III (1953), 436.

viewing.[11] Instead, he finds an isolated comment here and there, such as: "The irrationality and usually unconscious motivation of scapegoating makes work with it especially difficult."[12] This, of course, does not carry the worker very far. In the last analysis, in developing his own interventive techniques, he comes to rely largely on his own knowledge of behavioral dynamics and the accumulated experiences of colleagues.

Such a worker in the Group Work Department of Boston Children's Service Association, better known as the Department of Neighborhood Clubs, finds himself in the midst of a group of practitioners who expect to face this problem in their groups every day. The department's *raison d'être,* the integration of the alienated child with his "normal" peers, and its procedure of forming "normal" neighborhood groups around the children referred to it for treatment, make it almost certain that scapegoating will be a central issue in the department's practice. These workers, then, are inevitably pressed to engage in a continuous exchange on the subject of scapegoating.

At various points in the department's history these exchanges have been formalized and peer group supervisory sessions instituted on the matter of scapegoating. What follows is a distillation of the concepts and techniques advanced by department workers during the course of these sessions.

The patterned presentation of the results of their deliberations cannot really reflect the intensity and, at times, confusion of their self-questioning about scapegoating. Classification of behavioral nuances and their meanings and of management techniques is not easily achieved. It is not surprising that nowhere were we able to find a scheme for classifying either forms of scapegoating or types of targets, let alone notions about "handling." We hope that our efforts to outline such a scheme will stimulate further attempts at classification. Without classification, we clearly lack a necessary condition for planful treatment.

Function of the Scapegoat

The scapegoating phenomenon appears both on a person-to-person level and within the multirelationship context of the group. Although social group workers are primarily concerned with dealing with it in a group situation, we must establish our base first on the intrapsychic level to examine how individual needs and dynamics generate and feed the scapegoating process. Then it will be possible to understand better how various individual patterns are combined to create and in turn be affected by the interactional process and the structure of the group.

11. David Wineman, "The Life-Space Interview," *Social Work,* IV, No. 1 (1959), 10.

12. Gisela Konopka, *Social Group Work as a Helping Process* (Englewood Cliffs, N.J., Prentice-Hall, Inc., 1963), p. 58.

THE SCAPEGOAT

The most commonly observed characteristic of the scapegoat is his inability to deal with aggression. A strong passive and masochistic mode is usually evident; uncomfortable with, or inept at, direct expression of his own angry feelings or burdened with guilt, the potential scapegoat finds it necessary to seek ridicule or rejection from others. He may act like a sponge, passively soaking up punishment, thereby maintaining his psychic equilibrium with negative outside support. On the other hand, there is the justification approach wherein the scapegoat must first provoke attack, thus externalizing responsibility for aggression and absolving himself of blame for his subsequent counterhostility. Whether or not the scapegoat's need is basically for atonement and confirmation that the outside is "bad," he requires the collaboration of his persecutor, and uses a variety of techniques to insure it.

Three principal facts lend credence to the idea that assumption of the persecutee's role is often purposeful. First, the individual tends to put himself into contact with situations, persons, and interpersonal sets which are easily definable by inspection or by history as injurious to him in a manner that is repetitive and gives no evidence of adaptive learning. As a matter of fact, he often intensifies his provocation or stays progressively longer in the dangerous situation, which may build to a crescendo of abuse. A case in point is a youngster in a group of six adolescent boys who week after week insisted on walking in an apparently unconcerned manner on the group's clean tumbling mat while wearing dirty shoes. This brought increasing abuse from the other members and finally physical attack, although the only observable change in the boy's behavior was a more dogged facial expression as he plodded fatalistically to the slaughter.

The second phenomenon frequently observed is that the scapegoat denies the existence of any pattern of persecution or that he is seeking it. Failing this, he may deny that there is any negative change, particularly on his part, in what is going on: "I was just fooling around." "The other guys don't mean anything by it." "I don't really mind if they don't like me."

The third test of purposefulness is that if the scapegoat admits that the situation is bad, he insists that it is beyond his control and hopeless. He may employ projection ("They always start it"), resignation ("Nothing will make them like me"), or helplessness ("I've tried to defend myself, but I just can't fight back"). All of these may be seen as defenses against altering the attack pattern, particularly if they are associated with no attempt to deal constructively with the situation or if they resolve into attempts that are repeated stereotypically long after they are obviously ineffective.

There are at least four other distinguishable types of vulnerability that may result in scapegoating action and which may not be purposefully provocative on the part of the scapegoat.

1. The first of these is confused sexual identity. We single this out because it appears so frequently and strongly in groups in American culture, particularly among males. Also, it appears to be associated with, and conditioned by—in terms of whether or not it provokes attack—the aggression factor. That is to say, in both male and female groups an individual who is confused in his sexual identity typically escapes attack if he is able to be actively aggressive in dealing with other group members or is a good manipulator in controlling group and individual interactions (particularly in employing diversionary techniques). In this respect, the identity variable is more problematic in male groups; an undefended feminine orientation is typically passive and susceptible to attack in addition to the fact that it arouses the fear of homosexual involvement. We note also that in most cases in male groups where attacks are based on sexual identity problems, there is a component of masochism on the scapegoat's part which brings about purposeful provocation. In this sense, the syndrome is directly related to the aggression-based scapegoating.

2. Second is an attempt at adjustment that evokes an unexpected negative reaction, a rider which is tolerated as a price for gratification of the original need. We might label this "secondary pain." The obese woman who craves acceptance from others in her group may go along cheerfully with humorous gibes about her size in exchange for the attention she gets in the process. This may be despite the fact that she does not get masochistic gratification from the gibes and may be made quite uncomfortable by them.

3. The third nonpurposeful persecution situation pertains where the individual is vulnerable by reason of a poorly organized or insufficient aggressive drive. Persons who make erratic, inappropriate, or ineffective forays against their peers provoke counterattack, albeit unintentionally; they are fair and tempting game for ridicule, domination, and exploitation. We might label this the "piranha syndrome." Falling into this general maladaptive mode as well are individuals whose energy is minimally or sporadically invested in others by reason of depression or schizoid withdrawal. Their mutism provokes the anxiety of others, and their ineffectiveness or passivity makes them in most cases easy prey.

4. Related to this latter class are the various types of unorthodoxy. We would apply here the concept of visibility; whether intentionally or not the person is identifiable in manner or appearance as being different. This difference may be on a cultural level; for example, a youngster may wear a yarmulke to his group. Physical appearance, such as skin color, obesity, physical deformity, may provide a target. Bizarre behavior is the most frequent target in social work and psychotherapeutic groups.

THE SCAPEGOATER

Here too we find a frequent element of purposefulness, a seeking out of a compatible object—in this instance, one that can be attacked. Indeed, the origin of the term is found in the ancient Hebrew practice of selecting once a year a goat upon whose head the sins and troubles of the people were symbolically laid.[13] The goat was driven into the wilderness, relieving the people, at least for a time, of their accumulated guilt and shortcomings. On an individual level, as we all know, people often have a need to get rid of impulses and self-perceptions which are guilt-producing or inimical to self-esteem. Where simple denial does not suffice and where other defensive maneuvers are not successful in maintaining psychic comfort, projection of ego-alien drives and characteristics onto another person may prove to be a rather convenient and satisfying operation. Bad, dirty, greedy, stupid, angry, weak, deformed, or dependent qualities of the self can be blamed on a visible and often acquiescent target. At the same time, punishment and ridicule of the scapegoat for his imputed badness provide vicarious relief for the guilt associated with the attacker's projected badness. Incidentally, the attacker may derive considerable secondary guilt-free gratification of hostile drives in the process. This latter phenomenon is noted particularly in persons who have strong moral tenets about being "good" but seem to find themselves continually confronted with evil which evokes their righteous indignation and wrath.

The other side of the coin is that, in addition to the need to reject and scorn these bad parts, the scapegoater usually wishes also to preserve, even cherish them. This cherishing becomes easier when the undesirable trait—and the onus—is figuratively riding on another person's back. Thus, the scapegoat may be both despised and loved, sometimes alternately, sometimes simultaneously. The former is typified in the Christ figure who is vilified and killed—and the blame for this is often fixed on "others"—then subsequently restored miraculously and deified. In this connection we note that the religious sacrifice is almost universally selected on the basis of his freedom from blemish, as an ideal representative of his species. Similarly, the scapegoater's use of the group clown or mascot shows his need to debase and dominate the ineffective, comical, or odd object and, at the same time, his desire to protect, preserve, and enjoy him. The loved scapegoat is seen most clearly in families where one member is identified as the "sick one" and is cuddled and catered to. Hostile feelings toward the sick relative may be denied vehemently even as his condition continues to deteriorate.[14] Conversely, all of us who have worked with groups have noted the extreme disappointment expressed by an overbearing group member when his punching bag fails to attend a meeting.

The second major dimension of the scapegoater's need is displacement. Since this includes the involvement of a third party—and note that we are moving from intrapsychic to diadid to group focus—we may say that external variables play a larger role in the process than in the case of projec-

13. Leviticus, Chap. 16.
14. Vogel and Bell, *op. cit.*

tion. It assumes basically two forms: displacement proper and deflection. For our purposes, we think of displacement as the psychic maneuver whereby the scapegoater, unable openly and consciously to express negative feelings toward another person (group member or worker) because of his affection for, or fear of, him, splits his ambivalence and selects a third person (or persons), the scapegoat, to heap scorn onto. The selection may be determined by the visibility-vulnerability factor, or it may be related as well to an association factor, the similarities between the avoided object and the attacked one. Similarity may be defined not only on the basis of physical appearance, cultural background, behavior, and the like, but in terms of group role, even special proximity. We are reminded of how often the member who is seated next to the worker is attacked by other members; sometimes out of jealousy, to be sure, but often as a target close enough to the power figure to satisfy but a lot safer.

Deflection may be thought of as a diversionary technique and is commonly associated with the familiar phenomenon of the pecking order. The individual, in order to avoid attacks from his peers, or in order to preserve his position in the group hierarchy, attempts by labeling as undesirable something pertaining to his victim or by attacking him to induce others to attack or devalue the person. This finger-pointing operates with varying degrees of complexity and subtlety. At times it may be as obvious as saying, "So what if I struck out three times? That dope Harry forgot to touch the bag when he rounded third." It is traditionally recognized that the low-status person often attempts to find a group member even lower on the totem pole onto whom attack can be deflected; the scene of a group enjoying a fight between the two bottom echelon members is a familiar one. Less recognized but fairly prevalent are the adroit manipulations engaged in by high-status persons as they juggle staff positions and personnel in order to preserve or improve their own status. Note in this regard the tendency in some social systems for persons in authority to surround themselves with associates who are censurable or dischargeable in times of crisis or dissension. It is interesting, for example, that the assistant principal of a high school is often assigned the role of disciplinarian, and thus becomes the major target of anger for students and parents.

CONGRUENCE OF TARGET QUALITIES
AND ATTACKER'S NEEDS

Other variables or interpersonal sets which in correct combination tend to produce scapegoating are such things as age, sex, and certain conditions of cultural, psychic, and physical stress: latency age boys attacking an effeminate boy; adolescents ridiculing peers who dress "differently" or who have physical peculiarities; adult cerebral palsied groups characterizing paralytic polio victims as "pushy"; psychiatric patients attacking bizarre or "sick" behavior on the part of a fellow patient; Negroes applying derisive labels to fellow Negroes with darker skin or kinky hair. These conditions may intensify, diffuse, or change focus with time, growth, or alteration in extra-group conditions.

The Group Dynamic

As we have said, both individual and collective needs are met through the process of scapegoating, and it may function in the establishment and maintenance of group stability.

GROUP EQUILIBRIUM

At the risk of being accused of oversimplification, we see an analogy between the psyche's need to preserve its integrity by maintaining a balance among conflicting internal drives and the group's need to do the same, albeit on a vastly more complex level. The network of interpersonal relationships which serves the needs of the group members presumes among other things a balancing between unifying positive and divisive negative affects. Where the equilibrium is threatened, so may be the ability of the system to meet personal needs. One means for keeping the system in balance is to find an object external or internal to the group onto which disequilibrating tensions can be displaced.

FOCUS AND LOCUS

What kinds of problems, tensions, and images are inimical to the group and where or to whom are they affixed? Examples of problems and tensions which provide a focus for scapegoating are: fear of entering into a group; anger toward, or fear of, the worker's power; fear of having weakness exposed; anxiety over affectionate feelings toward others; and interpersonal power arrangements. Locus dimensions are virtually endless and elaborate geometrically as group numbers and outside influences increase. The most familiar locus for scapegoating, of course, is the group as a whole picking on one member. However, if one accepts projection and displacement as basic mechanisms operating in scapegoating, it is easy to visualize a locus paradigm including the ordinates of member, subgroup, total group, worker, and outsiders, and predict all the combinations possible. We note, for example, how often in very cohesive groups potentially divisive and antisocial sentiments are displaced and projected onto a rival group, a nationality, "them," or the devil. Similarly, workers are familiar with subgroup scapegoating subgroup.

Once again, congruence of focus and locus determines to a large extent the efficacy of the scapegoat maneuver as a group-preserving technique. That is to say, if the focus of concern of the group is fear of physical awkwardness and there happens to be a particularly awkward youngster in the group, he is likely to be the locus of strong and consistent scapegoating, and considerable efforts to preserve him in this role may be exerted, even to the point of giving him subtle rewards to insure that he does not buckle under the pressure and quit the group. The converse of this situation, of particular interest to those who are involved in promoting the inclusion of the deviant or isolated child in the normal group or community, is that the character of the deviant's pathology may determine the area or focus of scapegoating and actually influence the tone of the total group experience.

The Individual Scapegoat and the Group

When considering the range of relationship patterns which develop between the individual scapegoat and the group, their effectiveness for all concerned, and their relevance for therapeutic intervention some typical sets may be delineated.

OSTRACISM

Driving out the symbol of what is distasteful or threatening to the group equilibrium and image may be only temporarily functional. Unless the memory of the excluded member can be effectively preserved and used, it may soon become necessary to find a new scapegoat. We note that recalling the faults of the former member becomes increasingly difficult and, without some attending ritual (such as a humorous song elaborating his failings) or material symbol (perhaps a picture or personal possession), tends to lose its power to satisfy or relieve projective needs. The only exceptions to this condition are found where the disparity between group and scapegoat is so great as to make continued association on any basis intolerable, and where the group subsequently finds another outlet for its tension or another means to resolve its intragroup problem.

INSTITUTIONALIZATION

A permanent place is made for the scapegoat in the dynamic equilibrium of the group. Pain inflicted on the victim is balanced carefully by social, emotional, or material reward. Easily identifiable examples of this arrangement are the perpetual club buffoon, the grateful errand runner, the team mascot, and so on. Sadomasochism may on the characterological level provide an important underpinning in this *modus vivendi*. Intervention potential in these cases is low, and the group equilibrium tends to be static with little flexibility in roles and little individual or group growth evident.

ENCAPSULATION

In this process the deviant is isolated within the group. In relation to the emotional structure of the group, he is a satellite, held suspended by the gravitational force of the worker on the periphery of the interactional network. This is a tolerable and often stable arrangement, particularly when the potential scapegoat is nonprovocative or emotionally detached. The group's guilt and sense of responsibility are satisfied. The deviant's needs are minimally met. Interaction and mutual threat are minimized so long as distance is maintained and no new pressures enter the system.

INTROSPECTIVE INCLUSION

Attack includes active examination of what makes the deviant "tick" and is usually followed by self-examination. This represents a movement away from the previous three static positions, and one notes attempts on the part of scapegoaters to get reactions from the scapegoat. A desire to understand the victim's behavior usually indicates a willingness to identify with him and examine one's own problems.

The Changing Character of Scapegoating

The focus and locus of scapegoating may change as various group developmental tasks and crises are encountered.[15] Examples of this are: rejecting the member who demands a great deal of closeness during the preaffiliation stage; picking on the member who appears physically weak or inept during the power and control stage; ridiculing the member who is most dependent or jealous during the intimacy stage. In the fourth stage of differentiation or cohesion, intragroup scapegoating should be at a minimum, although it is not uncommon for group members to emphasize at this time the inferiority of other groups. In the stage of separation, previous scapegoating themes and targets are likely to recur, sometimes in rapid and rather random succession. Also, members who indicate pleasure over the group's termination are liable to attack for rather obvious reasons.

Intensification of scapegoating or change in its quality or direction often presages developmental shifts or crises.

Similarly, we expect that scapegoating will generally decrease in intensity and frequency and that anger as well as affection will be more evenly shared among members as developmental plateaus are reached and as the group matures.

Reversing the Scapegoating Pattern

There are general conditions that operate for and against healthy resolution.

15. The concept of group development upon which these remarks are based is from James A. Garland *et al.,* "A Model for Stages of Development in Social Work Groups," in Saul Bernstein, ed., *Explorations in Group Work* (Boston, Boston University School of Social Work, 1965), pp. 12–53. Five sequential stages are proposed: preaffiliation, power and control, intimacy, differentiation, and separation.

As is true in reversing most pathological patterns of adjustment, one must consider first the satisfaction that sickness provides. We have indicated how both attacker and scapegoat derive mutually reinforcing gratifications from their sadomasochistic contract. Second, when hierarchical pecking orders are involved, investment in self-protection adds further psychic cement to the compact. Third, the defense of denial seems to be particularly difficult to penetrate. We have referred to the frequent assertions on the part of the scapegoat that "it doesn't hurt." Attackers, often in concert insist that the scapegoat "doesn't mind it" or that "we're only fooling." Fear of identifying consciously with the scapegoat or of being compared with him also makes it necessary to deny that he has feelings or that he is like "other people." Finally, outside pressures (family tensions, community threats, academic failure) not subject to alteration or diminution by the worker or group may provide continued impetus for preservation of the *status quo*.

One could make some naïve but basic assumptions:

1. In refutation of our previous point, preservation of the myth of the scapegoat's insensitivity and inhumanity becomes difficult when it is exposed to rational examination. As attack intensifies, it becomes difficult for the target not to admit pain at some point, or for attackers, when confronted, to maintain their position indefinitely.

2. Moral values of most people create pressure against "picking on people."

3. The multiplicity of group relationships offers diffusion and deintensification of both positive and negative cathexes; emotional escape hatches, so to speak. Note, for example, how often in adolescent groups "ragging" or "cutting down" directed at one youngster turns into a general humorous session where everyone gets his knocks in turn. With effective manipulation by the worker, displacement and deflection may be employed to break up pathological patterns as well as to preserve them.

4. There is an inherent propensity for change and growth in most individuals and groups.

5. There is also a tendency toward cumulative causation, for change to feed itself. As the deviant begins to act more appropriately, others tend to fear him less, accept him more. He, in turn, may respond to their approval, make attempts toward *rapprochement,* and so on. Strategic factors in this reversal process include: (a) choosing points of leverage in the system; (b) choosing appropriate techniques; and (c) timing and pacing.

How do we go about resolving the problem of scapegoating? There is a range of possible interventions.

SQUASHING

Scapegoating behavior may be stopped by moral sanction and threats and permitting no other consideration. This is probably undesirable on ethical grounds and unsuccessful practically. It frequently involves counterscape-goating on the part of the worker as he, the "stronger," imposes his will on the members, the "weaker," drives the problem underground, and invites battle.

COMPOSITION

While at first glance it might seem safer to pair the potential scapegoat with "healthy" peers, experience indicates that where there is little basis for mutual identification, we can hope for only an encapsulation or satel-lite arrangement. More successful in the long run, though initially more productive of strife, is the practice of involving other members who, while "healthier" than he, are not so dissimilar from the deviant in emotional ma-turity and achievement level as to prevent empathy and who at the same time represent desirable models for emulation.

GIVING INFORMATION

Information regarding the deviant's behavior prior to the group's begin-ning may be helpful. At the Department of Neighborhood Clubs, the prac-tice has been to give data both to parents and children regarding certain parts of the background of a disturbed child referred to a club and the be-havior that can be expected of him. The prediction that the normal mem-bers may react more positively to the child if he is disguised as "one of the gang" usually proves to be wishful thinking on the part of the group worker and may indicate as well a measure of denial. More often than not, when information is given, there is some initial shock and anxiety dis-played by the parents and children followed by curiosity and then by the revelation of some of the problems they themselves are having. Thus, in formed therapeutic groups, the stage may be set to preclude scapegoat for-mation by dispelling confusion and myths about the deviant member's be-havior and a progressive diminishing of the fear that their own problems are shameful or ununderstandable or must be hidden. We know that this initial information tends to be forgotten for defensive reasons for the initial period of group association and at times may even exacerbate scapegoat-ing for a while. However, in general, both denial and acting-out are signifi-cantly diminished, and the stage is set for open exploration of feelings and behavior of the normal members as well as of the deviant.

PROTECTION

The worker should intervene to prevent physical or psychic harm to the scapegoat or loss of control, especially during the time when power and control issues are most dominant. On the other hand, continual defense of the scapegoat to the exclusion of interaction may result in counterscape-goating (and countertransference) at worst and satellite formation at best. It is on this issue that the worker must be most nonjudgmental and, where possible, benign. He should be solicitous of the needs and fears of the members who are doing the attacking, even in the face of denials on their part that the problem has anything to do with them.

DIVERSION

Finding another outlet, either through physical activity (bowling, chasing grasshoppers) or by using another person as the target offers a diversion. The latter may be the worker himself (who is often, underneath it all, the "real" target) or, at times, generalized "outsiders." Usually picking on non-present teachers, political undesirables, or foreign devils is only temporarily helpful, for the anger quite soon moves closer and closer to the group itself.

REDUCING INTERACTION

This includes providing structure or activity to cut down contagion, stopping meetings to provide a cooling-off period, or limiting their length to preclude blow-ups.

EGO SUPPORT

Via skill training, feeding, and so on, ego support may be provided. Making attackers more secure, stronger and less in need of "pecking" is probably the single most important long-range strategy since, as we have indicated, projection and displacement occur most in situations where the ego feels powerless to deal with issues of autonomy and competence. Workers are tempted to throw their energies into dealing with obvious attack phenomena and to protect the underdog. What is needed is confidence on the part of the worker to intervene instead into the background issue of bolstering self-confidence through help in developing activity skills or acquiring autonomy through making decisions about group affairs.

An alternative is to make the scapegoat hardier, more competent in his own eyes and in the eyes of the group. This may include, for example, some extragroup practice in achieving skill in a high-status activity (guitar playing in an adolescent group) or in an aggressive activity, which may have implications for his ability to defend himself from attack or to bear up under the normal wear and tear of group life.

CLARIFICATION

The technique of clarification has to do with direct identification of behavior and its meanings on the conscious and preconscious level. Depending on what the group is ready for, the clarification may be accomplished with progressive specificity, directness, and depth. For example, the following comments may be made in response to provocation by the scapegoat and attack by the group: "Guys get excited sometimes." "We seem to be excited." "What do you think of Joe?" "Why do you think he acts that way?" "What is is that he does that upsets you?" "Aren't we all worried about this problem?" Where possible, the worker should identify the real source and target of the anger: help the group to recognize and express their anger at the worker for being late which has been repressed and displaced onto a member. This general area should include building up a repertoire of labels for affect-laden situations and important relationships. We note phrases which have special meaning to the collective life of the members, such as: "Al's gettin' itchy again." "We're picking substitutes again." "Don't pull a cover-up."

ALLOWING SCAPEGOATING TO FLOWER

In bringing the scapegoating into sharp focus and allowing clarification of underlying emotions, the group worker must be sure of his ground and of the limits of the controls of the group members. He must also be aware of his own countertransferences, lest he throw the scapegoat "to the wolves." On the other hand, this approach has the value of not distorting or watering down interaction.

HELPING THE GROUP TO CONTROL THE SCAPEGOAT'S BEHAVIOR

When the group appears ready, the worker should transfer to them the objective control of the deviant's inappropriate behavior. This presumes a generally positive relationship and mutual identification between scapegoat and group. Assurance on the part of the group that they can exert some control over the scapegoat's upsetting or frightening behavior may increase their positive feeling for him and free the worker from the role of overprotective parent. Also, reality testing on the part of the deviant is likely to be more successfully accomplished when confrontation proceeds from supportive peers than when it is associated with the worker.

PLAYING OUT THE SCAPEGOAT PROCESS

As is true with all interpersonal relationships, scapegoating can be acted out symbolically through "it" games, chasing, secret-keeping, aggressive competition, and conscious role-playing. Affording opportunities for experimentation with a variety of attitudes and feelings in a safe, nonretaliatory make-believe fashion provides release and diffusion of emotions, reality testing, social skill development, and sublimation, and induces empathy and identification.

REMOVAL OF THE SCAPEGOAT

Realizing the limits of tolerance and potential for identification and growth, temporary or permanent removal of the scapegoat must be considered. In this event, care should be exercised to explore feelings of guilt and fantasies that the group may have about what they have done to the scapegoat. He on his part will require help with his feelings of badness, failure, or omnipotence. This is a drastic measure, and the possibility of reforming a whole group for the nonreferred members as well as for the deviant youngster should be kept in mind.

Close observation and experimentation with these and other methods are needed to achieve better understanding and control of the pervasive and disturbing phenomenon of scapegoating.

19. The Life-Space Interview
DAVID WINEMAN

The present article describes an interview approach—the life-space interview—originated by Fritz Redl under specific conditions of practice with ego-disturbed children—and contrasts it with traditional interview techniques found in clinical social work practice.

The greatest single influence on the interview method in clinical social work has come, of course, from classical psychoanalytic treatment practice. *Content* most eagerly sought by the classical therapist is that which refers to the libidinal relationship to the parents and siblings of the client, on both conscious and unconscious levels. Interview *relationship and role structure* are most carefully guarded against contamination from either the therapist's or client's ongoing life experiences; neither the therapist nor the client may have such ties with each other as could involve either or both with the opportunity for gratification of the other or direct power over each other's behavior away from the interview setting. Finally, the *time-space conditions* under which all clinical events take place are strictly defined in an appointment hour (time) and in the therapist's office (space).

The original psychoanalytic model from which this is borrowed is best suited, and was originally developed clinically, for the classical adult neurotic. Although complexly disturbed, he sacrifices the least of his ego to his illness, as compared with other disturbance syndromes, and his principal *ego strain* is experienced in connection with his specific conflicts, leaving him free to cope with most other adjustive tasks in a normal way. How-

Reprinted with permission of the National Association of Social Workers from *Social Work,* Vol. 4, No. 1 (January, 1959), pp. 3–17.

ever, when we come to the child neurotic, things are a little different—even with the "classical" child neurotic. Redl[1] reminds us that Anna Freud herself explicitly recognized that certain modifications of adult therapy techniques were necessary because of the incompleteness in ego development and the nature of the child's relationship to the adult world. These modifications raised the ceiling on how far the therapist could directly invade libidinal, reality, and value spheres, as compared with adult therapy. Thus, one of Miss Freud's girl patients was seriously advised by her that while it was perfectly all right to use obscene language in telling her fantasies to Miss Freud, this was "out" anywhere else. Specific directions and suggestions of a management or training type could be made to parents. On the gratification level, candy bars, soft drinks, and cookies are far from infrequent in orthodox therapy with children of less than pubertal age.

Yet, in spite of these shifts toward more involvement in the libidinal, reality, or value zones of the child's life, classical child therapy—casework or psychoanalytic—sticks with *content* focus on libidinal materials of a historically determined type, becomes involved in ongoing reality areas only to "save" the therapy from oblivion, and, while permitting gratifications to the child, holds these down to the bare minimum required to involve the child in a relationship. Also the classical *space-time* condition of the office appointment is preserved.

So much for a brief structural analysis of the "classical" interview concept and its modifications for work with children. Now let us examine the origin and development of the "life-space" concept which in some ways only carries further the modifications begun by Anna Freud, and in others is clearly different along qualitative lines.

Life-Space Concept

In the early 1940's, Fritz Redl was operating both summer camp and winter club groups in the city for severely ego-disturbed children, who had been referred by various Detroit social agencies with whom the children were simultaneously in individual therapy. As experience accumulated in these projects, it was noticed that frequently a child might produce behavior (temper tantrums, swiftly appearing sulks and withdrawals, stealing, fighting) that required on-the-spot handling of an interview-like type, the responsibility for which was assumed by the adult in charge, usually a group worker or a group work-field work student. Upon analysis, the types of interviews[2] that grew out of this proved to hold a technical com-

1. Fritz Redl, "Strategy and Techniques of the Life-Space Interview," *American Journal of Orthopsychiatry,* Vol. 28, No. 1 (January 1959).
2. Redl first used the term "marginal" instead of "life space" for these interviews. The reasons for this shift are interesting but not crucial to this paper. One reason, as Redl wryly puts it: "The term 'marginal' lost the clarity of its meaning besides the low-status meaning the term 'marginal' seems to hold for some people."

plexity and meaning that any good casework or psychiatric interview might have, even though the locus of interview was much more a part of the *life-space* of the child, its content released by a piece of unplanned *life-space* dynamics and was being performed by an *"out-of-role" person who had direct life-experiential meaning for the child on reality, value, and libidinal terms*. Thus, while the classical approach would specify that reality issues should be handled only when they endanger therapy, the life-space approach would insist that with severely ego-damaged children they provide some necessary materials without which therapy could not go on. Yet–and this is important–it does not argue that traditional methods cannot also be of powerful assistance and readily concedes that both methods can be applied in the service of therapy with the same child. Thus, for instance, many of the episodes that were the target of life-space interviewing in the club groups were also picked up by the agency therapist later on, either being brought in by the child himself or raised by the worker who was always in communication with the project leader.

Beginning in this way, the life-space approach was further experimented with at Pioneer House (1946–48),[3] a residential treatment home for boys, at the children's ward and residence at National Institute of Mental Health in Bethesda (1953–present),[4] and at the University of Michigan Fresh Air Camp, a summer camp for disturbed boys (1950–present)[5] from which setting the clinical material for the present paper is drawn.

Goals, Tasks, and Levels of Function

The type of child around whose treatment life-space interviewing has been developed finds it virtually impossible to manage himself for a single day without the eruption of behavioral episodes representing in one way or another his disturbances in ego functioning. In this section we shall try to examine the ways in which these episodes may be used by the clinician as potential content for life-space interviewing, and the kinds of goals, tasks, and levels of function that have been tentatively worked out for this style

3. Fritz Redl and David Wineman, *Controls from Within* (Glencoe, Ill.: The Free Press, 1951).

4. Fritz Redl, "Strategy and Techniques of the Life Space Interview," *op. cit.*

Joel Vernick, "Illustrations of Strategy Problems in Life Space Interviewing Around Situations of Behavioral Crises," paper presented at the 1957 Annual Meeting of the American Orthopsychiatric Association.

Allen T. Dittmann and Howard L. Kitchener, "Life Space Interviewing and Individual Play Therapy: A Comparison of Techniques," *American Journal of Orthopsychiatry*, Vol. 29, No. 1 (January 1959).

William C. Morse and Edna R. Small, "Group Life Space Interviewing in a Therapeutic Camp," *American Journal of Orthopsychiatry*, Vol. 29, No. 1 (January 1959).

5. William Morse and David Wineman, "Group Interviewing in a Camp for Disturbed Boys," *The Journal of Social Issues*, Vol. 13, No. 1 (1957). Also, for the interested, this issue carries several articles on the University of Michigan camp and its operation.

of interview. As an opening illustration, let us take a look at Ricki,[6] one of our last season's Fresh Air campers in one of his "bad" moments.

> Ricki, an 11-year-old boy with a chain-style history of broken foster home placements, was a terribly deprived, bitter child with an insatiable, violent hunger for proofs of affection from the adult and an equally intense expectation of treachery and deceit. Imagine, then, his reaction when one day, after an acrimonious dispute between himself and another camper over the ownership of a walking cane which had been made in the camp craft shop, the facts supported the other child and we had to take the cane from Ricki and give it to the other youngster. He blew up immediately, had to be physically prevented from slugging the other boy, accused us of being in league with the other boy, and so on.

At the point of eruption of this "symptomatic" behavior, the adult on the scene will have to decide in which of two basic directions Ricki's interview handling should go:

1. He may simply try to "pull him through" the behavioral storm and sit it out with him until he is controlled enough to go about his regular business of life at camp. In addition to this protective waiting it out with him, we would also try to take the edge off his suspicion about our being in "cahoots" with the other boy by going over the facts again of how the mixup in the craft shop had occurred so that the other boy's cane had been mistakenly given to Ricki. And we would display our eagerness for him to have a cane by offering immediately to detail a staff member to help him start a new one, thus alleviating his frustration in having to wait until the next morning when the craft shop would be open again.

2. Our on-the-scene adult, instead of merely sitting it out with Ricki and getting him started on a new walking cane, might see this as a good opportunity to pick up this particular blow-up (which was a repetition of many that Ricki had already had) as a typical instance of his "problem," point out that this was the way he reacted *whenever* things didn't go the way he wanted them to, that we knew that even back in the foster homes he had these blow-ups, and so on. In other words, in Step 2 the adult tries to use this situation toward the realization of a long-range clinical "improvement goal." (Actually in this case we went only as far as Step 1 because Ricki was still too confused about himself and his problems to have enough "uninfected ego" on tap for use in picking up a useful perception of any part of the self in relation to a long-range goal.)

Redl has given these two major uses of the life-space interview characteristically descriptive titles.[7] Simply pulling a child through a tough spot (our Step 1) he calls "emotional first aid on the spot." If, in addition, the

6. All campers' names are pseudonyms.
7. Fritz Redl, "Strategy and Techniques of the Life Space Interview," *op. cit.*

incident is tactically aimed at the long-range goal (our Step 2) he calls it
"clinical exploitation of life events." However, the dichotomy is anything
but a tight one. Not infrequently, there may be a coupling of the two functions or a switch midstream in the interview. Following the dichotomy
with this warning in mind, let us now examine some of the subfunctions of
these two basic functions.

Clinical Exploitation of Life Events

Clinical "exploitation"[8] is a broad term. A clinical goal, upon inspection,
becomes a network of subgoals or tasks which therapy is trying to achieve.
Interviews along the way serve now one, now another, of these subgoals.
In the category under discussion, the following separate subheadings are
aimed at demonstrating this discreteness of function in the life-space interview.

REALITY "RUB-IN"

Many ego-damaged children are perceptually confused as to what goes on
around them either because they have already woven together a "delusional"[9] system of life interpretation or because they suffer from a peculiar
"drag" of a structural type in their ego development. In either case, many
times they don't seem to "get the hang" of a social interaction web unless
one puts it together for them with the special magnification aids of the "on-
the-spot" style of interview.

> Hank, 8½, is removed from his cabin at bedtime in screaming, hitting
> rage, having already socked his counselor twice in the side. "She didn't have
> no right to flip me on the floor," he yells, as we take him to the main lodge
> of the camp, giving in this way his rationale for hitting her. In the lodge, he
> sits broodingly in a thirty-minute sulk before he will say anything at all, while
> the counselor and I sit with him, the latter having been relieved by another
> staff member so she can stay with Hank and me. As his rage drains out and
> in response to our encouragement, he blurts out again, "She didn't have to
> flip me to the floor!" Then commenced a four-way interview between Hank,
> Lorie (the counselor), myself, and Dr. Albert Cohen, the camp sociologist.[10]

8. Throughout this article I am following the nomenclature of the life-space interview and its major as well as subfunctions originated by Redl and appearing in his
article "Strategy and Techniques of the Life-Space Interview," *op. cit.*, and also, in
part, in our joint volume, *Controls from Within, op. cit.*

9. The term "delusional" is used to connote a kind of persistent, perceptual distortion of a somewhat persecutory type which is frequently found in impulse-disor-
dered children. Since, however, many of them have really been badly handled by the
adult world, this is not classically paranoid. Yet in treating the "good" adult as
though he were the same as the "bad," they commit a delusional error.

10. All examples are drawn from the University of Michigan Fresh Air Camp
experience of 1958. In each instance the writer was the interviewer except where
otherwise specified. Each interview sample is the product of postinterview "selective"
recall. Both individual and group interviews are included and will be identified as such.

Lorie: (*replying to Hank's statement that she "flipped" him*) This is not the way it really happened, Hank. Remember you've been jumping on me, poking me, and pulling on me most of the afternoon and evening.

Hank: (*somewhat defiantly but smiling a little*) Aw, that was just in fun. You didn't even care about *that*.

Lorie: I asked you to stop many times.

Hank: Well, yeah, but you really didn't care though.

Cohen: Hank, let's talk about what happened in the cabin tonight. Here was Lorie trying to get you guys to bed—right?

Hank: Right.

Cohen: And what were you doing?

Hank: I was holdin' on to her.

Cohen: How?

Hank: I was grabbin' her around the middle from behind. I had my arms around hers (*pinning her arms*).

Cohen: And Lorie is busy trying to help the other guys get ready for bed.

Hank: Yeah.

Cohen: And the other guys may need things that she has to get or want her to do some things for them, too.

Hank: Yeah.

Cohen: Lorie is tired and she's been asking you to quit jumping on her most of the afternoon and evening but you're still grabbing her and won't let her go.

Hank: Guess so—but she didn't have to flip me.

Cohen: Did she *ask* you to let her go?

Hank: Yeah.

Cohen: How many times?

Hank: Three or four.

Cohen: So she *asks* you to let go. But you keep hanging on to her. Now, (*gently and emphatically*) she's asked you many times but you still hang on. She wants you to let go because she is tired of all the jumping and hanging on and has all these things to do which she can't because you're dragging on her. What do you think she should do?

Hank: Dunno.

Cohen: She has to get loose, doesn't she?

Hank: Guess so.

Cohen: So she spreads her arms forcing you to let go—right?

Hank: Yes.

Cohen: Could she have done it any other way?

Hank: (*without anger and quite readily*) No—guess not.

Wineman: Then you fell to the cabin floor?

Hank: Yeah.

Wineman: Then what happened?

Hank: The kids laughed and I got mad.

Wineman: I guess we can all see that that would be hard to take. And then?

Hank: I socked Lorie.

Wineman: Hank, right after you socked Lorie, how did you expect she felt toward you?

Hank: Sore at me.

Wineman: And because you thought she was sore at you, what else did you think about her and you?

Hank: That she wouldn't like me.

Wineman: And then?

Hank: I got mad all over again.

Wineman: And then?

Hank: I socked her again.

Wineman: That's about when I came into the cabin, isn't it? (*He nods.*) And she was havin' to hold you because you were so sore. Then I took you over here and at first you were still so sore you wouldn't talk or anything and still kept thinking that she had tried to flip you on purpose—right?

Hank: Yeah. (*By now he is smiling rather brightly; his mood has changed from sullen and defiant to cheerful agreement; actually he seems to enjoy the careful emphatic unraveling of the episode.*)

At this point, it seems that Hank has a much clearer perception of his own role in the production of the cabin situation and the "flip" by Lorie. At first he sees her as an aggravator and rejector, blots out entirely his own persistent, somewhat erotic, pestering of her and his blocking of her carrying out of her duties in the cabin in relation to the whole group. This series of perceptions is the target of the first part of the interview. Next he sees that the group reaction to his unfortunate fall "burns him up" and grasps the relation between this and slugging the counselor the first time. Finally, he understands that once he has "socked her" he expects retaliation from her in the form of rejection (Note: He does not expect to get "socked" in return, showing his basically *correct* understanding of our policy against physical punishment). This, he sees, makes him even more angry *so he hits her again.* Then comes the finale in the lodge.

In terms of *goal,* this type of interview is both short-range and long-range in its intent: short-range, we want to help Hank stop mauling the counselor *as soon as possible.* Long-range, through the "injection" of many such interview episodes, we want him (1) to become more habituated and skilled in self-observation and (2) to step up his sensitivity to the feelings and emotions of people upon whom he is acting in an interpersonal chain. Hank's postinterview behavior in relation to this single item—mauling the counselor—improved, by the way, so that the short-range goal can be said to have been achieved. Obviously, as stated, only multiple exposure can attack the long-range problem but this may be seen as a link along the way.

SYMPTOM ESTRANGEMENT

Another characteristic of the children in connection with whose treatment the life-space interview has been developed is that instead of finding any part of their functioning strange or bothersome (as does the conventional "treatment-prone" neurotic) they have invested heavily in secondary gain ventures to such an extent that the whole ego seems to be allied with their central pathology rather than any part of the ego taking a stand against it. While this does not mean that the whole ego is sick with the same disease that we are trying to cure, unless its "uninfected" part can be "estranged" from the core pathology and converted into an allegiance to seeing that "something is wrong," the clinical battle cannot even get started. The life-space interview has shown itself to be peculiarly fitted for this crucial, initial task.

Don, 10 years old, is so intensely driven toward the image of a teen-age "hood" that he seems to have stepped out of a "cornier-than-life" Hollywood movie of this type of kid. He has been an addict smoker since the age of 6, steals, knows all of the crude sex terms and practices, and lies with the aplomb of an Alcatraz lifer when "caught with the goods." An adopted child of a near-to-middle class family, he has overwhelmed his adoptive father with the force of his "delinquent" identification, spurring the father into alternating fits of brutality and mawkish, sentimental surrender of a defeatist type. Any admitted perception on Don's part that he is ever scared, might need protection against more powerful kids, or that he might, in any cell of his being, have a "little boy" part seems to have been ruthlessly ground out of awareness. The following episode was one of the first clinical demonstration chances we had at camp to trap his ego into what might be considered a potentially "treatment positive" perception. It all happened as a result of Don's having sadistically teased one of his cabin mates by shaking a tree branch that this boy was perched on, in spite of the other one's terrified screams for Don to stop, and, then later on the same day, ripping up another cabin mate's Sorry cards because the second boy would not give Don a snake he had caught. These two seemingly unrelated events were "stitched" together in the following interview in such a way that Don's fear motivation was made visible to him.

Interviewer: Don, do I have this straight—when Terry was yelling for you to stop shaking the branch, you kept on doing it anyway?

Don: Yep.

Int.: And then what would Terry do?

Don: Keep yellin' for me to stop.

Int.: But the more he yelled the more you what——?

Don: Shook 'im.

Int.: Why do you suppose he was yelling?

Don: Because he was scared.

Int.: Yet the more scared he got, the more it seems you felt like shaking him.

Don: That's right.

Int.: I wonder why you'd want to do that—make him scared?

Don: I dunno.

Int.: That'd be something I should think you'd want to know about yourself—don't you agree?

Don: (*uneasily*) Yeah.

The interview then moves on to the second incident of the same day—tearing up the Sorry cards.

Int.: Don, how come you ripped up Rusty's Sorry cards?

Don: (*indignantly*) Heck—he promised me the next snake he caught and after he caught this here snake he never gave it to me.

Int.: Well, I guess he should've gone through with his deal, although I'm not saying you had the right to tear up his cards because he didn't. Anyway, how come you don't catch your own snakes?

Don: (*indignantly again*) I'll bet you'd like to get bit by a snake on yer finger?

Int.: No, I wouldn't. You mean you are scared enough of snakes that you try to get Rusty to give you one of his? Not take the risk of catching one yourself?

Don: Yeah, boy.

Int.: And yet when Terry is up in the tree you do everything you can to make *him* more what——?

Don: (*disgustedly*) Scared!

Int.: That's right Don, scared. So now I begin to wonder to myself. Maybe Don wants to make other guys scared because if he can be such a guy as *can* scare other guys, then he doesn't have to be so what ——?

Don: (*spits it out*) Scared!

Int.: Yep—that's right again—scared.

Don: (*blustering*) Yeah—yeah (*in his most "gravelly" voice*). Next time my ma comes I'm gonna ask her to bring two of my buddies, *they'll* tell you I don't get scared.

Int.: Easy, boy, easy! I'm not saying you're chicken or that you get scared all the time. Heck, anybody gets scared about certain things—there's nothing wrong with that. But you—you don't like to admit you get scared hardly at all. Go around actin' like you're a teen-ager, smoking, stealing and all that. You *do,* don't you? We've been through that before.

Don: Yeah.

Int.: So all I'm sayin' now is that maybe some of that stuff is mixed up with your tryin' to make out that you don't scare easy—see? That's about all I'm saying. And you're already in plenty of trouble back home on account of doin' that, aren't you?

Don: (*unhappily*) Yeah.

Don, of course, is far from happy with any of this. In fact, he is "burned up." The clinical issue, however, is the question: is he any *wiser?* We think he may be—a wee, but crucial, bit. Also, it puts us in a much more favorable position to urge Don to take more seriously the camp caseworker's attempts to get at his problem as well as to take a new look at what his worker in the city is trying to do for him. This, followed by continuing interview coverage which explores his fear motivation, is an important step in working back to his whole tough-guy reaction formation against being little and helpless. (Of course, there is a hard possibility that Don cannot be helped by anything short of residential treatment anyway, but that is another story and not for these pages.)

VALUE REPAIR AND RESTORATION

The ego-disturbed child handles still another major adjustive task very unskillfully: that of bringing about a proper balance or synthesis between values and behavior. This is a complicated issue and there is not enough space to give it the "phenomenological respect" it deserves. Briefly, with the children under consideration, there are three aspects of this problem:

a. There may be some *deficiencies* in value content: certain pieces of superego have never been formed.

b. There may be some *uniqueness* in value content: certain pieces of superego are formed but are different, sometimes to the point of opposition, from the value pattern of the dominant, surrounding social environment.

c. Regardless of what value content there may be to begin with, the *superego is incompletely introjected,* still depends in its functioning upon the presence of "adult enforcers," and is feared and fought by the ego.

These three possibilities are not necessarily mutually exclusive; in fact, with the type of children being discussed they are usually interwoven. The resulting clinical challenge involves us in the task of helping them become more sensitive to the demands of whatever superego has already been built into the personality, or rebuilding it or modifying it as the case may be. Since the admission of guilt is often fought off by these children out of fear of peer-group derision or rejection as "adult lovers," it is especially important to reconnoiter their myriad interpersonal squabbles and feuds for "clean" issues where potentially culpable children can be spared this expensive prestige payment in front of their buddies.

A group of 11 year olds was being seen with the purpose of trying to help them figure out why they were continually at each other's throats, battling, cursing, teasing each other with cruel tricks, and, in general, unmanageable by their counselors. As typically happens, at the outset they all heaped responsibility on a particular youngster who served as chief scapegoat.

Interviewer (Al Cohen): What are some of the things Larry does that make you guys think he causes all the trouble?

Chorus of voices: Calls us "mother names,"[11] spits at us, wakes up early in the morning and yells—stuff like that.

Int.: Tell me about the last time he did that.

Joe: This morning I was sitting on my bunk before flag-raising—and I asked him for one of his comics—so he says: "Yer mammy."[12]

Int.: And what did you do?

Joe: I says, "Yer sister."

Int.: And then?

Joe: He throws a shoe at me.

11. A complicated form of verbal teasing by accusing each others' mothers of obscene sex practices.

12. The unspoken, but understood ending to this expletive is "Yer mammy is a *whore.*"

Int.: And then?

Joe: I climbs up on his bunk and slugs him—that's what!

Chuck: (*a third boy*) Yeah, and he *always* does stuff like that. That's how we get in trouble.

Int.: Who else had fights today?

Sam: (*a fourth boy*) I did—with Chuck!

Int.: How come?

Sam: Aw, we come out of the swim and he calls my mother a name.

Int.: Chuck, is that right?

Chuck: Yeah—'cause that bastard [Sam] flicked his towel at me!

Sam: The hell I did—I just threw it over my shoulder!

Bill: (*a fifth boy*) 'n this so-an-so (*pointing at Jim, a sixth member of the group*) flicks his towel at *me*.

Int.: What was Larry doing all this time?

Group: (*Silence*)

Int.: You mean he wasn't involved at all?

Voices: Naw!

Int.: Look. First you guys start off by saying that Larry starts all the trouble, but here are Joe, Chuck, Bill, Sam, and Jim all at each other, yelling mother names, slugging with towels, spitting—and Larry wasn't in on it at all. He sure couldn't have started this one, could he? I wonder how fair it is to accuse him of starting "everything."

Group: (*Amazed silence, then agreement.*)

Joe: (*his principal accuser*) Boy, it sure wouldn't be easy to be him!

It is clear that this quite amazing pinpointing of a piece of group unfairness could hardly have emerged so cleanly without a close "life-space probe" resulting in clarification of the behavior chain involved in this particular incident. That the original goal of the interview (to help them achieve some insight into their mutual goading of each other) was only lightly covered detracts hardly at all from the unexpected value lesson so deftly pulled out of the interview by the interviewer. In fact, it hit at one of the contributing factors to the group control problem which was one of tax-exempt shifting away of blame from the self on to the scapegoat. This evasion became much harder for them after such a clear admission of unfairness. The reader may be reminded by this spontaneous interview development of an earlier comment about the difficulty of deciding ahead of time as to exactly which goal a given life-space interview is to be focused upon.

NEW TOOL SALESMANSHIP

In this very aptly named subfunction of the life-space interview, Redl has emphasized that one of the severe hazards faced by the ego-disturbed child is linked to the marked impoverishment of his reaction techniques. An important clinical goal, then, is defined by this particle of his pathology: situations must be salvaged from his ongoing experience which can be used to give him a vista of "new tools" that may be applied in moments of problem-solving breakdown.

Chick, a delinquent boy of 9½, who had been booked by the police many times in his short life for larceny and armed robbery—among lighter offenses such as truancy—was a very assaultive child. Early in the camp season, we faced a critical problem in his tendency to slug his female counselors on what appeared to be light provocation. Detailed exploration of these encounters proved that the attacks upon the counselors took place when sudden floods of rage and fear confronted the ego based upon Chick's anticipation of rejection or physical attack from the counselors whom he really liked very much. This seemed to be a severe transference style reaction stemming from a lifetime of exposure to violence and fear at home. However, complex though it was, the transference reaction was not the immediate problem but rather that when Chick was in a fear state, reality-justified or not, the only thing he seemed to be able to do was to use his fists or a nearby weapon. Thus, the first problem we attacked was not the reality distortion of his counselors' feelings and motives toward him, but his need to use his fists to begin with whenever he had such feelings. Partly he was *aware* that he was caught in a web of confusion to begin with, which fact he conveyed to us directly once after we had said, "Chick, you know the counselors aren't like *that*" (meaning that the counselors neither wanted to hurt nor reject him). To which he replied, "Yeah, but sometimes you just *can't believe it.*" Our tack with him then became: "Chick, whenever you have those kinds of feelings, use *this* (*smiling and lightly putting a finger on his mouth*) instead of *these* (*touching his fists*). He gave his "crooked" smile and seemed to understand.

Of course this had to be repeated many times—it was not easy to wean Chick from using his fists. Ironically enough, the very next incident, after the above attempt to sell him "word tools" in exchange for slugging, involved his being brought in for *biting* the counselor and then claiming he was using his mouth instead of his fists as he had been asked to! But gradually, and ultimately with pride, he substituted crude verbal statements of fear and rage for action demonstrations as far as the adult was concerned at least.

MANIPULATION OF THE BOUNDARIES OF THE SELF

One of the job achievements that proper ego development assures to the individual is that of helping him to learn effectively where he "ends" and other people and/or their rights, privileges, and processes "begin." This is one sector of the larger process of distinction between the self and the non-self that developmental theory posits as one of the major critical achievements of ego growth. Unclear and complex as this process is, it is a certain fact that it is blocked and hamstrung in the type of children under discussion. Thus, in addition to having a core pathology of severe, uncheckable impulsivity, they seem to have much more than a peripheral, additional problem in dealing with other people and situations with the proper degree of autonomy and self-determination. Breakdown of this ego subfunction results in two widely opposite responses: (a) either other people's excitement quickly becomes theirs, other kids' mischief or aggression quickly racing toward them and covering them as a leaping flame with a gasoline-soaked rag; or (b) quite the reverse, their own feeling tone, whim, or prejudice is narcissistically, sometimes even megalomaniacally, forced upon another individual with no apparent awareness of or concern about the boundary between the own self and the other person, his rights, privileges, and so on.

In other words, in the first reaction, (a) the ego permits itself to be invaded by a "foreign" ego and then functions as though the motivational trend of the invading ego were its own. In the second reaction, (b) the ego invades a "foreign" ego and then functions as though it were the motivational trend of the invaded ego. The pathology is the same, the direction reversed, just as having the delusion that one is dead or is the last person on earth who is living are examples of the same pathology.

An interesting example of the second reaction, as well as a beginning attempt at influencing it, may be found in the following fragment of a long interview with Slim, a violent, but verbal and intelligent 13 year old. It so happened that Slim intensely disliked a peculiar trait of one of his cabin mates: a habit of walking on his toes whenever he was barefoot.

> Slim: He (*other boy*) always stands and walks on his tiptoes. I don't like that. I don't know why but it seems to be just one more reason for not liking him. So I decided, and I told him, that every time I caught him doing that I would snap him with my towel. I'm trying to break him of the habit.
>
> Int.: Do you really feel you have the right to inflict pain upon him just because you don't like it.
>
> Slim: Yeah (*slowly and deliberately*). I really think I do.
>
> Int.: You mean your conscience goes along with this?
>
> Slim: No, it doesn't. I know it's wrong to do but sometimes when I don't like something I feel I have the right to attack it.
>
> Int.: Even though you know it isn't right according to your conscience.
>
> Slim: My conscience can't control me when I get mad.
>
> Int.: I guess that's the real problem, isn't it, Slim? You really can't control this, even when your conscience tells you it's wrong. Seems to me that this is where you need special help.
>
> Slim: I know it. . . .

In this interview the goal is to stake out the problem as clearly as possible when Slim is not caught in one of his megalomaniacal episodes and to promise "lend-lease" to the superego-identified part of the ego in its struggle with the narcissitic infantile part. Obviously, there will be a need in the long-range treatment of Slim to attack many more issues than this one.

Thus, the special motives and feelings into which this particular ego weakness plays and which form the central core pathology have, of course, to be dealt with. However, this narcissistic blurring of ego boundaries does stand as a formidable clinical problem on its own and there is a question as to whether entree can be gained or waited for into the deeper pathology without tackling this piece of it first. Thus, for instance, by talking with Slim about Whitey's walking habit, it was possible to explore with him the possibility that Whitey was disliked by him for still other reasons, or served as a target for other problems, and in this way Slim's pubertal, phallic competitiveness with Whitey came out. Then it was suggested to him that perhaps his dislike of Whitey's walking on his toes was based upon a fear that Whitey would leap upon him and hurt him—in this way proving he was stronger than Slim. It was interesting that this markedly paranoid boy was relieved by this "theory" which reduced his fear of Whitey. Now of course this does not cure his ego-boundary problem or his paranoia, but it does aim at giving help to the uninvolved part of the ego for dealing with both if continued in balanced doses over a long enough time.

These have been some few, rough illustrations of the use of life-space interview on the level of "clinical exploitation of life events." There is no implication that a completely investigated instrument of change has been evolved or that any of the children in this setting are being treated until the correct terminal point in their therapy will have been reached. In each case, only a *piece* of the total pathology is being demonstrated as it has been contacted through the interview by picking up a life event or a series of life events packed together in a relatively short time exposure.

Emotional First Aid on the Spot

As mentioned earlier, another major function of the life-space interview is that of simply pulling a youngster through a tight spot without any specific intention or clinical motive toward cure. Its aim is to offer to the ego hygienic protection and support which aid it in overcoming a temporary, sometimes critical, loss of function. Here, too, Redl has offered tentative categories aimed at clarifying some of the subfunctions of this style of life-space interview. Broadly, these differentiate between interviews which aid the ego in moments of (1) acute frustration, fury, guilt, or panic; (2) throw support around the ego when it is faced by sudden violent retreat from relationship; and (3) help a child steer his way safely through some complicating and confusing "social and behavioral traffic jams" and decision-making crises. For space reasons, we shall confine ourselves to samples showing two different subfunctions classifiable within these three groups. The apparent simplicity of such moments conceals their complexity and to some of our more orthodox clinical brethren may make them "undeserving" for admission to the elite status of "the interview."

Interview Support in a Moment of Panic

Chick, whom we have had occasion to describe a few short examples back, was watching a camp movie, "Bad Day at Black Rock," when his counselor observed him get up in a restless, agitated way and walk out of the lodge with the kind of expression that she had learned to read as "trouble." Tipped off by her I followed him out. He said nothing when I asked, "Hey, Chick, what's the trouble?" but strode purposefully along to his cabin. I jogged along by his side in as friendly and relaxed a way as I could. He got into his cabin, climbed up in a bunk, pulled up his blankets to his chin. "I ain't goin' back to that movie or the campfire later or nuthin'." "How come?" No answer. I stretched out on an empty bunk across from his, leaned back, folded my arms under my head and waited. A few minutes later, he got up just as purposefully as he had come in, pulled his blanket back, got down, strode out of the cabin. There I was again by his side. Not a word between us. He walked to the boys' "john." I waited. He came out and went back to the lodge. Instead of going in, he sat down on a bench near the door. I sat down next to him. About a minute passed. Then he said, "Some Western that is . . . no shootin' or anything!" "Oh" I said, "there'll be shootin'—wait 'till that one-armed guy catches up with the bad guy. The one that killed his buddy which is why he came to this town." "Oh," says he, "that I gotta see," and walked in. I went with him and sat by him in the movie. In a low voice I sketched out what was happening in more detail: how Spencer Tracy, the "one-armed guy," had this friend in the army who had come to this town and been killed by a gang of crooks. Some men in the town who had gone along with the killing—like a weak sheriff—had a bad conscience but were afraid to do anything about it. Now the one-armed guy was going to show them that they didn't have to be scared. He was "giving them back their guts." Then they would take care of the bad guys. Chick relaxed, exchanged comments with me, and appeared to enjoy what was happening. After a bit I "faded" away, leaving him on his own. The rest of the evening was uneventful—campfire and all.

In this encounter, Chick seems to be upset by the subtle violence of this movie as contrasted with the explicit violence of the usual Western—"ain't no shootin' or nothin'." He withdraws and finally returns after two clear-cut "regression" behaviors: climbing into bunk and urinating. In making the plot and actions *explicit* for him—like an interpretive subtitle—and throwing "proximity" protection around him, the ego is able to recontact the fear-inspiring situation and master it. This illustration would seem to be in line with Redl's category of interview helps in the management of "panic, fury, and guilt."

Is this really a "simple" situation that could have gone unhandled? Far from it! Chick, on his own, would have parlayed this momentary threat into an aggressive attack on somebody during the balance of the evening.

Yet no attempt is made here to deal with any underlying causality for the ego's inability to meet this situation without fear—this is what differentiates this type of life-space interview from "clinical exploitation."

Interview Support in Moments of "Relationship Decay"[13]

One of the most dangerous maneuvers of the sick ego is its tendency to draw back into the communication-bereft world of autism. While the more intactly delinquent child rarely finds this complete a retreat necessary, using mainly aggressive exploitation of the surrounding world as his major approach to all problems, there is a category of prepsychotic-like disturbances marked by explosive types of acting out intermixed with dependency and passivity, with strong superego and id forces pressing against a thin, underskilled ego, where sudden psychological retreat happens more easily than the clinician finds comfortable to behold. Such a boy was Jon, 13.

Whenever Jon became threatened by aggressive or sexual feelings regardless of whether they were set off by some action or language of other boys in the cabin or from "within" by his own feelings or fantasies, he acted like a virtual hebephrenic: cackled like a rooster, smirked, rolled his eyes, screamed wildly, attacked stronger boys recklessly, shouted obscenity. One day, after a day and a half of such behavior which was almost virtually impossible to bring under control, his whole cabin blew up at him and in their words: "We're goin' to kill the bastard!" The whole gang came in for a talk about it and in the interview room Jon continued to display the whole panorama of behavior described. Finally I asked him in a firm, decisive way: "Look, do you want to work this out or not?" He looked at me and said very calmly, "Well, Dave, you see I've been like this for three years" and then, bang! He was "off" again. Only this time he added to his previous paraphernalia of "goofiness": running out of the room, coming back, hiding under the table, getting back out again and throwing some sunflower seeds he was eating at one of the toughest kids in the cabin. Then, in response to my pressure, he would "come back again" with a few rational statements about himself and his feelings only to follow this with a fit of wildness.

After this happened about six times and it was all we could do to keep the other kids away from him, we let them go and kept him with us since it was dangerous to release him under these conditions. Dr. Phil Spielman, a visiting participating psychiatrist (on a busman's holiday from Dr. Redl's residential treatment unit at Bethesda) and known to all the boys, had been sitting in with us during the group talk and at this point said to Jon: "How come, every time you make a sensible statement about yourself, you immediately go off your rocker and act like a wild man? There is something that is bothering you but you can't come close to it without running away. Why don't you tell us what

13. Fritz Redl, "Strategy and Techniques of the Life Space Interview," *op. cit.*

it is?" At this point I left Phil (as he was known to all campers) alone with Jon.

About an hour and a half later, I saw them coming down to the waterfront for a swim. Jon was literally like another person. Phil had "got to him." This particular episode, Jon had finally told Spielman, was caused by his fear of Biff, a much tougher, more primitive adolescent from a neighboring cabin who had come into Jon's cabin one day when the counselor was out for a brief while and started some rough sexual horseplay with him which involved grabbing for his genitals. Jon, quite calm now, told me later that this scared him—that he had never seen "stuff like this before." I told him I would talk to Biff and make clear that we would not tolerate anybody forcing other kids into play like that which, in my role as one of the "camp bosses," it was possible to do as far as Biff was concerned.

In this sequence of events, neither the interviewer nor I made any attempt to get at the reason as to why this upset Jon so much. This would have involved opening up on a deeper clinical level than the camp was able to engage in with Jon. The whole purpose was simply to try to get him back into communication and relationship which necessitated that he face his sexual excitement and fear that Biff had released. Also, obviously, it was important, then and there, to prove to him that we could *protect* him from Biff, which also played a decisive role in the restoration of control and the relinquishing of the bizarre borderline behavior which masked the anxiety.

In summary, these samples of "emotional first aid on the spot" type of life-space interviews are aimed at demonstrating (1) the difference between this function and "clinical exploitation of life events" and (2) differences between some subfunctions of the "first aid" type. It should be obvious that all the classifications of function are anything but airtight and mutually exclusive, a warning that has been stressed right along in this discussion. For example, both Chick *and* Jon were involved in panic reactions but Jon's was of a deeper and more devastating type and threw him into a more dangerous channel of defense. The reason for subclassifying them is only to trap the different quality of challenge to the interviewer and not to imply that true compartmentalization of ego pathology and interview function really exists in a rigid sense. This same fluidity exists, as has also been stressed, between the "clinical exploitation" and "first-aid type" of interview, too, and there are many interview moments where the two major functions are converged into a single broad interview effort or alternate with each other at different time segments of the interview. This should not surprise the classicist in therapy because the same procedural fluidity exists there, too. For instance, frequently the neurotic has to be "soothed" in the very same hour as a dream is interpreted, or he has to be sympathized with or emphatically reassured of the therapist's continued affection and support even though he has death wishes toward the therapist. These are similar to the mixtures of "first aid" and "clinical exploitation" that exist on the terrain of the "life-space" approach.

Finally, it is necessary to point to a serious gap in the present discussion. Again because of space, it has not been possible to describe various critical factors that determine the ways in which the life-space interview is to be used. Issues such as *timing,* the particular *role* of the interviewer in the life of the interviewee, the *nature of the ongoing activity* within which the episode to be used for life-space interviewing may develop or even the *particular physical location* circumscribing such an event are all of vital importance. Beyond offering the assurance that the relevance of all such factors is assessed in relation to each instance of use of life-space interviewing, no more can be described.

Implications for Practice

What, if any, of this is translatable for general agency or outpatient clinical social work practice? The fact that life-space interviewing has been developed and tested in a relatively restricted area of institutional or quasi-institutional design and that even in such settings there is much for us to relearn and modify makes this a most speculative and tentative issue.

First, it must be clearly stated that the moment we talk about outpatient practice we should be simultaneously shifting our sites to a different type of clientele than the severely disturbed children described thus far. For them the life-space approach holds no new answers in extramural settings. There is no cheap solution for the grim lethargy of the American community in providing a tragically needed expanding front of intensive inpatient treatment designs of a variety of types for severely disturbed children and adults.

Beyond this, for appropriate practice of a clinically oriented type with properly selected clientele, one general, underlying meaning of the life-space approach would involve the development of a *tool-conscious* interest in the ongoing life experience of the client and how various segments of it may be carried into the therapeutic situation more meaningfully. We must recognize that this has been going on silently for some years in agency practice. However, since many of the life experiences of the client are made known to the worker only through the clients reporting of them, there has been reluctance to rely on these as compared to other forms of more indigenous data about the client—fantasies, fragments of emotion, attitudes toward and perceptions of the worker, behavior in the interview situation, and so on. This is a real problem and cannot be dismissed. Still, much of what we do tactically with the client is governed by what we *believe* is achievable and reachable. If there had been no theory about the importance of dreams, no one would "dream" that such ephemeral and diffuse data could ever be recovered from the far-off corners of the psyche and converted into pragmatic materials for therapy either, and a whole magnificent skill area would not have developed. However, agency practice will, itself, have to define its adaptation of the life-space approach through appropriate experimentation and in advance of this nothing more specific should be said.

Leaving the typical agency setting and thinking of certain special, but still noninstitutional designs of practice, life-space findings may hold more concrete applicatory meanings. In *detached worker* settings with the hard-to-reach and in *school social work practice,* a very clear entree for experimentation with these techniques is immediately visible. In such settings, the worker in varying ways and degrees is *already embedded in pieces of the client's life-space to begin with,* is perceived as such by the client, and has available for interview use life events in close proximity to their actual occurrence.

Finally, life-space interview findings remind us once again of the crying need for planned experimentation—and I mean in practice!—with combinations of group work and casework. What *did* happen to casework and group work as a clinical blend anyway? Fritz Redl, Gisela Konopka, and S. L. Slavson have written about it for the last twenty years, at least, in publications too numerous to mention. Yet today there is the most abject resignation in our field to the extinction of professional group work, a shaking of heads over the fact that "Group work is a dying field!" If child guidance and family casework agency practice were widened to articulate these two approaches, a badly needed gap would be filled in treatment resources for certain types of problems. Although they do not require institutional therapy, clients with such problems are still not reachable without making available for treatment life experiences that can be created on the group scene and are clinically useful there as well as in the interview situation. Shall we disentomb group work?

Perhaps most fascinating—and admittedly most speculative—is one last issue: what does life-space interview suggest for a *fact and theory* base in social work? Right now our field is exhibiting a frantic lionization of the social scientist in the parlor and a frosty tolerance of the backyard romance between the kitchen maid and the local psychoanalyst on the beat. This is symptomatic of our embarrassment over having buried ourselves (and *we* did it!) too deeply in the id. There may well be an equal and opposite danger that we may, via social science, launch ourselves too swiftly into space. In either case, the client is still left in the dark where he started, poor fellow! It seems to me that life-space data suggests that in *ego processes* are wrapped up the vital connections between the person and his "inner" and "outer" worlds. The ego seems to be a continuum with one end buried (but alive and "kicking"!) in the slumbering roots of the person and the other proliferated into a sensitive network involved in sleepless radar-like contact with the world around it. The resultant picture is that of an enormous, multifunctional plasticity about which we still know pitifully little. This is where we have found—in the "life-space circuit"—our most fascinating clinical challenge. Obviously, we have had to become involved most elaborately with special features—social and nonsocial—of the environmental terrain. However, *the ego is not its environment,* not even that part that becomes specialized for the task of dealing with it. It is always "attached" to the person who "carries" it—even when its "radar" is madly clicking in space with varying, and variable, influences from without.

In our "knowledge rush" toward social science, are we remembering that ego function is a *personal* function? The gap between the data of social science and individual psychology is by no means closed and it is treacherously possible to intermingle carelessly perceptions arising from these two discrete modes of observation and description. The view, for example, that the proper goal of social work is the "enhancement of social functioning" already seems to carry an imagery leaning toward peace with the offerings (and critiques of social work!) of social science. The auxiliary concepts that are lined up with this goal-concept: *role, interaction, environment,* also speak out for this orientation. What is the view of the person that is coming out of this? It is a view of man as *social-man* as opposed to *id-man.* Ego psychology will not, in a manner of speaking, "have" this. The ego—as a function of mind—is no more "loyal" to social-man than it is to id-man. In short, the type of involvement that social work is developing with social science may leave us—as did our handling of psychoanalysis—with a *half-man.* It portends a violation of the concept of the *total person.* If, as seems to be the case, a smooth conceptual model for the determinants of the total person are not yet deducible from social science and individual psychology, this is our proper cross to bear and, operationally speaking, our practical functioning in relation to the client world must reflect, clumsy though it may seem, a tortuous fidelity to two oracles instead of one.

20. Life-Space Management of Behavioral Crises

NICHOLAS LONG, VICTOR STOEFFLER,
KENNETH KRAUSE, CHARLES JUNG

In the latter part of 1954 and early months of 1955, six boys between 8 and 11 years of age were admitted to a closed ward in the Clinical Center of the National Institutes of Health. They had been selected for their aggressive, hostile, antisocial adjustment, and for the next four and a half years were the subjects of a prolonged research study in the residential treatment of such children. From the outset their program included four hours a week of individual psychotherapy, special in-hospital school, and intensive milieu therapy with emphasis on "life-space interviewing" around disturbed behavior.[1] While the severity of their symptomatic behavior necessitated emphasis on programing within the hospital milieu, closely supervised experiences in the community were planned as often as possible. A caseworker assigned to the group maintained contact with members of each boy's family and arranged visits at the hospital or at home when either of these seemed advisable.

By July 1957, these boys had improved sufficiently to move out of the closed hospital ward into a specially built "halfway house," officially called the Children's Treatment Residence. This structure was located on the hospital grounds and was designed as an intermediate stage in the boys' socialization and treatment. During their two years' stay at the residence the boys became increasingly community-oriented through their attendance at public schools and participation in such community activities as teen clubs, Little League baseball, Boy Scouts, visits with friends, and so forth. At the residence they continued to live in a carefully planned milieu

Reprinted with permission of the National Association of Social Workers from *Social Work,* Vol. 6, No. 1 (January, 1959), pp. 38–45.
1. The life-space interview is a therapeutic technique developed by Dr. Fritz Redl in which the patient is confronted with his symptomatic behavior when an issue arises that can be clinically exploited in terms either of long-range treatment goals or of providing immediate ego support and emotional first-aid. *See* Fritz Redl, "Strategy and Techniques of Life Space Interview," *American Journal of Orthopsychiatry,* Vol. 28, No. 1 (January 1959), p. 29.

program geared to support and develop newly achieved gains, as well as to continue to provide protective limits on impulsive behavior. The boys also remained in individual psychotherapy. Inside of a short time one of them was well enough to be discharged, while the other five continued in treatment at the residence.

In the early part of 1959 we learned that for various administrative reasons our project would be terminating, and the boys were to be discharged sometime that summer. On Friday, February 13, 1959, this information was announced to them. In the following two weeks there was a progressive increase in quantity and severity of acting-out behavior.

The purpose of this paper is to illustrate how this increase in acting out was clinically exploited by means of life-space interviewing. Though our focus will be primarily on the interview technique, we recognize that the total impact of our treatment plan was the result of the combined approach of all facets in our milieu. Individual psychotherapy, limit-setting, and special programing, as well as interviewing, contributed to the effect we obtained. This presentation will include a discussion of (1) *precipitating factors* in the series of acting-out incidents, (2) *strategy-planning* in the handling of these incidents, and (3) the *life-space management* of them.

Precipitating Factors

On Friday, February 13, we announced to the boys that the residence would close that summer and they would be discharged. Some of the boys responded immediately with aggressive remarks, expressing mainly concern about leaving the residence and questions about possible placements. By Tuesday some acting out had begun. Ed became disorganized—sloppy eating habits, swearing, verbal obscenities, a disheveled appearance, and a "you-make-me" attitude appeared. He required a staff member with him constantly to help control his behavior. Tony stole some things from a neighborhood store.

The staff moved in with a highly structured program, tighter controls, and closer supervision. By Saturday some of the acting out had leveled off. On Sunday, however, after family visits which aroused anew feelings of separation from the residence, the boys again became nearly impossible to manage. Tony grabbed restricted dietary food off the table faster than we could tell him to stop. Bruce clung leechlike, and made impossible demands on everyone. Later in the evening when the program director asked the boys to turn off the TV and retire to bed, Ed blew up and kicked him.

The next day Ed's disturbance was so severe that we moved him to a closed ward in the adjacent hospital. This gave him the security and boundaries he needed. Because of staff concern with the management problems he presented, a staff meeting was held in which handling techniques were discussed. An outgrowth of this meeting was the conversion of our craft shop in the basement into a "settling room."[2] Arrangements were made for additional staff if this should become necessary. When Ed returned to the residence three days later, a highly structured program was prepared for him which included assigning him to a "special"—*i.e.,* a person who stayed exclusively with him and was totally responsible for his program and management.

The other boys perceived the attention given to Ed as a form of rejection of themselves. During the rest of the week they reacted both to their own feelings about separation and to the special attention being given to Ed. The latter returned to the residence on Wednesday and within four days each of the other boys had individually and collectively acted out. Tony stole from school and was more aggressive with staff members. Frank smoked and fought at school, missed his cab pickups from activities, and it was suspected that he was stealing at school and at the residence. Clif was involved in sex play with Frank. All the boys but Ed were involved in fire-setting, playing with matches, and other destructive behavior. Tony, Frank, and Bruce broke into the medical supply cabinet, damaged a blood pressure gauge, and took medical supplies. Only Ed remained out of it all, content and secure in his new program.

After a very difficult weekend, a shaken staff returned the boys to school on Monday. It seemed miraculous that there were no major problems at school during the day, but that night the acting out reached new heights. Bruce had a temper tantrum and had to be held for an hour and a half. The other boys, too, were anxious and presented difficult management problems: Clif pushed a counselor down some stairs; Frank was found smoking at the residence; Tony became angry at a staff person when he was sent to his room, flew into a rage, pushed out his window screen, and broke his cupboard door. Ed, who had just returned from a closed ward, reported that someone had taken his foreign coins from his room. The senior staff member on duty recorded seven life-space interviews with the boys as he tried simultaneously to settle their immediate problems and keep them from exciting each other to new ones. The staff was becoming exhausted and it was obvious that something had to be done to cut through this steady increase in acting-out behavior.

Planning Strategy

By the next day at regular staff meeting, staff morale was low and concerns over the current increase of acting out, along with personal feelings about

2. This was a room which had no windows or furnishings other than two mats on the floor. Here two or three staff members could comfortably restrain a boy, while he would neither destroy any property nor receive secondary gratification from acting out in front of the group.

termination of the project, were freely expressed. Two of the staff members were on sick leave; others were fatigued to the point of demanding relief. It was understandable, therefore, that when this meeting opened, the predominant feeling tone was one of depression mixed with open hostility. The meeting started with the staff examining all the incidents that had occurred during the past week. A staggering series of incidents relating to each boy were grouped separately and recorded on the blackboard.

Once the incidents were listed, two questions emerged: (1) What were some of the underlying reasons that led the boys to act in this way? (2) What could we do, as a team, to help the boys become aware of these reasons while we sustained them and made them feel that we were not going to let them destroy the gains they had worked so hard to achieve?

After considerable debate, the staff decided to use a dramatic approach in order to shock the boys into looking at their behavior and to demonstrate to them the deep concern over their acting out. Accordingly, the following plan developed:

1. As the boys returned from school they would be met by a counselor, escorted to their rooms, and told that they would meet individually with the entire staff to discuss their behavior.

2. The housemother would bring each boy his regular after-school snack and try to reassure him if he was becoming upset.[3]

3. The living room chairs were to be arranged in a circle, with a large paper pad on a portable easel placed at one point in the circle. Each boy's name with the list of incidents in which he had been involved during the past week would be written on a separate page. Each boy in his individual interview would sit directly across from the easel and between the housemother and the social worker.[4] The rest of the staff would sit in the remaining chairs while the director stood next to the easel.

4. After his interview, each boy would return to his room with a counselor until all five boys had been seen. Then all the boys would be called down for a group interview to review what had gone on in the individual sessions, to emphasize the common problem of separation, to assign each boy a counselor and senior staff member for a follow-up life-space interview, to announce a limited special program for the next five days, to plan for a formal evaluation at the end of that period, and to answer any questions.

Despite ambivalent feelings about the plan on the part of various staff members, it was adopted and went into effect when the boys returned from school. As the boys returned to the residence, they were sent to their rooms, where they were told about the meeting. They complained about this re-

3. The housemother, Eve Citrin, a professional social group worker, lived in the residence and was the assistant director.
4. The social worker, Walter Sceery, did casework with the boys' families and was responsible for finding new placements.

striction and threatened "to bust the hell out" if they were not allowed to
leave immediately. They were reminded that this was the kind of attitude
about which the staff was concerned, and were told that they would have
to remain in their rooms until they were called.

Individual Interviews with Total Staff

Since it is not possible in this paper to give a verbatim report of each interview, only the first is described in detail; the other four are summarized.

Frank is an intelligent, controlled, hostile boy who plays hard at being a
tough delinquent. As he enters the living room, he is momentarily taken aback
by the elaborate room arrangement and the number of staff members present.
Slowly he counts the number of staff persons and says smugly, "Twelve against
one, it looks like I don't stand much of a chance against this jury." The staff
laughs and the director says, "While it may look like a trial to you, we are
not here to pass out verdicts, but to see if we can understand what has been
happening to all the boys these last two weeks." Frank asks in a hostile way,
"Why are all the staff in on it?" The director explains that since this is such an
important meeting, he has asked everyone to attend. The director points to
the first page on the pad. On it is written the date, "February 13." "Frank,"
he says, "It's been a little over two weeks since you were told that the project
is ending. Since that time there has been a lot of acting out. Let's take a look
at the kind of situations in which the boys are involved. Perhaps you will get
a better picture of how serious and alarming it is. What we want you to see
is that this acting out of feelings is not just your problem but involves all the
boys." At this time, the director slowly and seriously reads each list of incidents. Frank seems impressed by the lists and shows some genuine concern
over the amount of acting out. When the director finishes reading Tony's list,
Frank comments, "Humph, Tony is in worse shape than I am."

The director flips to Frank's page and says, "Why don't we go over your
list again and see if there is any pattern to it." As the director repeats the
items Frank slips into his delinquent defense and starts to argue that he was
not involved in breaking the blood pressure gauge. The director replies that
Frank will have plenty of time this evening to go over each of the incidents
with one of the senior staff members. The director continues, "Frank, if you
look at this behavior and compare it to the way you behaved four years ago,
you'll notice a lot of similarity. It's really wild stuff and is seen in a locked
ward and not in an open setting like this." The director pauses but Frank
does not respond. "If we try to understand what is behind all this acting out
it seems that some of the boys are saying, 'I can't trust you any more,' 'I'm
getting the short end of it.' 'I'm being kicked out, so what the hell!' Perhaps
these feelings are very close to the feelings they had when they had to leave
their parents." Frank appears depressed. His head is bent and supported by
his hands. The director continues, "We all know that this has not been easy
on any of you boys. We know that you have questions about where you'll be
placed, when you'll be leaving, and many other questions. If you recall, Frank,

Dr. Noshpitz[5] told you that Walt (Walter Sceery, social worker) would be talking to you about your future plans." Walt describes in detail the one treatment residence he visited and gives Frank a list of the places he will see the following week. Walt adds that Frank's placement to some degree depends on his behavior during the next four months.

The director asks Frank if he has any questions. Frank hesitates and then asks Walt if he can find a place for him nearby. Walt answers that he has no way of knowing right now, but that his plan is to visit many places and select the one that will give Frank the most help. Frank accepts this, walks over to the easel, and reads his list of incidents. The director then asks Frank if he has any further questions. Frank replies that he does not and starts walking out of the room. Suddenly, he turns, walks to the director, puts his hand in his pocket, pulls out a cigarette lighter and says, "I found this in school today." The director accepts it and Frank returns to his room.

The other four interviews followed the same general pattern, although they varied considerably in terms of their effect on the boys:

Ed, 14 years old, weighing 216 pounds, was just back at the residence from a closed ward. He reacted to the pressure of the interview in a severely infantile fashion. He ran to his chair, sat down, grabbed the rungs, got up holding the chair as though it were stuck to his seat, and walked around the circle like an elephant. Finally he dropped the chair, made some animal sounds, rushed around the circle, and shook hands with each person. It was only after much assurance that we were not going to hurt him that Ed settled down. The director commented that Ed had just gone through a difficult period and that since his return to the residence he had been trying hard to maintain controls. Ed was able to ask several questions about placement. When they were answered, he seemed to realize that he was being taken care of and quietly returned to his room.

Clif, a tall, good-looking boy with a schizoid-like makeup, approached the meeting with a sullen anger. He glared at the staff during the first part of the meeting. The only thing that pleased him was Tony's long list of incidents. He laughed and said, "All the stuff isn't even there." Walt commented that he planned to see him and his mother every two weeks to plan for his return home. Clif said bitterly, "I don't wanna go home." Walt asked where he would like to go. Clif shouted back, "To hell." Walt commented on Clif's fear of returning home, but added that he had to face the fact that he had to go home. Clif answered, "I don't have to do anything," and froze for the rest of the session.

Tony, like Frank, was overwhelmed by the number of adults, and responded by becoming very silly. When the director presented the material, Tony mimicked him, using baby talk. When the housemother refused to

---

5. Dr. Joseph Noshpitz, chief psychiatrist of the Child Research Branch, was the person who had announced the termination of the project to the boys.

allow him to sit in her lap he clung to her. The social worker replied that his home would not be able to provide him with the help he needed. Tony became angry and said, "The way they treat me here, I'll never be ready to go home." Tony started to swear at the staff and had to be taken to his room.

The last boy seen was *Bruce,* who reacted to the session seriously and listened attentively. He asked what he had to do to get ready for a foster home placement. The social worker asked Bruce to see him after the meeting so that they could spend more time discussing this question. Bruce read over his list of incidents again and asked if he could tell the entire staff about his part in them. The director told Bruce that there was no need to make a public announcement and that he could wait and talk later with one of the senior staff members. Bruce then asked to have his interview with a senior staff member start immediately. He was told it could take place after the group session, and returned to his room.

Group Interview with Total Staff

According to plan, the entire group was called back to the living room after the individual interviews. Initially there was a great deal of confusion: Tony jumped on the backs of staff, Clif sat in a corner refusing to join the group, Ed crowed that he wasn't in any trouble like the rest of them, Frank threatened to punch Tony in the mouth, and Bruce screamed that the meeting should start. Finally, all the boys were sitting around the circle while the director reviewed the individual sessions, underlined the separation theme, and emphasized the need for the boys to pull themselves together. He stated that, in order to protect them from further difficulty, the boys would remain in the residence or in the immediate area for the next five days, except for the time they were attending school and their individual psychotherapy sessions. He further stated that at the end of this period each boy would be seen again to evaluate whether he had been able to gain some understanding of his part in the acting-out incidents and whether he was able to modify his behavior. Bruce wondered whether he could return to community activities if he worked everything out in two days. The director replied that it would take time to work through the problems and the earliest a boy would be allowed to assume responsibility for his own behavior in the community would be Monday. The director ended the meeting after answering a few anticipated complaints.

Individual Life-Space Interviews

After the group interview with staff, each boy was seen individually by a member of the senior staff along with the counselor who was to be with him during the evening. Generally, the goals for these life-space interviews were:

1. Interpretation of underlying anxieties as motivating factors in the acting out of symptomatic behavior—in this case mainly the feelings around separation, rejection, and sibling rivalry.

2. Resolution of the acting-out incidents, or at least open discussion of them, in order to relieve unconscious guilt which could in itself become a motivating factor for more acting out.

3. Demonstration of protection and security through the control of impulsivity, along with a feeling of adult interest and physical closeness which would serve as counteragents against the separation anxiety.

4. Discussion of separation feelings in order to set the tone for follow-up interviews.

Frank. One of Frank's major problems was the conflict between his identification with his delinquent social and family background on the one hand, and the value system presented by our institution on the other. In order to justify and maintain his delinquent image, Frank used an elaborate defense system employing techniques of denial, projection, rationalization, and displacement. In dealing with these defenses we were frequently in the difficult position of having to prove Frank's guilt in some given situation. If we could not do this Frank would perceive this as an admission of his innocence. This established, Frank would maintain that we had no grounds for pursuing an incident any further with him. If we persisted, we would be feeding his paranoid fantasy of the persecuting adult. Moreover, when Frank succeeded in his manipulations of us, his pathology was reaffirmed and our ability to help him greatly weakened. Worst of all, the omnipotence of the aggressive and hostile forces within were reinforced. We had learned through hard experience that we could work with Frank most effectively when we were able to avoid his manipulative defenses and approach him on the more vulnerable level of his underlying motivation. We could strengthen our approach by offering him protection from the dangerous breakthrough of his own aggressive impulses through a tightly structured program with clearly defined limits on behavior.

Thus, we handled the interview according to our pragmatic knowledge, avoided defensive traps, and mentioned areas of improvement since hospitalization as well as the upsetting factor of separation. As the interviewer made interpretations, announced limits, and outlined the program for the next five days, Frank's rigid posture and tense facial expression gradually relaxed. He curled into a fetal position on his bed and fell asleep shortly after the interview.

Ed. This boy had had his eruption the week before and was the only one not involved in the current episode of acting out. The interview was therefore designed to support what we could of Ed's observing ego, and to anticipate with him the potential stimulation from the acting out of the other boys. The interviewer planned with Ed a number of activities to support his positive self-image. By design, many of these took place in the community, where Ed would be contagion-free from the other boys.

Ed's extreme anxiety concerning the interview diminished as he began to feel secure within the structure of the program and as he anticipated the gratifying activities. At the end of the interview, Ed responded with a determined, "Don't worry about me, they're not going to suck me into their problems," and left with his counselor for a trip to the store.

Clif. Despite Clif's hard core of hostility he was frequently able to behave pleasantly and acceptably. In interviews, and particularly in the face of confrontations, Clif related in two major styles: either by a flat response of indifference and unconcern along with total denial of affect, or by an eruption of hostility of such proportions that meaningful exploitation of the incident was impossible. The aim in this interview was to find some middle ground where a connection could be made between underlying feelings and acting-out behavior.

After meeting some initial passive resistance, the interviewer changed his approach and asked Clif if he recalled what made him push a counselor down some stairs the day before. Clif said that he did it because he was angry. The interviewer allowed that angry feelings made Clif do such things as pushing staff around and setting fires, but that there were better ways to handle such feelings. He suggested that Clif was angry partly because he had seen Ed getting a lot of attention following his "blow-up" the week before, and partly because he had been told that the residence would be closing and he would be going home. Clif said again that he did not want to go home, and followed this with many questions about his school friends, his baseball team, what would happen to the residence, the staff, and so on.

In contrast to his individual session with the staff, throughout which he remained sullen and hostile, in this interview Clif talked with some freedom about how he felt in the face of the impending separation. The interviewer assured Clif that the staff would help him learn how to cope with many of his difficulties before he left for home. Clif was able to accept this and the specialized residence program without protest.

Tony. Tony seemed to operate out of guilt patterns based on deep feelings of rejection and oral deprivation. As a rule, any stimuli which activated these underlying feelings provoked a wave of impulsive aggression. This in turn created more guilt, which led to even more acting out. The staff had found that the most effective way to break into this vicious circle was, first, to bring all the misdeeds into the open and come to some resolution of them through discussion, and then to interpret and try to handle whatever current pressures were stirring up the underlying feelings. Thus, a meticulous discussion of each of the thirteen incidents ensued. Resolutions for each one ranged from working out a system of repayment for broken items and planning for the return of stolen goods to labeling an incident as having been "out of line." All told, these resolutions required three interviews, each about forty-five minutes long, which took place throughout the evening. Tony, anxious to get out from under the load of guilt, pitched in co-operatively in working out each item.

After all of the incidents had been discussed, the interviewer spoke approvingly of Tony's participation, but added that they really hadn't touched on what was behind this behavior. Tony's reply was his stock answer, "I don't know, I just felt like it." The interviewer remarked that since the announcement of the discharge, all the boys seemed to feel that they were being let down and that we didn't really care about them. One could understand why Tony felt this way in view of all he had experienced with his parents and the many feelings that came from their rejection of him—the sense of not being wanted, of not being cared for or fed enough—and finally of being sent away. For a moment Tony looked startled and sad, then quickly covered up this unusual display of true emotion with a strained grin. Feeling that no more discussion could be tolerated at this point, the interviewer briefly explained the specialized program and terminated the session.

Bruce. In order to protect a vulnerable core of dependency strivings, Bruce had developed a highly effective defense of manipulativeness. In action, he was a "behind-the-scenes" operator. He was frequently an instigator, indirectly involved but seldom guilty of the misdeed itself. He would often stimulate episodes of acting out, but he always withdrew at a strategic moment.

The interviewer began by enumerating the incidents that Bruce was involved in along with Frank and Tony. Bruce responded by claiming that he had been drawn into these incidents by the others through no fault of his own; which was true, insofar as it was the others who actually perpetrated the deeds. Bruce carried this line of defense to the point of creating an impression of having been threatened by the others as a potential squealer. He complained that staff were failing to protect him from the others; indeed, it almost appeared that we were the guilty ones rather than Bruce.

The interviewer said that all the boys, including Bruce, had been involved in these incidents and that maybe they all were reacting to the same thing—the prospect of having to leave the residence. She said that this was something all the boys had to face, and that we would help them with this problem as we had helped them with other problems in the past. The housemother answered Bruce's questions about possible placements and said that he would be kept informed of things as they developed. After talking out some of his concerns about leaving, Bruce was able to accept the housemother's discussion of his participation in the incidents.

Follow-up

Following the interviews, each boy spent the evening in the company of the counselor who had been assigned to him. The usual residence evening routines went smoothly and without incident. Through the next five days we conducted a special program. Since the boys could not go out for activities and we did not want them to view this restriction as punishment, we brought the activities to them. We provided some new athletic equipment, some quiet projects such as model-building, and two full-length movies which were shown during the weekend.

During this interval at least three life-space interviews were held with each boy. These sessions were intended to continue the working through of the various incidents, to lend the boys additional support, and to examine any further difficulties that might have arisen. Ed was seen once in order to interpret to him how the others had begun to scapegoat him in an effort to lure him into acting out.

Finally, on Sunday, each boy was interviewed individually to evaluate his behavior during the five days. In each session the interviewer recapitulated the causes of the boy's previous acting-out behavior, the behavior he had displayed during the last five days, and the progress he had or had not made. All but one were allowed to resume their regular schedule of activities; Tony seemed to need more time to work on his particular problems. In his evaluation, Tony was able to accept the fact that he would still be limited to the residence and would be closely supervised.

Aside from the lowering of patient anxiety, staff morale had been lifted considerably. It was generally felt that a combined staff effort had succeeded in bringing a useful therapeutic design out of what had seemed like complete chaos.

PART FIVE

STAFFING AND PERSONNEL
IN A THERAPEUTIC MILIEU

21. The Child Care Worker

HENRY W. MAIER

Neither child care work nor parenting as basic child development activities have so far been either defined in the dictionaries or explicitly researched in the behavioral sciences, although economically, socially, and culturally these activities encompass the largest occupation in the world.

The child care worker, including the group living counselor, residential worker, cottage or house-parent, may be defined as *the person responsible for the daily care and the nurturing living experience of a specified group of children and youth in a child-caring institution.* He is the primary nurturing agent in twenty-four hour group living, as the parent is in family living. Child care work includes four dimensions:

(1) Nurturing care and management of children's recurring everyday requirements;

(2) Therapeutic care and extraordinary management of specific requirements of children in socially engineered living situation;

(3) Leadership and management of the living group; and

(4) Partnership in the implementation of the total organizational program (13).[1]

Reprinted with permission of the author and the National Association of Social Workers. From *1971 Encyclopedia of Social Work,* New York.
1. Numbers in paranthesis refer to bibliographical resources—see References.

Practice Tasks

While the actual child care work may differ with children served and from program to program, the tasks common to all child care work practices can be viewed for their *instrumental* or *expressive* components. By the emphasis upon one or the other component child care work becomes differentiated. For example, the task of "awakening children in the morning" might be valued more either for its *instrumental* component of getting the children up and ready for the tasks ahead of them, or for its *expressive* component of making personal contacts with the children and the starting of a day together (18).

The four dimensions of child care work establish the following clustering of child care tasks with the instrumental and expressive functions inherent in each:

1. *Care and maintenance of the children's everyday requirements.* The child-rearing activities immediately associated with physical care (feeding, clothing and the like) habit development (personal hygiene and social patterning), and self-management in interpersonal relations (discipline). Also, practice tasks associated with the children's planning, playing, working and the introduction of creative experiences into their daily lives.

2. *Therapeutic care and extraordinary requirements of children.* Personal counseling, tutoring, first-aid, life-space interviews.

3. *Leadership and management of the living group as a cohesive unit.* Leadership tasks involving the overall planning and working with the children toward the betterment of group functioning and relationship among group members. Management of food provision, clothing maintenance, and the unit's facilities; arrangement and coordination of the use of space and time.

4. *Implementation of the total institutional program.* Planning or consultation with other staff members on the institutional program, writing reports, and managing community contacts (6, 9, 13).

The Child Care Worker's Psychological Position

The child care worker is the "hub of the wheel" of residential care. A child's everyday life experiences—from receiving food, personal care, and a place of his own to the predictable assurance of having a person and a unit to belong to—are immediately linked with his interactions with the child care worker. In twenty-four hour residential care, the worker is the parent surrogate, regardless of his competence, because of the child's basic dependence upon him (6, 13, 14).

The living units of a residential institution make up basic primary and organizational groups of the institution as a whole. As the leader of a living group, the child care worker accomplishes or fails to accomplish the basic mission of the institutional program. Even in programs where the children associate intimately with other key persons—teachers, psychiatrists, indigenous group leaders, or staff leaders—it is the child care worker's personal influence that either sanctions or negates the impact of these other people.

The Child Care Worker's Sociological Position

Sociologically, the child care worker is an "outsider" in the living group. His position in the institution is dependent upon the administration of the institution, not on the living unit; his value and power are closely tied to social systems other than the one in which he works. But the child care worker is also dependent upon his base of work, the living unit. He can only have an impact upon the group if he is recognized by its members and his power and values are validated by them. He is apt, therefore, to adapt to the demands of the group living situation. His effectiveness, consequently, is directly related to the degree to which he can become an "insider" in this living group and how well he balances the values of the living group and those of the institution as a whole (18).

Despite the important part the child care worker plays in residential care, in most programs he is apt to be one of the lower status positions educationally, socially, geographically within the institution, and economically. He tends to be at the bottom of the hierarchy of decision-making, and most important, the institutional policies and procedures tend to by-pass him in the allocation of prestige—in attendance at key staff and case conferences, in location of offices, and in representation to the outside world (9, 13, 19).

The Child Care Worker's Professional Position

In addition to the conflict between psychological importance and sociological impotence the child care worker has as yet no professional reference group of his own (9, 17). In Canada and many European countries child care workers have a national organization of their own. In the United States, there is no national organization, although thirty-one states have organizations, for personnel employed in child-caring institutions. Many of these organizations devote most of their activities to the training of child care workers (4).

In the literature the child care worker is denoted as a professional (2, 9, 13, 16, 17, 20). Yet, child care work in the United States can be only described as a discipline-in-the-making. There is however, a shift from a preoccupation with the child care worker's role clarification and search for professional alignments—with what he ought to be as a person—to a concern with competence development. Whether he is to become a part of social work (13), education (12), or a professional discipline of his own (19) remains a debatable issue.

Training of Child Care Workers

Since the mid 1950's a trend towards professionalization of child care work has been intertwined with the emergence of educationally centered training programs. In most European countries professional preparation for child care work has been established for several decades (10, 12). In this country institutions of higher learning in twenty-one states offer child care courses. These vary from short-term institutes as part of university extension program to fully accredited undergraduate or even graduate courses (4). There is no clear curriculum pattern for the education of child care workers; there has been however, a distinct shift from programs patterned after social work training to more eclectic educational programs (12, 13). Opinions are presently divided between junior and community colleges or four-year colleges as the appropriate educational institutions for child care work training programs. The training for day child care and twenty-four-hour child care work tends to be viewed more generically and within one educational program (4).

History of Child Care Workers

The "ancestor" of today's child care worker was the matron of the orphanage and almshouse of the nineteenth century. She served as the overseer of the children's moral training to assure them respectability and usefulness (15, 21). The interest in child development, the perception of the child as a product of his environment, and the child welfare field's emphasis on family and foster care over institutional care in the first half of this century brought the shift from matrons to housemothers and houseparents for the care, rather than mere overseeing, of children. Congregate living was replaced by small living units, and *residential care* became the appropriate term for institutional service. Yet, this very emphasis upon the importance of the family living and the interest in small "family-like" living units also rendered the position of the child care person less desirable. Institutional care was seen as the last resort and only advisable when neither family nor foster care was attainable. The child care worker then became a secondary rather than an alternate child-rearing person; a perspective which still affects currently the appraisal of the child care worker (15, 21).

After World War II, residential programs were modeled after the orientation of educators, psychiatrists, psychologists, or social workers with the child care worker serving as auxiliary worker. In some respects, these helping professionals enhanced the practice repertoire of child care workers. Most important, they were responsible for the child care worker's role shifting from one of caring for the children as if he were the parent to the one in which he could have a therapeutic (change) impact. This shift introduced the eight-hour day, and gave the child care worker importance based upon his work rather than his personal involvement with the children. In other respects, these helping professionals diminished the position of the child care workers. Though further removed from the children's everyday life, the professionals became the high-status persons, assuming primary responsibility for the institutional program, as child care workers became further removed from the actual formulation or the care and treatment program of the children. Recently there has been a realignment. Child care workers are becoming recognized as on a par with other professionals, which is resulting in all the professionals becoming more centrally engaged in the residential aspect of the children's life (6, 14, 16, 21) and with the child care worker's specialty in bolder relief.

The Child Care Worker Today

The following sample data provide some indicators of the status of the estimated 100,000 child care workers in the United States. Approximately 50 percent work in institutions for emotionally disturbed and dependent children, 25 percent in institutions for the retarded, 15 percent in correctional institutions, and 10 percent in institutions for physically handicapped, homes for unwed mothers, and group homes. Two-thirds of all child care workers are women, less than one quarter of whom are classified as "never married." A somewhat larger percentage of the men are listed as single (9). A bimodal curve places the major age groupings between 26 and 35 and 46 and 55. Fifty percent of all child care workers have a high school education or less; 35 percent have had a year or more of college education; and 15 percent have had a college education or more (3, 9). Surveys of 1969 place the salary ranges of basic child care staff in public institutions at $4260 to $9930 (median $7830) (7), and in private institutions at $5000 to $12,000 (median at $6700) (5).

The Child Care Worker and His Future

The child care worker has clearly established himself as a decisive agent in twenty-four-hour residential service programs. His professional development is apt to follow a twofold trend: (1) an increase in his competence in treating and caring for children in group living situations, and (2) a broadening of his discipline by bringing persons together as social welfare personnel—group care workers, day care workers, migrant center children's workers, and foster parents—all those everyday-life workers involved with children and youth who need to be cared for while removed from their ordinary caring persons. The challenges are to improve the methods of caring for these children and develop training programs that will concentrate less on the role of the child care worker but more on the specific tasks he has to pursue as *the* child caring person.

REFERENCES

1. Berman, Samuel P., "A Project on a CLWA Pilot Project to Train New Child Care Workers," *Child Welfare,* Vol. 49, #3, March 1970, pp. 156–160.
2. Burmeister, Eva, *The Professional Houseparent,* New York, Columbia University Press, 1959.
3. Calvin, Ralph W., Hylton, Lydia and Rothschild, Barbara G., *Salaries and Manpower in Child Welfare,* 1966, New York, Child Welfare League of America, Inc., 1967.
4. Child Welfare League of America, *A National Directory of Child Care Workers Training Courses,* New York, Child Welfare League of America, Inc., 1969.
5. Child Welfare League of America, *Salary Study 1969,* New York, Child Welfare League of America, Inc., 1969.
6. Child Welfare League of America, *Standards for Services of Child Welfare Institutions,* New York, Child Welfare League of America, Inc., 1963.
7. Department of Institutions, *1969 Salary Study,* Olympia, Washington, Department of Institutions, State of Washington, 1969.
8. Grossbard, Hyman, *Cottage Parents—What They Have to Be, Know, and Do,* New York, Child Welfare League of America, Inc., 1960.
9. Hromadka, Van G., *Child Care Workers on the Road to Professionalization,* New York, The Hawthorne Center for the Study of Adolescent Behavior, 1966. (Mimeographed paper.)
10. Hromadka, Van G., "How Child Care Workers Are Trained in Europe," *Children,* Vol. 11, #6, November-December, 1964, pp. 219–222.
11. Hylton, Lydia F., *The Residential Treatment Center: Children, Programs, and Cost,* New York, Child Welfare League of America, Inc., 1964.
12. Linton, Thomas E., "The European Educateur Program for Disturbed Children." *American Journal of Orthopsychiatry,* Vol. 39, #1, January 1969, pp. 125–133.
13. Maier, Henry W., "Child Care as a Method of Social Work," *Training of Child Care Workers,* New York, Child Welfare League of America, Inc., 1963, pp. 62–81.
14. Maier, Henry W. (Editor), *Group Work as Part of Residential Treatment,* New York, National Association of Social Workers, 1965.
15. Maier, Henry W., *History of Trends of Child Care in Children's Institutions,* Minneapolis, Minnesota, University of Minnesota, 1957. (Unpublished paper.)
16. Maier, Henry W., and Kamps, Franz X., *Consultation Report on the Proposed Marin County Residential Treatment Center,* San Rafael, California, Marin County Printing Office, 1963.
17. Mayer, Morris F., *A Guide for Child Care Workers,* New York, The Child Welfare League of America, Inc., 1958.

18. Polsky, Howard W. and Claster, D.S., *The Dynamics of Residential Treatment,* Chapel Hill, North Carolina, The University of North Carolina Press, 1968.
19. Schwartz, William, *The Practice of Child Care in Residential Treatment,* Cleveland, Ohio, Bellefaire Symposium, 1968. (Mimeographed paper.)
20. Trieschman, Albert E., Whittaker, James K. and Brendtro, Larry K., *The Other 23 Hours,* Chicago, Illinois. Aldine Publishing Company, 1969.
21. Whittaker, James K., *Planning for Child Care Institutions,* Minneapolis, Minnesota, University of Minnesota, 1970. (Unpublished Doctoral Dissertation.)

22. The Parental Figures in Residential Treatment

Morris Fritz Mayer

One of the purposes of residential treatment is to neutralize or inactivate temporarily the influence of the child's parents and simultaneously to put the child under the care of adults who can become—partially and temporarily at least—substitute parental figures. While one predominantly conceives of staff members, such as houseparents, as carriers of these parental qualities, it is obvious that there are many potential parental figures within the institution who have a different degree of parental influence and authority.

Every child placed in a residential treatment center is to a certain degree a dependent child. The relationship to his own parents (if they are still available) continues to be the primary relationship. Some of the processes of search for and interaction with substitute parents are the same for the dependent child who lives away from home for mainly social reasons and for the disturbed child who lives away from home for psychological reasons.

The intensity of the trauma of separation from parents, present in all children placed away from their own homes, varies with each individual. There is no categorical difference in the reaction to trauma between so-

Reprinted with permission of University of Chicago Press from *Social Service Review,* Vol. 34, No. 4 (September, 1960), pp. 273–85.

called dependent children and disturbed children. The immediacy and intensity of the trauma requires attention. Without this attention treatment of the underlying problems is limited and sometimes impossible.[1]

One of the important ingredients of residential treatment is the warm, supportive, and, at the same time, controlling influence of parent substitutes. Hospitals have designated this ingredient in the somewhat elusive formula of T.L.C. (Tender Loving Care). Its content, dosage, and timing cannot be defined adequately. The effectiveness of this ingredient depends on the emotional capacity not only of the child who receives it but also of the adult who gives it.

While there are a large number of potential parental figures for each child in the institution, and while any adult with whom the child comes in contact can actually be selected and invested with parental functions, there is in most institutions a pattern of administrative assignment of such parental functions. Thus certain staff members are given a greater responsibility and opportunity to fulfill these functions previously carried out by parents.

The administrative structure of the treatment institution, the patterns of living, the treatment program, and the mode of integration of all services condition the development of the parental roles in the institution and set a climate which may be called "parental."

The term "parental" presents certain limitations and lends itself to the possibility of misinterpretation. I have indicated elsewhere that the inclusion of the term "parents" in the institutional staff nomenclature is improper, as it prejudges the role of the child-care staff.[2] Yet, while the institution cannot arbitrarily predetermine who will become a parental figure, it must provide staff ready to fulfill the parental role. The manner in which the child relates the role of the institutional parent to that of his own parent significantly affects the progress of his treatment.

The child brings with him to the residential treatment center the reality of his own parents. The institution confronts him then with three different levels of parental figures. The child must, therefore, deal with four levels of parental figures. The first is his own parents. The second we like to call the "care parents." These are the people who live with him and provide his daily needs. The third group we call the "power parents." These are the people who have power over the care parents and who determine, at least as the child sees it, his destiny in the institution. The fourth group we call hesitantly the "transference parents," namely, the therapists, although other people in the institution can become parental images to the child through transference.

1. Esther Glickman, *Child Placement through Clinically Oriented Casework* (New York: Columbia University Press, 1957), p. 328.
2. Morris F. Mayer, *A Guide for Child-Care Workers* (New York: Child Welfare League of America, 1958), p. xi.

The Natural Parent

It is impossible to discuss the role of institutional parents separately from the role which the natural parents have played in the past and continue to play while the child is in the institution. The parents who have been involved in treatment of the child in their own home have already struggled with the acceptance of treatment and the surrender of authority. They have had to accept the therapist's direction and to consent to a limited self-expression in the home.[3] They have had to defer to the therapist's authority in at least five areas: (1) They have asked to accept responsibility for physical arrangement for treatment, i.e., getting the child to the therapist, payment of fee, organization of time. (2) They have had to submit to the therapist's decision with regard to duration and frequency of treatment. (3) They have had to abstain from interpretation of causes and consequence of symptomatic behavior of the child while he is in therapy. (4) They have been asked to change certain modes of their own behavior upon the therapist's request. (5) They have been asked to accept certain changes in the distribution of roles between themselves. Very often treatment in the home has been discontinued because one or both of the parents could not accept the surrender of authority.[4]

In placement, of course, a much greater amount of authority has to be surrendered by the parents. They actually have to give up the child. This includes the surrender of the right to determination of his daily living and routines, his health care, his educational program, his psychotherapy, of the intensity of his religious training, and, above all, of the right for uncontrolled T.L.C. Two questions arise instantly: To whom do they surrender all these functions, i.e., who are in loco parentis (with or without legal sanction)? What parental rights do they retain? The answer to the second question is, Very few. Even the right to communicate with the child must, if necessary, be abolished. The degree of parental participation and the areas of such participation have to be determined by the institution. The area, however, in which parental authority remains intact is the *future*.

Parents must be assured that the surrender of authority is only temporary, that during the child's stay at the treatment center they should become ready to assume their parental authority after treatment is completed. The more sure parents are of their ability to resume their parental role in the future the more ready they usually are to surrender their authority for the present. The degree and mode in which parents can participate

3. Chester R. Dietz, M.D., and Marie E. Costello, "Reciprocal Interaction in the Parent-Child Relationship during Psychotherapy: Workshop, 1955," *American Journal of Orthopsychiatry*, XXVI (April, 1956), 376–91.
4. Ben O. Rubenstein and Morton Levitt, "Some Observations Regarding the Role of the Father in Child Psychotherapy," *Bulletin of the Menninger Clinic*, XXI (January, 1957), 16–27.

in the treatment institution and exercise some part of their parental function while the child is there depends on the organizational structure of the
institution and its philosophy. Some institutions have been creative in stimulating parents' constructive participation while the child is in placement.[5]
By supporting the parent's ego in this period ways can often be found to
guarantee a continuity of the parent-child relationship. It is the institution's
responsibility to facilitate parents' participation, by assuring such things
as regular visiting and regular correspondence, by planning for visits, and
above all by casework with parents to help them with the very problem of
surrender and ultimate resumption of parental authority.

For the child the surrender of parental authority is very hard to understand. The very fact that parents had to "give up" on him by placing him
in the institution may mark the parents as weak and helpless or as hostile
and selfish. As the child recognizes the tremendous amount of authority
which the parents have surrendered to the institution, the feeling about
parents' powerlessness, helplessness, and emasculation outweighs any
other feeling. Whenever possible, the child must be helped to see that the
reduction of authority does not mean the reduction of love from the parents. The feeling of numbness or of hyperactivity that we often observe in
children in the first weeks of institutionalization, or the disappearance or
increase of symptoms, may often be related not only to the panic of abandonment by the parents but also the shocking recognition of the institution's power over the parents, of the institution's quasi-omnipotence versus
the parents' impotence. The powerlessness of the parents handicaps the
treatment process itself. The parents' inability to exert authority in the
child's daily living may remove not only the immediate source of the disturbance but also the target of the child's hostility and therewith the guilt
emanating from these hostile feelings. These feelings are projected onto
other people who exert authority in the environment, on the care parent,
the power parent, and the therapist. The child often forgets the original
causes of his discomfort and disturbance. He is free to fantasy about his
remote parents, to invest them with wonderful qualities which they never
had. Only as the treatment proceeds and as the child can look back and
remember the parents in their reality can he see the parents again as
powerful sources of discomfort and disturbance. The more alive the reality
picture of the parents remains during the child's stay in the institution, the
more hopeful is the process of treatment. Therefore, methods must be
found to maintain this reality picture, short of giving up the child's protection from the parents' narcissistic interference with his welfare and his
treatment.

For the child, too, it is of paramount importance that he knows that the
stay at the residential treatment center is temporary and that his parents

5. Milton Willner, *An Institutional Approach to the Parent-Child Relationship* (New
York: Child Welfare League of America, 1955).

will resume their function as parents as soon as possible. This knowledge enables him to overcome the feeling of abandonment, to retain the parents as a concrete reality in the treatment process, and to relate his progress in treatment to the goal of returning home. Perhaps more important is the fact that he can see himself as a person who came from a family and returns to a family. He can see his stay at the center as a bridge between a past and a future, rather than as an end itself. It is almost impossible to treat younger children in a treatment center unless they have the feeling that they can return home. With children who cannot return home, either because the home is broken or undesirable or unavailable to them, treatment in an institution is very difficult. The fact that an agency is available is only a small and cold comfort. The uncertainty about where to go from the institution may bring about an indefinite delay of treatment readiness. With these children it is necessary to discuss future placement as soon as treatment permits it. This is especially difficult when the child and parent still nurse the illusion of ultimate reunion. Time must be allowed to work out such fantasies and to introduce reality. Some institutions have established, not only foster homes for children after they leave the institution, but foster homes to be, which are maintained long before the child is ready to leave the institution. Foster parents receive a standby fee and are remunerated for expenses involved while the child spends weekends and vacations with them. They are committed to accept the child after he leaves the institution. Such a plan seems particularly necessary for the younger, dependent child. For the older adolescent the problem is not as desperate, since independence, college, and the armed forces are often acceptable or preferred alternatives to any form of family living.

As the child gets ready to return to his own home, a gradual increase of parental authority is desirable and necessary. This increase should grow naturally out of parents' participation during the child's total stay in the institution.

Parent Substitutes

To whom have the parents surrendered their power? When the child wonders about this, it is not easy to give him a simple answer. He is virtually surrounded with parental figures. He may receive orders from a great many people, sometimes from as many as three or four in his living unit alone and from others who supervise his health, recreation, education, or religious training. Within this multitude of parental figures the child-care worker will soon emerge as the most significant to the child.

THE "CARE PARENT"

Child-care workers, counselors, nurses, houseparents, by the very nature of their assignment, become authority figures and parent substitutes. They protect the child in his daily struggle with his inner and outer environment. They organize the overwhelming muddle of daily events for the child in a non-punitive, affectionate way. They observe and respect the pace and tempo with which the child can deal with the biological and social demands of his life and try to adjust this pace gradually to the requirements of reality. In this process they become very meaningful to the child and the child may become meaningful to them. However, their authority is qualified. They receive their information and direction from others on the staff who know better the child's history, his family interaction, and his mental and emotional capacities, and who have more authority to direct the course of the child's treatment. They are asked to bring order into the child's life without really having the authority and capacity to organize it. They are asked to bring values into the child's life without really being certain what values are sought. They are asked to give love to the child and at the same time to maintain a distance which will make it possible to deal dispassionately with his negative behavior and his leaving. This kind of paradoxical assignment limits their authority, their security, and also their gratifications.

Child-care workers need something more in order to succeed in the struggle for the child's health. Clinical assurance of the child's ultimate treatability is not enough. There must be another force, an additional personal investment. This additional investment is not usually as clearly and consciously a part of the culture of the institution as is the one described by Jules Henry.[6] There the "idea-emotional factors" operating within the culture promote an atmosphere in which "the counselor's incentive to work parallels the child's struggle toward sanity, and ultimate reward for child and counselor is similar." Most institutions have a more multiply motivated staff. Most treatment centers are not as purposefully oriented toward providing emotional maturation and self-realization to their staff.[7] Yet, in a less homogeneous and more diffused way many child-care workers have this additional motivation. The simplest word that comes to mind would be "faith" in the child. It is a form of investment which the child-care worker makes either on the basis of strong superego command, religious or ethical convictions, or libidinal investment in the child similar to that which parents make.

The people who make this additional investment on the basis of moral demands and personal needs may on the other hand play with fire and expose themselves and the child to dangerous situations. Their "faith" may drive them to act against treatment plans. They may see themselves as the

6. Jules Henry, "The Culture of Interpersonal Relations in a Therapeutic Institution for Emotionally Disturbed Children," *American Journal of Orthopsychiatry,* XXVII (October, 1957), 725–34.

7. Bruno Bettelheim and Benjamin Wright, "The Role of Residential Treatment for Children: Symposium, 1954; 8: Staff Development in a Treatment Institution," *American Journal of Orthopsychiatry,* XXV (October, 1955), 705–19.

saviors of the child pitted against the "cold-hearted" professionals. In this way they may scuttle the treatment, may subtly steer the child away from the therapist, may set themselves up as the "good parent" versus all the other "bad parents." The administration can take measures to reduce these dangers. It can enable the care parent who brings this faith to the job to define his own parental function with each child, unless the care parent is rigidly fixed in his beliefs and investment. The administration can encourage the care parent to bring his own concepts of behavior expectations and social values to the formulation of treatment goals. The administration can help the care parent to develop his own "gestalt" of the child and the treatment process. For example, a care parent was described as follows:

Mr. Baxter is the son of very religious parents. While circumstances never permitted him to finish college, he has been a self-learner, with an unfocused but intense thirst for knowledge and a somewhat omnivorous intellectual curiosity. He is married, has held responsible jobs in business, but was always searching for something more fulfilling and essential than "selling pajamas." He started at the center by helping on week ends, became fascinated by the work, and finally decided to become a full-time counselor. This meant a sizable reduction of his income, which could be offset only through offering living arrangements to him and his family. Mr. Baxter has an unusual ability to relate to children, even those hard to reach. He had his own ideas on education and treatment, which deviated in a number of points from the philosophy of the professional staff in the center. He felt the therapists were "too distant," "too objective," and "too pessimistic." Some of the professional staff members questioned the risks involved in Mr. Baxter's tendency to be "in business on his own," but most of them felt that his tremendous interest and readiness to learn would outweigh all these risks, under the guidance of an imaginative supervisor.

Unfortunately, too often the care parent, who comes to the center with this faith and capacity for personal investment, does not receive the help he needs. It may be that this significant quality is not even discovered. It may be that the supervisor is so threatened by the neurotic component in this investment that he cannot utilize it constructively. It may be that the institution is not able to make available the intensive supervision and staff training which such development requires. It may be that the care parent's fear of the experts that surround him may cripple his confidence in his own convictions. Realistically we must face the fact that the majority of care parents are not possessed of this additional force of personal motivation. The average child-care worker is satisfied to be a channel through which parental care is dispensed, to take orders, and to submit to the experts. The most natural route to the child's spontaneity and intuitive expression is thereby blocked.

The care parents face another problem—their confusion about the institution's values. It is difficult for them to differentiate between methods of treatment and values. They may mistake tolerance of aggressive behavior, of swearing, of masturbation, for lack of moral standards. They may suppress the conflict between their values and those of the power parent, but stay in a state of latent rebellion against the supposed values of the institution. They are not then free to set standards and demonstrate values of their own, nor can they be expected to transmit the institution's values which they have not themselves incorporated. The failure to set standards is illustrated in the following incident:

> Mr. Handler, a rather unsophisticated new counselor, took Mike to a downtown drugstore. On the way back he noticed that Mike had pocketed a flashlight. Instead of handling it with the boy directly, he waited until their return to the institution when he took the boy to the supervisor. Questioned later on why he had not taken any action himself, Mr. Handler became very defensive and stated: "You allow a child to do everything else here. I thought perhaps stealing was also permitted."

Since children can take over values only through the process of identification from adults who have themselves incorporated these values, this care parent is severely handicapped in his role of ego ideal. It is this very role which has long been established as one of the most important tasks of the child-care worker.[8]

The major limitation of the care parent's authority comes from the fact that the child is in therapy and that a great number of controls over his life are set by the therapist and the people who coordinate the therapy program. The therapist has the right of intervention in many areas of the care parent's functioning. While the child usually is not aware of this intervention it still limits the authority of the care parent. We have seen that there are some major concessions of authority which the parent has to make while the child is treated in his own home. Five such concessions have been specifically mentioned. An analogy between the parents' and the care parents' role in this respect is very obvious. Care parents, too, must see that the child gets to the therapist at the right time. They must relegate decisions regarding length and frequency of treatment sessions to the therapist. They too must usually abstain from interpretation of causes of behavior. They too must adjust certain modes of daily living in accordance with the therapist's recommendations. They too must arrange for changes in their own role distribution upon therapeutic recommendations.

The care parent's authority is affected by therapy in many other ways. Since treatment infiltrates all areas of the child's life at a treatment center, the handling of clothing, food, recreation, education, or allowances may be altered according to the treatment plan for the individual child.

Another factor reducing the authority of the individual care parent is the

8. August Aichhorn, *Wayward Youth* (New York: Viking Press, 1943), p. 235.

necessary sharing of this responsibility by several child-care workers. The size of the group and the attention required by individual children make the coexistence of several care parents unavoidable. While one child-care worker must be responsible for the major care of the child, the presence of the others lowers the parental powers of each.

To the child over ten years of age the limitations of the care parent's authority becomes apparent. He recognizes a new social structure in which the person who gives the orders does not initiate most of them and has no power to amend them or to revoke them. Least of all has the care parent power to answer the most pressing question: "How long will I have to stay at the center?" The child also soon recognizes the real powers in the center—and leaves the care parents in no doubt about his awareness. Quite frequently the care parents themselves are eager to minimize their own power and to defer to the therapist's or the power parent's supposed instructions even in areas in which they themselves have jurisdiction. Their fear of the child's aggression, of the therapists' criticism, and of the power parent's disapproval may lead them to surrender more authority than necessary. An example of surrender of authority follows:

> Mrs. Lowe was on duty on Saturday when Jack demanded vehemently a substantial sum of money from his account to buy a rather expensive tie clip. There was also some reason to suspect that he would use the money for a runaway. Mrs. Lowe denied him the money because "the supervisor would not like it," implying that she by herself might have given the permission. The boy immediately called the supervisor for his approval because "Mrs. Lowe says it's up to you." In reality, Mrs. Lowe is authorized to use her own judgment regarding the youngsters' use of their allowance.

The younger child does not usually readily recognize the power structure at the institution and expects the care parents to be totally and fully responsible for him. He needs a long time to understand the limitations of the care parents, oftentimes long enough to have established a meaningful and important relationship with them, so that the recognition of their powerlessness can be more readily absorbed.

The relationship with the child is the care parent's major inherent power. If this relationship is not established, or if it breaks down, the authority of the care parent is jeopardized. He must invoke the authority of the institution, i.e., of the "power parent." Whenever he does this—and it is frequently necessary for him to do so—he appears weak and dependent to the child. Thus the child in a residential treatment center feels confronted not only with helpless natural parents but also with powerless care parents.

THE ''POWER PARENTS''

Who are the people who hold the power in the institution? From whom do the care parents derive their authority? Who determines how long a child is to stay? Who can fire the care parents and the therapist? These are some of the questions children and staff ask themselves soon after arrival.

Actually, the larger an institution, the more difficult it is to answer these questions. The social structure is so complex that often the ultimate power carrier remains anonymous. The board, the department of mental hygiene, the agency, the parole board, or the hospital—all are more or less anonymous powers of whom the child has no concrete concept. Younger children are usually even less aware of the extramural power structure than they are of the intramural ones. The older children somehow know that nobody at the center has the ultimate power, that there is an anonymous power behind the throne. At times they are concerned about how this anonymous supergovernment is informed about them. At times of distress and anger with the parental figures, they project upon the distant anonymous power carrier qualities of understanding and empathy ("if they only knew about me and what is going on here") or qualities of total indifference ("they do not care in the downtown office what happens here") or qualities of counter-hostility ("they would like to keep us here until we rot, as long as they can keep their jobs").

Actually children often forget this power structure if they are comfortable at the center and feel the strength of the institutional power parent and if the authority of the institutional power parent is not challenged by outside forces. Then it is only in crisis situations that the authority of the institutional power parent will be challenged by the children. If, on the other hand, there is no strength, if the authority of the institutional power parent is frequently interfered with from the outside, if frequent changes occur within the administration, the role of the institutional power parent will be challenged by the children and a great deal of confusion and insecurity will be the result.

The impersonal power structure does not answer the child's questions: "How does the person in power know about me?" "How does he decide when I am ready to leave and where I am to go?" "How does he know about my behavior?" Even in centers, therefore, which are headed by an administrator with rather limited authority, the child usually invests the administrator with powers far beyond his real assignment. However, in most well-run centers the man in charge has sufficient real authority to justify the children's expectations. The children regard him as the powerful parent within the institution who has his critical and protective eye on everyone—staff and children. He makes ultimate judgments (at least the children think so). Children need to be sure of his benevolence. He is the parental image—the parent of parents, the expert of experts. They have all kinds of fantasies about his age, his wisdom, and often about his personal possessions. Many times they think that this person "owns" the property of the institution, and often they do not readily recognize that he is bound by decisions of people who are more powerful than he. This need to have a powerful parent is very striking, especially with adolescents. They can accept limitations from this powerful but remote parent with greater ease and less fear of emasculation than from the care parent against whom, in daily struggle, they must defend their growing masculinity and onrushing adulthood. On the other hand, the power parent often becomes the object of the children's tremendous hostility and fear. Onto him they can project all the angry thoughts and death wishes not expressed against the natural father. Since he is remote enough and powerful enough, it is safer to have and to express these death wishes against him rather than against the care parent. Children essentially feel that the power parent is indestructible.

At times children invest the power parent with qualities of magic, of omnipotence and omniscience which he may use arbitrarily either for them or against them. It is necessary to dispel these fantasies, to help the children realize that their therapeutic needs and their educational interests are the compelling criteria for the power parent's decisions. They must know that the power parent sees them as individuals and recognizes their individual problems. They must know that he is carrying out a joint plan in which the therapist and care parent also participate. This is not easy since the very structure of the institution nourishes the children's fantasies about the power parent. For instance, John, a rebellious adolescent, has broken the cottage rules. He has seen a number of intermediary staff before he sees the director. Interviews with others have already weakened the force of his attack, softened his defiance. Actually he is ready to give in before he enters the power parent's office. A few kind words by the power parent and the issue is settled. Yet in the eyes of John, the other children, and perhaps even the staff, the legend of the power parent's omnipotence is confirmed.

Sometimes the power parent himself nourishes this legend. He enjoys the role of the magician, the *deus ex machina*. He lets the children believe that he knows all about them, that he can look through them, as it were, that he can solve their problems when no one else can, that their fate is in his hand, as in the hand of God. Such a power parent may surround himself with a weak staff, dependent people who do not look for self-fulfilment but for protection and perpetuation of their dependency relationship. Such a power parent often has a fear of the experts similar to that observed in the care parent. He cannot accept other staff members as equals and cannot permit them the independence they need; basically, he sabotages their work. The nature of residential treatment will not permit such a power parent to retain his power for long, since the need for intradisciplinary expertness and for interdisciplinary equality requires a strong integrator. The head of the center must be relatively powerful, since he must be a leader to the staff and a vigorous interpreter of the program to the community. The qualities of foresight, compassion, courage, patience, militancy, and judgment must be outstanding parts of his personality. These qualities, as well as his status role, enable him naturally to become a parent figure to the whole institution. As the main parent figure he is also the main value setter. His values are predominant in the institution, and he is, at least by indirection, the supreme ego ideal. Although standards and values may be partially set by the anonymous power carrier, they can become real to the children only as they have been adopted and incorporated first by the personal power parent and then in turn by the care parent.

The size of the treatment center may well be a handicap to the power parent. Although he can never be as close to the children as the care parent, and although he derives a part of his power from his remoteness, he has to be close enough to be well acquainted with every child and to be able to assure every child that he knows him and protects him. Otherwise, children may know him only in crisis situations when their own defenses are considerably higher or lower than usual. The power parent may then have to make decisions in support of the care parent with whom the child may be in conflict at this time. The child must be sure that the power parent knows him sufficiently to empathize with him at all times, particularly in crisis situations. Children who frequently see the power parent surrounded by or in conference with many adults must feel that they themselves have access to him. The treatment center has to be small enough that such assurances can be realistically given. In the larger institution, compromises must be found which allow the children to relate to the power parent.

THE MIDDLEMAN

There are three forms of compromise. The simplest form of compromise is to divide the institution into independent smaller units. If these units are geographically independent the head of each unit may take over the role of the power parent, and the head of the total institution may remove himself into greater anonymity.

If the units are on the same campus or in the same building, the head of the unit becomes a middleman between power parent and care parent. At the present stage of development of these attempts at decentralization, it is difficult to say what the sociopsychological role of the middlemen is. Do the children see them as "qualified power parents"? In what areas is their authority final? What fantasies do the children have about them and about the man behind them? These questions cannot be answered yet.[9]

Another form of power delegation is made through the role of the assistant—the man who sits in the office adjoining the director's. What part of his authority the power parents delegates depends on many factors, in-

9. Morris F. Mayer, "The Unit Social Worker," *Child Welfare,* XXXV (December, 1956), 23–26.

cluding personal and professional qualifications and community demands on his time. The surrender of the parental rather than organizational functions to the assistant can negatively affect the structure of the treatment center and the security of the children. More study and investigation is needed in this area.

It is important, therefore, whatever the areas of delegation are, for the power parent to back up the middleman and to refrain from interjecting himself within the areas of delegated authority. The primary purpose of delegation of authority is to facilitate the children's access to the accepting and benign authority figure. It certainly is not to confront the child with still another powerless parental image.

THE ''TRANSFERENCE'' PARENT

Every object relationship to parental figures is in a way an unconscious transfer of feelings which originated in the relationship to the parent. The causes for this transfer of feelings are unconscious.[10] The child unconsciously expects the objects of his affection to react to him as he feared, or hoped for, or remembers or fantasies the reactions of his parents. An institution which is full of adults offers many opportunities to the child for such a transfer of these unreasonable, inappropriate feelings. Gardener, teacher, cook, or nurse may be the objects of these fantasies. But, since their roles within the institution force them to fulfil a concrete function in the child's environment, transference cannot really develop. They become participants in the child's reality. They may become objects of identification but not of transference. It is only the therapist who can permit the transference. Not only can he permit the child to fantasy that he is an imagined parent figure, but he can allow him to relive in the therapy session some of his relationship with the parents. The therapist becomes a parental figure through transference.

Transference is of course not the only basis of the relationship between the therapists and the child. Contracts between child and therapist may be based on many different forms of transference.[11] Especially in the treatment center, the therapeutic utilization and interpretation of transference phenomena may be possible only in a limited and flexible way. The absence of the parent represents a considerable handicap to the development of transference. In the process of psychotherapy, the therapist must often use detours and byways in order to reach the essential area of the child-parent relationship, which, while the major original source of the child's trauma, is somewhat anesthetized by separation. Nevertheless, the child at

10. Ralph A. Greenson, M.D., "The Classic Psychoanalytic Approach," in *American Handbook of Psychiatry,* Silvanvo Arieti, M.D., Ed. (New York: Basic Books, 1959), II, 1407 ff.

11. Sara Kut, "The Changing Pattern of Transference in the Analysis of an Eleven-year-old Girl," *Psychoanalytic Study of the Child,* VIII (1953), 355–78.

the institution will try to cajole, seduce, coerce the therapist into assuming in reality the role into which he fantasies him. He will want him to be not only the "super-parent" but also the "super-care parent" and the "super-power parent." If the therapist is persuaded to fulfill this function, if he tries to "mix in" with the management of the child at the center, he may not only impair the development of the treatment relationships and of transference in particular but also seriously handicap the child's relationship to the other parental figures at the center. He has to remain a "parent" in the child's fantasy only. Sometimes the inadequacy of institutional management, the inadequacy of personnel, and his own anxiety or lack of confidence in the institutional staff provoke the therapist into taking direct action rather than operating through existing channels. The child's urgent request for a new jacket, piano lessons, or a trip to the zoo brings forth parental impulses in the therapist which impel him to meet these requests rather than have the care parent meet them. If the institutional budget, or its red tape, delays the fulfillment of these requests, the therapist may at times feel compelled to show the child his support, or he may be sufficiently angry to want to take action himself. He then sides with the child against the parental figures, becomes the "good parent" who gives love versus the "bad parent" who does not give love. Basically the immediate gains of such intervention are far outweighed by the long-range losses.

This, of course, does not mean that the therapist should not significantly influence the child's environment. Indeed, only to the degree that the influence of therapy on the total milieu is significant can residential treatment be carried out. A therapeutic milieu inheres in the structure of the treatment center, in the plant itself, in the choice, distribution, and training of staff, and in the educational, recreational, and living program. Only if the therapist can feel assured that a therepauetic milieu is being maintained can he work with individual children. Once he starts working with the individual child, he has to accept the therapeutic milieu as a reality. Only thus can he help the individual child to react and adjust to this reality. He must influence this environment by indirection rather than by direction. Otherwise, he becomes just one more parent substitute in the child's life at the center.

The Transmission of Therapeutic Direction

This brings us to some of the problems of transmission of therapeutic direction. We have discussed the transmission of authority and the transmission of values from the power parent to the care parent. The transmission of therapeutic direction is more complicated. In a treatment center the therapist has to have direct and continuing contact with the care parent. The care parent receives therapeutic direction from both the power parent and the therapist. The need for harmony and understanding between power

parent and therapist is, therefore, obvious. Together with planful staff selection, careful staff supervision, and strong co-ordination, the guiding
principle guaranteeing staff harmony seems to be mutual trust. Only if this
trust is established, only if in crisis situations power parent, care parent,
and therapist support one another, and only if in day-by-day life-situations
they give each other the benefit of the doubt can the treatment center provide a therapeutic atmosphere.

The power parent has to be in command of all therapy in order to create
a therapeutic atmosphere and to play his important role with the children.
He cannot be the chief expert in all of the many disciplines needed. He
must surround himself with experts and give them the freedom they need
to carry out their jobs, and he must consult with the experts on all decisions. He must, however, remain the chief "sponsor of treatment."[12] He
must transmit to the care parents the concepts of treatment in all the many
areas with the treatment principles so that treatment is total. The institutional parent figures then will become parents who are motivated not only
by a need for self-fulfilment, and by a desire to heal but by the deep
knowledge of how to use the tools of everyday living in the healing
process. This may ultimately bring about an application, on a wider basis,
of Fritz Redl's "life-space interview," so that events and emergencies of
everyday life can be therapeutically handled, as they occur, by the people
who live with the child.[13]

The child in the institution is surrounded by parental figures. Most outstanding among them are his natural parents with whom the child contin-
use to have a primary relationship. Because of their surrender of authority
to the institution their image appears to the child to be, at least temporarily, weak. The people who take care of the child during the day, the "care
parents," are very important figures, although the structure of the institution and often their own personality needs let them appear as weak. The
person in charge of the institution, the "power parent," plays a remote but
very important role to the child. Actually from him emanate authority,
values, and therapeutic direction. The degree to which the therapist of the
child becomes a parent figure depends on the pathology of the child and
on the particular form of therapy. The therapist cannot become a real parent figure and at the same time retain the therapeutic role that will enable
the child to develop a transference relationship. The integration of these
parental figures into a harmonious and constructive influence is one of the
most difficult functions of the institution.

12. Donald A. Bloch, M.D., and Earle Silber, M.D., "The Role of the Administrator
in Relation to Individual Psychotherapy in a Residential Treatment Setting," *American Journal of Orthopsychiatry*, XXVII (January, 1957), 69–74.
13. Eveoleen N. Rexford, M.D., *et al.*, "The Life Space Interview: Workshop,
1957," *American Journal of Orthopsychiatry*, XXIX (January, 1959), 1–44.

23. Communication and Cottage Parent Supervision in a Residential Treatment Center

John Matsushima

In the residential treatment center, cottage parents are highly influential in providing a therapeutic living experience for the children. Emotionally disturbed children are sorely in need of mature adults who will protect them from their own and other's aggression and impulsivity.[1] Educating them in the means toward self-control and more acceptable behavioral standards is a major responsibility for the cottage parent.

One would think that staff members who carry out such important responsibilities would be well integrated into the treatment team. And yet, more than those in any other specialization in the residential treatment center, the cottage parents are a frequent source of administrative concern:

> Suitable people are hard to find, and often a rapid turnover in such personnel is considered inevitable. And their failure to become integrated produces innumerable problems in a treatment program, such as a breakdown in communications, creation of staff tensions, and a defective program of child care and management.[2]

Cottage parents indicate resistance in more immediate ways by missing conferences, using therapists' advice only limitedly, and not reporting cottage incidents of treatment significance. As the cottage parents' morale deteriorates, they come to feel less identified with the institution's purposes, and they may be convinced that the "powers that be" do not appreciate them. Discouraged, they tend to become less conscientious about cottage life, and some drift into a compromise with the children's methods of managing themselves. Erosive subcultures among the children, complete

Reprinted with permission of Child Welfare League of America, Inc., from *Child Welfare,* Vol. 43, No. 10 (December, 1964), 529–35.
1. Howard Jones, *Reluctant Rebels* (New York: Association Press, 1960), p. 104.
2. James F. Berwald, "Cottage Parents in a Treatment Institution," *Child Welfare,* Vol. 39, No. 10 (1960), 10.

with status prerogatives, differentiated roles, and enduring values, may work in direct opposition to the treatment goals for which the institution exists. But sanctioning and manipulating the children's influence patterns may result in more peaceful living for the cottage parents, so that treatment considerations may give way to expedience.[3]

Clearly, treatment is dependent on integrated efforts among all segments, professional and nonprofessional, of the institution staff. Because such harmony is obviously so much to be desired, its tenuous nature in institutions has provided a fascinating subject of inquiry for researchers and practitioners. It has been pointed out that cottage parents feel threatened by their relative lack of formal education and their modest socioeconomic backgrounds.[4] Other authors state that it is difficult for cottage parents to adjust their methods of caring for disturbed children, since they constantly contrast recommended procedures with their personal experiences in child rearing. Grossbard stresses that the influx of professionals into residential treatment has complicated the cottage parents' responsibilities.[5] Consequent role confusion is seen as a reason for rivalry and dissension.

Whatever the specific remedies proposed, one must recognize that any institution is a community composed of human beings in personal interaction. As human beings, all of the staff have the need for respect, recognition, and appreciation, as well as achievement.

> An institution is a highly organized arrangement whereby human beings can live together and meet each other's and their own needs in a relatively predictable way. . . . The people who compose [it] are not automatons devoted only to attaining the purposes of the [institution]. . . . They carry out the prescribed activities not only on the institution's terms, but also on their own terms. They gather information, think, appraise, and want to try out things that are new. Human beings are always difficult if one tries to *fit* them into a framework of some mechanical institution organized only to fulfill some explicit goal. . . . Failure to meet the needs of any people, be they patients, staff, or community, will lead to suppression, and resulting challenge of the institutional structure. The very existence of the institution depends upon the fact that to a large extent it meets the needs of all the people in it.[6]

Investment in Cottage Parents

Among the immediate needs of cottage parents are improved salaries, clearly defined job assignments, better living quarters, and shorter hours.

3. Howard Polsky, *Cottage Six* (New York: Russell Sage Foundation, 1962).
4. Ivan Belknap, *Human Problems of a State Mental Hospital* (New York: Mc-Graw-Hill Book Co., 1956).
5. Hyman Grossbard, *Cottage Parents: What They Have To Be, Know, and Do* (New York: Child Welfare League of America, 1960).
6. Alfred H. Stanton and Morris S. Schwartz, *The Mental Hospital* (New York: Basic Books, 1954), p. 28.

Beyond these, however, are the less tangible but equally important aspects that contribute toward staff morale and sound institution functioning, such as respect, support, and recognition in *fact* as well as intent.

Some of the more effective means of working toward the avowed goals with cottage parents are the development of an intensive staff training program, supervision by professionals, and an associated communication structure that fosters exchange of views among all segments of the staff. The desirability of such a program is widely acknowledged, but its content, design, and rationale need further study. The attitude underlying the *way* in which educational-supervisory efforts are carried out is crucial to its success. If the professionals respect the cottage parents and demonstrate it by being helpful and investing a substantial amount of time, their example speaks far more strongly than the most ambitious of administrative pronouncements.

Our experience at the Children's Aid Society of Cleveland has shown us how important educational efforts are as a means of improving services to children, strengthening staff identification with the institution's goals, and promoting communication among all services. With full awareness of the significance of cottage parents in the total treatment effort, staff training and supervision were designed for the aforementioned purposes. The medical director, individual treatment staff members, and the cottage parent supervisor all invest a sizeable proportion of their time in regular weekly meetings with the cottage parents. The meetings with the medical director, which include all cottage parents and professional staff, center on the broad aspects of child development, emotional disturbances, and management techniques.

> Many subjects reappear for discussion fairly often: for example, discipline and punishment (we do not permit physical punishment), eating problems, runaways, stealing, sex play. But the cottage parents also . . . bring up many other things—gripes about each other, about the administration, about the food and their work schedules. When the gripes are legitimate, steps are taken . . . to rectify things.[7]

The individual treatment staff members confer weekly with each cottage parent to exchange pertinent information regarding the children, their families, and cottage observations. Because the workers concentrate on evaluating the child's behavior in the cottage and giving practical advice, many of these contacts are of immediate tangible benefit in management.

It is the third element in our educational-supervisory program that will be reported in detail in this paper. This element consists of weekly group supervision of cottage parents by a senior social worker. Group supervision as a communicative method per se bears close study. We are particu-

7. Berwald, *op. cit.*, p. 9.

larly interested in its content with relation to nonprofessional staff in an institution setting. The supervisor serves as a communicating link between the cottage parents and professional staff. This is only one of several integrative links, of course. Still, as the professional representing the authority of the medical director to cottage parents—and as the member of the professional staff most broadly in touch with the management specifics of cottage life—the supervisor occupies a key position.

Rationale and Focus of Supervision

Our selection of supervisory aims and techniques was based on the training needs of the cottage parents, on agency expectations, and on a recognition of the priorities of integration among staff in an institution setting.

The cottage parents' role at the Children's Aid Society is that of parent surrogates within the cottage-living experience. The accent is on providing necessary controls on antisocial behavior and encouraging the children to deal with dangerous and destructive feelings in a constructive way, such as by verbalization instead of action. A major means to these objectives is the presence of a cottage atmosphere in which management is based on an understanding of the behavioral manifestations of the children's problems. Education toward acceptable behavior is a direct technique that is used by cottage parents, one element of which is the placing of limits and the withdrawal of privileges. Supervision was needed to translate theory into practical, usable "action" terms.

Another important determinant in the design of supervision was the personal background of the cottage parents. Those who have performed most satisfactorily in this agency have been lay people. We sought adults of stable character who had a healthy interest in children. "The amount of their formal education seems relatively unimportant. Some of them are older persons, married or widowed, who have reared children of their own . . . others, younger, draw upon [an] unusual capacity for empathy with the children."[8] Capacity to limit without rejecting, to control without coercing, and to love without demanding was essential to the management of the impulsive, aggressive children that comprise our population. At times, young college graduates who were interested in preprofessional experience have served as cottage parents. But usually, maturity, stability, and judgment were more characteristic of the adults who chose to be career cottage parents.

The chief social worker, the original cottage parent supervisor, selected group supervision as a method because she recognized that communication among cottage parents was fully as important as the content of supervision. Each cottage is assigned four or five cottage parents, but their working

8. *Ibid.,* p. 8.

shifts are such that only two are on duty at any time. There are some individual conferences, but the weekly meeting with the supervisor is the only
collective discussion opportunity for the full staff of each cottage. With a
combination of parent surrogates sharing such an emotionally demanding
common assignment, disagreements among them were inevitable. Group
supervision offered a means of airing differences and attempting to resolve
them before they grew to more serious proportions.

The Supervisor as Translator

One of the supervisor's responsibilities is to give specificity to the child
care principles outlined in cottage parent meetings with the medical director. The supervisor is particularly watchful for misinterpretations in view
of the complex content and the cottage parents' lay background. The psy-
chiatrically sophisticated techniques that they must learn may be quite
foreign and difficult to reflect in performance, and rigid adherence or resistance to principles may become common. Since most of the cottage parents have reared their own children, it is only natural that they have strong
convictions about the best management techniques. Direct contradictions
to their firmly established attitudes are avoided when possible, and the
rationalization that disturbed children are entirely unique is not always
challenged.

An example of a professionally sound principle that may result in misunderstanding by cottage parents is the therapeutic desirability of children's verbalizing aggression. To tolerate open defiance is extremely difficult, particularly for those cottage parents most anxious about preserving
group control. Because the professionals tend to anticipate the cottage parents' counteraggression to the children, they may often emphasize the prohibition regarding the cottage parents' feelings and overlook the possible
consequences to group control. In the interests of literal adherence to instructions, the cottage parents may adopt an attitude of noninterference
with widespread defiance, although their unstated resentment may be apparent in supervision.

The supervisor clarifies the principle as being a general guide, since,
otherwise, the cottage parents' frustration may easily mount into a conviction that the professionals do not truly appreciate the pressures in cottage
life. Although the unconscious basis of their frustration involves more than
the misconception of a principle, it is nevertheless possible to enable improved management via educational techniques.

Encouraging the children to express strong feelings, such as anger, in
words need not require the cottage parent to stand by helplessly and be
abused. Neither does it require him to ignore a child whose continuing defiance may threaten to precipitate the others into open violence. Specifically, the child *can* be sent to his room or *can* be separated from the group

with the explanation that his being upset does not entitle him to agitate all of the other children, too.

In short, the supervisor indicates specific ways in which the principle can be followed without prohibiting verbal aggression or precipitating rebellion among more children. These measure are based on prudence and common sense, although the distinction must be drawn that separation is based on protective rather than on angrily punitive grounds. As well as the cottage parents may absorb this principle, however, the supervisor must still offer continual guidance. Relationship, after all, is an emotional exchange rather than an intellectual process, so that the staff who participate in highly charged interactions must be able to rely on the objectivity of the supervisor.

It is incumbent upon the supervisor to report cottage parent reactions and misinterpretations to the other professionals and particularly to the medical director. Subsequent full-staff discussions can then emphasize the management (rather than the therapeutic desirability) of verbal aggression. In this way, the content of the meetings can be attuned to the cottage parents' desire to effectively handle the children according to professionally acceptable techniques—instead of implying a need to protect the children against the adults' counteraggression.

Another example of misconstruing principles involves the management of soiling. Soiling is described to the cottage parents as a symptom of an emotional problem, the overcoming of which may not be within the mastery of the child at that time. The provocative nature of this symptom is discussed in order to help cottage parents understand the futility of punitive measures. Simply requiring the child to report such incidents and to clean himself and his clothing are standard procedures. Furthermore, cottage parents are encouraged to indicate their concern and to urge the child to discuss such instances in treatment.

The unconscious bases of soiling may be so literally accepted by some cottage parents, however, that they may respond with sympathy and over-attentiveness—thus, in effect, *rewarding* the child for retaining the symptom. Such misinterpretations can also occur around symptoms and problem behavior such an enuresis, open masturbation, mutual sex play, etc. The supervisor emphasizes that understanding is not equivalent to ignoring, and he supplements his clarification with unambiguous, exact instructions.

Fostering Communication Within the Cottage

Through group supervision, the supervisor helps the cottage parents to learn, to discuss, and to voice disagreement if indicated. Experience in work with groups is helpful to the supervisor because resistant subgroups can be sensed, competition felt, and the cottage parents' feelings of loyalty to one another respected. A proposed change in cottage routines, for example, may be brought up because of genuine concerns or as a move representing other conflicting staff issues of long standing. Competition for added status or implied criticism of other staff may be additional motivations.

Diagnosing the circumstances may prompt the supervisor to impose an immediate decision, pose alternatives, or encourage discussion, as the situation requires. Under the best of conditions, harmony is difficult because the children exploit disagreements and attempt to manipulate the staff. As in any family, the "parents" are hard put to avoid occasional differences in dealing with the children.

Criticism of associates, disagreement with therapists' advice, or discouragement with the children can be handled by recognition of pressures, explanation, and, at times, direct authority. Here again, the cottage parents' lay background is a strength. In most instances, the cottage parents come to their job having learned the need for self-discipline in any work relationship. The lack of psychiatric and teamwork training, even though it may prompt difficulties, is accompanied by a willingness to follow instructions even in the absence of complete comprehension. As mature adults, too, many of whom are parents of grown children, they are able to appreciate the institution's philosophy that places children's welfare above all other considerations.

Oftentimes, in preference to giving direct instructions, the supervisor outlines a problem and involves the cottage parents in contributing to an acceptable solution. Because decisions by consensus always stand a greater likelihood of being effective, group deliberation is sought when appropriate.

In one recent instance an excitable, highly provocative child was consistently successful in promoting bedtime riots among the other children. Removal of privileges, extra work, temporary exclusion from the dormitory, etc., had all been tried (at the supervisor's instruction) and had failed.

The cottage parents had become increasingly frustrated, angry, and almost dared the supervisor to propose a remedy to this "insoluble" problem. In these circumstances, their response to the boy's provocation literally precluded the success of recommendations from any authority. As the supervisor reviewed the problem, he moved into the role of discussion leader rather than outside authority. He encouraged them to call on their own impressions and experience, and he urged their joint efforts toward an acceptable solution.

The energies that were formerly expressed as resistance were now turned toward the cottage situation. A number of proposals were made, the final decision being to make some strategic shifts in the placement of the boys' beds in relation to one another. Peace returned at bedtime, and it seemed that success resulted just as much from the cottage parents' favorable response to the decision-making process as from the decision per se.

Handling Intracottage Staff Tensions

Instances of disharmony among cottage parents are more difficult to resolve. With each cottage parent feeling that criticism of one another, no
matter how justified, may result in strained personal relationships, most
staff members prefer to overlook all but the grossest incidents. The very
loyalty that is fostered to promote unanimity in handling the children
handicaps the cottage parents in relation to personal disputes. Because the
institution is their full-time community, it seems logical that cottage parents are reluctant to risk antagonizing their peers. One can readily understand their attitude: "There isn't much satisfaction in being right if the
other person is going to be mad. We have to live here, but you don't."

Details such as folding and putting away the children's laundry, turning
in clothes for repairs, and ordering needed supplies are cottage routines
that may become issues when a staff member neglects his duties. The others may quietly take over the responsibility, but they eventually become
resentful if everyone does not take his proper turn. Changes in bedtime for
the children, giving paying jobs, etc., can create even greater confusion if
each cottage parent does not clear with the others before instituting a
change. Resentment mounts as the cottage parents hesitate to complain to
the person involved. The supervisor may not be informed because for a cottage parent to do so might be construed as disloyalty by other cottage parents. The result often is that resentment festers while the cottage parents
silently await supervisory intervention or open conflict.

The supervisor's handling of intrastaff situations varies from the use of
individual conferences to pointed group discussions. In most instances the
latter is favored, since communication must be achieved among all concerned. The cottage parent who neglects cottage routines must correct his
practice, but so, too, must his associates who allow potential disagreements
to grow without making communicative efforts. Supervisory intervention
that stresses mutual responsibility, then, is aimed toward eliminating the
issue while simultaneously avoiding undue embarrassment to any one cottage parent in the presence of his peers. The supervisor concentrates on the
issues rather than the personalities, and he gives priority to the effect of
staff disunity on the children rather than the personal needs of the staff.
Here again, if the staff has perspective on the institution's purpose, compromises regarding personal differences become more palatable.

Cottage Parent Supervisor as Communication Link

Another important responsibility of the cottage parent supervisor is his
function as a link between the therapists and the cottage parents. The over-
all communication structure stresses regular and substantial contacts

among all staff, and we make an extraordinary effort to integrate the treatment and management aspects of the program. The meetings with the medical director, however, include all of the cottage parents so that content
cannot routinely concern only a single cottage. The conferences with the
individual treatment staff center on a limited number of children, and
much of the time goes toward keeping abreast of current incidents of significance to a specific child.

In contrast, the supervisor's meetings are structured in such a way that
the cottage parents in each cottage are seen as a separate group. Several
factors combine to distinguish these meetings: (1) the cottage parent
supervisor's authority originates with the medical director, but differences
with official policies are more easily voiced to the lesser authority; (2) the
limited number of participants allows greater freedom of expression; (3)
management questions can be answered in detail as applied to certain children or subgroups of children; (4) intracottage issues among children or
staff can be more comfortably and appropriately discussed.

It is of paramount importance for the cottage parent supervisor to communicate summarized, pertinent material to the medical director and the
rest of the professional staff. When each therapist is kept aware of the flow
of cottage life, he can more effectively maintain a grasp on the reality aspects of a child's reactions in treatment. When the medical director considers priorities for staff training meetings, knowledge of specific issues
that are currently occupying staff time helps to supplement his own observations.

Equally important is the supervisor's direct responsibility to the cottage
parents. The latter must feel confident that their supervisor will continually evaluate the appropriateness of expectations that are held for them by
the professionals. Thus, if there are treatment recommendations such as
extended individual supervision of certain children, more private living
quarters for some cases, or bringing resistive children to treatment interviews, the therapists must clear with the cottage parent supervisor. This
procedure is formally structured under the medical director's authority as
a protection to the cottage parents in meeting many separate responsibilities, and it is the supervisor's task to exercise decision on an appropriate
basis.

In essence, the cottage parent supervisor's authority in the residential
treatment setting, as in all supervisory relationships, is as effective as the
degree to which the staff remains voluntarily responsive. In addition to the
usual expectation of fair and objective attitudes, the cottage parents have
every right to expect the supervisor to identify with their interests as well
as those of the children and the institution. Authority must serve as an enabling, supporting, and educational function as well as a directive one. To
the extent to which the supervisor fulfills his role in concert with the rationale of the educational-supervisory structure, the cottage parents can be

helped to function on behalf of the children and the formal institution purpose.

24. How Child Care Workers Are Trained in Europe

Van G. Hromadka

Persons who work with children have long recognized that the child in institutional care can be helped to make a healthful adjustment to life by being treated as an individual and not just as a member of the group. The child has to be exposed to the benefits of group experience—but this group experience should not keep his individual psychosocial needs from being met.

This approach assumes that the child's total living experience should be therapeutic and, therefore, be planned and managed in the interest of his healthful adjustment. Child care workers, often called "cottage parents," "house parents," or "counselors," hold a key position in this new approach to care: They have the unique opportunity to observe the child in an informal setting in his hour-to-hour living experience.

With this approach has come the realization that child care staff usually lack the professional know-how and status for the responsibilities they carry. As director of a research project to find ways of upgrading child care staff, I have found a growing awareness among institutional administrators of the importance of the child care worker's role. Nevertheless, people coming into the field have extremely limited or no child care training. Moreover, the rivalry between so-called professional and nonprofessional workers is still strong. The efforts made in this country to remedy the situation are inadequate and lack a uniform approach. Most of the training is carried out through local inservice training programs or short-term extramural courses, seminars or workshops, which usually deal mainly with a specific local emergency. Experiments in employing child care workers with professional training in some related discipline have had mixed results.

Reprinted with permission of Children's Bureau, U.S. Dept. of Health, Education, and Welfare from *Children,* Vol. 11, No. 6 (November-December, 1964).

The situation is somewhat different in Europe—or at least in those European countries with the more advanced child care programs. Judging from my own research and from reports made to the United Nations, the International Union for Child Welfare, and the International Association of Child Care Workers, such countries would include Austria, Belgium, Denmark, England, France, Germany, Holland, Switzerland, Sweden, and Yugoslavia. Except for Belgium and Sweden, I have studied the approach to training of child care personnel at firsthand in all these countries and have found more similarities than differences among the various systems both in philosophy and practice. In this article when I speak of Europe and European ways I am referring to these countries.

The first thing that impressed me in Europe was the cohesiveness of staff in those child care institutions which had an interdisciplinary team. The representatives of the various professional disciplines seemed like a homogeneous group; they spoke to each other on equal terms and respected each other. In explanation, I found that: (1) most of the psychologists, psychiatrists, social workers, and teachers on these teams had some direct experience in taking care of children in institutions, or, in addition to their original professional training, they underwent the same training courses as the child care workers; and (2) most workers who took direct care of children were graduates of comprehensive training programs in child care which were never less than 2 years in duration.

The other difference I noted between practices here and in Europe relates to the overall scope and concept of child care. While in this country we tend to emphasize services to children who are physically or emotionally handicapped, in European countries there seemed to be much less differentiation between types of children for whom services were provided and a greater emphasis on giving equal importance to all children. This emphasis dates from World War II, when Europe was confronted with the problems of evacuation, mass mobility, and the care of children separated from their families. Europe was unprepared for this task and had to use every human resource available and make many improvisations. Inexperienced workers shared the burden with experienced workers; both learned a great deal from each other. In this process, newly recognized or discovered methods, tools, work habits, and activities were found useful in the child's rehabilitation.

The empirical knowledge derived from the experimentation and research of World War II was used to develop the postwar child care programs and training. Two ideas particularly were emphasized:

1. *A child is always a child, regardless of his personal handicap or living circumstances.* He is never less than that—not a thing (a case), nor an animal, even when he acts like one. He is never more than that: he is not an adult, even when he acts like one. Therefore, child care programs and training for child care should be concerned with the normal child, taking

into account, of course, the special needs of the handicapped child. The handicapped child's deviant ways should be understood and dealt with in close line with normality. Frequently, similarities rather than differences should guide the rehabilitative process. A handicapped child should not be treated as an oddity or freak, but as a child. The range of activities for the handicapped child should be broadened, not limited, to include truly stimulating, creative, and useful activities—meaningful for all children. (Often in this country special activities arranged for handicapped children seem planned more for the worker's than the child's convenience.)

2. *Residential care and care outside the residence should be treated equally.* The basic training for child care workers in either area should encompass most of the same knowledge and skills. Similarities rather than differences guide the shaping of a program structure. Unless the worker is trained thoroughly in child care, he is not adequately prepared for work with children, within an institution or outside as a street worker or parent counselor.

European Programs

These two ideas are generally accepted by all the European programs I have studied. Their training efforts usually have the following pattern:

1. Both fieldworker (who works with children and youth and their parents in the community) and residential worker in schools or child care institutions take the same basic training averaging about 2 years. A specialized course follows for persons who choose to work with severely handicapped and delinquent children. An advanced course produces the child care specialists and also trains for teaching, administration, and research. In some countries these training steps are handled in different schools; in some, they are all parts of one program.

2. Many subjects taught correspond with material presented in training programs in this country, but there are four areas of wide difference:

• The degree of emphasis on teaching child care workers how to observe a child and how to learn from observation. European training could not put more stress on this than it does now. Most of our training programs for child care workers barely touch the subject, if at all.

• The stress put on creative and activity therapy. The emphasis is not so much on developing the worker's skills or know-how in leisure time or vocational activities as on appreciation, understanding, and the therapeutic use of creativity and various forms of human expression and communication. One French school devotes a whole semester to teaching the child care workers how to appreciate modern art. What we in the United States do in this regard varies: Too often we have a lecture on activity, list games to keep "kids" busy, or suggest traditional needlework, wood or metal work for rainy days.

• The emphasis on teaching "pedagogy" and "defectology" in European programs. A course in "pedagogy" instructs workers in how to handle the child in various situations and to help him learn new knowledge and build new standards and values. Courses in "defectology" teach methods of handling children who are afflicted with mental or physical impairments.

• The emphasis in Europe is on the child care worker's personality development, so that he can make use of the knowledge he has acquired. Talking about love and affection is not enough. Real understanding comes when workers are convinced of the fundamental goodness of human beings, when they are prepared for disappointments, and when their ability to give and receive love is increased. To meet this goal, the prospective child care worker is, first of all, carefully screened before he is enrolled as a regular student. While in training, he is required to live with other students and is subjected to experiences in group dynamics. His adjustment and growth are continuously evaluated and discussed with him. In some schools the student is also expected to subject himself to personal analysis or psychotherapy, which is available to him for a nominal fee. The short training courses provided for institutional workers in this country can hardly include these provisions.

Child Care Worker's Status

The graduates who complete all phases of such European programs are considered professionals with all the privileges. In an institution for delinquents outside Paris, I saw a staff composed entirely of such graduates in action. In full charge of their living units, they also functioned as caseworkers, group workers, and group therapists, and maintained contact with the community and family. All child care workers, working as a team on an equal basis, were directly responsible to the director, himself a senior child care worker. The position of supervisor in our sense was unknown. The staff held daily consultations and received consultation from a psychiatrist. Also, they had an analyst, a psychologist-therapist, available to them whenever they felt they had a personal problem that might affect their work—or when they felt the pressures of work might affect their personal lives. The exchange between analyst and his worker-clients was confidential.

The multiple functions and professional status of child care workers in this institution are not, of course, typical. Other institutions in Europe have a true interdisciplinary team approach. Division of labor and interprofessional rivalry exist as they do here. But there are differences. In Europe a fully trained child care worker giving direct care feels much more accepted than he does here: (1) because he does not compete with the social worker, whose function is less broad there than here and who less frequently carries the therapist's responsibility in a residential setting; and (2) because the European psychiatrist is differently oriented. At the administrative level, however, advanced child care workers are in pronounced competition with schoolmasters and educational psychologists, who, traditionally, have been in charge of schools for the handicapped and are not ready to see this changed. This competition, however, has an historical basis and does not imply lack of recognition of the child care worker's capability. In fact, schoolmasters and educational psychologists enroll in courses for child care workers.

From the foregoing, it would seem that the child care worker in Europe "has it made"—he gets thorough training, his contributions are recognized, and he enjoys status. This is not quite true. European workers are still striving toward complete professionalism and continue to scrutinize their training programs.

Goal of Training Programs

The European experts in the child care field see their child care training programs as helping to fashion a new profession, one at the juncture of nursing, social work, teaching, and psychiatry—drawing from these disciplines but evolving as an entity. They believe that new knowledge and concepts of child care remain to be discovered, and that there is need for research, experimentation with method, international exchange, and the development of a literature. They also believe that all the disciplines, unless supplemented by additional specialized training, do not qualify a person for residential work.

What should the training curriculum include? Many European experts seem to agree on these points:

1. *The central theme should be the development of the enrollee's personality.*

2. *There should be a constant connection between theoretical knowledge and its practical application.* The schools and institutions should work closely together in selecting the desired experience and in evaluating the student's progress. The institution, not the school, should supervise the student in placement. (As yet, however, institutions do not have trained supervisors to do this.)

3. *The curriculum should include the following courses* (in some countries it already does): (a) those which give knowledge about people, their environment, culture—psychology, social psychology, sociology, anthropology, ethics, medicine, and hygiene; (b) those which instruct in useful methods—pedagogy and defectology, case work and group work, nursing, homemaking routines, observation, diagnostic evaluation and treatment planning, reporting and recording; (c) those which relate to running an institution—social services, administration, budgeting, supervision and consultation, legislation, community work, research; and (d) those which develop appreciation of creative vocational and leisure-time activities for children.

For example, in art classes the enrollee learns not only to understand, appreciate, and teach art for its own sake, but also how to use it in life situations and other learning experiences. He also learns how to promote a child's interest in tools, materials, and various art forms and how to use art to stimulate interest in other school subjects—chemistry, through chemistry of pottery; history and geography, through history of foreign crafts; mathematics, through study of pattern designs. Classes in language development provide a clear understanding of the interactions between linguistic development, general mental development, and formation of attitudes toward life. Nature study teaches the worker how a child's urge to explore may be partly satisfied through the study of nature, and how to use environment in planning recreation.

4. *Thorough training in psychology is needed, especially depth psychology.* This training should have two aims: to enable the child care worker to look at himself and to study the condition of others. There is, however, some recognition of the dangers of developing "pseudo-therapists" or of upsetting beginning workers with large doses of self-discovery. Many persons concerned with these training programs see child care workers as developing an ability to carry out supportive and developmental therapy, but not correctional therapy. As to teaching methods, European experts consider the traditional classroom lecture less effective than group discussions or demonstrations.

Selection of Students

In order not to discourage applicants, the European training programs seldom have specified educational requirements. However, applicants are usually expected to have a level of formal education that compares favorably with 2 years in an American college. To enroll in the basic course, no previous child care experience is usually required, but the applicant's attitudes and overall ability to work with children are assessed. This is done through a short placement in a child care institution where he works under close supervision and lives in a students' dormitory where his behavior in a group is observed. Persons enrolling in advanced courses are usually required to have 3 years' experience in residential care.

The applicant's personality and motivation for child care work are regarded as very important. European child care experts believe that no single method of screening applicants for training for child care work is reliable; that a combination of methods should always be used. Psychological testing, though used by some schools, does not seem popular. The combination of methods favored by most experts is: an application form designed to detect personality traits and attitudes; personal interview with at least two members of the admissions committee; and a pre-enrollment institutional placement.

Once selected, the student is continuously evaluated for academic learning, application of knowledge to practice work, and personality growth. Some schools give written tests or assignments; in most places, the student is evaluated on class participation alone. At the end of the advanced course, however, students are almost always required to write a paper.

In the countries I visited, the reported average age of students in the basic course is middle twenties; in the advanced course, middle thirties. The maximum age for enrollment is 45; the minimum is 18 for women, 24 for men, and 23 for women who wish to work with adolescents.

A Summing Up

At present, I have no way of evaluating completely the European approach to child care and comparing it with the general approach in this country. I cannot say which is better or more advanced. There are differences in philosophy and practice; there is some good and bad in both. There is no single blueprint for good child care. All we can do is experiment and learn from the experience of others—and we and they are doing it.

We are constantly searching for new ways to help children, particularly in residential treatment of emotionally disturbed and socially maladjusted children. The idea of developing a new kind of staff of child care practitioners is under study. It is imperative that a good program for their training be formulated.

I believe that the National Institute of Mental Health project, "Formulating Training Program for Child Care Personnel,"[1] is a very important step. However, much more must be done. Reassessing the entire child care program in this country and the philosophical reeducation of all concerned is also important. To do this, free of historical biases, we should try harder to regard child care not so much as a functional problem as an emotional and intellectual challenge. We should think of it not so much in terms of corrective therapy as in terms of restoration and reeducation of children toward more healthful living.[2]

1. U.S. Department of Health, Education, and Welfare, Public Health Service, National Institute of Mental Health: Formulating training program for child care personnel. Project No. MH 631. (Sponsored jointly by the Jewish Board of Guardians, New York, and Teachers College of Columbia University.)

2. Child Welfare League of America: Training courses for cottage parents. New York. November 1960.

25. Training Child Care Staff: Pitfalls and Promises

James K. Whittaker

The growth of training programs for child care workers in recent years has been concentrated mainly in the area of junior college and university programs. Unfortunately, not enough has been said (or written) on the subject of in-service training for child care staff. Hopefully, this brief paper will shed a few rays of light on this most important subject, by outlining a number of specific guidelines for the establishment of a child care training program, as well as by exploring several potential pitfalls inherent in undertaking such a venture.[1]

To begin with, we must ask ourselves the question: "Training for what?" That is, we must begin with a very clear statement of our institutional goals and the various methods by which we hope to achieve those goals. It goes without saying, that *what* the child care worker does in an institution should be based, in large measure, on the problems and needs of the children in his care. Too often, *what* the child care worker does has more to do with organizational expediency, or with professional needs, than with the needs of the children. It would appear that whichever professional group occupies the position of leadership in an institution, that a great deal of time and energy is spent in maintaining rigid status hierarchies and role distance between the various professional groups. It has reached the point where the quality of an institution is often judged solely on the number of different specialists which it employs. In recent years, the elevation of so many of these "specialities" to professional status has, in many ways, served to the detriment rather than to the benefit of the children in care. In the course of a single week's time, the child might be expected to see his: psychotherapist, group therapist, family case worker, occupational therapist, recreational therapist, music therapist and so on, ad infinitum. We

Reprinted from *Mental Hygiene*, Vol. 54, No. 4 (October, 1970), pp. 516–19.
1. Based on the author's clinical experience as assistant director of the Walker Home for Children in Needham, Massachusetts and as a member of the senior clinical staff of the University of Michigan Fresh Air Camp.

expect this of the child, despite the fact that relatively few problem children come to the institution with such neatly encapsulated and well defined problems.

What all this means vis a vis child care training is that in such an institution the child care worker's role would actually consist of little more than that of a good traffic manager, who makes sure the child is ready for his string of daily appointments. Training child care staff would probably cause more problems in such an institution, than it would solve, as the individual child care worker is not allowed to do anything in the first place. A far more fruitful approach would be to begin with the problems of the children in care and to design the child care worker's role as the key role, since he is the person who is closest to the child and has the greatest opportunity for potential influence on him.

Having asked the question: "Training for what?" we must immediately ask another question: "Who shall be responsible for the training?" Again, we must report that in many settings, the choice of supervisor is more a reflection of professional needs than it is of the training needs of the child care worker.

Consider, for example, the plight of the beginning child care worker who really needs to know a great deal about how children function in a 24-hour-a-day setting, but who ends up being supervised by a social worker, psychiatrist, or clinical psychologist whose only contact with the child may be in the context of the 50-minute therapy hour, within the sanctuary of his office. One obvious way of avoiding this problem is to use senior child care workers as supervisors. The senior, more experienced worker possesses just the kinds of information that the novice child care worker needs to know in order to carry out his duties within the institution. These include such things as: a knowledge of the rules and routines of the institutions, some knowledge of the individual children, some simple behavior management techniques and some suggestions about things to do with children for fun. Later on, as the new worker becomes more proficient and secure in his role, he may seek added explanations from other professionals as to why a child acts in a particular way, or what the family dynamics are in a given case. Ideally, the institution should provide for different levels of training, ranging from direct line staff supervision, through informal meetings with agency professionals, up to and including participation by line staff in case conferences.

Whoever undertakes the supervisory task, a certain number of pitfalls are evident and should be avoided:

1. It should be the responsibility of the supervisor to define for the child care worker what will be the basis for their supervisory relationship. This could vary from an intense involvement in what amounts to personal psychotherapy, to a problem solving, teaching centered relationship. It is imperative that whichever format is used (there are many more than the

two previously mentioned), the child care worker be made aware of it. To do otherwise is to be faced with the situation of some child care workers who entered supervision expecting some sort of insight producing psychotherapy, feeling cheated when they do not receive it and of other child care workers who feel they are being unduly "caseworked," when all they really wanted were some concrete suggestions for how to manage a child's behavior.

2. A second point to make regarding supervision is that the supervisor should be aware of the various "games" people play in supervision.[2] For example, a popular child care worker game is: "Be Nice to Me, Because I'm Nice to You." This is essentially "seduction by flattery" and is indicated by such phrases as, "You're the best supervisor I ever had," or, "I look forward someday to being as good a supervisor as you are." A variation of this game is called: "Evaluation is Not for Friends," in which the supervisory relationship is redefined purely as a social friendship. A final child care worker game might be called: "Protect the Sick and the Infirm," or "Treat Me, Don't Beat Me." Here the child care worker would rather expose himself than his work, so he asks the supervisor for help in solving his personal problems.

In fairness, supervisors are not without games of their own: "I Wonder Why You Really Said That" and "One Good Question Deserves Another" are two favorites with supervisors who see all probing questions as threats and interpret all honest disagreement as psychological resistance.

Most of the games child workers play in supervision are designed to reduce a perceived knowledge, or power gap between themselves and their supervisor. They attempt to "bring the supervisor down to their level." For example, how often have we heard statements like: "He may have a degree, but he doesn't know what it's really like to work with those kids, or "All he ever talks about is theory, he never gets down to the 'nitty-gritty.'" In effect, the child care worker is saying to the professional:

> Look, you may know a great deal about individual dynamics, but you aren't able to help me with my biggest problem which is how to live with these kids all day long, manage their upsets, help them through the routines of the day, and work with them in games and activities. You can give me a long list of reasons as to *why* Johnny gets into fights at bedtime, but I'm the one who has to deal with him every night and you don't help me with that problem in the least.

While this might be somewhat of a caricature, I believe it describes accurately what many child care workers feel about supervision. One solution already suggested is to use senior child care staff as supervisors; another is to make use of "life-space supervision" by the professional staff.

2. Alfred Kadushin, "Games People Play in Supervision," *Social Work,* Vol. 13, No. 3, (July, 1968), pp. 23–33.

Life-Space Supervision

In this form of supervision, the professional moves through the life-space of the ward, or cottage offering assistance and support to the child care worker as he is invited to do so. In this way, he is given an opportunity to actually model a desired way of managing a child's behavior, rather than just talking about it in "office supervision." Care should be taken, of course, to move in on a situation only when signalled by a child care worker. The method of life-space supervision is not without its hazards, particularly for the professional. Once outside the sanctity of his office and the protection of the 50-minute therapy hour, the therapist's halo becomes slightly tarnished and his fallibility and mortality become plainly visible to all. In the life-space of the institution, the children act as the "great levellers." They are singularly unimpressed with Ph.D.'s and ACSW's and couldn't care less how well versed one is in psychological jargon. In what is often a painful moment of truth, the child care worker sees that it is not easy for his supervisor to calm a writhing child in the throes of a temper tantrum, or stop a fight, or put an end to a scapegoating session, or convince a timid child that it is alright to join an activity. The child care worker will see his supervisor: make mistakes with children, get angry, say the wrong thing, have nothing to say, and, literally, fall flat on his ACSW when trying to help restrain a wildly angry adolescent. In short, the child care worker will see the supervisor experiencing all those things which he himself finds so frustrating.

Given the fact that a supervisor has a strong enough ego to operate sometimes in the "fishbowl" of the milieu, the type of training that the child care worker receives will in the long run be most beneficial and lasting. It drives home the message to both supervisor and child care worker that there is no easy way of dealing with all of the problems which disturbed children create in an institutional setting. It tends to narrow the gap which child care workers so often feel between themselves and their supervisors and above all it sensitizes both supervisor and child care worker to the special problems which each faces in working with the children and creates a climate which makes working together more than just a nice sounding phrase.

Staff Training for All

It is entirely possible that an administrator could set up an excellent child care training program and still be missing a significant amount of interaction between children and adults, if he concentrates his efforts only on those people who work directly with the children. For those of us whose business it is to relate to children, it is sometimes difficult to admit that certain children will prefer the company of the cook, or maintenance man to our own. Unless we make some attempt to include this group in our staff training, we essentially lose all control over what happens in these encounters. Polsky[3] and others have pointed out the potential dangers in an institution which rigidly separates its professional and child care staff from its housekeeping and maintenance staff. Often the special techniques needed to work with emotionally disturbed children are a source of bewilderment to untrained maintenance and kitchen staff who raised their own children under the maxim: "Spare the rod and spoil the child." For this reason alone, they should be included in some part of the agency's training program.

Group Supervision

Many of the points made under the heading of individual supervision hold equally well to supervising child care workers in groups. Perhaps the most important of these is the necessity of making abundantly clear from the outset what will be the nature and purposes of the group. For example, will the leader assume a directive teaching role, or will he take a more laissez-faire stance? Will staff be urged to bring up criticism of each other's work, or will this be left for individual supervisory sessions? Will the group focus mainly on the children, or on staff relationships?

Another point centers around group decision issues; here, the leader should make clear to the members of the group that there are different phases of decision making in groups:

1. A phase of *Orientation* in which the members acquaint themselves with the various facets of the problem.
2. A phase of *Evaluation* in the various alternatives for action are discussed and compared.
3. And finally, a phase of *Control* in which the members decide upon an action strategy and take steps to implement it.[4]

Problems often occur in staff groups when child care workers try to arrive at a "quick fix" solution, without first becoming knowledgeable about all aspects of the problem and all of the avenues open for action. Child care workers eager for concrete suggestions may come away grumbling that, "All we ever do is talk about problems, we never decide anything." It should be pointed out by the group leader that a very fruitful session can be held in which the staff simply tries to find out exactly what is happening, without settling about any immediate solutions about "what to do."

On a related point, it is essential to make clear to staff groups exactly how much decision making power they have and in what areas they may exercise it. To do less than this is to invite ill feeling and create barriers be-

3. Polsky, Howard. *Cottage Six*. New York: Russell Sage, 1963.
4. Bales, Robert F. and Fred L. Strodtbeck, "Phases in Group Problem Solving" in *Group Dynamics*. Cartwright and Zander, Eds. New York: Harper & Row, 1960, pp. 624–638.

tween the administrator and his staff. It is the author's personal feeling that while the child care staff should play a major role in decision, a children's institution cannot be run on the model of a participatory democracy. Some decisions must be reserved for the clinical, or executive director and these should be made clear from the beginning. Typically, they would include ultimate decisions on intake and discharge of children, the hiring and firing of staff and matters of major policy change.

A Final Note

One of the paradoxes in the whole question of child care training is that the problem seems to be less with the people we would like to train and more with ourselves who would do the training. Certainly at no time in recent history have there been a larger number of bright, motivated young people who wish to make contribution in a service connected organization. Their very idealism and openness would seem to preclude any major impediment to learning.

The problem lies more with the administrator who thinks that staff training consists of subscribing to a few professional journals and having a few of the child care workers sit in and listen to a case conference now and then. It is with the therapist who sees no room in his narrow conception of the treatment model for child care workers to be anything more than custodians who provide a benign environment for children between psychotherapy sessions. It is with the case worker whose only venture outside of his office is to refill his coffee cup, because to do otherwise would be outside of his "professional role." Indeed, the problem is with any of us—regardless of our professional orientation—who refuse to accept the fact that the single most important and influential person in the institution is the child care worker. If we truly participate in helping him to work with the child for all of the other 23 hours—making available our expertise, while drawing on his vast practical knowledge and skill—then "training" in the formal sense of the word becomes less of a problem and we will be well on the road to developing a truly therapeutic milieu.

PART SIX

THE PLACE OF ACTIVITIES
IN A THERAPEUTIC MILIEU

26. Prestructuring Group Content

SALLIE R. CHURCHILL

At the NASW Institute on Group Process in Psychiatric Settings held in June 1958, an attempt was made to answer the questions: "What is the content of a group?" and "What determines the content of a group?" The definition of content arrived at included both the activities of the group and the inter- and intrapersonal relationships. Some of the many determinants of content were itemized: purpose of the group; the age, sex, and clinical diagnosis of the members; the climate, the current interaction, and the natural history of the group. One of the most important determinants of the content of the group is the social group worker. The purpose of this paper is to illustrate the way a social group worker influences the content of a group by describing the planning for a group meeting.

A word about the role of a social group worker in a child guidance clinic, the setting of the group to be described. It has three important areas. First, the worker consciously uses herself and her ability to interrelate with children. Thus, unlike the work described by Slavson,[1] relationship is a major tool. Second, the worker makes interpretations to the chil-

Reprinted with permission of National Association of Social Workers from *Social Work,* Vol. 4, No. 3 (July, 1959), pp. 52–59.
1. S. R. Slavson, *An Introduction to Group Therapy* (New York: International Universities Press, Inc., 1943).

dren regarding their behavior and reality events which are ego-level interpretations based on an understanding of the unconscious motivations. This is described in an article by Patterson, Schwartz and Van der Wart.[2] Third, the group worker, in relation to each group member, collaborates with a social caseworker, psychiatrist, and clinical psychologist.

The group to be described is a treatment group of five midlatency boys which has met at the Pittsburgh Child Guidance Center for a year. It is an activity group with programing based on Fritz Redl's concept of programing for ego support.[3] All members live at home in intact families; all attend school. All mothers and fathers are involved in treatment at the clinic.

Basic and Temporary Roles of the Children

The first step in planning a meeting is to identify the group roles of each child: his basic continuing role and the specific role that may be anticipated for him at the given meeting. A short description of each boy will precede a description of the basic roles of each member.

John, almost 10, is a small, strong Jewish boy. He presently meets life with impulsive physical aggression and sexual profanity. He has been in treatment for two years and has begun slowly to internalize feelings so that he is moving from a severe behavior disorder to a neurosis.

Freddie, 10, is the oldest boy. He is large, obese, and awkward. He also is Jewish. He is passively aggressive and negativistic and constantly has an unpleasant odor. An important clinical observation is Freddie's unlikableness to his peers, his parents, and to the professional staff. His self-description is, "I have bad ears, bad eyes. I wet the bed and I have no friends."

Mike, 8, is Roman Catholic. He is both immature and impulsive. Although referred for destructive and asocial behavior, Mike is frightened and hypoactive in the group.

Stevie, 10, Protestant, is psychotic. An extremely sensitive boy, he has used two years of treatment well, so that he now has few periods when he is out of contact. These periods are marked by fear and distortion of people's feelings toward him.

Norman, 8, is an Orthodox Jew, who attends parochial school and frequently wears his yamilke to group meetings. He is impulsive, hyperactive, and destructive.

John is the core member, the indigenous leader. He is the best liked, yet the most feared. All children actively seek his friendship. This is partially

2. Gerald Patterson, Rene Schwartz, and Esther Van der Wart, "The Integration of Group and Individual Therapy," *American Journal of Orthopsychiatry,* Vol. 16, No. 3 (July 1956), pp. 618–629.

3. Fritz Redl and David Wineman, *Controls from Within,* (Glencoe, Ill.: Free Press, 1952).

out of fear, for John is quick-tempered and impulsive. He is also sensitive to the needs and feelings of the other children and usually responds with a protective gentleness.

John is a close friend of Stevie's. He is particularly sensitive to Stevie's moods, frequently reassuring Stevie that he likes him. These two boys are the only permanent subgroup. Stevie plays the role of protected child. Group mores do not permit Stevie's being hurt or teased. He is not laughed at in his fearful mood; rather he mobilizes the other members to the helping role. He is a pleasant youngster when not upset, and he can give to the other boys, particularly in his uninhibited way of expressing his liking for them and his wanting them to like him.

Mike is the baby of this group. Not only is he the youngest, he is also the smallest and his behavior is infantile and regressed. He is whiny, uses baby talk, and has difficulty reaching the craft or game levels of the other children. Mike is allowed to be a baby, but he is not given protection for this position as Stevie is. He may suck his thumb and have whiny temper tantrums, and drink from the baby bottle. These are not remarked upon or laughed at but tolerated. Mike does not feel liked and frequently asks, "Why don't children like me?"

Norman is the only contender for John's leadership position. He has not made any inroads, for his bids have been onesidedly aggressive. For a long time Norman tried to be a good boy by anxiously inhibiting all aggressive interation. Now his impulsivity and anger are beginning to break through and confuse his peers. Because he uses his Orthodox religion in a distorted manner to separate himself from the other boys, he is a recipient of hostility from the two non-Orthodox Jewish boys. Norman's father is also one of his problems in peer relationship. One might say this father has become a marginal member of the treatment group. He maneuvers himself into many positions where he has a negative contact with group members at least once a meeting. There is an open feud between this father and John. Norman's closest relationship is with Mike, with whom he shares an individual therapist. Norman seems to be trying to win Mike's affection (by assuming a protector role), as if this positive relationship to Mike would be rewarded by the therapist.

Freddie is the isolate. He is actively disliked by the other boys. His attempts at buying their friendship through gifts have failed. He operates in the group but is not of the group. He is on the edges, and his admission to the group circle is brief and usually initiated by action on the part of the worker. Negative interaction takes place as all boys try to use him as a scapegoat. Freddie, preferring negative relationships to none, frequently refuses the worker's protection.

In anticipating roles for a meeting, the worker considers the most recent history of the group. Factors in the previous meeting, which may affect interaction are reviewed. The worker consults other staff members to determine what individual therapy or parental interviews can offer in predicting possible group behavior.

At the beginning of the meeting preceding the one for which planning is described, Norman's father and John had a disagreement in the waiting room, and the father had bawled John out, telling him that he was a bad boy. John had not overtly reacted to Norman's father and had come along with the group on a scheduled trip. At the end of the meeting, however, John had run up to the worker, had said he was leaving, and had run home. A second later, Norman had approached the worker with tears in his eyes, complaining that John had knocked his ice-cream cone to the ground. Norman was not too angry, commenting that he supposed John was mad at his father. The situation with John could not be handled at that time, but the worker bought Norman a second ice-cream cone. Later in the week, John discussed the incident with his psychiatrist and requested a special appointment with the group worker. Until this time, John had steadfastly declared, "No one will ever get an apology from me." His feeling was that saying he was sorry would weaken him, put him in a spot where anyone could make him do anything. When he came to the group worker's office, with great difficulty he blurted out a request that the worker tell Norman he was sorry, John felt sorry but did not think he could tell Norman. He wanted to give Norman his refreshments to make up the loss of the ice-cream cone. Although the worker did not feel it was necessary for John to give up his refreshments, after discussing this with him she agreed to the plan John had made. (This example of the use of a marginal interview shows how a group worker assists a child with a group-centered problem which could not be best handled in the group itself.)

With this knowledge of anticipated roles, based both on basic roles and on immediate past history, the activity tentatively planned was evaluated. To what extent would this apology affect the activity planned, specifically in relation to the children's roles? The worker had planned that the group bake a cake for refreshments. In the history of the group each boy, at infrequent intervals, had an opportunity to bake a cake for the group's refreshments. This act allowed him to give to the group. In the session being planned for, it would have been Mike's turn to make, cut, and distribute the cake. Three boys were directly affected: Mike, who would make and give the cake; John, who wanted to give Norman his refreshments; and Norman, to whom John wanted to apologize. The worker did not know whether John could carry through his resolve to give Norman his refreshments. Yet, since it would be therapeutically helpful if he could, it seemed unwise to set up a situation which would make it difficult for him. On the other hand, it was important for Mike to give to John. Mike very much wanted John's friendship, and he would see John's refusal of his cake as rejection. Mike also might not want Norman to have extra cake, or if he did, he might wish to be the person making the gift.

In the planning of every activity, the effect of group interaction on each member must be considered. An essential concept in group treatment is that, though a specific activity may not be helpful to all members at a given time, there may be no activity which is harmful to any child. Since either Mike or John might have been harmed by the baking, the baking was postponed and cookies and Kool-Aid were planned instead.

Having considered the effect of the children's "anticipated, specific roles," the worker proceeded to the next step in planning: the choice of an activity which could foster positive group interaction. For every meeting the worker had to determine the degree of individuality versus the degree of group conformity desirable. Again she reviewed the last meeting, a trip to a nearby museum—an activity which forced high group conformity, because all the boys had to remain together and each had to accept the trip if he attended the meeting. That this was difficult for the children was demonstrated by the fact that each boy regressed in his behavior controls from those usually demonstrated in the group room. Norman dashed across the street without looking at traffic; John made "nasty cracks" to passing adults; a storekeeper yelled at Freddie for an attempt to steal a candy bar; and Mike and Stevie fearfully held the worker's hands. This regression determined, in part, the temporary roles the children would be expected to play.

The ability of a group of children to submit to high levels of group conformity depends upon the comfort of each child. Since the boys had been upset by their reduced group adjustment, an activity that would emphasize individual experience was desirable. Interaction could be derived from physical proximity. A familiar activity such as a craft that the boys liked was necessary, for in their regression they would reject new ideas as "stupid" (anger at the worker for reducing the protection inherent in the familiar room free of unknown people) or as "babyish" or "too hard" (loss of self-confidence and anxiety about trying). The group worker wished also to rebuild the self-esteem that had been temporarily dislodged. Therefore, she wanted to remove unnecessary areas of frustration. The craft should be easy enough for all the boys, and also preferably one where boys with varying levels of skill could experience satisfactions based on real achievement. This meant not only that a poor job could be satisfying to some youngsters, but at the same time a child could sense that he was improving. Second, sharing should be reduced as much as possible; tools or equipment needed should be immediately available to all without sharing. Construction of plastic model airplanes met these criteria: it was an individual project, well liked and familiar, requiring little skill but with different opportunities for greater skill and demanding no sharing of tools.

An important asset of this craft for this particular group was that building model planes is Freddie's only skill that the other boys accept. Requests for help can be referred to Freddie: "Maybe Freddie could help you" or "Maybe you could ask Freddie." For brief periods during crafts it might be possible to have Freddie admitted to the core group and for him to have short periods of acceptance by other children—an experience which might help improve his painfully distorted self-concept.

Placing children in situations demanding high levels of conformity, illustrated by the trip to the museum, has special usefulness. For the worker it offers three diagnostic opportunities: first, it shows how well gains made within the protection of the clinic stand up outside and allows more adequate future protective structuring; second, it reveals new problem areas in social behavior which may only become evident as other problems are mastered; third, it brings unexpressed concerns into the open. For example, in respect to the last point, a trip to an art museum or zoo may focus sexual concerns or a swimming period may focus fears. For the child there is the fun, the opening up of a new experience, as well as a special privilege. There is a chance to evaluate his increased ability to handle new situations. The presence and the activity of the worker affords him protection and understanding of his behavior, enabling him to manage the experience. The negative factors inherent in enforced group conformity may be balanced by a trip to the store, where each child regains some sense of individuality and self-importance as he chooses a vanilla or chocolate or a strawberry ice-cream cone. Such group shopping with the worker also represents a gift from her, which can confirm his feeling of being liked.

Amount of Physical Activity

Returning to plans for the meeting, the amount of gross physical activity was considered next. Since it was raining, the meeting was limited to the group room, a large playroom. One side has three tempered-glass windows; the opposite has two doors to the hallway and shelf space. At one end there is a wall at which balls may be thrown; the other end has a sink area and a large one-way screen. The boys are familiar with the room and know they may do "almost anything that is sensible." They know where balls may be thrown and what things may be climbed upon or into. Since this group has been in treatment for a year, some equipment has by now become invested with special meaning, and with this meaning certain inherent rules (either peer- or adult-initiated) have been formulated and internalized. Some of these rules are strong enough so that they are unspoken and inviolate and are group mores. Others are verbalized, so that the boys assume responsibility for ordering conformity when peers violate. The gym mat is an ordinary plastic mat (7 × 10 feet), always available to the boys. It is used to box, wrestle, or lie upon. Sometimes the boys roll up in it.

When the children wrestle or box, a part of the body off the mat stops the fight immediately. Children do not play on the mat with shoes on. The worker instituted these rules for safety as well as cleanliness and protection for the mat. This group has invested the mat with inviolate safety rules so that the worker was angrily rejected when she suggested its use for the game called "King of the Mountain." Since the worker foresaw from her knowledge of the group's regression that the children would be hyperactive, the mat was put out on the floor. Spatially, it naturally limited hyperactive running, and it would help the group to exert self-control.

The other special equipment is a large cardboard barrel. The limits on using the barrel are primarily child-instituted as opposed to the worker-initiated limits of the mat. Yet at this point in this group's development, both sets of rules are accepted by the children. The barrel can be ridden in and on. Children can sit in the barrel or put the barrel on top of them. Occasionally it is used in place of a basketball hoop. The children also use the barrel as a means of isolating themselves when they need to be alone. Group mores prohibit disturbing a child who has removed himself by jumping into the upright barrel. A child often participates in uncomfortable discussions productively from inside the security and closeness of the barrel. If the barrel is on its side and a child gets in, however, this is an invitation to be pushed or for another boy to join him inside and roll about on the floor. Interestingly enough, Freddie has never been able to climb into the barrel and it still holds fear for him. For this meeting, then, the barrel was present as a comfortable self-isolation technique and as a possible spontaneous nonverbal invitation to subgroup interaction.

Total room arrangement can also be used to control the amount of gross physical activity desired. The mat on the floor is a spatial limit—a physical aid to self-control and a reducer of adult-imposed limits. This concept is in a sense an opposite of Redl's gadgetorial seduction.[4] Since delicate craft work was planned, worktables were placed so that they were protected from reasonable ball play. (Nothing protects from "accidents" on purpose.) Since the group worker decided that the children should be allowed much individual activity, no group games were planned. Rather, some equipment conducive to group interaction was available. Selection of this material, while fairly permanent for the group and not changed from meeting to meeting, contributes another factor to the worker's plans for the content of the meeting. Activities such as hammering, nailing, and painting are ways of expressing hostility, withdrawing from group activity, or, occasionally, of doing task-oriented projects, and are therefore available. A wood plane was purposely introduced to help the boys learn that adult limitations are not always arbitrarily and unfairly placed. The boys know that they are not to turn the knobs and that if they take the plane apart they are unable to put it back together. Objects introduced for such a pur-

4. Ibid.

pose should have some prestige, but they should not be objects by which an angry child's behavior could destroy total group enjoyment.

In some therapy it may be a helpful technique to allow children to spill paint on themselves and their surroundings without restraint. Such permissiveness does not, however, fit the concept of ego-supportive group treatment. The parents co-operate with the group therapy program, but they cannot tolerate consistent destruction of clothing. Not only the parents but the children become upset. Since the worker knows that the boys cannot use paints without sloppiness, in this group only tempera paints are used. Rather than trying to impose limits they cannot yet handle, they are provided with a material which is not damaging if misused.

Other standard equipment are balls, bean bags, crayons, table games, and a rope hanging from the ceiling. The rope, like the barrel, is a seducer to companionship since it is difficult for these boys to climb the rope or to swing by themselves. Taking turns pushing and swinging seems to come naturally but painfully. Arguments, fist fights, and tears result, but part of the group worker's role is to provide these activities and to be available as a mediator and a conscious-level interpreter. Crayons and paper allow a child to isolate himself, so that at points of inner tension he can involve himself in acceptable, pleasurable behavior. Card games and other table games offer the worker or the child a chance to invite another to a needed "one-to-one" contact.

Interpretation and Discussion

Having completed the plans for craft and physical activity, the worker considers the verbal aspects of the meeting, interpretation and discussion. Interpretation here means ego-level interpretation rather than interpretation of unconscious material. It is used to help the individual child understand the relationship of his feelings to his behavior, of his behavior to the response provoked from others, and to help the group understand a given member's behavior. It is often used to universalize feelings and to give general behavioral suggestions. Discussion involves the group's talking a particular situation over and is used for group planning and talking over common problems. Interpretation may take place independently or as part of a discussion. The process of interpretation is a continuous, unplanned part of a meeting, although the worker has in mind for each child certain behaviors which should be noted and interpreted if they arise.

Frequently a boy is seduced into a fight, needing to defend his honor against the insult "He's afraid." In such a case the group worker stops the fight and points out that the boy is afraid. Boxing is for fun, and a boy does not have to box in the group room when it is not fun. The worker points out that every boy is afraid of something, though not necessarily of boxing. By universalizing fears, the worker involves all the children. The group worker tells the child that the worker is sorry he is afraid, but that it is all right for him to show he is afraid and that the clinic will try to help him. As the worker speaks, not only one child but the whole group hears. Fears are established as legitimate in the group. Children are enabled to accept the no-boxing rule for one child, since the interpretation assures them of like understanding in relation to their own fears.

In this example the group worker has not delved into unconscious meaning of the fears, although she may have understanding of them. She will suggest that the child talk to his psychiatrist about his fears. When a child has handled the unconscious material generic to the fears, he is frequently left with an established "fear pattern." The group can offer him support as well as remedial help in trying to change. In individual sessions Stevie had dealt for many months with his fears, which had markedly inhibited his learning. One day John offered to teach Stevie how to climb the rope. With some coarseness, hiding the gentleness in his voice, John ordered him to put his hand here and his foot there. Stevie made numerous unsuccessful attempts. John reassuringly commented, "You're doing fine, Stevie. I couldn't hold my foot on like that the first time." "You really can't learn everything the first time, Stevie." "You have to make mistakes." For three weeks the lessons continued and Stevie was finally able to climb four or five inches. The fourth week, John announced that he was going to teach Stevie the way his violin teacher taught him. He proceeded, "You can never learn to climb, you're too stupid. You're all toes instead of fingers." Stevie didn't do well, but he told John that he was a much better teacher than his violin teacher and that he thought John might learn to play the violin faster if he had a teacher like John had been before.

Symptomatic behavior is a nonverbal communication. When the worker indicates she understands its meaning by putting it into words, the child can be freer to change his behavior. A special group phenomenon is that interpretation can be directed to one child and heard and used by another child for himself or to help a third child later. For example, Mike broke several safety rules when he felt unwanted in the group. The group worker told him that she knew he was upset because the children didn't like him, but that the boys did not like the things he was doing because they were dangerous to them. Later, when Mike threw a ball too close to Stevie, the latter said, "Mike, I want to like you but I get mad when you scare me." Another day Norman said, "Mike, I feel like hurting people who don't like me, just like you do."

There is a tendency to think of discussion as taking place when children sit down in a circle and talk about a specific subject. With this group such a method of discussion is generally unproductive. Some discussions do arise when the children are sitting together eating, but generally the group prefers to have a story read or to play "chance"-type table game. Discussion arises spontaneously and usually does not involve physical proximity. For example, the group worker was holding some wood that Freddie was hammering and told him that she felt things were coming along better for him.

Freddie commented, "Yes, maybe they are, but they're not going very fast." John, sitting at a table some distance away, commented, "Well, what do you expect? I've been coming here for two years and you've only been coming a couple of months." Norman commented, "Maybe it's because you're so sick, John, that you come so long." The worker commented that John has a lot of problems but that he's been working well in therapy and that we all know that each of the boys in the group still has work to do. Mike wondered then if anyone could tell him why the boys don't like him. The general consensus was, "We do like you, Mike, but we wish you weren't such a baby." Mike sighed and suddenly the activity resumed and the discussion was dropped. On another occasion John, very angry with his therapist, screamed, "I hate Dr. Reed, I hate her. She makes me talk about things that I shouldn't talk about. I hate her." Stevie replied, "But John, that's what we come here for. I talk about things to Dr. Thomas and he helps me to understand."

In general, the worker plans to introduce certain topics for group discussion, as well as spontaneously facilitating discussion of material the children introduce. For this meeting the worker brought up the children's difficulties experienced on the trip to the museum, and she was prepared to facilitate a discussion of feelings related to apologizing, remembering John's difficulty with Norman.

Sometimes group discussion, rather than being helpful, takes an anxiety-producing turn, and then close contact and communication between individual therapists and the group worker is necessary. John began to give distorted sexual information in a group meeting. Because of the excessive concern of the other boys, the group worker stopped John, pointing out that this was an area of confusion and concern to him. She told him that this was something he should discuss with his doctor. She pointed out to the other boys that they seemed to have problems about this also and that they could talk about it with their doctors, too. As in physical activity, the worker serves as a guard in seeing that the primary concept of group therapy—that what goes on in a group may not at any given time be helpful to all children, but what is harmful to any one child must be prevented—is maintained. The content of John's misinformation was communicated to all the therapists involved so that they could be ready to handle this material. In collaboration with these therapists it was agreed that the group worker would continue to limit attempts at discussions of sexual matters in this group. Discussion of sexual matters in a group may, under different conditions, be a helpful and supportive process.

Summary

The content of a group meeting has been planned for in terms of the basic and temporary roles of the children, the degree of conformity to the group desired, the amount of physical activity, the equipment available, and the interpretations and discussions desired or anticipated. Nothing guarantees what will happen in the group session. But the planning described, focused toward providing an ego-supportive experience and based on principles of social group work, gives a meaningful framework within which these goals may most likely be accomplished.

27. The Impact of Game Ingredients on Children's Play Behavior

Fritz Redl

For this discussion* I would like to concentrate, not on some of the more recent material that has come out of our present study groups, but rather on something a little more detached. I have chosen "games," and for two reasons: partly, because last year's discussion with Mr. Bateson (1) led us into quite a few fascinating speculations about play, work, and games, and some other phenomena somewhere in-between. I do not think we have even come close to exploiting this trend of our discussion enough, especially as far as the group psychologic implications for the play life of children are concerned. The other reason for choosing games is that it seems to me that games are a sort of little "universe in miniature," something nearly like an experiment of nature with the creation of social systems, activity structures, and many other potent ingredients; we would have a lot of trouble mixing them together in the right way unless the folkways of the human species had done some such mixing for us. Most of the considerations that go into an experiment for a miniature social structure and activity design for a specific group of patients, or normal people for that matter, seem to me also implied in the pattern of games, and there is the advantage that they can be varied at will, can be inserted for 10 minutes, then unhooked again, with group as well as game structure still examinable afterward. In fact, a lot of experimenting can be done in that way with factors that would be too hard to manipulate and too heavy to move around, were

Reprinted with permission of Josiah P. Macy Foundation from *Fourth Conference on Group Processes,* New York, 1958, pp. 33–81.

* Participants included: Howard S. Liddell, Bertram Schaffner, Donald H. Barron, Gregory Bateson, Ray L. Birdwhistell, Helen Blauveit, Jerome S. Bruner, Erik H. Erikson, Jerome D. Frank, Erving Goffman, Robert J. Lifton, Konrad Z. Lorenz, Margaret Mead, I. Arthur Mirsky, Harris B. Peck, Fritz Redl, John P. Spiegel, H. Burr Steinbach.

we trying to experiment with the total life structure of a whole institution and the people in it.

In short, the choice of games for our discussion seems to me to have a special advantage, as long as we remember that we really are not trying to exhaust the analysis, but that all this is meant to be a warm-up exercise for something else. I also have planned a discussion of the question of why games are so important in the treatment of children, but I shall deal with that later.

I will now give you the following list of twenty items. They are items which I believe to be relevant in the analysis of games. My giving you this list should not be construed as an attempt to report on the study in which they were prepared. I am merely using fractions of that material for specific purposes of illustration in our discussion here today:[1]

List of Game Dimensions and Ingredients

1. "Challenge" or "Theme"
2. Chance Skill
3. Competition
4. Institutionalized Cheating
5. Permanence of Alliance
6. Personalization of Game Props
7. Potential Sexualization Range
8. Outcome Clarity
9. Timing
10. Role-taking Factors
11. Interdependence of Players
12. Volume and Distribution of Participation
13. Pleasure-Pain Content of Winning or Losing
14. Spread of Winnership
15. Penetration by Rewards and Penalties
16. Trust Dependence
17. Nature of Obstacles
18. Mirroring of Life Themes
19. Rigidity
20. Rule Complexity

Before looking at this list with you, however, I should like to illustrate what it is about, by selecting a particular game, taking it apart, and raising the question: just what is in this game? And I shall raise this question purposely from a very limited, one-sided point of view, *i.e.,* from the point of view of the poor fellow who has to survive such a game with a bunch of ex-

1. This list is an abstract from more comprehensive mimeographed materials taken from the early work-sheets prepared by Dr. Redl, Dr. Paul Gump, and Mr. Brian Sutton-Smith in connection with the Wayne State University Research Project, financed by the National Institute of Mental Health Grants Program.

tremely lively youngsters. Please allow me such willful narrowing of focus
for a moment. The game I am choosing for my illustration is rather amus-
ing, and perhaps not too typical of games children play in this country in
the streets. In fact it probably would not be played unless some adult in a
settlement or playground project initiated it. Any of you who grew up in
Europe may remember the game called "Plumpsack geht um"; that was the
Austrian name for it. In this country it is played either without a name or
under the name of "Beatle" or "Beetle" or "Beadle." Game books don't
seem to be in agreement on the name.[2]

This is how it goes: A group of children stand in a circle. One has a gadget to hit someone with, preferably not a lead pipe, but perhaps a sock
filled with soft stuffing. He walks around the circle.

Fremont-Smith: He is outside the circle?

Redl: He is outside the circle. The children stand in a circle with their
hands behind their backs. He goes around the circle for a while, sup-
posedly aimlessly, to heighten the suspense. Then, whenever the spirit
moves him, he gives the gadget to one child, while he continues walking
on as though nothing had happened. The child who has the "beetle" now
also pretends for a few moments that nothing has occurred, but then the
official ruckus starts, for suddenly he turns around and he has not only the
right but the obligation to hit his right-hand neighbor, even though this
may be his best friend. His right-hand neighbor has not only the right, but
the duty, to run away as fast as he can, to avoid being beaten, irrespective

2. Editor's Note: In an effort to determine the exact name or origin of the game,
the names given by Dr. Redl were looked up in Webster's New International Dictionary, Second edition, unabridged, published by G. and C. Merriam Co., 1952. On
Page 236, the following definitions are given for "beadle":
1. One who proclaims or summons; a herald. *Obs.*
2. A messenger or crier, as a court crier or usher, summoner or servitor, under
   bailiff, warrant officer, etc. *Obs.*
3. An official attendant whose office it is to walk before dignitaries; a mace-bearer;
   specif.: a. An officer in a university, who precedes processions of officers and
   students; spelled *bedel* at Oxford, *bedell* at Cambridge. b. The apparitor of a
   trade guild.
4. An inferior parish officer having a variety of duties, as the preservation of order
   in a church service, the execution of the orders of the vestry meeting, etc.;—
   called in Scotland *bedral, bederal. Chiefly Brit.*
The word "beatle" was not found in the dictionary.
"Beetle" was defined as follows: (p. 245)
1. A heavy hammering or ramming instrument, usually with a wooden head, used
   for driving wedges, ramming pavements, etc.
2. Specif.: A wooden pestle or bat for beating linen, mashing potatoes, or other
   domestic uses.
3. A machine in which fabrics are finished by being hammered over rollers, as in
   cotton or linen mills.
In all probability, the game is known by various names in different locations. One is
tempted to think that "beetle" may be the correct name since the definition of a beetle
is that of an instrument for hammering or beating. Since Dr. Redl prefers the spelling
of "beetle" and since Dr. Mead prefers the spelling of "beadle," the word will be left
in the form that each prefers, in his own discussion.

of pride and prejudice in favor of bravery or of defending a just cause. They chase each other around the circle for a while. The round is terminated when the chased finally has enough or is decent enough to give someone else a chance; he then goes back into his old groove. At that moment, the hitter has to stop hitting, and walk on to give the "beetle" to someone else.

This is a somewhat oversimplified description of the game, and it leaves out details of variations that can easily be found. These details are entirely irrelevant to the point toward which I am building. Let us simply take this game apart in terms of its potential impact on the players in terms of issues such as contagion potential, etc.

Frank: What does the child who is holding the sock do after he gives it to the next man?

Redl: He goes back into the line somewhere.

Frank: Just goes in anywhere?

Redl: He goes back to his former place.

Fremont-Smith: Doesn't he go into the chaser's place when he jumps out?

Redl: There are different ways and different varieties. In "Three deep," a similar game, the chasee doesn't have a space left, but stands upon his return in front of the other two. I am trying to remember, but I am not sure just how this part of it goes.

Birdwhistell: Dr. Redl, you say they can keep on going around. In most of the places I have seen it played in the United States, they only go around once.

Redl: They are not supposed to run around long; this is one of the things I especially want to come back to. There are certain aspects of the game that vary, and what is and what is not fixed in the game pattern also may vary. This is important for the adult who is in charge of children's groups to know, for, if children play it differently somewhere else he should know. A lot depends on which issue in a given game is well fixed, and which is left to chance and therefore open to free-wheeling umpiring by the adult leader from case to case. If an issue is fixed, the adult leader should watch out, for even details in game ritual may be viewed by the players with the emotional weight of a religious issue. Some of it has implications for work situations as well as for games, but, again, I shall come back to this later. What I want to show at the moment is this: Every game basically has two sides. Of course, it has more than two, but I am now referring only to a purposely narrowed down issue, namely, to assess what the internal balance between impulses and controls within individual players will be like. I am raising the question, if this is what the game permits or demands, just what will the individual player, exposed to such permissions and demands, have to handle within himself? For in all those cases the individual player has something done to his impulse and gratification system, but he also has something done to his ego, and the game may or may not offer him the additional supplies for ego-support which he may need while exposed to its gratification lure.

Let us now look at this game and ask the simple question: What is the source of fun in it? This, by the way, still bothers me the most, and has never been answered to my satisfaction. In our own studies we were never able to find a theoretically clear and practically satisfactory formulation for this. It is hard enough to come to a reasonably well defined philosophy of what fun is or should be, and which sublimation levels are culturally acceptable or not; philosophical definitions, as long as they stay wide enough, are not too hard to get. For the practicing clinician, however, they remain useless unless they can help us also to decide how we know which child gets what type of fun on which level out of a given phase of the game. Different consumers of the same game activity going on in the same group may get very different gratifications out of entirely different aspects of the game at the same time.

Cutting it all down to very crude statements and going back to the "Plumpsack" game, we could readily list a few "gratification potentials" that seem to be almost built in: First, there is the opportunity for running, and even the mere practice of some simple "functions" or activities of body or mind may be pleasurable in its own right. Then, there is the gratification, obviously offered in this game as one possibility, of the expression of aggression "on a mild hitting level." You can't get mean, cruel, or nasty; this game is not a good outlet for such needs. But you can, for the duration of the game, have the fun of getting in a few good socks, even at an adult, provided the adult has the courage to become a "player" himself. In fact, and we shall try to make more of that special point later, the game not only permits, it seduces one into expression of aggression on a "mild hitting level." Thus, it may actually force a person into enjoying a potential impulse he may really not have felt very strongly just at the time that "beetle" got around to him—

In short, games have a certain "seductive element" in them. For the duration of a given phase of a given game, one is not only permitted, one is even supposed to have certain impulse potentials gratified—and not be a "sourpuss" who only goes through the motions. One had better really enjoy it while it lasts. Thus, one side of the game involves the offering of opportunities for certain gratifications, as well as a certain amount of seduction into that specific type of gratification.

In this case, certainly, if children are to get fun out of playing the "beetle" game, they had better be ready to enjoy a certain amount of fun out of running and hitting, being chased and trying to evade being hit, and of course, not minding too much if they fail somewhat in either.

Fremont-Smith: A high level of anticipation, then, is one of the aspects you are speaking of here. Anticipation is having to be ready, isn't it?

Redl: Not all games have anticipation in the foreground.

Fremont-Smith: But you implied that any game with "You'd better be ready" in it has anticipation.

Redl: I didn't say that. What I was trying to say was, unless you are ready to get that gratification, the game won't work.

Fremont-Smith: Then, in order for the game to work, there must be a high level of gratification?

Redl: On the contrary, sometimes it is much better if a specific game comes in sort of "suddenly." But, of course, there must be a high level of potential need in that direction. For instance, if the children have been sitting quietly for a long stretch, you can see their tension mounting. In that case, an active running game inserted at that moment will not need any "anticipation" element in it to offer relief.

Fremont-Smith: They have to anticipate the next step in the game.

Redl: You mean they have to know the next step?

Fremont-Smith: You used the phrase, "They had better be ready." I say this means a high level of anticipation. You say "No." I don't understand why you don't like the word *anticipation* which seems to me inherent in what you are talking about.

Redl: I was worried about the term *anticipation* because I thought, although I may be wrong, that you implied they have to be prepared for it.

Fremont-Smith: When you say "They had better be ready" it means they must be prepared for something, and they had better be ready.

Redl: I take the word "ready" back. What I wanted to imply is they are not ready now but they had better be equipped, or better be the type of person who enjoys being chased.

Fremont-Smith: When the man or child goes around the outside, it seems to me what you have there heightened is a level of suspense or anticipation.

Redl: Yes.

Fremont-Smith: Which always has some degree of anxiety in it.

Redl: Yes. This is on my list. This is suspense, and anticipation is part of this game.

Fremont-Smith: That is what I am talking about; for this game it is essential. Not all games have that. There is the whole period where people go through the phase of suspense. It is figuring out when destiny will come. Will it or will it not, or not yet knowing it, and maybe being hit. This is a specific ingredient which this game, in forms of anticipation or potential suspense, has.

Birdwhistell: We start out with the assumption, do we not, that this is a moral game in the sense this fits the American-Western European game pattern; that is, it contains the element which is characteristic of games from baseball to run-sheep-run and hide-and-seek. There is a threatener who goes out and threatens, who attacks a man who, in turn, becomes a threatener. Being "it," in a sense, is to be, for a period, the threatened. You are first infected by the "threatened"; you will, in turn, then be forced to infect someone else with the role. There are elements which don't have to be anticipated; they are built into the whole system of training games.

Redl: I hope to be able to show that there are about seven different types of themes or challenges, and that all games contain one or another. This game has the chase in it. It isn't really attack, it is a chase. There are other themes in other games. It need not be of this specific nature. I am not sure I made that part clear. If you mean in terms of just this game—

Birdwhistell: No, if you start out with what is a moral game and you say—

Redl: I said that?

Birdwhistell: No, I did. A moral game is one derived from a pattern into which a major proportion of the games of a given culture fits. If you discover in a given area that a major proportion of the children will spend a major proportion of time engaged in playing such a game, you already have a pattern built in the socialization process. Such a pattern anticipates the particular situation and prehandles the anticipation.

Mead: Dr. Fremont-Smith's point about the readiness within the game is nicely summed up in "One for the money, two for the show, three to make ready, and four to go."

Erikson: What age children do you have in mind, and do you have in mind both sexes?

Redl: You mean in this specific game?

Erikson: This particular situation.

Redl: You might find children playing variations of this specific game between 7 and 12 years of age.

Fremont-Smith: Both sexes?

Redl: And both sexes, but that may depend, naturally, on how they do it or whether this is part of the program.

Buhler: Does your own study include these ages that you mentioned?
Redl: Yes.

Erikson: You are just talking about boys in your own experience?

Redl: We had girls, too. Girls also play the game. But at the moment this doesn't bother me. We are far enough advanced in our discussion even to raise the question of "boys versus girls."

The chasing and being chased is in it. Then there is, of course, a gratification potential through well limited limelighting, limelighting as different from other games. By that I mean that two people are somewhat in the focal performer position while the others are relatively passive. Many games have this situation as a core; other games have none of it; others again have it as a side issue, but it isn't the real focus of the game. In this game it isn't either, but it plays some part. There is some emphasis on the special gratification potential for some of the players that may lie in the fact that everybody looks at you, watches how skillfully you pursue or how cutely you evade. I plan to come back to this point.

At this time I want to focus on an entirely different and much more important angle, namely, that the game also imposes certain peculiar demands and at the same time offers some very helpful defenses. For instance, if one of the players in your group is bent on the gratifications of being a bully, he is out of luck. For no matter how much he might want to grasp the opportunity, he cannot beat his victim. He can't hit him too hard, he can't chase him into the bush; he has to stay around the highly group-visible circle area, and if the victim should mind too much, he has to remain a good sport and lay off, even though he feels that he just has gotten going. On the other hand, the victim, who might be the kind of child who is viewed by his gang as simply a prestigeless receiver of a lot of aggression, can now become the "cute" actor, admired for his skill in coyly evading his persecutor; actually his otherwise all powerful persecutor may become the one to receive temporary group ridicule. There is, of course, some form of vicarious gratification built into the role of the other players while they are in the role of circle-forming onlookers; they have all the leeway of choosing which of the gratifications of persecutor or persecutee they may want to enjoy vicariously, even while temporarily inactive, watching a show with a lot of suspense and fun in it. Even while they are not running themselves, they have a sort of television show to keep them from getting bored.

At the same time, the identical issue that I have listed here as a gratification potential may also come back like a boomerang, and at the next moment become the source of trouble and frustration which make the game break down or motivate a player to abandon it in disgust. For instance, if children have to watch an excitement-producing performance beyond a certain amount of time, the fun goes out of it, their own excitement gets hold of them, and the very fact that they are in the watcher's role becomes the one issue that creates disorganization. They get "higher than kites" as we say, and game rules are blown to the wind. They begin to feel like people in a ball-game audience who at certain moments simply have to jump up and yell, just short of getting into the act itself. Then the game leader faces the problem of how to keep them in the temporary onlooker role.

Liddell: Do you have television facilities in your play group, so the children can see the other children?

Redl: I am sorry I used the term television. I didn't mean it literally; I only thought of it as a comparison. I wanted to mark the difference between visualized gratification of others, vicariously enjoyed, and the gratification by actually being in a game. There is a dual element in this process: in a way you have access to some of the watched actors' enjoyment and share in the excitement about it; on the other hand, you are also exempt from the worry and anxiety that may go with the real participation.

I was primarily trying to stress the fact that even the onlooker role at times comes very close to the action threshold, and this in itself may be a clinically most important prediction for someone who works with aggressive children to be able to make.

And this leads us squarely to one of the really big problems I hope to get to in a moment, namely: what ego supports are needed for given children in a given group in a given game-moment, in order to support that action-threshold, so it doesn't get thrown overboard by the excitement which you so wanted them to have, without which they would simply be bored? In short, we want them excited even though not active, but we also want them to remain able to limit themselves to onlooker-excitement, instead of throwing the switch into acted-out behavior. Which elements in a given game guarantee this task?

Torre: Do you know why they call the game "beetle"?

Redl: No, I don't.

Bavelas: Is it understood that the chasee will not select the chaser again?

Redl: That is right; that is another limitation, at least most of the time. As I mentioned, game customs vary, but on the whole the chaser will not be expected to select the same chasee again after he returns into his groove. There are conditions, however, under which this varies, and a chaser may elect the same chasee for the very purpose of surprise. If he does so too often, though, he will elicit group censure in no uncertain terms. It is in the interest of the course of this game that two dangers are averted: one, you don't want the same people as actors all the time, for reasons of fatigue, overexcitement, as well as participation fairness. And you don't want the same person left in the same role too long, or the masochistic chasee and the sadistic chaser might use the game simply for their own mutual pathologic gratification, or they might get stuck in either role beyond the point of endurance and with no face-saving way out left to them. All this psychiatric wisdom is sometimes buried in the outspoken "rules" of a game; more often it is relegated to the unspoken but strong code of fairness about playing the game.

Bateson: Is it *beadle* or *beetle?*

Mead: Beadle. It comes from the word "beadle" b-e-a-d-l-e, a church official who carries a staff.

Birdwhistell: This is called "Pass and slap" in parts of the country.

Mead: There is something soft on one end of the beadle's staff.

Goffman: Is this always a supervised game? Can children play it without an adult or a scout leader present?

Redl: The chance that children might play a game of this sort is relatively low, because our youth activities are very adult-dominated. At most playgrounds there is always some supervising person in charge. In the era and country where I grew up, this type of game would be played spontaneously much more often by any group of children to their own devices.

I want to come back, though, to a very important issue, if I may, of which these questions remind me. This game is so designed that, under reasonable conditions, the group control which is imposed on the players by a number of elements which I listed is actually quite sufficient to take care of all danger potentials. A reasonably well put together group of children playing this game in a reasonably relaxed mood will not need any umpiring by an adult or child play leader. Game geography (the circle) sees to it that all players are always in plain sight; random turn-taking, as demanded by the game, excludes usurpation by despots who want to play favors; the chance to terminate one's own chasee-role by going back into one's groove without loss of face offers the player a self-regulatory safety device against embarrassment or panic; the demand to be a good sport keeps the excitement of the chaser from going out of bounds; and the decency demand of giving others a chance sees to it that no one pair of players is likely to be exposed to action-excitement for too long a stretch at a time. In short, you would need leader-umpiring only if some of these built-in structural devices of the game itself should prove insufficient, and if player morale, individually or in groups, should break down for one reason or another.

This whole question of ego-supportive devices by which a game secures individual impulse-control balance as well as a reasonably healthy group atmosphere is a most fascinating issue, and I hope to get into it later in the discussion.

Steinbach: In line with Dr. Goffman's comment, this type of game is a very old game in this country, but it has disappeared in the last 25 or 30 years. "Drop the beanbag" is one variation; there were a number of games played mostly in my youth, at church socials of the Epworth League, etc. I would suggest, as one of the reasons that the games may still persist in Europe and not in this country, that they arise only within a very rigidly structured society where children are brought up according to rules. I believe that the same components of the game exist in New York now except that lead pipe is used, and instead of going in circles the children go in blocks. But we have had this marked shift during the past 25 or 30 years in the organization of children and the rigidity with which they operate. I suspect that is quite a good reason why the game did not at once seem familiar to everyone from your description. We more or less had forgotten the conditions under which those games used to arise. I believe a very necessary component is a rigid set of behavior rules for children which we now no longer have in this country.

Fremont-Smith: I wonder how many in this room remember having played this or a closely analogous game? I certainly can remember playing several games that fitted into the category. Is there anyone who doesn't remember ever having played a game like this?

Walter: We used to play a party game like this at Christmas.

Fremont-Smith: It apparently is a common memory experience of us here to have played this or an analogous game.

Steinbach: My children played it in England but they don't play it here.

Birdwhistell: We observed children playing this game about 5 months ago, without any adults around. The boys were in shorts, and they played with a wet towel. They were between 12 and 14 years of age. It was a very rough game.

Steinbach: Was that a Y.M.C.A. or Boy Scout camp?

Birdwhistell: Yes.

Steinbach: This is a traditional Boy Scout game. They put a knot in the towel.

Lorenz: I thought that it was entirely an Austrian game and I am quite surprised to find that it seems to have world-wide distribution.

Birdwhistell: I think we should be careful about presuming internationality in games. Having watched Hopi games, I cannot imagine any game among those people that is comparable to this one. Nor would I expect to find such a game played among the Kootenay Indians.

Lorenz: I meant, obviously, these games must be derived from a mutual ancestor in cultural development.

Mead: All the children's games that are found in Europe are, of course, very widespread. They are found in the Pacific and Asia, also. They are apparently very easy to communicate from the members of one society to another. We can assume that all the elements Dr. Redl is suggesting are quite deeply human.

Lotspeich: At the risk of bringing up Jung's name, do these games follow symbolic structure patterns, such as dream patterns follow?

Lorenz: Some do. For instance, the game "Who's afraid of the black man?" It is one of the "infectious" games, in which you put a group of children at one end of a long alley and one single child, who represents the black man, at the other; then they must change places. The whole group has to get to the other side of the alley, and the black man has to touch one or more of them who, in the process, are thus converted into black men. I have been told by the Austrian educator, Meister, that this game was a symbol of pox and that it was played as a sort of religious ceremony symbolizing infectious disease.

Fremont-Smith: There get to be more and more black men?

Lorenz: Yes, until all of them are on the same side. The more children have become black, the less chance the rest of them have to escape being infected with blackness.

Redl: There is one element in what you mentioned in the preceding discussion that is close to one of the points I have been trying to make. All the rest of these speculations and the issues you mentioned are very important too, but at this stage I really wasn't trying to talk about variety or which trends show where, because I haven't had a chance to finish my list under the first item. There is one thing in that game which you mentioned that I would list as a "danger potential" to any game leader who would ask me whether a given group of children is or isn't ready for playing it with enjoyment; namely, the game you described requires a player to become a turncoat. It means that he was playing on one side in the beginning; then, suddenly, he has to switch sides.

Let me suggest that with some really good, group-conscious gangsters on the child level, I couldn't play such a game. They couldn't take it. They are not going to betray the group they just joined and go to the other side. I won't go into the reasons for this, nor into details as to just how I know which child is or is not in that stage of sensitivity about his own even game-temporary group loyalties. For the purpose I had hoped to demonstrate, I only want to use this idea: Certain aspects of a game may have a very important impact on the question of just how the players, individually and as a group, are going to take it. The same item that for one situation may be a great asset may be the very one over which another child or another group breaks down completely. There is something like a "mental hygiene assessment" of game ingredients, which is an issue in its own right.

Coming back to the illustrations you used, the issue of aggression, hostility, and competition is an especially sensitive one in this respect. In professional work with disturbed children, for instance, many a game that looks wonderful on the surface becomes negatively "loaded"; there may be too high an intensity of competitive challenge in it, which then produces either hostility between the teams, or throws the individual players into too much panic about losing, or too much excitement about winning, which results in their loss of control. Or the forms of aggression involved in a specific game activity may be too frightening, or special features, like the "switching of sides" mentioned above, may create trouble.

As to the game mentioned, there are many of a similar type. There are some similar games with chants, such as "Who's afraid of the big bad wolf?" some with a little verse in front of them, and some which seem to rely primarily on simple running and tagging. As to "Who's afraid of the big bad wolf," I really don't want to try to discuss early origins, as it would lead us even further from the point I am trying to focus on, but since it has been mentioned, my own first thought is that it may have been the devil who caught some of the children on the "good" side and then forced them to help him against the remainder of the "good" ones. However, I hope you consider this an irrelevant side remark, and won't hold it against my theory of games in the vital areas which I hope to sketch.

Lorenz: "Pantoffel, Pantoffel, der Himmel ist offen, Pontur, Pontur, die Höll' ist zu." That is a little song accompanying the Lower Austrian peasant variety of the same game in which, obviously, the little chanters sang their own condemnation.

Bateson: Translate the chanty.

Lorenz: Pantoffel and Pontur do not seem to mean anything here. The rest means that at first Heaven is open and Hell is shut, and later Heaven becomes more and more shut while Hell opens with the number of children converted to evil.

Lotspeich: You have the same thing in game, "Ghost." Somebody gets to be a third of a ghost, a half ghost, and then a complete ghost. When you are a complete ghost, you can't be spoken to. So, all sorts of elaborate structures are built up to communicate with the fellow who is a full ghost.

Birdwhistell: In your question about symbols, we have been using the concept of what we call the vampire type, in which there is the threatener and the man who becomes a threatener. In the vampire situation, each man, in turn, continues and the number of vampires is spread. By being infected, you continue, and you stay infected until everyone is infected, and the game ends. This is contrasted to the game in which by infecting somebody else you get over your infection, which is the standard myth situation. In one variation of this, there is the myth that you get over syphilis if you have intercourse with a virgin. These two groups are still within the range of the moral game in which there is a threatener. There is a difference in the way the game ends. The one game ends when everybody is infected. This other game is just as characteristic, but the question always maintains, how does one stop it?

Redl: This last issue you mentioned, namely, the assessment of which game for what situation, assumes great importance. For instance, the Beetle game has many advantages in terms of termination, for it is acutally a sequence of little games. Each round, in a way, is another game course. You can terminate it any time. Nothing is left unfinished or undone when the game is terminated because the whole game process has been gone through as soon as one round has been played. This is quite different from the type of situation where there may be a 20-minute intermission and then a game has to be started, the first round of which was never over. In a more complex game, with a more clear-cut long-range goal, such as "Capture the flag," the interruption-hostility produced in the children, when the leader has to terminate it prematurely, is much greater. This is why, with disorganized children, it is much better for a long time to select games whose interruptability is easier, for with such children, any argument as to why interruption is important, any promise that the game can be played again later, is of little avail. Therefore, if easily terminable games are selected, less collective hostility is produced against the adult who has to terminate them. On the other hand, if you stick to this principle too long, you never build up in children the concept of long-range goals or the perception of the enjoyment potential of games with higher complexity, again a toss-up. The same issue may become a criterion in favor of, as well as against, game selection, depending on who the children are, what the nature of their group is, and what the goal in the whole game-exposure is, to begin with.

It certainly is important to emphasize, though, that games themselves come in different sizes, so to speak, in respect to this item of "terminability."

Freeman: I wonder if our colleagues are implying these games have a moral and symbolic value, that they have such values for the children playing them? I would question that seriously. The implication of what has been said here is that these games were played by children who somehow sense the moral and symbolic significance of what they are doing.

Redl: I didn't say that.

Freeman: No, you didn't, but I get that impression from what is being said around the table.

Lotspeich: I was thinking of its being an unconscious thing in the sense that symbol structures occur in dreams. I was thinking of them as being part of the cultural pattern where things are done without a conscious chase of that symbol.

Mead: Children begin to understand the morality of their own society before they can talk, for instance, "You give it to me" and "I give it to you." We see the whole basis of proper reciprocity built up before the child can even talk.

We are not using "moral" in a Sunday school sense or in an articulate, verbalized sense, but having to do with children getting the ethical essence of interpersonal relationships as a characteristic of growing children in any culture. That was the sense in which Dr. Birdwhistell meant it, wasn't it?

Birdwhistell: Yes.

Freeman: I might accept that for giving and sharing, but I am not so sure of that either. On the other hand, I am not at all sure these "ghost games" and the "black man games" and the "taboo individuals" have the significance for children that we think they have, or that we read into them. They might, but it doesn't seem to me they do, necessarily.

Lorenz: Dr. Freeman, if I may answer from personal experience, I have good recollections of my early emotional responses. I think I may, with conviction, assure you that the symbol of being caught and eaten by the predator, or turned into a ghost, was so vivid with me, at pre-school age, that I got highly excited about it and really felt bad when I was being eaten or turned into a ghost. And in the more elaborate fighting games, playing police and criminals, or Indians and cowboys, Indians being chased by cowboys, etc., we actually felt such strong emotions, such as the need to escape that we were led to take high jumps; we jumped from one tree to another, and I shudder to contemplate, in retrospect, what we did under this emotional pressure. In running from the Russians during the war, I did not do anything more daring than I did as a child in running away from the "police." I think that the symbolism of death and perdition is grasped very early in the emotional life of a child and reacted to as seriously as the real thing.

Birdwhistell: Dr. Freeman, I don't know what you mean by the word "sense" in this case. Answering your question, if one of the functions of a game, and you certainly see the pattern cross-culturally, is to teach children a kind of patterning response, they may not be "aware" of what is happening in the performance of the game but they are quite well aware of it when they break the performance. If they break the pattern, they are immediately warned and a portion of the pattern becomes explicit.

One of the functions of games may very well be to provide a systematic pattern in experience, in which the child learns not to break certain kinds of patterns and in which the lesson is driven home as to what he has done that is wrong. This may not be any kind of explicit message. But every time the pattern is broken, there is an organized, active "putting him into line." You either invent a new game, add a new rule, ostracize the man, or isolate him by never passing him or never catching him. If the man won't obey the rules, he may be isolated from any further play.

There is probably about as much awareness about the implicit patterns in games as there is in religious ritual. They gain, very often, the significance of the ritual at the point of breakage of the ritual.

Freeman: Within the game itself.

Birdwhistell: Within the ritual itself.

Lotspeich: What do you mean by "breakage"? Can you give an example? Do you mean talking to a ghost when you are not supposed to, or getting up in church and shouting, or something like that?

Birdwhistell: Yes.

Mead: Taking an apple to church and eating it.

Birdwhistell: Or praying too long.

Bavelas: I think it is one thing to talk about a moral game in the sense of morality play but a different thing to ask is it a moral game, in the sense that it is ethical or it is proper. A few years ago a group of us were looking at a book of ancient games. These were all board games, however. Some were war games, some pursuit games. For instance, on a board that is divided laterally into a series of spaces there are five white counters and eleven black counters. If this is put in the middle of the table and a group of people are brought together and asked, "What do you suppose this game is, and how might it be played?" they will spend a lot of time trying to arrive at a good game. A good game turns out to be a way of making it fair. If one has eleven black pieces and the other has five white pieces, the man with the black pieces must be constrained, in some way, so he can move less freely. The more moral or ethical rules that are broken, the more the game is played in the spirit of a game. So this game could be called "immoral."

Mead: This is the sense we meant.

Birdwhistell: I didn't mean to confuse. There are some games and rituals which make a "morality" statement. But by "moral" here I am talking about a broader concept. The morality play game would be subsumed under the morality which relates to the way the game or ritual fits the patterning of the society.

Kramer: I am interested in one aspect of the games which relates to the evolution of emphasis of particular elements of the game. For example, in this game you mentioned some five elements. There is a version of it which we all know, namely, the beanbag game, in which there is no aggressiveness; in other words, the aggressiveness is left out. Instead of the participant being selected by whacking, a beanbag is simply dropped behind him, which he picks up, and the chase begins. The question I have is this, and I want later to give one other variation of the game which I have seen played, to emphasize it: to what extent is that variation imposed by the adult supervisor, to the extent, for example, that the adult supervisor cannot stand the aggressiveness in the game, and then makes it a "nicer" game, in which there is no aggressiveness? And to what extent is the evolution of elements of the game derived from the children or the participants themselves?

For example, at the Munich-American Elementary School, in Germany, there was a version of this game which surprised me. Children sit around in a group; the main elements of this game are suspense and touch contact. They all close their eyes. One member is selected by the leader. Instead of a whack or the beanbag selecting the participant or the chaser, the leader simply indicates "You"; it is just a sign, with no verbalization. There is only this pointing, to one of the children playing the game, to start. This child gets up, walks around—they all still have their eyes closed—and simply touches, in any way he wants, another child. This may become aggressive. Sometimes some of the children introduce aggressiveness into it. Instead of touching or caressing the other child, they poke. But, normally, the main element here is contact; there is no chase. The child that has been touched then gets up and goes around to different children and has to guess, from the touch, who has done the touching. In other words, there are different elements of emphasis, which become, as you say, ritualized in the game. I wonder to what extent the ritualizations are child-based, *i.e.,* grow out of the needs of the child, and to what extent they grow out of the supervisor's needs? Do you have any information on that aspect of the variation of games?

Redl: Yes, but I refuse to be seduced into discussing that part of it now. All I have tried to do was to put one single and not too complicated game on this table, take it apart before you, and try together to see what is in it. Of course, there is a wide variety of different games. Of course, they may contain different forms of aggression: in some it is in the foreground; in some it seems nearly left out; in others different gratification potentials seem to be more in the limelight, etc. I really want to postpone the discussion of this question, for if I start on it now I will be hopelessly pulled in an entirely different direction.

The issue of modifiability of game ingredients as such is a very important one, indeed, especially in work with disturbed children. I certainly want to know if I can modify game ingredients, so that one ingredient which for a given group may be too "heavy" can be cut down or left out. It is often, for instance, essential to reduce the amount of competitiveness or forms which a game originally involved while one wants all the other gratification potentials left in. In fact, this very idea of developing a "pharmacopoeia" of game ingredients so as to know which combination will have which effect on a given child or group is in the foreground of our most cherished hopes. Even so, I would like to underline the point that even with all that in mind, it is often quite difficult to go against the folk-lore halo of a game, beyond a certain point. Some games are factory-made anyway; there is no reason why practically every aspect of them cannot be modified. Other games are part of an inherent cultural expectation of the children, and if an attempt is made to modify too much, they would say that the game is not the same game any more. Sometimes I can still get around the tribal resistance against such modification, provided I am careful enough to call the game something else. In short, sometimes I can modify even tradition-loaded games so that they do fit exactly the prescription of ingredients I want the children to get, but still children may not accept the new prescription.

Kramer: Is that element that they will not go beyond the rules and regulations?

Redl: It depends upon the type of game, the type of children, and their awareness. Sometimes it is quite fluid. Games vary in terms of how much the original pattern can be violated. Some of it should be left in its original shape; touching it is like meddling with religion.

Peck: Studying different groups, you could compare them as to their readiness to accept games with rigid rules.

Redl: Yes.

Buhler: What has made certain games into folklore games which are played all over the world in very similar ways is really an interesting question. And what makes other games so flexible that no one cares whether the rigidity is broken is also an interesting question. Have you investigated that?

Redl: No. I would like to go back to this very simple issue: Here is a given game. I want to inspect that game as to its potential impact on the gratification needs of the children, I want to assess the likely frustration impact parts of the game might produce, and I want to inspect that game as to "built-in ego control." I have said a few things about gratification potentials. Next, I shall say a few things about the assessment of frustration impact of a game. No matter how much "fun" a game is in general, I do have to figure out during which phase the children might get too bored or so overexcited they cannot handle themselves any longer, or so frustrated they might "blow up." As to those frustrations, they may lie in most unexpected areas. With some groups, for instance, the need to unhook the origi-

nal pecking order and switch to a different status hierarchy for the duration of a game can be too frustrating to risk. For instance, if I want to play
the beetle game with Cabin No. 5, it may be quite all right. For the time
being I might dissuade my counselors from getting Cabin No. 7 into it.
Cabin No. 7 happens to have a pecking order of high rigidity, and with
powerful child-leaders who do anything to avoid having it upset; it also has
frightened group members who panic as soon as their rigid positional order
is upset, no matter how much they suffer under it. In a circle game like
"beetle," the social structure and pecking order demanded is quite different. Every player is even; there is no "tough boss" and no "lieutenant" to
carry out his orders and no "fall guy" to take the rap, etc. In order to have
fun playing such a game, you would have to abandon your accustomed
position. You are supposed to be able to take some ridicule and not mind;
you are supposed to let a weaker child hit you when his turn comes, without hitting back; you are supposed to lose with grace and without retribu-
tion. You have to surrender your position in the power hierarchy, or else—

   Liddell: How long have you had to delay that?

   Redl: It varies. I have to delay until the over-all spirit of the camp
culture—

   Liddell: It may take weeks?

Redl: It may take a few weeks or a few days; it varies. It depends on
how many older children are in the same cabin, because they are part of
the previous camp culture, which keeps it from being face-losing. While
you live in this camp, you don't have to do certain things; you can't lose
status; you get your status back the moment you get home. Even though
you surrender, you get it back. It was only a 20-minute game. As long as
that gets across, I can begin to play.

   Goffman: Could I ask you to distinguish between altering the status
structure, and scrambling or randomizing it? In the games I recall, playing
always involved an alteration of status, but a *mere* or random alteration
would often have spelled failure. You can in fact take a given pecking
order or hierarchy that applies outside the game and rearrange this within
the game in such a way as to guarantee that the game will fail to "come
off." So a game does not merely involve any alteration in the status pattern,
but rather an alteration that makes it possible for the game to become fun.

   Redl: Yes, that is right.

   Goffman: On the face of it, a game provides its own internally determined status and power structure, cutting across the wider one to which
the players belong. In the case of a simple game, where one person hits
and chases, and other person tries to avoid the blows, an allocation of
power is established for the duration of a turn; then, this is changed and
the chased becomes the chaser, while the previous chaser gives up his
claim to the limelight. At the moment of tag, the tagger must automatically
surrender his power position, and in fact if he was not prepared to do so he

wouldn't be much good for the game of tag. So that even within the world of the game, there is an alteration in status, and often a very rapid one. Apparently players often feel that the internally generated structure has no intrinsic bearing on the external, wider one outside the game, and this fiction may have to be sustained even though the game would fall flat if in fact random alterations tended to occur.

Fremont-Smith: If you happen to be a slow runner and you are "it," this becomes a frustrating situation, and now you are not in the power position, but everyone else who escapes you is in the power position. This is a reversal of the role.

Redl: That is right. By the way, you might even turn that into an advantage, provided the group is ready for a high degree of deviation. The chance to taunt the group may substitute for another gratification part. But in the usual situation it is a disappointment when you have to give up power and actually are on the receiving end of the line.

Fremont-Smith: Having been there, I remember it very well.

Goffman: There is always a best accidental order of people within the game. You can't draw the order out of a hat or the game is likely to be flat.

Redl: Yes. The only reason I brought all this pecking order and status hierarchy problem in here was to illustrate the idea that an assessment of the frustration impact of a game may have to go as far afield as that. For, customarily one would think, among frustration risks, of things like playing the game so long that the children get tired, demanding too great a performance which the children can't achieve, or keeping them bored and passive too long a time. I wanted to point to the fact that under an issue like "frustration potential" of a game you may go that far afield, since exposure to a social structure which is new and frightening, or to a pecking order which demands too many new adaptations, may be as "frustrating" for children as getting tired out or having to sit still too long. This type of frustration, too, may produce temper tantrums or withdrawal, depressive defeat or manic elation, and may lead to the breakdown of the game or to disorganized behavior in the players just as much as if I had forced them into a charade which contained arithmetic tasks way above their grasp.

This is the only context in which I pulled this complex issue of social structure into the picture at this point. I am still really talking about the same point I started with, *i.e.,* the inspection of game ingredients for the assessment of the potential impact on the players who will participate in a game at a certain time and place.

Peck: Isn't it necessary to introduce some caution when one is talking about the ability of an individual to tolerate a particular game? Is this determined only by the conditions that we ordinarily think of as being within the game itself? For a moment we might consider some elements we usually think of as being outside the game. For example, the ability to tolerate a particular game for a given individual may depend on whether he suggested the game or whether someone else did. The ability to tolerate a team game, for example, may be determined by how this person participated in the choosing of sides. In a sense, we have games within games.

Redl: This assessment of what is in a game that is potentially relevant for the players, goes far beyond anything I have said. I am only selecting a few illustrations that might apply.

Your point brings up something that perhaps I should have said at the outset. I do want to make a sharp difference between blind analysis of the game, and prediction of the processes going on within the recipient at the time of the game exposure. I cannot dissolve the concept of the game as an organism in its own right, into merely the question whether children playing it get wild and excited because of the impact it has on them. These are two different issues. The game itself is still there, irrespective of its effect on particular players, as a structural entity. In this respect a game belongs in the same category as the concept of "milieu" or "environmental stimulus" or such. By just looking at the game and its ingredients, even before it is "played," I can predict certain potential effects upon players, certain danger points and certain special properties. Whether these danger points become an issue with a specific group of children or not is a question of a separate nature. For that assessment I have to look at children, the nature of their group, etc. It is a little bit like deciding whether a given combination of chemicals will have a "good" effect on a given stomach, or not. In order to decide that, I take into account just what that particular stomach is like at the time I put the drug into it. However, the drug is also an entity in its own right and I can make a lot of statements about its potential impact on organisms and their parts by analyzing its chemical properties.

Of course, we must not carry this analogy too far, for it could lead us into the narrow corner of pathology which we don't want to get into at this moment. But I still insist that just to observe how children act when they play a game and then to say, out of our experience, it is a difficult or frustrating game would not be enough. I also want to look at what the game is composed of; its bones, its organs, its physiology, etc., because it has all that in it. What a given game pattern will do to a specific group of players is a separate question in its own right.

For the moment, I would like to continue to look at the game as such, before the children even start playing. On the one side of the ledger, we discussed at some length the gratification and frustration potential side of the picture. Now let me change to the other side of the fence: Just what are the built-in ego controls a game may offer its participants? I shall list them briefly. I think there are about four major parts in any game structure which are meant, so to say, to play special tricks upon the participants in terms of making the game process possible and safe from destructiveness. First, any game offers ego support through certain arrangements as to timing, arrangement of space, and conditions for the use of props. I use the term props here purposely and must leave its precise definition for a future opportunity, as there certainly would be a great deal to discuss. For the moment let us be satisfied with referring by this word to anything that is being used as a gadget in a game.

In Monopoly this would be the board and the dice. In baseball, it is the baseball and the bat, or whatever other props are involved. In the beetle game, by the way, there is only one prop that is the beetle with which you hit the right-hand neighbor when the round starts.

The question of props, by the way, is indeed fascinating. Sometimes even people may become "props," as for instance in certain games where one player has to stand with his face toward the wall while the others take turns swatting him. There are moments when the individual player really stops being a person playing a role. He actually becomes something like a "live prop."

As to the use of the term "ego-support" here, I include anything the game does that helps an individual player or the group to keep a reasonable balance between impulse gratification, emergent anxieties, frustrations or excitements on the one hand, and the behavioral demands of the game process itself on the other. The reasons why we have so much trouble defining just what is meant by ego support is a complex story in its own right. It goes back in part to the lack of therapeutic vocabulary, which has few good descriptions for any form of ego support that isn't directly verbal in nature, and it is complicated by the fact that we have paid little attention to the question just how people outside the therapy room offer ego support to children who need it—*e.g.,* a camp counselor or a mother—and that we have paid too little attention to the ego-supportive properties of the setting in which people operate. It is our contention here that besides anything people may do who lead a game, the game structure itself has certain "built-in" properties which are meant, by game nature, to be ego-supportive in effect.

It is those properties which enable even an excited group of players to survive a game without being torn to pieces by conflicting urges, without unmanageable panic, or action-barrier flooding excitement beyond what the game situation or the players can endure.

The second ego support is derived through role definition, power arrangements, group structure, and the imposition of action-ceilings on individual behavior. The third ego support is through built-in group-code demands. The fourth ego support is for emergencies through a special machinery for settling disputes and keeping recalcitrants in line. Not all games have all of these equally developed. Some games, for instance, leave certain aspects to chance, or to the judgment of the leader, or just assume that matters won't get out of hand. Other games have built-in provisions to meet special hazards to which their specific nature seems to expose the players. The wisdom with which folkways often have anticipated psychological complications for players which we think only our present day psychiatric theory could have thought about, is an amazing spectacle to behold.

Lotspeich: When you talk about ego support, are you referring to the ego of the individuals in the game, or to the group ego?

Redl: This is a difficult question and I hope I can come back to it later. At the moment I am thinking primarily of the individual player, but of course the question also needs to be raised for the group. As to the individual player, the group itself may be the very factor that offers the support. On the other hand, I am interested in the game's effect upon the individual player not only for his own sake, but also because it will be quite decisive on the further course of the game itself. I am eager for the game to give the individual player so much ego support not only so that he can have fun without "blowing up" in the process, but also because I want the game left undisturbed by whatever crisis it might have produced in him. These are two levels of equal importance, but they should not be confused with each other.

If a game is really to give ego support, it must help the individual to keep his own balance between impulses and controls in reasonable shape and must do it in such a way that the individual still remains a potentially constructive player in the over-all process of the game. Not all games do enough of both.

Goffman: Is that what we mean by a good game? Is it this double function that is taking place when children say, "This is fun?"

Redl: The reason I have trouble answering is because you brought in children. But I think I understand what you are trying for, so let me try to answer you this way:

If there is enough balance between gratification and frustration avoidance, plus some frustrations the coping with which is fun in its own right, on the one hand, and then good ego supports built into the game on the other, then it will be the kind of game you seem to have in mind where children will say, "it was fun." But they will say so only if the elements were well mixed in that way. For, if the game were only impulse-gratifying it would most likely become too confusing and lead to breaking up; the complexity of the game couldn't be maintained. If it were full of ego-supportive factors but without gratifications on the level on which children can take them, they wouldn't like that either. There are some exceptions to this, by the way: there are some games that make the mastery of anxiety or danger, or the control of one's will by somebody else, the major "fun." "O'Grady," a game frequently played in Boy Scout troops, seems to fall into that category. One of its major gratifications is voluntary submission to clear-cut regimented patterns and quickness of "uptake." There are some drill games which have less "trickery-gratification" and suspense built into them than "O'Grady," where pride in mastery of control when submission is demanded seems to prevail.

Freeman: In speaking about this O'Grady game, you say that gratification comes from subjecting oneself to control. I suspect that that is an adult interpretation. How do we know it is what you interpret it to be? Couldn't it come from the mere kinesthetic satisfaction, from the mere ability to respond quickly? What makes you say it is subjecting oneself to control?

Redl: I shouldn't have used this illustration. In my haste, I tried to use one and the same game to explain two theses, and it is apparently backfiring now. The gratification involved in O'Grady has two different angles: One is actually a sort of "fooling-response," being vigilant so as not to be trapped into the wrong "answer," so to say. This was not the one I had primarily in mind at the moment. I was referring more, when I spoke about "control," to that phase of the O'Grady game that it has in common with other marching drills, and the gratification there is in not just walking, in leg movement or body co-ordination as such but to marching with a clear-cut prescription, turning when told to, following a pattern in quick and obedient response.

Freeman: That is control of body activity.

Redl: That is right.

Freeman: As in ballet dancing.

Redl: But I don't mean the *mastery* of body movement. I am referring to that visible feeling of being very proud of being able to react to a command quickly and correctly; it is very evident on the faces of children in a good marching drill. There is some real enjoyment of subjection to command.

Fremont-Smith: It is more than subjection; it is capacity really to win this game, of not being thrown off base by the other fellow. So that, actually, it is your own mastery of the situation rather than subjecting yourself to someone else's mastery. There is also the matter of winning the game. The game is, can the other fellow throw you off? If you are master of the situation, nothing he can say to you will do so; therefore, you remain master of your situation, and the subjection is really only an apparent subjection.

Freeman: There is another element, namely, the satisfaction of going the thing itself, as in all kinds of athletics, for example, swinging a racket and hitting a ball gracefully. Good tennis players and good ball-players are graceful dancers. I don't think it is just a matter of competition. Physical discipline is involved in this, but emerging from that is the satisfaction of doing well the thing itself. I think this factor is often ignored.

Kramer: There is a type of subjection or submission to outer forces or outer elements, which is natural, for instance, in something like sailing. When you sail a boat, you are completely aware of the movement of the water and the speed of the wind. These factors are reflected in the position and tensions in your body as you sail and you guide the boat, really, in complete submission to those forces outside of yourself. Even though you are completely submitting to the elements, there is tremendous pleasure in being able to do that, just to be in tune, and to pick up this change in wind direction or that change in water speed, and to guide the boat in accord with the outer changes, and skillfully.

Fremont-Smith: It is mastery-submission though; there is a mastery involved in the submission.

Lorenz: Dr. Freeman means the mastery of the coordinated efforts. There is a tremendous joy in doing anything gracefully, in doing it just as it ought to be, joy of the highest order. What you say is actually the same story on the afferent side, that you rejoice in the subtlety of your afference, and the fine poise of your responses. I quite agree to what you say, that there are many things in which the joy lies in submission to afferent processes.

Walter: If you are going to bring in physiologic terms, there is a new concept in physiology in which movement and perception are considered to be very much more under the control of the higher central nervous system than was at first believed. In the control not only of voluntary movement but also of postural movement, there may be specific pleasure of a type which the physiologist can investigate quantitatively, either in submitting to or modulating this semi-involuntary control system which is called the "gamma-loop." Previously, physiologists thought vaguely of all movements as starting as an impulse from a Betz cell. It may be that they begin as a change of bias outside the brain, in the effectors. Directing this bias and accommodating to it may give us very specific pleasure.

Freeman: I agree, but the performer may not even know he has a brain.

Walter: No, he is not conscious of it; of course he doesn't know. But I mean the specific nature of certain pleasures of skilled perception and effector action may be associated with the operation of the bias system. It may be an important aspect of playing these games, round games or team and group games.

Goffman: Let's not overestimate this factor of mastery of one's body in motion; it fits too well the "Academy's" image of exercise. No doubt there is something to this kind of analysis, but let's be very suspicious of it. It is the sort of thing university people have been shoving down other people's throats for many years.

Walter: That games are good for you?

Goffman: Graceful performance, fine dancing, sailing, and all that. I for one would want us to feel a little suspicious about this. Let's not overstress it. We've mentioned it; that's enough, let's go on.

Mead: It is interesting to note that if there is one person in this group who spends his time with children and knows how they feel and act, it is

Dr. Redl, yet while he is talking and trying to make abstract comments, he is challenged as though he were a university professor. That, I think, is a little strange.

Redl: I am tempted to get into this fracas, but I think I should try to finish what I started to talk about. I shall make a few more remarks about the four ways in which games offer ego support on the spot. I should like to add a few illustrations, and I am not going to try to separate the four issues as I go along. For instance, how does the beetle game avoid the confusion an excitable group of children might easily run into when playing the game? Let us select just one item, the circular structure of the game. The circle arrangement has much psychological importance in it, for this game has no provisions for a captain or a group or game leader. Whatever controls may be needed, therefore, have to exist right in its very structure as much as possible. Through the circle structure, two conditions are guaranteed: You are supposed to run around that circle, and stay there. You are not supposed to chase your opponent off into the bushes to take care of him there; you are supposed to stay right in proximity to the group. That circle rule means that the group is taking no chances. It trusts you, but only that far. Who knows but what the latent sadism of one player might suddenly flare up in the excitement of the chase and lead to hitting beyond the level that the game group would approve of? Who knows whether one or another little masochist might not be tempted to goad his persecutor into more violent action and then accusingly complain if he gets what he asked for? How could one be sure that children themselves, while playing, would have the ability and sense to watch out for such events? Therefore, the circle arrangement sees to it that the group remains in the saddle, and has a chance to perform the watchdog functions which a game leader or umpire would otherwise be expected to exert. The other guarantee the circle structure provides is the assurance that there will be turn-taking. No matter how involved the players may get while they are at it, the group can terminate any pair-interaction that lasts too long for anyone's comfort.

There is another wonderful device built into this game which I should like to single out for attention, a device for face-saving, together with a generously ready alibi. For instance, if you are the fellow who is being chased and for some reason have had enough of it, you have the built-in safety place guaranteed to you. You can terminate the persecutor's action simply by going back into your groove. This, by the way, is a device many games of similar nature have well worked out. In this game, however, there is apparently an extra bonus to be had. Let us assume you want to stop because you actually have become anxious or embarrassed about the teasing you got, or hurt by the roughness of your persecutor's vehemence, or what not. As you still don't want to seem a poor sport, your own ego ideal might force you to keep at it to the point of real exhaustion, breakdown, or despair. The beetle game offers you a guarantee against that. Going back to your original place is, by the unspoken standards of the game, viewed as a generous act; you go back because you are a good sport and want the others to have a chance. Therefore, besides providing you with a safe place to terminate exposure to play action, the game also provides you with an alibi for possibly less heroic motives in your behavior, and you can use this alibi against possible accusation by others, and still better, even against that voice from within yourself.

In addition to all that, the game has a built-in safety device for the as- surance of turn-taking. This is needed in order to assure the ability of the passive players in the circle to hold on to themselves. Without such a semi- official rule for taking turns, onlookers in the circle might easily be help- lessly exposed to overexcitement or boredom, or other secondary conse- quences, such as a captive audience in an assembly program is exposed to when someone on the stage doesn't have sense enough to terminate the program. Besides the need of this device for the distribution of participa- tion in the game, it also serves as a supportive device for the temporarily inactive players so that they will not be exposed to more impulse-flooding or anxiety or impatience than they can stand.

Coming back to our original assumption of a fictitious play leader who may have to decide which game to play with a given group of highly ex- citable children, I would want him to know such things about games, so as to make wiser choices and to anticipate better what a fix he will be in once a certain game gets rolling. For, in those items where the game has already built in available ego-support devices, he will not have to worry unless things get far beyond what a built-in device can be expected to handle. However, every game also contains many spots where no built-in devices are available. In these he, himself, will have to do the ego-supporting, and he should know what will be needed. For instance, in the beetle game there is no built-in device against excessive taunting of either of the run- ners; there is no unspoken limit to what the rest of the children can say or yell while the chase is on. There is an expectation that all players be good sports and take some ridicule without getting too upset about it, but there is no built-in suggestion as to just where bearable ridicule should stop. Therefore, the game leader should watch for such issues from the outset; it will be up to him to see that the group doesn't lose its sense about it and that the game is protected from breakdown in that direction.

When I mentioned four types of ego support built into games, I also mentioned the "group code." This item actually has two subdivisions. On one level we may think of a group code as regulating behavior in the in- terests of the game proceeding. In this respect, it is deemed "unfair," or at least poor sportsmanship, to hog too much time, to keep others waiting, to hog the ball when another player would do better with it, and so forth. This built-in demand that the group makes on the individual player contains primarily issues which would likely endanger game progress. On the other side, there are also many wildly assorted and not always clearly placeable items of fairness, decency, as well as clearly moralistic or ethical demands. It certainly would not be considered fair by many groups if one player acted especially unkind or downright mean toward another. Yet, this is not "code-expected" in exactly the same way, as if he for example broke out of a waiting line in a relay race. Only in our loose use of language do we throw both issues into the concept of "group code."

Of course, each group of children has special codes of its own, over and beyond the fact that any group will accept the built-in code of a game they like as binding. It is important to know, where game-demanded code items do not coincide with the "native group code" of the players. We ran into something along that line in the early phases of treatment, when youngsters on our ward would engage in Chinese checkers. There are many rules about the game which make it clear which move is fair and which not. I couldn't find any rule anywhere which stipulated that you can't steal the marbles. The game just hadn't thought of that. When we play that game in winter or in the middle of summer, we usually have no trouble with it. The marbles are merely "props" and considered as such. But let us not go on thinking we can play Chinese checkers in Spring! Spring is the marble season, and then a marble isn't just a prop; it is a prized possession whose value varies greatly, depending on whether it is a "purie" or not, or on whatever issues the marble market happens to emphasize at the time. During that season also the greed for possession of the best marbles is so universal in our group that it would be hard for any one child to view a marble as anything else. Therefore, Chinese checkers in Spring simply means that the marbles will all be stolen before the game has even begun. In Spring, the group code would remain as indignant about a false move in checkers as in any other season. The taking of the marbles as such, though, would not produce indignation, except in a child who wasn't fast enough to get as many as the next fellow. It is more or less expected that each will try to get as many of the prized possessions as he can get away with, while the basic game rule of fair play still remains intact. The marble illustration is also a good example of the problem of "prop dominance," but that isn't why I used it here.

In general, some games have more built-in ego supports against exploitation of other players through ruse than others; many games leave this issue entirely to the control of the captain, umpire or the group.

Liddell: About the props, do you dare let the children play "Monopoly"?

Redl: Yes, but for a while Monopoly money disappeared into the children's cash boxes, until they were really ready to enjoy the game. Sometimes a group is ready to play chess, and they leave the chess pieces alone, before a game of Monopoly would have a chance of lasting. In answer to your special question, we have quite a bit of Monopoly money around during the early phases and expect most of it to be hoarded, until finally the more complex pleasures of the game begin to sink in. Sooner or later they all have so much Monopoly money hoarded by legal or illegal means, that it is de-contaminated enough to be used reasonably for the duration of the game.

By the way, I should like to exploit this opportunity, since we are talking about Monopoly money, to smuggle in another comment about the role of props. With Monopoly, for instance, it is bad for us, during the early phases of therapy, if we get game props that are too alluring. As you know, in Monopoly the figures that the players move on the board are quite attractive; there are shoes, cars, etc. During the phase of early therapy I often wish the game was sold merely with buttons of different colors. Here, again, the toy value and the symbolic value of the different game props often produce such trouble for a given child that the game never has a chance to get under way. For some children it becomes so important that they have the shoe versus the car, or whatever the choice may be, that pre-game emotion rises sky high before positive or negative feelings about the game even have a chance to develop.

I should like to add one additional point here: All that has been said about games also has important implications for other areas of activity, such as arts and crafts, boating, swimming, cookouts, trips, shop settings, etc. Again the question of what props will be involved, what they will mean to the game, and what they will do to the children, is of similar relevance. Also, built-in ego supports, outspoken rules of deportment as well as tacitly assumed ones, need to be analyzed; the group code of the specific player needs to be inspected along similar lines as were suggested here for games. In fact, what I said about games was meant primarily to offer an opportunity to point out facts which seem to me equally relevant in the mental hygiene appraisal of all settings and environmental factors, of all "milieu ingredients" in the wider meaning of the term.

Goffman: Aren't all games board games? There is great variety but basically isn't some form of board always involved?

Redl: In a way, yes. You may call everything a board, but there is still a difference. This by the way leads us close to what I would like to get into now. In some games, for instance, there is clearly the theme of a "chase." Under some circumstances, whether it is a chase with wooden figures on a board or a chase meaning running in the woods is irrelevant. The question is: are the children ready for and in need of an experience of chase? Under other circumstances the issue of relevance may be that very difference between a board chase using representative props versus real running by live persons. Either of these deliberations may be decisive depending on the concrete problem at hand.

Peck: I don't know whether the attempt to define when a thing is a prop and when it is "real" can also be extended to other than inanimate objects. This might be crucial in determining when a game is no longer a game, when it is play and when it is not play.

If I may take a rather big jump, this question brings to my mind the fury with which a therapy group reacts to a new member who says something to the effect, "You shouldn't get so angry." He may say this because he doesn't understand that the game that is being played makes the assumption that "It is all right to be angry because this is only a prop by which we are going to do something else." In other words, not knowing it is a prop, he is unable to define the boundaries of the "game," and it creates a tremendous reaction in the older member who may regard the new member as breaking the rules.

Walter: Dr. Redl, approximately how many good games do you think there are?

Redl: There is no such thing as a good game.

Walter: In classes. You talked about this as if it were a good game.

Redl: This is not a good game; chess is not a good game. I want to talk about the indications or contraindications as to suitability of a given game, with regard to the specific games of a given group.

Walter: I mean in large categories. You said most games involve some sort of pursuit which, of course, is true, but not all games do. I wanted to know how many categories of games you think there are, roughly, two, five, ten, a hundred?

Redl: That depends. I have thirty categories. You can categorize them in terms of how games look, or in terms of any aspect of the game. If you were to categorize as to whether they are table games or running games, you get one kind of division, for example.

Walter: That is not quite the sort of classification I meant; I am curious about the parameters of play. I should like to be a little more clear as to the range of your categorization of games. We have spread over a rather wide range of games in the last hour.

Redl: I don't understand.

Fremont-Smith: Why is it important to know how many categories of games he has in mind at this time?

Walter: Just to get an idea of what he thinks is possible in game behavior, what the repertoire might be.

Fremont-Smith: Wouldn't this depend upon *with respect to what?* And, depending upon with respect to what, there could be an infinite number or only one.

Mead: Dr. Redl is not giving a lecture on games, as if he were primarily interested in games and had looked at them cross-culturally and determined how they fitted with ritual, and all the different kinds for which we would need a set of parameters. He is only using the game to get on to some other matters. Therefore, he is not responsible for having thought out the whole range of games.

Walter: I appreciate that. I only said "approximately." I would just like to know what you might have in your mind, as a hunch, what you think the repertoire of game behavior in your children would be, in this particular field of inquiry. I don't mean in all the world or cross-culturally, but in this particular group, how many sorts of games would they play, roughly?

Redl: I can't answer that.

Fremont-Smith: Very interesting! You stumped him completely.

Redl: It is a question that floors me, unless you ask me about game behavior in what respect?

Walter: Within the framework of your particular inquiry and discourse, about how many modes of behavior does your group have? What is the repertoire of your group within the framework?

Peck: Another way of saying what Dr. Mead said, and perhaps it has to do with the difficulty that Dr. Redl and some of us feel, in response to this question. We are saying, "You don't understand that Dr. Redl is only playing a game with games."

Redl: No, we are also interested in games, or else we couldn't find out enough about them to lend use for what we want to do with children. I will still have trouble in answering the question in a general way, unless I first get the basis on which you want me to.

Birdwhistell: Perhaps the answer to this, if we are not going to be trivial, is that there are really only two kinds of games. There are the games children of a given group play and games which they won't play.

Walter: That is the first answer.

Redl: Then I can make innumerable kinds of categories. I could say there are only seven different, basic factors, and that practically any game contains one of them. Then I could say, there are five different games, games which are related. You may have to use a prop as a substitute for yourself, and there are also games where you yourself are involved. I could say there are that many games in terms of games which have an interaction pattern in the group structure, etc. I would still need to know, according to *what* criterion?

Walter: Mathematicians say there are 1,152 algebras, which at first seems to be a nonsensical statement but it is actually quite an interesting one to algebraists. I think my question is a better one than it seems, but the answer might, in fact, come out in the course of your presentation. I think the answer might be rather interesting in relation to the analysis of the behavior patterns you are speaking of.

Fremont-Smith: I think what has happened is that you have brought in a frame of reference which, from Dr. Redl's point of view at the moment, is irrelevant and can become relevant only when you define your frame of reference more specifically. I think it would be interesting to see whether you do get an answer during the course of the day and, Dr. Walter, I hope you come back to it.

Walter: Yes.

Mead: He wants the answer.

Walter: I would like to have it.

Buhler: It depends upon how many games you are going to play.

Walter: Approximately. That would be the first step.

Fremont-Smith: The answer is "many."

Redl: In order to answer that, when do you call one game different from another? Is it different according to basic ingredients?

Fremont-Smith: You have asked a general question without indicating with respect to what.

Walter: I wasn't quite sure, with respect to what he said. He asked the question this time.

Mirsky: He said "thirty games." [Laughter]

Kramer: Maybe we will return to that when Dr. Redl mentions the seven basic ingredients.

Redl: For the next part of our discussion, I have *purposely* selected some of the earliest and most worrisome attempts we made to bring some system into this, simply because an early and confused attempt has a better chance to elicit a fruitful discussion than handing out well organized, whitewashed category systems ready for publication. The people who worked with me on this, especially Dr. Paul Gump, Mr. Brian Sutton-Smith, and Dr. Jack Kuonin, are as aware of the inadequacies of this attempt as I am (2–6). I only wish they were here today, for they are much more familiar with many of the details in the mass of materials, on the basis of which some of these categories were established, and they could answer questions about specifics of research methods much more adequately than I can.

What we were trying to do was simply to see whether we could separate out everything that *might* become relevant in the assessment of a game for its clinical use, and to see whether we could eventually get some systematic order out of the wide variety of items that emerged from our observational studies.

I should like to start with the "challenge" or "theme" concept. Dr. Paul Gump deserves credit for having pushed for its relevance most vehemently and for tracing its various manifestations most consistently. It is also the item on our list which drew the most excited responses when I discussed this material several years ago with other scientists and clinicians. It is a strange kind of angle, which does not impress one at first. Whether or not it is the most important one we are not ready to say.

Most games, like plays, have an actor, an action pattern, a counter-action pattern, and somehow a "theme," the resolution of which terminates the game. We think the Race, the Chase, the Attack, the Capture, the Harassment, the Search, the Rescue, the Seduction, are all typical "Themes." If you can find some more which we can squeeze in among these, I'll be very happy. The important issue about a theme is that the form in which it takes place can be ignored for the time being. If it is a chase, it remains the same theme, whether you run after your partner's figures on a checker board or whether you run after him in the woods. Just what this thing is we are talking about, we are not quite sure. We were tempted to call it the challenge or sometimes the theme, but let us forget about nomenclature for a while. Whatever it is, it seems to deserve the status of a game dimension in its own right. To illustrate some of this, let's pick the "race" for a moment. By race we mean a situation in which one person has to move and the other tries-to overtake him. The resolution of this challenge occurs when, at a certain point, the overtaking has taken place. In a race, both players attempt to reach the goal; no interaction is required between them.

This is quite different from, let us say, the "capture" theme. In a race the issue is to get there first; it simply consists of two individual actions which are parallel. But the issue is for one of them to stay ahead, for the other one to overtake.

This describes only the nature of the theme or challenge. Whether this is the most important thing to consider in a given game, remains a question in its own right. In many situations it may be more important to be concerned with whether the children chase each other over a checkerboard or in the woods; in others it may be more crucial whether they should be exposed to a race situation rather than a capture one, irrespective of whether it happens through props or directly, in the woods or in their cabin.

What had been pointed out to me before is, that there seems to be an amazing parallel between these themes and the major events in primitive man's life. I think it was Dr. Mead who mentioned that these themes seem to be basic problems of human actions running all through Life, but let us leave this speculation out for the moment.

In the chase, there is an attempt by one to catch, tackle, or tag. The other has to outdistance, dodge, or elude. This implies that there are two quite different gratification patterns offered here. Only one at a time can be the dominant one for a player, but he can switch roles later. Of course, the chase can also be done via props. It can be done in a wide field, in a room, in a guessing game, etc.

Peck: It is more likely to involve interaction?

Redl: It ends up with interaction. It aims at some interaction because, finally, you have to tag somebody or try to avoid being tagged yourself.

Walter: Do you insist that within this framework, these various activities should be within some board or court or track or course? In general, a race is run within certain limits. This seems to be the case in the games described. In other words, the area of play, which may be on a board or may be in the open, is delimited by some arbitrary convention. Is that so?

Redl: Now you are ahead of me, you are referring to some of the other categories of rule coverage and spatial distribution.

Walter: This is an essential condition for this to be a game and not "real" activity.

Redl: What I am trying to point out is that once you have any one of these dimensions, you will still have all the others in there somewhere. I am only trying, at this moment, to bring out one dimension at a time and to classify them somewhat. Of course, everything else is still in it too. For instance, in order to have a successful and gratifying chase, quite a variety of gratification potentials must still be involved; many frustration issues must be considered; also, some built-in ego supports are needed; limitation of space will probably be quite essential, and many more factors enter in.

Goffman: This is important in baseball, where finding a field big enough to serve as a diamond may constitute a problem.

Redl: If the terrain is difficult, you must make your over-all rule sharply. Then you must have extra penalties or extra premiums for staying within a certain space, and the rule complexity increases.

Goffman: In jails there is often a question of what to do when the ball hits a jail wall. Often a rule has to be worked out, governing how many bases to give when the ball hits the wall, and how to count catches made off the wall. Here the high wall clearly has a special role to play in the game.

Walter: In most Public Schools in England there are special games where the degree of constriction is determined; for example, Eton has a special wall game. The rules have been built up from the constriction.

Usually the constriction exploits the boundary of legal activity, *e.g.,* a wall. You have to use the wall as part of the game, and reembody in it a part of your play rather than as part of your constriction.

Lifton: In these challenges there is also a relationship to ideology and tradition. When children play cowboys and Indians for instance, usually the cowboys are the "good guys" and the Indians the "villains"—all related to the American ideology of the frontier.

Redl: That is another dimension; I think I have classed that under "mirroring of life themes." Some games seem to be quite detached from actual life allusions while others seem to have clear roots in a historical or contemporary pattern in life in general or in the fantasy world of contemporary society.

Lifton: There is also the solidifying of a deep-seated idea, a traditional one, so that the unconscious patterning around it is made more conscious, in which process the game serves as a transition.

Redl: Your assumption is, in the minds of such players, consciously or not, even though it looks as though it was a race it is still the cowboy riding?

Bavelas: There are some people who do not play chess, but like to solve chess problems, and there are some problems which are extremely unpopular with most chess players, problems in which, instead of white having to mate black in a specified number of moves, black forces white to mate him. It is called a "sui-mate," which is short for suicide mate. This goes against the grain for many chess players. It does not feel right.

Liddell: I should like Dr. Blauvelt to tell you about her little boy playing Wild West and cowboys, and how he was frustrated when the girls came in.

Blauvelt: A Cornell professor was writing a book on the role of woman in American culture. As he looked up from his writing he saw his three youngsters and my 10-year-old boy playing a Western game in which each child chose his role. The boys had chosen to be lieutenants of the U.S. Cavalry, the girls were the ladies of the saloons and had a wonderful time dressing up for the part.

Later, I asked my son if they rescued the ladies. He thought a minute and said "No, as a matter of fact, we needed to be rescued from them."

Redl: This reminds me of the demarcation line. Where is the demarcation between fantasy play and games? There would be a lot of fantasy in playing house, but it does not necessarily fall in the category of a game. When a game becomes a game is something we have spent many sleepless hours over. I don't know yet.

The attack means overcoming a barrier, entering a guarded area. It can be in the form of a board game or in any other, *e.g.,* overpowering a defense, or injuring, psychologically or otherwise. Attacks may be obvious or undercover. Then the counteraction is on the other side.

Capture means to take, either to take a person or a symbol. It includes swiping as well as open grabbing. There are some games, like "Steal the bacon," where the issue is to take unobserved and not to be caught, or to avoid being taken; to avoid loss of symbols.

I heard of an interesting incident[3] about one child who could never play chess or checkers or any of the games where any of the personalized symbols of the player would be taken away; however, he was expert at playing "Hex." "Hex" is a game which has hexagonal figures in which you do not take away your opponent's "pieces" or "men"; you merely block their moves. Each partner tries to surround the other so that his men are cornered, but no one takes anything away, symbolic or otherwise, from anyone else. This particular youngster became an expert in this game at a time when he still found it unacceptable to play a game necessitating the elimination of an opponent's men or jumping them. This, by the way, is only meant as a side remark; I don't want to get into discussion of special therapeutic issues at this time. So much about "capture." Not all games contain this theme, but some do; others have it as a major focus.

Another such theme is that of harassment. Many games seem to contain elements which suggest that a player lure his opponent into the wrong move, or taunt, tease, or trap him into unsuccessful attack. We concluded

3. Bettelheim, B.: Personal communication.

that this "game element" should be elevated to the level of a major theme in its own right. The counterplayer must then see through the trick, to avoid being caught laughing when he shouldn't, to bide his time for the moment of successful attack, to move suddenly and punish the attacker by countersurprise, etc.

The "search" is another interesting and very frequent theme in games. It usually implies finding either by chance or through following cues; there are many variations of it. Charades, by the way, is a game of search in which a hidden meaning is to be found. Here again we run into the question of by what activities the search is to take place. In many instances the question whether the players should search for the hidden meaning of a charade sentence or for buried treasure in the woods is more relevant than whether the major theme of the game should be a search or a race. In other situations, the importance may be the other way around.

The "rescue," another one of our challenges or themes, is sometimes only one part of a game; many games switch themes or have several themes. Many capture games have the rescue motif as one part. The constituent performances demanded of the actors, then, may be to "spring the prisoners" on the one hand or to be the jailer and to guard the prisoners on the other.

By "seduction" we refer to the theme which implies tempting the opponent to a forbidden act.

Peck: Under rescue, aren't there three roles? What about the person who is rescued? You have used the person as a prop.

Redl: Yes, the rescue as a theme. What happens to you when you are in any one of those themes?

Peck: You have chosen, in this particular example, to make this a two-role kind of thing.

Redl: From the game's point of view.

Peck: And why have you done this?

Mead: Why have you left out the rescuee when you have a chasee?

Redl: We don't have a chasee here.

Mead: You had a chasee a while ago. When you are talking about chase, you have a chasee.

Redl: I see. I don't know why.

Birdwhistell: In rescue, this is the thing that is characteristic of football. If you contrast soccer and Canadian football with U.S. football, you discover the difference lies in the special role of the blocker. The ball carrier is not actually a prisoner but the blocker in U.S. football makes possible the ball carrier's performance. This is stressed in the whole series of American games, and reduced at least in terms of extent in the British and Canadian games. Would the blocker's performance come under rescue?

Redl: I would have to think about this.

Mirsky: The blocker would be the counteractor in the attack.

Birdwhistell: No.

Redl: Perhaps rescue doesn't belong here but somewhere else.

Peck: The interesting thing to me is that Dr. Redl has chosen, which indeed he can, to make this a two-role affair; whereas in certain of these things it is perfectly evident there is no reason, intrinsic to the game, why he had to. The whole question of when a game is a game may relate to this. One possibility that occurs to me is that it becomes not a game for Dr. Redl, when there are no longer two clearly defined roles and the prop is no longer behaving like a prop but like a third role; this may spoil the game for him.

Redl: This is one of the things I was worried about. I was also worried about the seduction and the harassment. There is a lot of overlapping in it, which bothers me.

Torre: Does "Post Office" involve gratification which children can't get outside of the game?

Redl: The question of gratification leads into another category.

Buhler: What about all the games which are played in a circle, where there isn't the role?

Redl: That belongs under the question of role.

Buhler: When a piece of paper is handed from one to the next, and each writes something on it, the whole thing is resolved. What about sales games? You take only structured games here. What about unstructured selling and buying?

Redl: This, I would call "play." You mean if the children play, let us say, drug store, and there is some selling and buying?

Buhler: Yes.

Redl: This we wouldn't put in our definition of game.

Buhler: Game is only structure?

Redl: The other is structure, too. It is quite difficult to draw a line.

Frank: In this game, someone wins.

Buhler: In "Silent Post," nobody wins. It goes around the circle.

Frank: In beetle there is momentary winning and losing.

Lorenz: I think there is an important point that has not been made, that in beetle there is momentary winning or losing. It is hardly discernible but it is certainly there.

Redl: Why don't we pick that one up? It belongs in our category of "winnership"; it is among those dimensions I referred to before. I purposely started out with the challenge or theme, because that is what we had most trouble in figuring out a place for, where it should be included. All the others, such as winnership, social structure, and role distribution, somehow seemed easier to fit into some semblance of order. We are still totally at sea as to just where it belongs; we are only sure that it is an issue in its own right, and a point to be checked on by whoever is responsible for selecting games for a specific purpose with a specific group of children.

Lifton: Upon "seduction" you suggest "to be controlled and not influenced." Could you illustrate that?

Redl: It would mean to "remain" controlled and not be influenced. It is a careless formulation. An example might be in the game where one player is supposed to be a statue, while others try to make him laugh or move out of role. The purpose then is to remain under control and not to be influenced by the taunters. I personally disagree somewhat with the separation made between harassment and seduction; I felt that somehow the two have much in common.

Fremont-Smith: To remain controlled, in control of yourself?

Redl: To remain in control.

Fremont-Smith: In self-control, then?

Mead: If you use the term "provocation" you really cover both. Harassment is a little bit too excessive.

Redl: Yes.

Frank: Your listed questions show both "blocking" and "winning" together under the heading of "competition."

Redl: We had a terrific discussion and disagreement about competition. I have trouble with that because, in the process of the game, while there is some competition necessary, someone has to win or lose, but the gratification or the main thing that people get out of playing may not be the competitive part; it may be any one of the sub-parts, or may be what you go through while you do all this. The fact that, by description, in most games there is some kind of competitive element does not necessarily mean that the major gratification comes out of that phase of the game. Therefore, I should still like to consider the competitive admixture that is in a game and the styling with which competition takes place as a separate issue, even though some of us felt that competition as such is an essential part of all game arrangements.

Mead: Have you made a list showing *where* you are when you are making any one of these categorizations? I think this comes back to Dr. Grey Walter's question; one minute you are looking at this as a therapist, the next minute you are looking at it as one of the boys, the next minute you are looking at it as a classifier of games, and the next minute you are handling the game as a microcosm of life. You have given us a mass of parameters, all taken from different, unspecified positions; you have been moving around through space here.

Redl: That is because of the space that surrounds me. You got me multifaceted for the moment! However, let us look at competition *per se.* There is something to that issue of "centrality" of winning and losing. A game like beetle has a series of little competitive episodes, but no one really wins or loses. It isn't like winning in a chess game or such. In Poison pin, the players join hands and encircle a bowling pin; each tries to pull the other so that he touches the pin and is then out. There winning is central to the purpose of the game.

Birdwhistell: Why?

Redl: Eventually the one who ends up without having been trapped, wins the game. It is similar to Musical chairs.

Birdwhistell: My question "why" asks, is this the way the game ends, by having a winner?

Redl: By the nature of the game.

Birdwhistell: The question I am asking is, perhaps the only way you can stop a game like Poison pin is by being the last man, but to make the assumption this is the simple purpose of the game may obscure the game.

Fremont-Smith: It is a matter of definition of the term "purpose."

Redl: Sometimes the children only play it to a certain point. But my thought would be that there is something in the whole design of the game that makes it a purpose to get everybody else out and to be the only remaining survivor. The fact that you may sometimes stop the game before it has fully run its course is another question.

Fremont-Smith: How is the word "purpose" used?

Redl: I should remember what Dr. Mead tried to remind me of previously in the discussion. I am sorry about the confusion in words. I don't really mean "purpose" in terms of a built-in purpose as defined by the nature of the game.

Mead: As defined in the structure of the game itself.

Walter: You mean activity becomes a game when there is a winner?

Redl: Only this game. I wouldn't generalize.

Walter: Which game?

Redl: Poison pin or Musical chairs.

Mead: You would include this sort of structural analysis, Dr. Redl, also, in Farmer in the Dell, where no one wants to become "the cheese." It is a central game, to a degree, but the last person is the victim, instead of the winner; but it does also have centrality.

Redl: Or if you play Russian checkers, where the purpose is to get rid of your stones first.

Mead: You would include that?

Peck: A good way of finding out what the purpose of the game is, is to find out how the game is ended, how one terminates the game. Is that right?

Redl: Yes.

Peck: It may not always work, but most of the time it would work.

Redl: Provided you stay within Dr. Mead's categories. Dr. Mead wants me to stick to categories—

Mead: I don't want you to stick to anything; I just want you to tell us where you are at any given moment.

Redl: I don't want to raise the issue of whether the purpose of the game was fulfilled, meaning the reasons I had why I got the children into that particular game to begin with. I am now defining purpose as the inherent, built-in course which a game is to take by the way it is defined.

Goffman: The internal or contained world of the game.

Blauvelt: You spoke earlier of the wisdom of some games, their effectiveness in meeting the needs of your children. We have had comment on games which people cannot tolerate. You spoke of using games, of manipulating them to meet more nearly the needs of your children.

The terms with which you describe these games, "capture," "harassment," etc., are so primitive that they occur in animal behavior, too. My question is one which has interest in the behavior of young animals.

A group of young goats will often change their play activity suddenly. This means that time and space relationship between the kids as they act is changed. Often one animal leads in this change, but analysis of this group process on moving picture film makes it impossible for us to say whether the group sets the leader off, or follows him, or both.

Can you know this in your children? As your children move from one game to another, without your help, what group capacity is there to change the game?

Redl: This you find very often. Children do their own reshuffling of ingredients.

Blauvelt: Can you know when the game may shift? Can some player manipulate this?

Redl: If you say "can" I would say yes, but if you ask me just which game or under what conditions, that I couldn't answer.

Blauvelt: Does the game form an environment chosen by the group to fill its needs?

Redl: Let me try another illustration, though I am not sure whether it will answer the question satisfactorily. We couldn't play football with certain children for a long time, for a certain reason. However, the process of tackling was quite important for them. So, we made a special game of it. We said, "We are not playing football but we are going out to tackle." As long as that was clear, it was fine. If we pretended we were playing football, while we actually knew that all they could do was tackle, the rest being too complex for them, there would be a terrific disappointment issue. So, we said, "Let us not pretend it is the full game; let us pick a phase and make a game of it." One may want to modify the amount of competitiveness in a game, or the winnership. I am getting into other categories, and I shouldn't do that. But let us look at the emphasis on winning or losing that may be contained in a certain game.

You can play certain games with less premium placed on who wins or loses. Even though the game basically has such an issue, you can soft pedal the end result, for instance, by the type of prize you use. Everyone can win either a first, second, or third prize; everyone gets some candy. Thus the original issue of the game, that it should end with one person, is blurred or obliterated by my counter-maneuvers.

Mead: I believe Dr. Blauvelt is asking, if one took the natural history of an afternoon with children who were not very disturbed, but who had to be manipulated, because there had been so much chase and the chase had gotten a bit out of hand, will the children shift to another game, or shift within the game to another version of the game? That would be a very important thing then, to have a number of different ways one could play the same game. Then one can say, "Let's not play it by those rules; let's play it by these other rules for a change," something American children who move from one town to another do. They know three or four versions, and they shift.

That was the sort of question you were asking, wasn't it, whether the children themselves might use the game structure to meet their needs?

Blauvelt: Yes. When a group of young goats seem to change spontaneously their type of play activity, young animals with lowered vitality may not be able to function with the group. They cannot time their movements to the change of pace. Often this appears to be an inability to wait till the right moment for action. They will be in constant rhythmical movement which is ill timed, and therefore ineffectual. Is this true in children you have observed?

Redl: My reaction to that would have to be different, depending on whether I am talking about normal or disturbed children. With normal children I would expect a high capacity to make spontaneous switches and variations in their games. If you watch them closely, what you see is that they actually manipulate their own play life quite effectively, and they switch to another play pattern if one seems to be exhausted or gets too close to anxiety or stress for their own comfort.

If you talk about very disturbed children and let me limit myself for the moment just to the type of children I now work with, then I would say this capacity is very low. For with those children, either game excitement has a terrific impact on their control machinery and throws it out of gear or they get so involved they can't let go, even though the panic and frustrations they push themselves into more and more end up with their being left out, withdrawing, or drifting into side play, roughhousing or general diffuse bickering and hostile aggression. It is a certain amount of resilience in spontaneous restructuring of game and play situations which seems to me to be an ego function in its own right, and one which is happily visible in the well adjusted child and which we have as yet studied much too little.

Birdwhistell: We have a laboratory for this, since teachers trained to be recreational directors take jobs on Indian reservations to teach Indian children how to play games. We know a good deal about the difficulties these teachers encounter when they try to teach the Hopi; and we know about the willingness on the part of the Hopi to play the game *as long as* teacher is looking. The only competitive game permitted among the Hopi is the race, although this definitely creates a winner. Football was introduced, but it did not work. Wrestling and tackling were introduced, but these led to considerable anxiety. They performed well, but the Hopi were less concerned with winning than with playing together. In order to get along in the school situation, the children would rapidly restructure the game. As you observe a group of Hopi playing basketball, particularly the younger ones who do not quite understand it, it is clear that the children get so delighted in making the ball roll around that they don't play the game, unless the coach or recreation director is watching. These games and the formal recreation programs provide us with the laboratories for observing and testing both cultural and individual behavior.

Lotspeich: What about lacrosse?

Birdwhistell: In certain Eastern groups. In other groups its violence would be revolting, "Nice people wouldn't play such games."

Lotspeich: Is that game played among the Hopi?

Birdwhistell: No.

Lotspeich: It is an Indian game.

Birdwhistell: Hopis would say "Them Indians play it! We Hopi don't."

Redl: This reminds me of another caution I should voice. I purposely left out a wide variety of dimensions, such as sex role; I left out any consideration about which games only girls play or only boys play, etc. It is a justified issue of debate whether this should be left out or not, and it seems to me an issue which, again, applies in different degrees to different types of games. With some games, the sex role issue seems to me to be more detachable than with others.

Mead: If you include the age role, you make it easier to test, for instance, in what is happening in this country now, since kissing games have moved down into the sixth grade, as well as other games which had well-established rules. Formerly, they were played with the lights on, or the lights were put out for only a minute, and everyone had to stay in the room. The controls of older people, usually young married people, were included in the game, and a few really engaged people, so no one could go too far in kissing someone else's girl; all of this had been built into American culture. Now these games are played by pre-adolescent children, with parents excluded, or rules such as that a boy must kiss a girl a hundred times, an appalling rule that wears people out and has no sense to it at all. The children get into a sort of pre-adolescent counting coup like Plains Indians. Under these circumstances, they break the furniture. Sometimes people get hurt too. A game that once had excellent rules for one age group, has sunk to an age group where it does not fit. I think age is an even better criterion than sex for testing out this particular problem of whether you should or should not include these in the sociological study of the game.

Redl: In fact, if you know that, you could use the game as an assessment tool for the psycho-social maturation rate.

Birdwhistell: Age grading is the point, and not age-level. You had older children in it.

Mead: To keep the thing steady. The age variation is knocked out, the parents can't come in, and the thing has gone wild.

Kramer: Why do games such as kissing games among twelve year olds go wild when an older group or the parents are not present?

Mead: The safety device was the presence of the parents and the older people. Children would not go too far; they wouldn't do anything they shouldn't do, because the older people had told them not to kiss girls in the haymow, and because they could kiss them when the plate was spun. Protection against panic was built into the rules of the game.

Goffman: Were the parents in the same room or merely in the same house?

Mead: It varied in different places, also how far one could go.

Redl: I think the reason why a game might end up, without adults present, in sex behavior beyond what a game legitimately permits, varies with the pre-adolescent. This has to do with the psychology of the pre-adolescent. The way of coping with one's own awakening libidinal onslaught is through manipulative restlessness, acted out aggression toward the outside. It it also the age where, if a pair falls in love, the girl is tormented; she gets pinched. It is the defense against libidinal onrush, and it happens in terms of substitution with aggressive mauling; it is shown in external behavior, which is not necessarily the same defense in—

Kramer: Would you say the libidinal onslaught or onrush of excitation that goes with it also excites the aggressiveness and the potential destructiveness which has been kept down? In other words, when you excite the organism, do you not only excite the libidinal, but excite all the other qualities or properties which are kept down?

Redl: At the point of excitation, it becomes diffuse.

Kramer: This may already be an indication that when the organism is overexcited, it does not know how, or is incapable of keeping the particular behavior patterns or elements in order. The "orderliness" works only as long as the organism is kept at a low level of excitement.

Redl: Still another element for brief mention only, is this: if one's excitement gets high, one's "contageability" goes up, with the result that even though one or another child by himself might not be so violent as to break furniture, the mere fact that they are all highly excited may produce that stage of "group psychological intoxication" which I have described elsewhere and which may then end up in violence for which each member alone would not have been ready.

Fremont-Smith: Dr. Lorenz, I know you are going to bring this in later but don't you have some comment to make here, not only in terms of the confusion between aggressivity and sexuality, the interflow across one onto the other, but also on this matter of getting high and the contagion of it?

Lorenz: What Dr. Fremont-Smith wants me to say is that I always have a certain feeling of compunction in using the term "general excitation."

Even if you take into consideration the fact that, let us say, some general physiologic hormonal state may lower thresholds of very different activities simultaneously, I still have some compunction about calling this "general excitation" because, physiologically, it really is an increase of excitability and not real excitation. Many thresholds coming down simultaneously may produce a state which, in a sense, mimics general excitation which I really don't believe exists.

Walter: This is a very important paradox. As you say, it is very difficult, in studying the whole animal, to tell whether excitability has gone up or down. It is very hard to define a crucial experiment, a whole animal experiment, in which this can be decided, unless you are going to pry into the brain and other organs. There is no simple way of telling whether excitability goes up or down, because a rise in threshold may break the system up into small domains of intense local activity.

Lotspeich: Like epilepsy.

Walter: A rise in threshold may induce a state of extreme activity in many small domains. This may result in better goal-orientation.

Lotspeich: It is hard to think in terms of excitability.

Walter: We don't.

Lorenz: My way of putting that is that there is only one state of general excitation, and that is convulsion—cacophony.

Walter: It isn't cacophony; it is symphony.

Fremont-Smith: It is "symcophony"!

Walter: This concept of a threshold is very important in another context, because when you talk about competition, winning, and goal direction, this seems to bring in the possibility of describing the situation in terms of thresholds and shifts of law in certain planes. The notion of winning is really a question of emphasizing a threshold. You either win or do not win. A great deal of the pleasure and gratification of these games seems to derive from the emphasis on thresholds, on abrupt transitions. This is true also of natural phenomena. People will go a long way to see the ocean shore, a sunrise, the Grand Canyon, a tornado, a volcano, something which contains an abrupt transition.

In games, people enjoy working in one space of activity and suddenly sliding off into another one and working in another space.

Goffman: "Bases loaded" sort of thing?

Fremont-Smith: This has to do with rate of change.

Walter: Yes; we are dealing with sensory organs which have marked thresholds and respond mainly to rates of change. These properties introduce enormous difficulties in any formal analysis. What you are doing is groping to find a way of dealing with a nonlinear system in which there are abrupt transitions which may, as you say, be between one game and another, or between one phase of a game and another, between the pursuit and the imprisonment or seduction. These seem to be the essence of this game behavior. The game should emphasize thresholds and, of course, a good game does come to a neat end in some way; it doesn't have to be terminated by the clock.

When you try to invent a board game, you usually end up with a game that does not end. Monopoly is just on the borderline. It can go on a very long time. Chess is an excellent example; it can finish in 10 minutes.

Birdwhistell: We recently had the opportunity of watching a group of 12-year-olds having their first dance. We were very cautious and had the dance outside on the driveway. The record-player was going and the driveway was lit by a "bug" light, to keep the bugs away. There were fourteen 12-year-olds, all sixth graders. The girls had organized the affair. The equipment they had to have included plenty of records and four cases of coca-cola.

The dance began. Most of the participants attended dancing school but, as they said, they didn't dance at dancing school; they learned to dance at dancing school. Only three boys danced regularly, eight girls danced, and a number of the girls did not dance at all. As the party proceeded the dancing got more and more hectic. Those not dancing began to move around. As the fourth record was played they began a competitive drinking of coca-cola. The dancing went on. Suddenly four of the boys broke off and ran around the block. They came back huffing and puffing. Considerable discussion followed this run, then more dancing. Then seven ran around the block. Finally the oldest girl ran around the block with the boys. Then they quit dancing and one would-be social worker tried to organize a circle dance, in which they were to go through a ritual in which everyone would be included. They quit this immediately and drank a tremendous number of bottles of coca-cola, and broke four of the bottles. This was then followed by one couple sneaking off and kissing. Several of the group got very upset and came in to tell us. Then all of them began to look at their watches and say, "Oh, we only have 15 minutes. We have to do a lot of things." They ran around the block. Then their parents came.

REFERENCES

1. Schaffner, Bertram, Editor: *Group Processes.* Trans. Third Conf. New York, Josiah Macy, Jr. Foundation, 1957.
2. Redl, F.: Group emotion and leadership. *Psychiatry V, 573 (1942).*
3. Redl, F., and Wineman, D.: *The Aggressive Child.* Glencoe, Ill., The Free Press, 1957 (pp. 318–394).
4. Gump, P., and Sutton-Smith, B.: The "it" role in children's games. *The Group* 17, 3 *(1955).*
5. ———: Games and status experience. *Recreation 48, 172 (1955).*
6. Gump, P., and Yueng-Hung, M.: Active games for physically handicapped children. *Physical Therapy Rev.* 34, *171 (1954).*

28. Spontaneous Play in Resolution of Problems: A Brief Example

JEROME STYRT
MARY O. STYRT

Play is an effective approach to the resolution of problems for children. Homburger-Erikson[1] has explained that "to 'play it out' is the most natural autotherapeutic measure childhood affords. No matter what experience has threatened the child's psychic integrity, he attempts to restore it by mastering in play a sphere of reality in which his acts are physiologically safe, socially permissible, physically workable and psychologically satisfying ..."

The importance and role of play for the child at home is noted in relatively nontechnical and parent-aimed writing from time to time, as well as in more theoretical and more specialized work. Spock,[2] for example, speaks of young children at play as "hard at work learning about the world," and goes on to say about the pre-schooler, "Meanwhile, he's been learning to take out his violent feelings in *play* form."

To see the clear and spontaneous expression of a psychic problem in the play of a normal child at home is a vivid experience which may not be rare but is seldom shared. The occurrence of an active and concentrated playing through of an experience threatening to the ego, carried through to the point of psychologic satisfaction and acceptance, is a striking event—to observe the activity of the threatened child setting out to "do a job" of dealing with the emotional situation and conquering it, individually and spontaneously, makes "more real" the functioning that is already understood from other sources. We here describe two play incidents in the life of one particular child.

Reprinted with permission of The National Association for Mental Health, Inc. from *Mental Hygiene,* Vol. 49, No. 3 (July, 1965), pp. 405–407.

1. Homberger (-Erikson), Erik, In Section on "Play Therapy." Maxwell Gitelson, M.D., Chairman, *American Journal of Orthopsychiatry,* 8(3):499 (1938).
2. Spock, Benjamin, *Baby and Child Care.* New York, Pocket Books, 1957.

Betsy, now 6½, is four years younger than her sister, her only sibling. She is attractive, bright, large for her age and, in general, a very "normal" child. In spite of the boundless energy which she expends in roller skating and bicycling (and sometimes, it seems, in ceaseless motion), she used to sit quietly for long periods to be read to, and later to read to herself. In many ways she is a sensitive child. On the one hand, she is capable of raising quite a storm about an article of clothing that does not feel quite right when she puts it on. On the other hand, she sometimes comes out with surprisingly perceptive statements about feelings and people. As a first grader, she once expressed her own feelings about having a group of neighborhood children appear to play just after her return from school by saying, "Don't they *know* when I've been with twenty-five other children all day I want to be by myself for a while? I want to go out and rollerskate!"

When Betsy was five, her maternal grandmother—who lived a thousand miles away—suddenly died. Betsy's parents had to make quick plans to go there, and left the two little girls in the care of an adult whom the children knew and liked and who had previously stayed overnight at their house. The only comment Betsy made at the time was to tell her kindergarten teacher the next morning that "Grandma died." But three months later (some twelve weeks after the parents had returned from the funeral and the normal family pattern had been reestablished), Betsy began making significant comments about mothers. Thus, in the car on the way home from school, she would say, "You are our mother and Grandma B. is Daddy's mother, but *you* don't have a mother any more." This occurred three or four times, with very strong affect. It was usually responded to in such terms as, "No, but we remember her, don't we?" Presence of the voluble 10-year-old sister restricted continuation of the topic.

Much dramatic play was going on about this time, involving the sisters and one or two neighborhood children in make-believe related to family life, in addition to the playing of story characters. Instead of following familiar patterns, Betsy suddenly began saying, in her play, "I'm not going to get married," and "I'm not going to be a grandmother—I'm going to be an aunt." (Betsy has a maiden great-aunt about the same age as her grandmother.) This was not addressed to adults, for discussion, though it was said in the presence of adults.

Betsy's father felt that this move in her make-believe was related closely to mother's absence and grandmother's death, and suggested that the subject be approached directly with her. At a quiet bathtime, Betsy's mother asked her whether she had been bothered and confused about the events of that time. She reminded Betsy that she knew Grandma had not been well for a long time and had been taking medicine when she had visited; also, Grandma was 75 years old. Mother further mentioned that of course nobody had to get married, and named some unmarried friends of the family. She went on to say, however, that whether one was a grandmother or an aunt had nothing to do with dying, and that married people actually lived longer than people who were not married. In general, an attempt was made to encourage comment and to "clear the air" briefly and directly.

It was immediately noticeable that Betsy's play went back to the usual sorts of family situation make-believe, and "I'm going to be an aunt" was not heard again. Betsy also began to speak naturally of grandfather and to talk thoughtfully and understandingly about visiting him, and about the fact that grandmother would not be there. She showed no further signs of disturbance. A year later, when the family went to visit, she was able to talk in a direct and undisguised way, with tears in her eyes, about the fact that grandma was no longer there and grandpa was alone.

When Betsy was 6½, it became necessary for her to go into the hospital to have a small tumor removed from her nose. She knew the purpose of the operation. The pea-sized bump was just inside a nostril and was an irritation to her. She was reasonably well prepared for hospital procedures and her mother stayed with her. What had not been anticipated by her parents was a bit of plastic surgery. At the end of the operation, Betsy had both a bandage on her nose (all the surgery had been inside her nostril) and a bandage on the upper part of her thigh, where a bit of skin was taken for a free skin graft. It was necessary for her to stay in the hospital a day longer than originally expected, and she had to stay away from school for a few additional days because of the skin graft.

Betsy's doctors were thoughtful and reasonable in their approach to her. She was not subjected to unnecessary routines or procedures. Sinus x-rays were done and there was a single blood test. Half an hour or so before she went to the operating room, Betsy had her only injections: two, in quick succession, in the buttocks. The nurse gave her the disposable syringes, minus the needles, and Betsy eventually took them home with her.

It was explained to Betsy, both by her mother and by the plastic surgeon, why she had a bandage in the area of the groin as well as on her nose. Nevertheless, when the plastic surgeon at the first change of dressing asked her if she knew why she had the second bandage, she said, "No." It was then explained again.

The day after her return home from the hospital, Betsy began to show interest in the syringes. She brought them to lunch with her in a large kitchen-dining area of her home. Using a paper cup of water, she experimented with squirting with the syringes. She was mildly told not to squirt water in the food, and she appeared to lose interest in this activity.

Late in the afternoon, Betsy returned to the syringes and the water. She squirted water the length of the table. Her mother allowed this, cleared the table of anything that ought not to get wet, and let the play continue. The child then squirted water all around the edges of the table. She squirted water across the room and arching high into the air. She squirted water on her favorite doll, which was lying on the table.

After this went on for some time, Betsy moved to the sink. She began to use the rinsing hose and nozzle to spray all around the sink. She sprayed some saucepans on the drainboard and squirted water on top of the mixing faucet and watched it run off the end.

A few limits were stated—don't spray a certain piece of furniture (tile floor, formica table top, counter furnishings and painted walls made a good deal of wetness permissible, fortunately); don't spray down behind the sink; it might be better not to spray the doll's head because her eyes might get stuck up and not work properly. These limits were readily conformed to. Otherwise, the play was allowed to go on in unrestricted fashion, with constant squirting activity. Both the room and Betsy got rather wet.

After more than half an hour, Betsy's mother, busy in the same room while all this was going on, remarked to Betsy that she was getting pretty wet, and that any time she wanted to, she might go change her clothes or, if she preferred, take off her wet clothes and get right into sleepers.

After another ten minutes, Betsy suddenly stopped her squirting and disappeared up the stairs, saying nothing.

A little while later she reappeared in the kitchen, neat and dry now in sleepers and robe. She announced, "I want to make some chocolate pudding for supper, and I want to serve it myself!"

Betsy, in this episode, clearly seemed to be working out anxieties about castration and damage to herself in relation to the hospitalization and her two bandages. She seemed to demonstrate dramatically that she was able to reassure herself that she was really all right. She could come to a resolution of this problem and take on again in comfort the role of a little girl and a feminine identification.

The earlier of these two episodes depicts the appearance in play of a submerged problem which then required adult recognition and adult responsiveness to the implied request for help.

The latter incident in particular seems to present vividly, in a spontaneous play situation, confirmation of dynamic theories of psychosexual development and a child's working through of a psychic problem to an ego-strengthening resolution.

29. Therapeutic Recreation for Aggressive Children in Residential Treatment

RONALD K. GREEN
WILLIAM P. CLARK

Recognizing that recreation, in one form or another, consumes the major portion of a child's waking hours in a residential treatment center, we need to make an effort to evaluate just how this element of the residential program can best be integrated into the total treatment milieu.

We have limited this discussion to the treatment of the aggressive child[1] —defining the term generally to include those children who symptomatically and consistently express aggression in their behavior, either directly as in the acting-out sense or by a more passive-aggressive orientation, and have experienced such trauma in their first few years of life that they relate to their total environment in a preoedipal manner. It is common knowledge that a large segment of the population of residential centers, not to speak of correctional facilities, is composed of these children.

We tend to describe dynamically, as have others, the problems of these children in terms of ego deficiencies,[2] and theoretically base our view of therapeutic recreation on this kind of dynamic-diagnosis basis. We see the lack of ego development daily in the aggressive child's lack of time orientation, feelings of omnipotence, confused concepts of cause and effect, and time sequences that allow the constant use of denial and projection as defenses. These ego defects—coupled with the usually weak, spotty, or other-

Reprinted with permission of Child Welfare League of America, Inc. from *Child Welfare*, Vol. 44, No. 10 (December, 1965), pp. 578–83.

1. *See* Sidney Berman, "Antisocial Character Disorder: Its Etiology and Relationship to Delinquency," *American Journal of Orthopsychiatry*, XXIX (1959), 612–621; Henry L. Burks and Saul I. Harrison, "Aggressive Behavior as a Means of Avoiding Depression," *American Journal of Orthopsychiatry*, XXXII (1962), 416–422; Gerald H. Pearson, "The Chronically Aggressive Child," *Quarterly Journal of Child Behavior*, III (1951), 407–448; Fritz Redl and David Wineman, *The Aggressive Child* (New York: The Free Press of Glencoe, 1957).

2. Hyman Grossbard, "Ego Deficiency in Delinquents," *Social Casework*, XLIII (1962), 171–178.

wise inadequately functioning superego—seriously interfere with the child's ability to control his aggressive impulses by sublimation or other appropriate responses. Hence, we are faced with constant direct expressions of aggression, or if direct aggression is thwarted, we are faced with the expression of passive aggression through resistance, avoidance, and passive defiance. Often these passive forms of aggression are even more aggravating to the staff than the direct expression of aggression.

When stated in these terms, it becomes obvious that the goal of any treatment program must include helping these children to develop inner controls through a process of ego development and integration, thus leading to meaningful self-identity. We strongly believe that such goals can best be attained (1) by fully utilizing all individuals who come in contact with this child and (2) by the thoughtful development of programs designed to enhance ego development and self-identity. Recognizing that there is not complete accord in the definitions of residential treatment and that the implications of this paper could go beyond the residential treatment facility, we write from a particular point of view that includes recognition of the basic importance of all areas of the program and understanding that if inner controls are to be gained through ego development, the child must have enough opportunity to express himself so that his ego can develop more adequately through a constructive interactional process. In other words, we feel that if all structure and controls are imposed from the outside, the child will have little or no opportunity for the development of identity and inner controls. In line with this view, we have found that it is most effective to create an atmosphere in which the child is held responsible for his actions in terms of the residential worker's expectations; but, at the same time, the residential worker accepts the child's limited ability to meet those expectations.

The particular experience upon which this paper is based consists of a therapeutic recreation program conducted within a treatment center handling primarily preadolescent children. The ability of the recreation worker to understand the particular needs of the individual child is enhanced by frequent and continuing contact with the child's caseworker and other related staff. The responsibility then rests with the recreation staff, who work out activity-based programs geared to the children's needs.

The Recreation Worker's
Role in Treatment

It is difficult to discuss the therapeutic recreation program without first turning our attention to the responsibilities of the recreation worker within the treatment milieu. The worker's primary responsibility is to provide the children with ego-supporting play experiences. When ego support is consistently provided and individual children begin to display minute feelings of self-worth, the recreation worker can then use the play experience as a tool to aid the children in developing internalized controls. Thus, the recreation worker—in his role as supervisor of a craft period, as participant in a kickball game, or as timer in a track meet—constantly manipulates the environment so that it will maximize ego synthesis for each child.

One of the basic goals of treatment must be the development of a productive relationship between the aggressive child and the worker. Here, his role as recreation worker provides both the child and himself with a common ground on which the aggressive child can safely test his new environment. It is, therefore, important that recreation workers have a real interest in developing individual relationships, since recreation becomes "recreation therapy" only when it provides the aggressive child with a positive means of contact through which he can develop significant relationships between himself and adults. Alt and Grossbard have pointed out that "in order to become meaningful to a child, the therapist has to become a real being, identified with concrete activities and experiences in the life of the child—with giving and doing things for him."[3]

Similarly, the recreation worker, by "doing" in the craftroom and by "giving" in his role as the keeper of recreation equipment, comes to be identified with those activities that have positive meaning for the child. Once this association has taken place, the recreation worker becomes an ego-ideal upon which the child models his own behavior. The worker can then support the child's efforts at ego synthesis by verbally providing wholehearted and genuine support of real accomplishments and by physically serving as a model of internalization of reality-based controls.

Since many recreation activities are group oriented and aggressive children tend to be impulse oriented, recreation workers often encounter problems involving conflict between group and individual needs. Although group experiences offer significant methods through which the child can develop a social awareness and some degree of socially based conscience, the acting-out child (who has not yet learned to control his own impulses) is hardly capable of subordinating his immediate impulses to the needs of the group. An experience illustrating this point occurred on the Eastfield campus after the older boys had seen a high school basketball game.

> Eric was shooting baskets with Joe (a recreation worker) when several boys, who had just returned from school, asked if they could also play. Eric, sensing that the counselor would be unable to devote his full attention to him, went into a rage, claiming that Joe hated him. The counselor assured Eric that he did not hate him and suggested that he and Eric play together as a team against the other boys. Eric then continued to play until the game broke up at dinnertime.

3. Herschel Alt and Hyman Grossbard, "Professional Issues in the Institutional Treatment of Delinquent Children," *American Journal of Orthopsychiatry*, XIX (1949), 285.

Eric's reaction to the other boys was characteristic of his inability to cope with competition. By suggesting that Eric join his team, the counselor met both Eric's need to have the counselor to himself and, at the same time, made it possible for the other boys to participate in the game without its being disrupted. In this way, the recreation counselor reduced the anxiety provoked in Eric and turned the situation into an enjoyable experience for all concerned.

The Therapeutic Recreation Program in Practice

We have found it beneficial for the recreation staff to plan and post the monthly recreation program. Posting the program provides the child with a sense of security in that he sees that the schedule is continuous and consistent; it also provides him with a better conception of time and place relationships. The four main areas of the program are: (1) crafts, (2) games of lower organization, (3) games of higher organization, and (4) off-campus excursions. To the degree that it is possible, each area of activity is geared to the individual treatment needs of each child as well as to the group as a whole.

CRAFTS

The craftroom is of particular importance, because in it the children can achieve gratification at varying levels of ability. Regularly scheduled periods of arts and crafts offer a wide range of projects requiring varying skill. It is our feeling that by providing time and space structure (i.e., 3:00–5:00 p.m. on Tuesdays and Thursdays) while allowing much content flexibility (i.e., work with clay, wood, paint, or plaster), we best combine consistent experience with ego-expanding creativity.

Adult assistance is minimized. The worker helps the child only when his assistance is requested; his job is to offer technical advice and to help the children master the various tools. The children initiate, plan, and carry out their own projects. In this way, the craft experience aids in the development of initiative, self-identity, and autonomy.

In addition to the important ego-supporting opportunities mentioned above, the craft experience also involves the group and interaction within it. Reality does not allow us to provide each child with a set of individual supplies and tools; therefore, the children must share paints, brushes, hammers, and other equipment.

Sharing again enters the craft experience when group projects are spontaneously developed by the children. For example, one Christmas vacation the children decided to paint Christmas scenes on the institution's windows. Each child painted his own scene; yet, the children later decided to connect the individual scenes by painting a background of snow. On another occasion the children banded together and built a fort. Such experiences in sharing, although short lived, lead to group solidarity and feelings of group satisfaction; and, when accomplishments are reinforced by genuine adult praise, the subgroup code seems to be less distant from that of the larger group and society.

The arts and crafts experience also provides our aggressive children with the opportunity for developing useful ego defenses. Many children have spent hours hammering nails into pieces of wood; others have temporarily escaped from reality by losing themselves in projects that require a great deal of skill and concentration.

The craftroom experience is valuable in helping the aggressive child to increase his frustration tolerance. He sees the other children handle their frustrations in appropriate actions; he sees the recreation counselor handle his frustrations by appropriate verbalization. The child soon learns that the worker expects him to be angry when another child spills paint on his project, but the child also learns that the worker expects a certain amount of self-control. "Hyperretaliation," such as spilling paint all over the other child, is not tolerated.

Care of equipment is another important aspect of the craft experience. The borrowing of a paint brush is accompanied by a responsibility to care for the brush; moreover, destruction of a brush would only be self-defeating for the child involved, since the brush would not be available to him for later use. Shortly before the end of the period, the worker begins to clean up, requiring only that the children clean their own equipment, yet supporting those who offer assistance in cleaning the craftroom.

GAMES OF LOWER ORGANIZATION

Games of lower organization, unlike games of higher organization, contain minimal rules and skill requirements. Here, we again find activities that are ego rewarding in and of themselves. One of the favorite games of pre-adolescents is "war," played by dividing the participants into opposing sides and attacking one another with guns and other toy instruments of destruction. Initiative is often displayed by both sides in planning and carrying out attacks. Besides their obvious sublimation value, war and similar games are important in helping the children to develop the ability of finding constructive outlets for their free time—an ability frequently observed on public playgrounds but more difficult to find in institutions.

Games like "kick the can" and "hide and seek" seem to be characterized by everchanging rules. In one game the first one caught might be "it"; in another, the last person caught is "it" for the next game. Such inconsistency is tolerated and left to the subgroup code for clarification, but differences in interpretation are somewhat resolved by discussing the rules for each new game *before* it is played.

Indoor games such as chess, checkers, Monopoly, and numerous card games are particularly popular in the winter months.[4] These games, like other games with rules, often stimulate counteraggression. Unfortunately, indoor games are based on structure and competitiveness; therefore, it is impossible to reduce competition in them without seriously affecting their meaning.

GAMES OF HIGHER ORGANIZATION

Games of higher organization consist of sports and games that have standardized rules and require a certain amount of skill. The highly organized game experience seems to be less intrinsically therapeutic than either crafts or games of lower organization, because rules and skill requirements frequently stimulate counteraggression. The competitive element (closely related and often leading to aggression) also reduces the therapeutic potential of highly organized games.

In a residential setting, the disruptive potential induced by competitiveness can be reduced either by direct or indirect control. In using direct control, the worker might organize the teams in a manner that minimizes competition between those prone to resolving competitive situations through aggressive means, or he might "bench" a team member whose activity is approaching direct aggression. In utilizing indirect control, the worker emphasizes the "fun of playing" and deemphasizes the importance of scoring.

If the recreation worker is skillfull in controlling the game and if the competitive element has been minimized when the participating individuals cannot tolerate competition, there are several advantages to the highly organized games. The innings of baseball, like the quarters in football, aid the aggressive child in developing time and sequence orientation. The games also contain what Redl has labeled "depersonalized" controls.[5] The basketball player, for instance, knows that there is an automatic penalty for fouling and that he loses possession of the ball when he steps over the boundary line. Group cohesion grows out of highly organized games, and the individual is thus encouraged by his own subgroup (and not by an "oppressing adult") to play by the rules. When a child is able to accept his subgroup code but not society's code, highly organized games may aid in combining the two codes to form one that is accepted by both the individual and society.

OFF-CAMPUS EXCURSIONS

We see value in allowing the children to determine where they go for off-campus activities. This, of course, can be done only with children mature enough to benefit from such group autonomy and who have knowledge of

---

4. We have included indoor games in the category of games of lower organization because, with the exception of chess, skill requirements are minimal.

5. Redl and Wineman, *op. cit.*, pp. 352–358.

community resources. For example, we allowed the older boys to plan a weekly trip. They discovered—on their own—that decisions were most easily reached through parlimentary procedure. It was a unique experience because many of the boys (who had had great difficulty in simply following institution rules) established rules on their own initiative.

Regardless of the activity—hiking, camping, or swimming—one factor not present in other recreation activities is important here: on these trips the children leave the protective atmosphere of the institution and enter into the community. Amazingly, the children seem to be acutely aware of the difference and, in general, control their behavior outside the institution much more consciously than when they are in the institution.

Camping is of particular interest because a certain amount of organization and work are necessary prerequisites to more enjoyable activities. If firewood is not gathered, there will be no fire. If there is no fire, there is no hot food or heat. Here again, we emphasize the importance of allowing the children as much freedom to plan and organize the day as possbile. Any laxity will be handled by nature without the interference of the counselor. Thus, camping helps in the development of cause-and-effect conceptions while taking the recreation worker out of the controlling role and thus maximizing the opportunity for positive relationships.

Concluding Comments

The importance of taking a sharp look at our recreation programs is aptly confirmed by the finding that 40 percent of the "high-level programs" covered in the Hylton study indicate little or no special attention given to the development of therapeutic recreation for the children they serve.[6]

We have attempted to give a theoretical framework within which to understand and further develop the institution recreation program. Although it is recognized that programs treat children with differing problems and that general philosophies of treatment may differ, we feel it is imperative that the area of leisure-time activities be taken out of the realm of pure leisure and be placed squarely in the realm of treatment. This paper describes some of our experiences in representing this theoretical base and emphasizing the use of time-space structure, the support of individual initiative in the craft period, the danger of competition, the importance of subgroup controls in games of higher and lower organization, and the experience (of their behavior in relation to the outside world) gained in off-campus excursions. We also feel that a much more thorough evaluation must be made of the relationship among the pressure to succeed, competition, and the means of helping the aggressive child handle his aggression through relationship with others.

6. Lydia F. Hylton, *The Residential Treatment Center* (New York: Child Welfare League of America, 1964).

30. Pets: A Special Technique in Child Psychotherapy

Boris M. Levinson

The use of a pet, a living tool, brings in new dimensions in child psychotherapy which, of necessity, must help crystallize new concepts and new ideas. Many child therapists accidentally discover that a pet is a valuable aid in child psychotherapy. However, their general impression is that while the pet is useful, he certainly is not a crucial factor in treatment.

I, however, believe that in certain case situations, pets *must* become a part of the treatment plan. I wish to reiterate a point made by so many mental hygienists that we have too many disturbed children and too few psychotherapists. Furthermore, treatment takes an interminably long time, and short cut is necessary. I believe that in many cases the use of pets in psychotherapy offers this short cut.

My experience with pets made me reject, very reluctantly, the maxim that if a child talks and develops "insight," healing occurs, or that if a child discusses his day in great detail, we have been successful in penetrating his inner defenses. I feel that something very significant may occur even though the child merely plays with the pet and does not utter a word throughout the hour. Appearances are very often deceiving. In therapy, things are very often not what they seem to be. Healing does not always occur where one would think it should . . . and it sometimes does occur in the most unexpected places.

I prefer the term "pet therapy" rather than "play therapy." The term "play therapy" is really a misnomer. The word "play" connotes a self-chosen activity which is largely absent in the structured setting of a clinic or a private therapist's office, where the purpose of the activities are predetermined, the time set beforehand, etc. What we are actually doing in play therapy is engaging in directed make-believe.

Reprinted with permission of The National Association for Mental Health from *Mental Hygiene*, Vol. 48, No. 2 (April, 1964), pp. 243–49.

This paper was presented at a symposium on "Special Techniques in Child Psychotherapy" during the 71st Annual Meeting of the American Psychological Association, held in Philadelphia in August, 1963.

There are two interrelated aspects of pet therapy. One, the pet's use as a therapy aid by the clinician in his office. The other, as aid to therapy; i.e., the directed introduction of the pet into a child's home.

Adults ascribe human attributes to animals; children reverse the process and attribute animal qualities to human beings. Contrary to the widely held impression, it is, in my opinion, easier for a child to identify with a human being than with an animal. However, it is even more difficult for a child to project life into and identify with an inanimate object. The great virtue of pet therapy is that it permits identification on this intermediate level. Further, experienced child therapists know that dolls, clay, finger paints and other appurtenances of the play room cannot be truly loved. They are not alive; they do not grow, digest, respond. The child intuitively feels that they cannot share his feelings with him. Unlike his reaction to a doll, a child can conceive of the pet as being part of himself, part of his family who goes through the same experiences he does.

It is well-known that through play a child may rehearse and try to re-solve some of his life's problems. A sensitive therapist can utilize the child's play with the pet to understand the child. This understanding of what the child is trying to convey strengthens his relationship with the child. Taking walks helps to offer motor release to some children. The pet can also help solve the problem of sharing, separation, and formulation of self-image.

In his use of pets a child goes through a maturational process. A pet that is adequate at one time may no longer be acceptable or useful at another. The differential meaning of a pet to a child thus has to be considered very carefully. There is a certain lawfulness within which pet therapy operates. There is a change in themes, not only in terms of the psychodynamics of the situation, but also in terms of the length of time the child spends in therapy.

In the beginning the child just pets or talks to the animal and engages him in imaginative play in which the pet does not participate at all but merely submits to being handled at the whim of the child. The child at this point disregards the therapist entirely.

In the next stage, the pet is the center of the child's fantasied activity and is made by the child to participate in the role assigned to him. The therapist is permitted to be of auxiliary service. After a while, the child begins to people his fantasied make-believe world with other activities in which the pet, while actively participating, plays a role subsidiary to that of the therapist. Finally, the pet is no longer needed in the therapeutic interchange.

It is often first necessary for infantalized children and those with be-havior disorders to gratify some of their needs before an attempt may even be made to approach their nuclear conflicts. A child who has been sadly deprived of love may find it most difficult to accept affection from an adult, but he is capable of receiving affection from a pet. In the child's relation-ship with the pet, we may see a reflection of the way he was treated at home. Eating with the pet and therapist, singing and dancing with the pet, etc., may satisfy the child and yet help develop a relationship with the therapist. I find that only after some children establish a relationship with a pet do they begin to relate to me.

I believe that "pet therapy" is specifically useful for the nonverbal, severely ego-disturbed child. It is well-known that most children learn about the world and the differences between self and nonself through the medium of their body. This is particularly true for the autistic child, whose contact with reality is most tenuous. A pet would serve to strengthen such a child's cathexis and would help him become aware of the cause and effect relationships.

It seems to me that if we trained pets to give bodily comfort to the autistic child in his crib or while he is a toddler and thus provided constant stimulation throughout his waking hours, it would assuage the autistic child's all-consuming anxiety and help him to establish a firmer grip on reality. Thus, while on the average, a child is seen in therapy only twice weekly, the pet can exert his healing influence on the child 24 hours a day. We will find that pet therapy will affect the very substratum of the child's emotions and his unconscious concept of self as being a desirable person. The therapist no longer would have to handle in toto the basic affectional needs and thus could work on a higher conceptual level.

Another implication of the use of pets, since they are so active, is that the main locus of therapy need no longer be in the playroom, but in the wider world in which the child has to function eventually—in the street or play ground or wherever the child's and his pet's fancy take them.

The effectiveness with which a child therapist utilizes pets will greatly depend upon his previous experience with pets, how comfortable he feels with them, his personality traits, and his philosophy of treatment. It is to be noted that some child psychotherapists feel uncomfortable when they no longer are able to offer facile interpretations and to interact on an intellectual level with the child. Another relevant factor is that a pet, unlike finger paints or a puppet, must be taken care of. He is alive, requires active care, compels attention, must be fed, medicated, exercised and loved.

Each pet has his own behavioral characteristics and moods which must be considered. For example, if one wishes to secure a dog as a psychotherapeutic aide, the immediate question is what kind of a dog to choose, since it is well-known that different dogs vary in their temperamental characteristics.

The pet chosen as therapy aid must appeal to the child and meet the psychodynamics of the case. It seems to me, on the basis of my experience, that children who have difficulties in relating socially to their peers prefer large animals; those whose difficulties are mainly intrapsychic prefer small animals.

Quite frequently the cat is preferred by some children who are undergoing an oedipal conflict and are resentful of authority. Young withdrawn children who are not yet ready or wish to enter into an "entangling" emotional relationship also seem to prefer the cat. These children are emotionally "burned," resent authority and being pushed; they therefore prefer a pet which is unobstrusive, independent, not demonstrative in its affection, and does not initiate or seek a friendship.

I have also found the manner in which children approach a pet to be of diagnostic importance. The child's approach to the pet, his attitude and behavior may give me many clues to the child's conflicts. Thus, the aquarium is a potent projective device for some children. Their looking at the fish is somewhat akin to one's looking at the fireplace. They watch the antics of the fish and weave many a fantasy which may later be acted out in the playroom.

To illustrate: I noticed that Richard, age nine, a new patient, was sitting in the waiting room with his back toward his mother and the aquarium and alternately opening and closing his mouth as if imitating the oral play of the fish. I took some fish food and motioned to Richard to help me. Like any other child therapist, I try to establish contact with a child whenever and wherever I can reach him.

Richard reluctantly accepted this assignment: I put the food in his hand and let him drop it in the aquarium. The child seemed concerned and perplexed when he noticed the lively competition for food among the fish. I casually remarked that the big fish do not devour the small fish but that they all live amicably in the aquarium but compete for the available food.

The next few sessions were devoted to the observation of the fish and a discussion of their names and habits. Richard's primitive fear of being devoured was thus a little assuaged; and some boundaries were established between what the fish seemed to be and the reality of their existence. Richard then wished to learn how to start an aquarium of his own. This was the crucial point in my relationship with him.

My philosophy of treatment is that since most of the child's difficulties originate in the home environment, this is where they have to be resolved. It is to be noted that throughout recorded history, the value of pets to children seems to have been particularly significant. Innumerable accounts of the beneficial relation between pets and children may be found described in the literature of almost every nation. It sometimes seems, when we peruse these accounts, that these relationships between pet and child are almost symbiotic in nature.

It is also a fact, attested to by many generations of parents, that when a pet dies, their child is affected almost as strongly as if a member of the family passed away. Yet, although most people have had a pet at one time or another, few have stopped to examine what the pet meant to them and still fewer scientists have considered the psychological significance of the pet to the child.

When a family accepts a pet, a subtle change begins to occur in the family's dynamics, in its very subculture. There occurs a dilution in a family's interaction and a reconstruction of the family's psychological potential. It seems to bring about a certain attenuation of the symbiotic relationship between mother and child and a redirection of these emotions toward the pet. This may be particularly true of the small family.

The discussion of the pet's antics is a subject in which all members of the family may participate. The mere discussion of what the child can do for the pet forces the child to turn his thoughts outwardly, and to think of himself in relation to his parents and his pet. The child may thus learn that he, too, like his parents, has to undergo many inconveniences for the sake of the loved one. He further learns that sharing a loved object, a pet, does not mean losing it or that the loved object loves one less merely because it also offers its love to others. The pet acts like a lightning rod, diverting the pressure on the child. After the child learns about the peculiarities of his pet, he can use him more constructively in his fantasy.

The following case, illustrating the use of pets in psychotherapy, is merely suggestive. The discussion of therapy sessions has, of necessity, been telescoped. Case data had to be changed to avoid any possibility of identification.

Miriam Lev, age eight, was referred for treatment by a day [Yeshiva] school she was attending, because she was a regular "tomboy;" her work was below her potential; she was abusive to teachers; she started frequent fights with boys; and yet she would burst into tears very easily. Mr. Lev was very reluctant to follow up on the school's recommendations as he thought that Miriam was merely lazy and too noisy. However, he had no alternative since the school threatened to expel the child. Mrs. Lev, on the other hand, felt that the school was justified in the referral. She thought that Miriam was stupid, constantly fought with other children, was disobedient, had no friends, and had frequent nightmares.

Mr. Lev was an extremely pious man who had arrived penniless in this country. He had managed, by dint of very hard work and clever business deals, to become moderately wealthy. He had lost his entire family in concentration camps. At age 50, he remarried. Mr. Lev was unhappy over the fact that his wife was "too young looking," was "too attractive and sexy," was a poor housewife and was unable to manage Miriam. He would constantly compare Miriam unfavorably with his sons who perished. Mrs. Lev admired and loved her husband. She was most unhappy that she could not produce what her husband wanted most, a boy. (Miriam was a "Caesarean baby" and Mrs. Lev could not have any more children). She felt indaequate, both as a wife, and as a mother and for the sake of family peace she did not support Miriam.

At the office, Miriam brightened visibly when she saw my dog. She confided that she had nightmares in which ghosts tried to kidnap and kill her because of her "sins." Her imaginary companion, David, tries to help her to chase the ghosts away, but to no avail. She then runs to her parents' bedroom, much to her father's displeasure. Miriam further told me that she always wanted to have a dog, but that her parents would not hear of it.

It later transpired that Mr. Lev felt that it was not proper for an Orthodox Jewish child to play with a dog. Miriam played with the dog at the office and took him for walks. It was her act of defiance. She felt that the dog was the long-prayed-for friend who was in league with her against her parents. The dog thus provided Miriam with a tolerated identification with an aggressive animal which supported her against the dangers which threatened her.

My impression that Miriam would benefit from having a dog of her own was discussed with her parents. I indicated that no prior agreement with Miriam for the care of the dog was to be a prerequisite. I felt that eventually she, on her own, would accept such responsibility. Initially, it seemed to me, it was unwise to burden an emotionally disturbed child with unwanted responsibilities for the pet, such as walking, feeding or combing him. I feel that at the beginning a pet should be enjoyed and not become another superego threat. I suggested that the Levs permit Miriam to assert her autonomy and that she be given the right to make provision for the dog. The dog was to stay in her room. She could rearrange her furniture to make the dog more comfortable and she was even to be permitted to sleep with the dog, if she wished to. Since this was a doctor's prescription, Mr. Lev reluctantly agreed to secure a dog.

May I add that a trying period followed for the dog, Miriam and her parents. The dog made a hole in a chair, chewed the family's best shoes, and had many accidents. Many a time Mr. Lev wished to get rid of the dog, but he met the opposition of both Mrs. L. and Miriam. Mrs. Lev constantly fussed over the dog. At one time when she brought him to the office, the dog had diarrhea and Mrs. Lev wiped him.

Miriam noted that the dog was loved, no matter what he did. She learned that she too might be "bad," rebellious and impertinent, and still be loved. She learned to accept her own "badness" and to feel that she could still be acceptable and loved. This realization that one may be doing "naughty" things at times and yet be loved, I feel, was the crucial point in Miriam's treatment.

Summary and Conclusions

I believe that pets may be useful in two ways: first, as psychotherapeutic aids; i.e., as catalytic agents helpful in speeding up therapy in the therapist's office; and second, as aids in psychotherapy; i.e., being placed in homes of emotionally disturbed children where they tend to restore a healthy communication between members of a family.

Pets are useful not only in homes whose emotional climate seems to promote dissension and poor mental hygiene, but also in the average home, where they may serve to promote positive mental health. Pets should be the *sine qua non* of any institution, and general or mental hospital. The aseptic environment of such institutions would disappear and the mothering contact and sensory stimulation offered by pets would tend to go toward overcoming their deficiencies.

Questions arise: What is the meaning of the pet to the child? How does the process of emotional healing occur? We do find that psychoanalysts and psychologists have done quite a bit of work in analyzing the meaning of animal symbols in dreams, etc. However, comparatively little work has been done and hardly anything is known regarding the meaning of an animal pet to a child, or what role a pet plays in child therapy.

Do we possibly have in pet therapy a tool which permits us to examine at great length and under magnification the elusive something which occurs in child therapy and promotes emotional healing? I believe that we do. However, it is not possible for us, with our limited clinical facilities, to give a more positive answer. What we now need is a clearing house and possibly a journal devoted to the exchange of experiences and research findings on the use of pets as therapy aids and aids in therapy. The research possibilities are limitless. What about the use, on an experimental basis, of all kinds of pets? This would help to establish and explore for each animal the parameters that affect the child's recovery. Thus, we may be able to arrive more rapidly at an effective methodology in the study of pets as psychotherapeutic aids. This will enable us to learn the most effective methods of pet selection, what pets are most useful and when and how they are to be trained.

In conclusion, I feel that the success I had in using pets in therapy has wider mental hygiene implications, which we cannot afford to overlook.

PART SEVEN
WORKING WITH THE FAMILIES

31. Parent-Child Separation: Its Significance to Parents

ARTHUR MANDELBAUM

Understanding the anxieties that parents suffer in separating from a child is essential if parents and child are to be helped. This paper is particularly concerned with the significance of separation to parents in the residential treatment of children. Of all problems the social worker encounters in casework with parents and children, none is more significant than separation. But is it not true that separation is central to all life experiences?

Albert Camus stated, "Separation is characteristic of the human condition. It is often the rule of the world. . . . It is in the essence of things that all who love should be separated."[1] Of course, Camus was speaking of the separation that inevitably accompanies all growth and development and is therefore impossible to resist: birth, infancy, childhood, adolescence, adulthood, old age, and death. Throughout each stage of this growth and development, from birth to death, there is a gradual giving-up of the old for the new in an orderly sequence within which there may be great variation but where the pattern follows a major form. Separation through growth and development is a process whereby parents and child learn to differentiate themselves from each other and to part gradually, a process

Reprinted with permission of National Association of Social workers from *Social Work*, Vol. 7, No. 4 (October, 1962), pp. 26–35.
1. Philip Thody, *Albert Camus* (London: Hamish Hamilton, 1957), p. 28.

made possible by the satisfactions experienced by each individual in the family which brings a sense of growth, achievement, and contentment. The transition from one developmental period to the next during the early years is smoothed by the ever consistent, ever present parents, who create a sense of outer continuity, predictability, and harmony which becomes transformed in the child into a sense of inner security. Erikson has described this as essential for giving the child an identity and a sense of inner goodness and basic trust.[2]

The mother, who gives early essential nurturing experience to the child, is assisted by biological, social, and cultural factors. After the child is separated from her body, holding him close and feeling his softness and warmth comfort her for the loss of sensations and unity that she experienced prior to his birth. The encompassing love of her husband and his consistent support and attention mean that the child is loved as well, because now, although the biological unity is gone, she and the child are, in the emotional sense, still one. The culture approves of her caring for the child and sanctions her motherhood as the major priority. If she is always present for the child, alert and responsive to his needs, and if he is somewhere within the circle of whatever major interests occupy her, then he will absorb into himself an image of his mother that will become deeply etched into his personality. He will then go on to relate himself to his father and others who enter his life. Wherever he goes, he will carry an image of his parents that will remain unshaken; because he knows he belongs to them, he does not have to be physically bolted to them. Such a child will be able to separate. Psychoanalyst Christine Olden has stated, "It could be that you renounce complete possession of the baby more easily if these first months were a satisfactory experience, if you are satiated and feel free to go on to different joys with your child."[3]

This long satiation experience of nurturing and dependency between mother and child is characteristic of the human species, in contrast to the pattern in lower animal life. With the latter, instincts transmitted from one generation to the other enable the mother to force a separation from her young after a relatively short period of time; then, instinctively, the young know how to survive and care for themselves. But the human infant, who is so long dependent on his parents, develops slowly and painstakingly, acquiring in the process a permanent capacity to learn from experience, which is a more creative and flexible way of existence.

Without a protected childhood in which there is time for play, mankind would probably never have arisen above an animal existence. Perhaps in the

2. Erik Erikson, *Childhood and Society* (New York: W. W. Norton & Co., 1950), p. 219.
3. "Notes on the Development of Empathy," *Psychoanalytic Study of the Child*, Vol. 13 (New York: International Universities Press, 1958), p. 515.

future, the playing of children will be recognized as more important than technical developments, wars and revolutions. . . . it was precisely the protection of children from the struggle to survive which favored learning and new developments.[4]

Some fear of separation is universal to children and their parents. When the young child enters kindergarten or when the young adult goes away to college, parents experience vague apprehensions and anxieties. In a study of a group of normal parents whose children were to begin school for the first time, the parents expressed concern that the streets were busy with traffic, the child would be bullied by older children, he would come home with ugly words expressing dangerous aggressive and sexual thoughts, he might even eulogize the teacher as attractive, competent, and omniscient. Many mothers expressed a sense of loneliness after the first few days of school, and both parents shared some concern that now there would be a real test as to whether they had done a good job of rearing their children during those first five years when they were all theirs.[5] Harry Golden, with great sensitivity and insight, expresses the dilemma of parents upon separation.

> I believe the most stirring moment in this experience of a parent comes on the day he leaves the child in school for the first time. This can be so sharp an experience that, where there are two or three children, this ritual has to be alternated between parents. I remember leaving one of mine there all starched up with a look of bewilderment on his face such as I never want to witness again. I held his little hand and got him registered. As we walked through the yard and corridors of the school he never took his eyes off me and never said a word: Then came the moment to put him in a line and—leave him.
> I tried to be nonchalant as I walked away but I quickly hid behind a pillar; he had never taken his eyes off me. He just looked and looked, but I could see that he filled up, but, since I am bigger, I filled up more. What an ordeal! Yet I know that the final decision could not be delayed for long. There was no law that forced me to keep watching him. I turned my back and started out slowly and then I practically ran out the door. You have to make a break.[6]

The Disturbed Child

The child who is considered a suitable candidate for residential treatment is not likely to have had the long satiation experience of nurturing and

4. Henno Martin, *The Sheltering Desert* (New York: Thomas Nelson & Sons, 1958), p. 140.
5. Donald C. Klein and Ann Ross, "Kindergarten Entry: A Study of Role Transition," *Orthopsychiatry and the School*, Morris Krugman, ed. (New York: American Orthopsychiatric Association, 1958).
6. Harry Golden, *Only in America* (Cleveland: World Publishing Company, 1958), p. 49.

security essential to the development of identity and basic trust. His world has been chaotic, inconsistent, uncertain. His family has suffered breakdown because of events happening to his parents: separation, divorce, death, physical or emotional illness, or imprisonment. He himself may contribute to family breakdown through physical or emotional illness, severe retardation, acts of delinquency, or a combination of some or many of these factors which in their interaction are so intense and malevolent that the family can no longer tolerate or endure their impact.

One outstanding characteristic of a disturbed child is that he cannot relate to his parents without demanding infantile, primitive gratifications. He explodes with rage and aggression when these needs are frustrated. His world is filled with glaring hatred, disorganized behavior, wildly fluctuating ego states, bizarre symptoms, and distorted realities. This child cannot bear separation except to withdraw into the loneliness of himself where the dangers of abandonment are less likely and where he does not have to depend on the whim and uncertainty of adults and their world of terror. Because of the illness within him and in the parent-child relationship, he requires residential treatment.

The purpose of residential treatment is to arrange life sensibly for those children whose lives have not been sensible, to bring order to lives which have not had order, to give an experience within a new framework of security where the events of each day and the child's reaction to them are examined for meanings which gradually will appear consistent and logical to him. George Santayana said that those who cannot remember the past are condemned to repeat it.[7] In residential treatment the child repeats his past—it is the only behavior he knows. But he repeats it to have it examined by himself and others in a heightened, ordered way so that he can take up once again the torn threads of his interrupted and halted development and, from the fragment left of his life, revitalize himself into a whole human being.

> The essence of the residential process is that as each child projects his inner world against the macrocosm of the residence, by and large the staff will find from each other and within each other, the strength to resist stepping into the role of the feared parents, and give the child the nurturing and protection he needs to restore his faith in himself.[8]

It is this knowledge and conviction about the purpose and value of residential treatment that the social worker brings into his process with the parents.

7. Clifton Fadiman, *The Lifetime Reading Plan* (Cleveland: World Publishing Co., 1960), p. 14.
8. Rudolf Ekstein, Judith Wallerstein, and Arthur Mandelbaum, "Countertransference in the Residential Treatment of Children," *Psychoanalytic Study of the Child*, Vol. 14 (New York: International Universities Press, 1959), p. 186.

Facing the Need for Residential Treatment

As the parents face the formidable question of the child's need for residential treatment, their great fear of separation brings a feeling of isolation and loneliness. Their impulse to act, to agree quickly to place the child, to make this profound decision impulsively, is slowed and eased in casework. Indeed, it is characteristic of resistance to placement that the parents wish to bypass an understanding of the child's difficulties and the problems that exist in their relationship with him as unfolded by the study. To understand the child and their problems with him is to understand themselves, and there is a wish to avoid this pain. But there is also a wish to avoid understanding the fearful recommendation of placement—to run quickly from the child and leave him behind. The decision to run away seems less intolerable than facing thoughts about losing him, and later the parents must undo their act by returning to claim the child.

The study process, which every family is required to go through prior to any admission, aims not at a decision for residential treatment but rather at a beginning understanding of the nature of the total problem. Once the parents understand this as the first goal, the first essential, they will not feel urged or pushed, and a major part of their anxiety will be relieved with their realization that their child will not be placed until he is understood and until they share in that understanding. It is only from such a process that the importance of the need for this kind of total inpatient care begins to crystallize. When the study process deeply involves the parents and when their rights for making any decision are held foremost, treatment once embarked upon is less likely to suffer disruption. Since residential treatment is a contractual arrangement involving considerable time and expense, there must be as much assurance as possible prior to placement that both the parents and the treatment center will abide by the treatment. The important questions are consistently examined: "Can the child live with you at home?" "Can you live with him?" "If not, can you find the strength in yourself to permit the child, for an indefinite period of time, to live without you?" "But can you also see it as more than a matter of living —that it is a matter of growth, too?"

If these questions are not carefully deliberated, there will be treatment disruption at the first sign of stress. When this occurs it constitutes additional trauma for the parents, the child, the staff of the treatment center, and the children already in residence (who suffer when one of them comes and goes unexpectedly and abruptly and then begin to doubt the power and wisdom of the setting to give them protection from disruption and the logic and predictability their lives require).

The study process is not accomplished by one or two hours of work. To think that it could be is to depreciate the many-faceted aspects of the parents' thoughts and emotions and the depths of their concerns; it is also to overevaluate casework, expecting a persuasive power and magic from it which can then only bring disillusionment and a futile search for new and magical treatment methods. The process begins from the moment the parents make contact with the setting. It continues through the evaluation and study of the child, in which both parents must be deeply involved. It lasts until the parents have given enough consideration to their conflicting feelings and have arrived at sufficient understanding to risk separation.

Before and After Placement

What are the feelings of parents who face the prospect of residential treatment for their child? During the study and later, during the admission procedure, a universal reaction is that the child's need of residential treatment reveals their inadequacy as parents. They have been found deficient in qualities of goodness. Their past and present anger has been evil and destructive to the child; their power to hurt him is unlimited. This anger has assumed such power, they believe, that it has damaged the child beyond repair and he will never recover. There is also anger at the recommendations (but perhaps relief, too) and a secret hope that the treatment center will fail, for if it succeeds, and the child succeeds, it will mean they have solved things in the past in the wrong way. These are forbidden thoughts that arouse guilt and the fear that if discerned further disapprobation will be brought on themselves and they will be rejected as worthless. On the other hand, if the treatment center should fail, it will mean that their own failure is less, for the child is beyond anyone's power to help.

Many parents consider residential treatment as meaning they have been of no value to their child whatsoever. The good things they have done for him, the warm, tender moments, are swept away by the totality of their bitter thoughts. They no longer have a useful function; their parental rights are entirely severed. They feel that the treatment center will now do all the work and this confirms their helplessness, their inadequacy, and their feelings of being unwanted. They feel that even if the child is given the opportunity to grow, to get well, he may fail, and perhaps it would be better not to risk this failure after a series of so many—why gamble and risk finding out that there is no hope whatsoever? And because some parents tend to undervalue themselves, they depreciate the child and his potential strength or undervalue the child and thus themselves.

Separation from the child means that he is irretrievably lost. "Out of sight, out of mind" was the expression used by one parent. The disorganized parent, whose internal personality organization is fluid and fragmented, fears that he will lose the image of his child (the inner picture-making mechanism is broken), and this is equivalent to death. Because he feels his inner self is so chaotic, he fears that the child has similar problems of disorganization and that during the child's absence from his parents he will lose his image of them, which is the equivalent of their death. They will die and he will die.

During the interim period (after the study of the family and before admission), the social worker continues to explore with the parents the meanings of their fears, doubts, and expectations. They learn to look forward to residential treatment with hope that this, at last, is the long-hoped-for solution. They see it as having value for the relief it will give from the intolerable demands the child makes on them, and perhaps the demands they make on the child. They partially recognize that some of the chains that bind them to the child are forged with anger and guilt. These feelings are so strong that the act of giving the child into someone else's care is felt to be an act of aggression on their part. They see this reflected in the anger and doubts of the child about leaving home and their fear that as he grows big and powerful he will retaliate and destroy them. But this is because they see the child as having failed to renounce the pleasures of his instinctual life and feel that they have failed to help him move in this direction.

As the parents continue to exchange thoughts with the social worker during this period, it becomes clear to them that they have one direct way to assist the child to begin the education of his instinctual life: by separating from him. This step calls for their work and sacrifice, the renunciation of whatever unhappy gratifications they have from the primitive aspects of the child's behavior. This renunciation is the decision for placement. Through carefully planned admission procedures in which grief reactions and depression are expressed, the social worker continues to help them understand and master their feelings. Once these are mastered, the parents are rewarded by the gradual recognition that they have accomplished something good for their child, because it brought him growth and growth to themselves as well.

After placement the parents fear that the great force, the great energy they have put into the struggle, will now be gone and that the vacuum created in their lives because of the child's absence will cause them to lose their momentum, their reason for struggle, their reason for existence. One mother said that her son was like a great wind against which she could lean and remain upright and strong; now, with him gone, she would collapse. Another mother wrote her son shortly after admission:

> Hello Honey,
> Well, we have had it around here. Workmen all over the place. And now the roof is falling in. Then the painters again. Then the gardener. If you lose me, just check the local nut houses—that's where I'll be!
> I missed you yesterday . . . there is no news here . . . worth listening to that is. I forgot to tell you my bathroom window is disintegrating and both balconies are gone. I tell you, Allan, I'm getting tireder and tireder. If there is no such word as "tireder" you can take your choice and you can have it. I love you.

The parents are also afraid that they who are "bad" parents will be replaced by "good" parents. This fear is sometimes reinforced by the residential staff.

> And it will be found that categorizations of good and bad, loving and rejecting, eager to help and uncooperative, which are used subtly to dichotomize treatment staff and parents are current in some measure in all settings where children are treated. . . . Some of the many seemingly insuperable difficulties which frequently beset the relationship between the real parents and the residential center can be linked to these feelings. Generally children who have endured a particularly unhappy life experience, or whose conditions call forth immediate pity, are more likely to evoke these fantasies and feelings in total staff with extraordinary swiftness and intensity.[9]

When rescue fantasies from the "bad" parents do occur among staff, these are accompanied by feelings of righteous indignation and passion, with the result that diagnostic and treatment goals are blurred. The parents, alert to negative attitudes, can only react with a deeper pessimism about themselves. They fear the residential staff will alienate the child from them with these hostile feelings. And attitudes of contempt for the parents are sensed by the child as an estimate of him, for he feels himself a part of his mother and father. The parents may soon develop counterrescue fantasies and wish to remove the child from this "bad, critical place," especially as the child in correspondence and during visits describes his anger toward staff, his loneliness, his wish to be withdrawn. The strength of the parents to resist the temptation to return to the former unhealthy relationship with the child is sorely tested. If these elements in the separation are carefully predicted in advance, if the parents are prepared for these actions by the child, and if the meanings of the actions are correctly interpreted, they are then able to sustain the treatment.

Some parents communicate their distress after the child is admitted by excessive letter writing and a constant stream of gifts and clothing. These mean to the child, "Do not forget me," or "I am sorry that I have sent you away, please forgive me," or "I do not wish you to forget that I am the major person in your life, you need me, I need you and I do not want you to relate yourself to others; please stay young for it is the way I love you best."

These expressions may also indicate to the child that he remains the only source of gratification for his parents, the only reason for their existence, and that they have no other avenues available to them for satisfactions and a fruitful life. Thus, loyalty struggles become inextricably confused in the process of separation. If the child is to get well, he must have his parents'

9. *Ibid.*, p. 189.

permission and be sure of their conviction that it is all right for him to love others, to have regard for himself, and, finally, to regard his parents with esteem, dignity, and without fear that they will withdraw from this healthy, mature expression of his need and love for them.

Working With Staff and Parents

It is one of the essential responsibilities of the social worker to convey to all staff his knowledge and feeling about the parents, giving a whole picture of them as they really are—vital, human, and tormented. Social workers may become angry when a child's spirit is mutilated, but if they go to the other extreme and turn this anger against the parents they fail to see the mutilation of the parents' spirits, and the negative effects on their own spirits as well. When the social worker succeeds in identifying himself sufficiently with the suffering of the parents and can catch a glimpse of the extent of their terror, he is better able to provide staff with a framework of understanding. Staff will thus know better what the child carries within himself of his parents, what his life has been before he came, and what he is likely to do and repeat; they will know what the parents have within themselves that corresponds to what is in the child and, then, how these forces continue to interact even though there is physical separation.

Mrs. B recalled that as a youngster she had been like the patient, whining and clinging to her mother, frightened of separation. When Mrs. B left her son with us, she was depressed, and at home she felt confused, disorganized, helpless and without strength to do much. In the residence, a child care worker who had noticed Mrs. B's son meandering aimlessly and morosely about reported: "Instinctively I put my hand on Ben's shoulder. He spun around and embraced me tightly. I sat down and still holding on he sat on my lap. He squeezed me for a moment and I commented on his wish to be small. He said, 'I'd like to be smaller than the youngest child here. I'd like to be one year old. No! I'd rather be no months old and be small enough to crawl back in my mother's stomach.'

"At this point he moved off my lap and sitting next to me continued, 'I'd like to be smaller than a dot.' I said, 'Maybe you'd like to start all over again.'

"Ben said, 'Yes I would so I could be in my mother's stomach and she would eat and eat and I'd get bigger and she'd get fatter and fatter; so fat, two by four, can't get through the bathroom door. And she'd try and try and she'd break down the wall of Southard School and get into the bathroom and then I could start all over and I wouldn't have to come to Southard School.' "

During the first months of residential treatment, the social worker listens to what the parents say, write, or telephone to him, translating back to them the essence of their concerns. Hannah Arendt has written, "True understanding does not tire of interminable dialogue and 'vicious circles,' because it trusts that imagination will eventually catch at least a glimpse of the frightening light of truth."[10] And if the social worker translates this light of truth with kindness, warmth, clarity, and intelligence, it will become clear that there are no absolutes. Placement is an intervention which at first may seem all injury, all loss. As the child struggles to be without his parents and solve his problems and as they struggle to live without him, antagonism and despair seem paramount. This is often revealed through correspondence.

> Dear Dr. W,
> Would it be possible for me to visit. It's hard not hearing from Don himself. I get the feeling that I have to see him before something snaps. Who says the world is round? Don is way out in Kansas and that may be beyond the edge of the disc, where things drop off.
> One if by land and two if by sea!

> Dear Mousie,
> Those hamsters are as smart as they can be. I guess it gripes them that we are just a little bit smarter. They have discovered that if they work real hard they can squeeze out of their cage. I had them out in the patio yesterday . . . All of a sudden, one of the little monsters escaped . . . Finally Daddy looked behind the wall, and there the little thing was trembling and looking all around. I guess he was kind of scared, being out in the big world all alone. Served him right . . . because now I won't let them out of the house again.

> Dear Cindy,
> It has been a tough day. I believe that I am getting old for somehow I get more tired more easily . . . What is more those things which used to act as incentives no longer do so . . . I am dog tired. It just seems as though things just pile up. Believe me Cindy, it is a tough life and no one knows it better than you do.

The feeling that all is lost is an extremely egocentric one. The parents attach to their feelings an absolute value that obscures everything but their own dilemma. This position is a massive defense and as long as it exists there is a stalemate in which no forward action is conceived as possible. When the worker indicates that placement is not the end, but the beginning, that their involvement is not only desired, but necessary, the parents are relieved; but anger comes from the opposite extreme position—that placement in and of itself does not absolve the parents of struggle, of the need to understand the child and themselves and to come together with him when there is a strategic need to do so. Slowly, parents are able to reenter the struggle, but now from the designed, protected position of carefully timed contacts in which there is no overloading of such severe emotional intensity that the parents and child are injured. It is as if once

---

10. Hannah Arendt, "Understanding and Politics," *Partisan Review,* Vol. 20 (July-August 1953), p. 392.

powerful magnets came together with such force that separation meant a ripping-apart rather than a coming-together and leaving when the life situation demanded it.

> Dear Mr. M:
> Nice to see you and talk with you again. I did have a good visit with Harry. Feel much better about him. At times he displays a good deal of hostility toward me. If he has that much then it is better that he can display it, although it is a little difficult to take at times. He is mighty precious to us, and we are so glad that you people took him. He would not have had a chance otherwise. Usually when I return, I am depressed for several days, sometimes for weeks. Now it is different. I get over things much more quickly. Each time I have more strength to walk. This was the best yet. I believe that slowly I am emerging from the woods.

Absence from the child is more than a matter of suspended animation, a continuation of old routines; it is a matter of healing and growth, too. For absence, sustained by the relationship with the social worker, has a healing power. When the parents are encouraged to assure the child that as he grows stronger they do not get weaker, and that he is not expected to return home in order to take care of them, they will examine this need and expectation from their child and trace its irrational sources. For some parents, the closeness to the child has served to ward off their fears of facing other relationships in which their own inadequacies might be uncovered; a fear of facing life situations whose demands would be too harsh, too perfectionistic. Placement gives the parents the needed opportunity and freedom to seek a reunion with each other, to test carefully available strengths, to relate to others, to enter new activities and pursuits. To their surprise, the collapse they expected to undergo does not occur. Much of the resistance of professional people to separation of the child from his family for the purpose of residential treatment is based on the fear that the family will disintegrate. The current crisis in the family brings so much to the fore that is regressive that underlying strengths of parents to sustain themselves are covered over and underestimated.

When the parents reveal their feelings that it is *they* who have been abandoned, these feelings are gently highlighted by the worker. The perception of the parents is then widened to permit them to assure the child that he has not been abandoned and that he has their permission to feel less lonely for them. Much of the unconscious protest of the parents about the child's growth seems based on the fear that should he achieve levels of maturity they have not been able to gain he will then be beyond their control and his power will be used destructively. Thus, sexual strivings are feared lest they go awry, and aggression and learning are feared because they might be turned into delinquent activities—all this corresponding to what is tenuous and poorly integrated in the personality of the parents.

But it is possible to master these fears as the parents observe the child mastering them in his new environment. And as they understand some of the barriers overcome by the child, to some extent they overcome their own.

What further gives the child freedom to move on is the confidence that his parents have other gratifications in their lives which occupy them. He is not the center of their universe and they are not totally stricken at his loss. The knowledge that he can crush his parents because he is everything in their lives is too awesome a power for any child. Once he is relieved of this power, a tremendous burden is lifted from his shoulders and he is no longer an omnivorous monster but a small child who wants care from powerful but safe adults. Further, the child must have his parents' optimism that a new world is offered him and that they are not jealous or resentful of it. "After all there is freedom in not being loved too deeply, in not being thought of too often. Possessive love makes most of the complication and nearly all of the unhappiness in the world."[11]

Life—Not Death

The interpretation in casework of these feelings in the parents does not deal with their unconscious. True, these are deep feelings, but they are sharply apparent as the parents react. They are expressed directly or through metaphor, analogy, displacements, and projections, but very close to the surface of awareness. As the worker urges the parents to think with him, crosslacing back and forth what the child does and its consequences to them, and what they do and its consequences to the child, the worker couches his language, thoughts, and feelings in terms of what is logical and consistent with societal expectations. And if these societal expectations are logical and consistent, they are consonant with principles of healthy growth and development. Through such a process, strength and positive feelings gain ascendancy. And as the parents lose their exclusive self-preoccupation and turn outward toward the child and toward work and friends as other sources of gratification, they do not fear loneliness. Separation is then not an act of death, but of life and growth. This is the contribution of the social worker in helping heal the parents. His efforts coincide and intertwine with those of other disciplines invested in residential treatment, where united energy in a collective enterprise frees the human gifts in parents and their children.

11. Ellen Glasgow, *The Sheltered Life* (Garden City, L. I.: Doubleday, 1932), p. 252.

32. The Separation Phenomenon in Residential Treatment

Victor R. Stoeffler

Some of the staff members of the National Institute of Mental Health recently had the opportunity to observe closely the phenomenon of separation in a group of boys in residential treatment. Such close study was much like looking through a magnifying glass, since it revealed the details of the boys' reactions to the experience of separation. The study included five boys, 12 to 14 years of age, all of whom had been receiving intensive treatment in a residential program for a period of five years.

During approximately three years, in the first phase of the program, six emotionally disturbed boys lived in a closed ward in a hospital setting. They comprised the group under study for severely hyperaggressive, acting-out behavior. The program included four hours a week of individual psychotherapy, special in-hospital schooling, and intensive milieu therapy. Subsequently, the same boys were moved to the Children's Treatment Residence, a homelike building constructed especially for the project. This was an open setting which provided the boys with a therapeutic milieu. All were enrolled in public schools and they also continued their individual therapy. After one year in the Residence, one of the boys was well enough to be discharged to a foster home. His separation will not be discussed in this paper.

In February of the second year of the Residence program, the boys were told at a group meeting that the program would be terminated the following summer and that they would therefore be placed elsewhere. Before they had come to NIH, all of the boys had experienced severe separation traumas. All of them had been physically or emotionally separated from their primary objects many times. Some of them had had several place-

Reprinted with permission of Social Casework from *Social Casework,* Vol. 41, No. 10 (December, 1960), pp. 523–30.

This report, with many others from the Child Research Branch of the National Institute of Mental Health, is based on a study conducted under the direction of Dr. Fritz Redl.

ments in foster homes and institutions before their eighth birthday, and all had suffered from loss of personal love and attention. Since many of the staff members had been with the project since its beginning, the impending termination added to the intensity of this new separation experience.

The staff recorded on the daily nursing charts all material related to the boys' reactions to the separation from the date when the termination of the project was announced until the last boy left the Residence in June. This material covered the boys' specific and direct references to separation as well as the staff members' observations of their feelings and behavior. This information fell into two areas: (1) the boys' reactions to separation, and (2) the boys' resolution of the problem and their preparation for their departure. We shall not attempt to judge whether the boys' resolution or the staff's efforts to help them were successful; our interest here is in reporting on the responses of these disturbed boys, who had been in intensive residential treatment for an extended period, to the impending separation.

Reactions to Separation

It is generally known that feelings of remorse, depression, and melancholy are often associated with the experience of separation. The well known studies by René Spitz have demonstrated the extreme unhappiness of children who are separated from the mother figure. It is also known that separation by death produces feelings of depression and remorse in close survivors of the deceased person.

Our study highlighted the element of depression and also pointed to other reactions which will be discussed in this section.

DEPRESSION

The boys in the Residence were being separated from parental surrogates and in addition were aware that the Residence was about to close. The closing of the Residence and the termination of the project symbolically represented a demise. These two facts created severe feelings of depression which the boys revealed in their actions and words. Depression became a major theme in the life of Bruce, one of the boys. On his daily nursing chart it was noted repeatedly that he was depressed, looked very sad, and seemed to lack motivation for any activity outside the Residence. We observed little actual weeping, but he manifested fear and panic as well as remorse. Tony, however, did break down completely when his counselor bade him goodbye at his new placement. The counselor reported:

> Tony had an excellent trip; however, when we landed at the airport he began to cry bitterly and begged me not to leave him. His new houseparents were there and told Tony that the boys in his cottage were playing baseball that evening and they needed him. Tony wiped away his tears and climbed into the station wagon, but he was waving out the back window until he was out of sight.

Characteristically, disturbed children have a pretty difficult time expressing their true feelings and thoughts. They tend to guard themselves against close relationships and as a result it is especially difficult for them to express feelings related to the actual loss, or the threat of loss, of love objects. Our boys showed such fears of expressing their sense of loss, but did so in a somewhat distorted, symbolic way because of their great need for such expression. Bruce's reaction was reported in this way:

> When Bruce heard where he would be going after he left the Residence he appeared to be in a state of shock. He wandered around rather aimlessly. At bedtime, he came downstairs and asked if he could have a piece of toast. The counselor replied, "Sure, and I'll sit with you." While waiting for the toast, he moved around the living-room slowly, caressing pieces of furniture, and asking what would happen to all the stuff and the things they had collected, such as baseball gloves and records. The counselor said that the boys could keep the things they had collected. This assurance satisfied Bruce and he went to bed.

It is interesting to note Frank's focus on an inanimate object as a symbolic way of expressing a loss of personal relationships.

> During an evening smoking period, Frank called a counselor aside and said, "See that old piano there? You may find nicer looking and better tuned pianos, but you'll never find one that's been used for so many things. That's a fact. We've used it for a table, something to write on, as a chair." He continued to enumerate its uses and added with a forced grin, "I'm going to miss that old piano." He leaned back in his chair and, with a serious and almost mournful expression on his face, fixed his eyes on the ceiling.

It was noticed that even the boys' sleep was at times shrouded in sadness. Bedtime was often a difficult period for the boys since it was in itself a separation—a temporary but nevertheless disturbing one. They frequently would ask someone to stay with them while they went to sleep. The approaching separation, so prevalent in their lives and thoughts, seemed to have a profound effect on their sleep. The night counselor reported:

> Tony slept quietly all night but with a somewhat sad-looking face. He must have been thinking about the termination when he dropped off to sleep. Each time I looked in on him, I had the impression that he was a very sad boy. Also, Ed slept very restlessly during the night. It was a repeat performance of his slumber after he had first been told of the termination. His general appearance was that of a preoccupied and worried boy; he had a very mournful countenance.

The above notations were made two days after we had told the boys that the Residence would be closing. These observations indicate that they had tremendous feelings of depression in relation to their separation from the people and environment they had come to like and accept.

RECALLING THE PAST

With the theme of separation so prominent in the histories of all our boys, it was easy to understand that the discussion of another separation would arouse old thoughts and feelings. In effect, the impending separation made them relive earlier experiences that once had been extremely disturbing. Staff members had never before heard Ed talk about his early life and about some of the painful experiences he had lived through. A counselor reported a conversation with Ed initiated by the boy.

> Ed asked, "Did you ever live with your father and mother? Which one did you see most? How long were you at home before you started knocking around for yourself?" As the conversation proceeded and the questions were answered, Ed asked if the counselor had ever read his record (social history) saying that, if he had not, he should do so sometime. "When you read it, you'll see how much I've been booted around." Ed then talked about his last foster placement, telling how he hated the people. He then went on to mention all his former foster placements. He said he had been taken away from his family at a very early age because they did not like him.

Such discussion of the past was a marked digression from the usual content of Ed's conversations with his counselor and indicated his preoccupation during this period. Another boy, Frank, repeatedly recalled his experiences at a training school where he had been placed at the age of eight.

In recalling their past experiences, the boys often reminisced about their early days at NIH. They spoke of the life in the locked ward and of the ways they had often misbehaved, mentioning the things the counselors had done to handle this misbehavior. One day, as the boys were being driven to school, the station wagon passed the Clinical Center where they had lived when in the ward. Cliff, Bruce, and Tony struck up a conversation recalling incidents of their misbehavior. Cliff referred to those times as "when the world was young." Bruce talked about his experiences, saying that he wished he could go back there to live. He said that he preferred the ward to the Residence, because the best staff members were there. He seemed to be saying that he wished he could retrogress to the state he had been in four years earlier so that he would not have to leave. One day when Ed said that he was feeling bad about having to leave and about not knowing where he was going, he commented, "When I first came to the ward, I was given a birthday party and had a big cake. It seemed bigger than me but, now that I am bigger, the cakes get smaller."

FEAR AND PANIC

Fear and panic, reactions basic to separation trauma, were present to some degree in our boys. We probably saw only a degree of their fear because we gave them maximum support. We told them repeatedly, and demonstrated in various ways, that we would take good care of them as long as they were with us and that we were trying to find good places for them to go. Their reactions of fear and panic were similar to those of a child who experiences a separation from his primary love objects—such as happens in attending school for the first time. The reactions of our boys were sporadic, rather than continuous. Their fear was evident after the announcement of the closing of the project and thereafter appeared only at times when the idea of leaving suddenly seemed to strike one of them. Then they seemed to be able to think only of the uncertainties of the new placement.

The following notation is an example of one boy's immediate reaction to the fear of separation.

> Bruce became very anxious right after he had been told that the Residence would be closing in a few months. The counselor had a short interview with him about termination, but he withdrew. He ran out the front door, dashed around the house, and finally came to rest for a moment in front of the housemother's apartment. She invited him in, but he rejected the invitation. After about ten minutes of this running around, another counselor cornered him and tried to help him settle down. It seemed that Bruce had to keep moving to release his overwhelming anxiety.

Three months after the announcement of termination, Tony was given definite information about his future placement, which was to be in another residential institution. A new wave of panic seemed to sweep over him that evening. He wanted to gratify all of his needs at once, as if he feared that he might never again receive anything. The housemother reported:

> Tony suffered from an acute case of deprivation and separation anxiety tonight. He wanted to buy a dollar's worth of bubble gum *immediately* (just after having bought twenty-five pieces), to drink all of his diet soda, to visit his tutor on her farm this coming weekend, to borrow 42 cents to buy a bat for Bruce, to settle the dispute about the bat this instant, and to go to the store at once. He wanted everything right now, as if there were no tomorrow.

The boys' fear and panic were related not only to separation but to the unknown factor in their new placements, especially when they did not know exactly where they would be going. One of the counselors reported Frank's dread of going to a training school. Frank said that he did not want any part of training school and if we sent him there, they would have to hold him every minute of the day. He said he had been at this school when he was a little kid, but since then he had learned to run faster and better so it would take a lot to keep him there.

CONCERN FOR STAFF

One of the first concerns the boys expressed, other than their concerns about themselves, was about what was going to happen to all the staff. They often asked, "Where is the staff going?" Also, they approached individual staff members, asking each where he was going to live or where he was going to work. Ed asked one counselor, "Where are you going to be two years from now? The counselor replied that he was still very much involved in the work of the Residence and was not yet making plans. Ed pressed for an answer, so the counselor finally said that he might be in the army. Ed said, "Aw heck, I hoped you could teach me how to drive." Every staff member was asked many times about where he would be and what he was going to do; often the boys would ask if he were going to do the same kind of work. They wanted to be sure that they could keep in touch with the staff after they left, so all the boys got address books in which they wrote the names and present and future addresses of all staff members. This was a symbolic way for the boys to keep in touch with all the people they hated to leave; it was not likely that all the staff members would be on the boys' regular correspondence lists. En route to the airport, where he was to board the plane which would take him to his new placement, Tony made a final check of his address book and announced that he had the address of everyone, including his teachers.

Tony also wanted to be sure that he could keep some bond with all his companions at the Residence. He fortified that bond by making or buying little gifts for everyone at the Residence. Before he left, everyone had received a picture or a plastic boat model as a "going away present." In essence, he was saying, "Please do not forget me."

REACTIVATING OLD PATHOLOGY

The announcement of the termination of the Residence not only precipitated a set of new reactions in the boys, but it also revived old themes in each individual's pathology. Immediately after the announcement, and during the following weeks and months, each boy displayed old bits of his former acting-out and aggressive behavior. The reaction to the separation was by no means limited to sadness and remorse. The boys manifested much bitter hostility toward staff members and engaged in suspicious testing of them. It seemed to them that we had taken away all the security they derived from the treatment milieu and that we would not continue to help them control their impulses. In response, they manifested behavior that had been characteristic of them before their admission to NIH or during their early treatment days. All the boys had been fire setters before they came to the hospital, but this behavior had subsided considerably. Shortly after the announcement all but one of the boys became involved in episodic fire setting and in playing with matches. Overt sex play appeared again between two of the boys.

Also, there was a great deal of aggression at the Residence. Ed and Frank fought at their schools to the extent that we had to intervene and work with the schools on this problem. The boys were often verbally aggressive toward staff members and sometimes struck out at them physically. Tony began to steal and we spent many hours returning articles he had stolen and talking with him about why he was doing this. In general, many old patterns of behavior that had not been seen for a long time reappeared. Some of the things the boys did after the announcement of termination were the very things that had gotten them into the difficulties that eventuated in their coming to NIH.

One day Cliff got into trouble at school, something quite unusual for him since his move to the Residence. He had hit a girl in his classroom and although she had not been hurt the incident created considerable difficulty. The significant fact is that it was just this sort of behavior that was described in his preadmission history.

Frank began to feel despondent and upset when he saw the security of his milieu crumbling. It probably reminded him of the impermanence and insecurity in his own home which had led to his pattern of running away at an early age, often not returning for a long period of time. Frank seemed increasingly to feel that things were going to pieces for him at the Residence and at school. He was threatened with expulsion from school, but we had assured him that we would arrange for him to complete the academic year at the Residence. Finally, he was expelled from school and he ran away. We had no knowledge of his whereabouts until his return to the Residence at midnight. This runaway was a repetition of his behavior before he came to NIH five years before.

FEELINGS OF REJECTION

These boys, who had experienced the security and attention of a clinical team for many years, now believed that they were being rejected and "kicked out." Their feelings of rejection were not always verbalized but they were manifest in the boys' acting-out behavior. Sometimes their feelings were directly expressed to staff members. In another paper[1] our staff has described the ways in which the boys expressed their feelings of rejection with special reference to their anti-social, acting-out behavior. A wave of fire setting, sex play, stealing, school problems, and aggression swept over the Residence within two weeks after the announcement of termination. The director, in pointing out the meaning of this behavior to the staff and the boys, said, "If we try to understand what is behind all this acting out, it seems that some of the boys are saying, 'I can't trust you any more. I'm getting the short end of it. I'm being kicked out, so what the hell.' Perhaps these feelings are very close to the feelings the boys had when they had to leave their parents." Bruce quite openly verbalized his feelings—more exactly, some of his feelings, because he also realized that he was not being kicked out. He said, "First they [the government, the staff, other responsi-

1. Nicholas Long, Victor R. Stoeffler, Kenneth Krause, Charles Jung, "The Management of Behavioral Crisis in Residential Treatment through Modifications in Interviewing Technique," accepted for publication in *Social Work*.

ble people] said that they were going to keep us two years and ended up keeping us four. Now we're getting used to it, and they decide to kick us out."

The boys also felt that, because the project was closing, everything would "fizzle out" and things would be different, that they would not be taken care of as they had been in the past. The staff members had to demonstrate and point out repeatedly that they were going to take care of the boys as long as they remained at the Residence. At one council meeting, a staff member was talking with the boys about some supplies they might need. Frank requested some new tools for the shop, and Bruce stated that since they were leaving they would not receive anything more from the counselors.

As might be expected, the boys endeavored to place the adults in a rejecting role. Tony insisted on a plan for one of the male counselors to adopt him, thereby putting the counselor in a position of apparently rejecting him.

Accepting Separation

The boys came to accept the reality of separation and to make some adjustment to it in various ways. In general, two main factors were important: (1) their positive feelings of anticipation about the new placement, and (2) their ability to face the facts about their own home situations.

POSITIVE ANTICIPATION

When some of the fears and uncertainties concerning their separations and new placements had been allayed, the boys began to look ahead to the future, wondering what it held for them. They tried to bring into focus an image of their new life. Although the boys did not want to leave the Residence, they were able, in general, to have constructive ideas about the change. It seemed as though their depressed feelings led them to reach out with hope for the gratifications they might find in their new placements. Cliff told how his own home, to which he was to return, had been reshingled and the rooms redecorated. He said that his family was going to get a new television set next Christmas and he then would get the old set for his room.

After a time the boys began to ask questions and talk freely about their placements with the other children and with staff members. While the boys were on their way to school or when they were sitting at the dining table, they often would start a conversation about their future placements. One of the counselors reported:

> En route to school, Tony told his peers that he might be going to a boarding school in upper Pennsylvania. Several derogatory remarks were made by Bruce and Cliff. Tony, however, defended boarding schools and asked the

boys to tell him what was so bad about a boarding school. They couldn't, so the conversation ended.

One evening when the boys were sitting around a table doing homework, Ed, in an elated way, said to Bruce, "Hey, do you know where I'm going when I leave here? I'm going to another Residence for a little while and then maybe to a foster home or boarding school. They're looking all over the country for places for me and Frank."

After the boys had given considerable thought to their new placements and to the separation and were able to talk comfortably about it, both among themselves and with staff members, they began to ask questions about what they could expect. Staff members both initiated and abetted such anticipatory discussions, always trying to be positive about the future.

One day while Bruce was waiting to go to a therapy session he began talking about a proposed boarding school, saying that he hated the place. When the counselor asked him where the school was located, he answered, "Vermont." The counselor asked if he had any idea where that was, and Bruce replied, "Up near New York." The counselor then suggested that they go into the study and look it up on the map. Bruce agreed, and after they traced the route, the counselor got out the encyclopedia and pointed out scenes in Vermont. The counselor said that he had been there last summer and told of the mountains and landscapes in that area. Bruce began to be fairly enthusiastic about the place but he also remarked that he would still like to go to a foster home.

FACING THEIR HOME SITUATIONS

All the boys with the exception of Ed had maintained contact with their families and homes on a fairly regular basis. The parents had made scheduled visits and the boys had gone home for a short stay on various occasions. During the last few months of the program we learned that some of the home visits had been upsetting to the boys so we then permitted such visits only after careful preparation. We limited the time to not more than twenty-four hours.

Throughout the period of treatment the boys had not been told where they would go after leaving NIH. Even if they had assumed that they would be returned to their homes they did not consider this possibility seriously since they did not know how long they would remain in treatment. They considered the Residence their home and thought of their real home as a place to visit. When we finally made the announcement that everyone would be leaving, the question of "Where do I go?" became a real one for all of the boys except Cliff, who knew he would return to his own home. Unfortunately, we could not tell the other boys where they would be going and this uncertainty created many problems for the staff. Because of the circumstances related to termination, it was necessary to tell the boys about leaving before plans could be made for their future care.

When a definite answer about the future could not be given to a boy, he was faced with the possibility that he might be returned to his own home. This prospect was frightening and aroused considerable ambivalence. It is interesting to see how the different boys reacted. Frank was told that he would go to another placement, probably to a place where he could continue treatment. Although this was fairly acceptable to him, there seemed to be some question in his mind about it, as if he wondered whether his own home were not the best place for him to go. Ed, who had had no contact with his family other than an occasional telephone call from one of his brothers, seemed to accept the fact that he would not go home. Nevertheless, he once asked in a joking, testing way, "Are you going to send me to a beer garden?"—a reference to the behavior of members of his family.

Cliff knew that he would be going home, and his immediate reaction was, "I don't want to go home and if I have to I want to be the last one to leave here." Up until the moment he left he constantly averred that he did not want to go home. He offered such excuses as, "I have made a two-year contract to play baseball with a league here and I *can't* leave them." Obviously, Cliff needed help in anticipating what it would be like to live at home again.

Bruce and Tony had to come to grips with some of the unpleasant realities of their own homes, which they had never faced before. We told both boys that we believed that a return to their homes would not help them, pointing out that they must avoid becoming entangled in the problems that existed in their homes if they were to continue making progress. We were firm about telling them that some kind of institutional placement was necessary. Bruce went into a rage when he was told this and his immediate comment was, "If you're going to send me to a boarding school you might just as well send me home." This remark seemed to be an admission that he really did not feel good about going home and suggested that he was confused about other possible placements. He then began the slow process of clarifying the issues and, while we could see his ambivalence as he talked about plans, it was clear that his choice was never that of returning home. Bruce did a lot of talking about returning home and asked for reasons why he could not return. We talked to him in a realistic way about the many problems he had encountered there four years earlier and let him know that they still existed. Later he asked about foster homes and other residential units.

Tony reacted to his home problems more dramatically than did any of the boys. Up until a month before Tony left the Residence he was defensive about his home, his parents, and the inevitable difficulties he encountered on his visits. He always had protested loudly when he had not been permitted to go home on a visit. Tony apparently accepted the fact that he would not return home to live, but during the spring he made several visits. While there it seemed to be impossible for him to stay out of difficulty.

After returning from a weekend visit, a month before his final departure, Tony engaged in impulsive acting-out behavior which did not end until we discovered what he was trying to say.

> Tony began to act silly at the table. He ate like a pig and grabbed a brownie from a plate (Tony was on a diet and was not supposed to eat anything other than what was on his diet tray). Since he seemed pretty upset, he was told to go into the study and wait until a staff member could talk with him. He quickly grabbed another brownie and ran outside. When the counselor got him back to the study, he said that they had better get to the core of the problem right away. Tony immediately started to talk about all the forbidden food he had eaten on his home visit. (He had had two bowls of chili, two hot dogs, six crabs, five pieces of French toast, three strawberry shortcakes, two ice-cream cones, and some soda pop). Tony's acting-out behavior increased during the interview. He began to hit the counselor as they got closer to the touchy area of his problem. The counselor had to hold Tony, who started to bite, first the counselor and then himself. The counselor stopped him and Tony said, "I used to bite myself when I was 7 or 9 when I was home." It was pointed out that since he had just been home on a visit, he possibly felt that home was the same now as it had been years ago. After some prodding, Tony finally blurted out, "I don't ever want to go home again and I don't care if I never see them again." Tony said that his father had taken him to a tavern where Tony got sick after consuming two sodas and a sandwich. Later that day Tony went to his grandmother's and had two ice-cream cones. In essence he was saying that it was no different at home now than it had been in the past.

In this interview the counselor tried to help Tony face some of the painful facts about his home and to help him realize that he could not live comfortably with his family, but might get along well in a new placement.

Conclusion

Obviously, many more details could be presented about the reactions of these boys to the separation experience. The techniques employed to make the break as easy and as comfortable as possible for the boys have been mentioned only incidentally. An analysis of the techniques, which would require study of different sources of information and of the subjective views of the staff, could not be encompassed in this paper. Our primary interest in this study has been to present the meaning of separation from a therapeutic residence to the boys themselves. Their reactions, their feelings, and the means they used to make the transition gave us a clear picture of what children experience as they leave the scene of a treatment setting. Although these observations are limited to one specific residential treatment unit, we believe our findings may be a guide to other persons who must deal with similar problems of separation.

33.   The Study and Treatment of Families that Produce Multiple Acting-Out Boys

Salvadore Munichin
Edgar Auerswald
Charles H. King
Clara Rabinowitz

"I lived with my mother, my father, and my stepfather, Joe, when we were at 120th Street, and then I lived with my mother in Brooklyn and two grandmothers, but one was a fake grandmother. And now I am at Youth House I think 16 weeks, or months, or 16 years," says a ten-year-old, intelligent Negro boy referred by the court, with the label J.D., to Wiltwyck School for Boys.

We have seen hundreds of these children who present a combination of childish dependency and negativistic bravado. They are full of resourcefulness and cunning about how to get along in the streets, yet they are hopelessly ignorant and illiterate after six grades of public school. They demand constant gratification but do not admit being gratified. They are children with no sense of the passage of time, who think and feel in action, and who see themselves constantly as reactors. They seem to others to be manipulators and exploiters, yet they perceive themselves as exploited and manipulated by an adult environment. They picture the adult as being unrelated to their needs but as possessing the materials for subsistence, which are distributed at the adult's capricious will. The importance and power of the adult as the executive is magnified in inverse proportion to the child's

Reprinted with permission of the American Orthopsychiatric Association from the *American Journal of Orthopsychiatry,* Vol. 34, No. 1 (January, 1964), pp. 125–33.

This study was made possible by National Institute of Mental Health Grant Number OM 745 (RI) MHPG(1).

The term "acting out" is used throughout this paper to describe a particular style of learned behavior in which impulses are expressed in activity without the intervening intrapsychic processes more characteristic of neurotic acting out.

The authors wish to express their appreciation to Braulio Montalvo for many helpful comments and suggestions.

perception of himself as powerless and insignificant. As participants in the field of interaction, these children remain blind to their impingement on other people and always see controls as arbitrary and external.

After working with these children, we began to ask what conditions were significant in their pathological development; how we could account for these children's blindness to their impingement on others, for their cognitive deficit about self and the way in which they function and for their global, inarticulate organization of their experience; and how we could explain their coexistent sense of powerlessness and sense of omnipotence.

These questions turned us toward the study of the families of such children. Literature told us little about the intimate operations of these socially very deprived families. Psychiatric researchers, for the most part, have avoided working with this particular group because the life stresses they undergo seem to make their co-operation unlikely. Additionally, the dynamics of interaction behavior and survival behavior are so interwoven that it is often difficult to know whether a given situation represents an adaptation to a sociological situation not of their own making, or is primarily reflecting intrapsychic phenomena.

We began our work with these families three years ago, first, with a pilot project; then, in 1962 we began this more extensive, three-year study. The lines of interest are many. This paper is confined to two areas, namely, what we have observed about how these families function, and the adaptations of therapeutic technique we have devised for clinical work with them.

The Subjects

Ethnically, our population at Wiltwyck is 70 per cent Negro, 15 per cent Puerto Rican and 15 per cent Caucasian. These people are of low socioeconomic status; approximately 70 per cent are on welfare. Very few parents have finished high school; most did not complete grammar school.

Seventy per cent of these families have only one parent, generally the mother. In more than 40 per cent, there have been two or three fathers and in 10 per cent, four or more, and one child or more has been conceived out of wedlock in 60 per cent.

The number of children ranges between two and eight, their ages between one and over 18 years. The great majority live in New York City slums in cold-water flats and walk-ups, in very crowded quarters without privacy. A very few enjoy the rare low-income housing projects.

We have defined the family as a household unit with at least one member in a parenting function, regardless of whether the children are or are not his (her) progeny.

In 37 per cent of our families, two or more children have been involved in some form of acting-out behavior. For our study, we chose families from this group because they might provide more information regarding the genesis of acting-out pathology.

In our early clinical work, we were impressed with a few basic characteristics of family structure which seemed crucial: (1) In a large percentage of the families, parents had relinquished their executive role, that is, the parental responsibilities necessary for the control, guidance, and protection of children; (2) a rarefication and breakdown in communication between the parents and the children facilitated the development of a distinct sibling subsystem and this subsystem tended toward autonomy and opposition to parental control; (3) this sibling subsystem acquired significance as a socializing agent far beyond the emphasis placed on it in studies of family functions; and (4) this sibling subgroup utilized power-oriented value systems seemingly drawn from the socially deprived and distorted subculture in which these families live.

In other words, we found a definite separation between parents or parental surrogates and siblings. It is as if parents and siblings exist under the same roof, but are autonomous entities in many vital aspects of living. The siblings frequently operate outside of the awareness as well as of the control of the parents. Frequently the parents deny responsibility for a child's unacceptable behavior on the grounds that they were entirely unaware of it, or that it had occurred only in the community outside the home, or both. They clearly state that, because their child's behavior was without their cognizance, it was therefore outside the boundaries of their ability to cope with it.

The Therapeutic Design

Our first job, then, was to design an approach that would (1) tap the operations of these subgroups in the family and help in understanding their separate dynamics and (2) create conditions within which the critical split between parents and siblings could be mended by bringing the sibling operation into the sphere of parental awareness. Our ultimate goal was the re-establishment of the parental control and guidance children need for their growth.

It seemed to us that our immediate diagnostic objective of knowing these two distinct groups within the family could be achieved through a procedure which first permitted us to see the total family as a unit. Second, we needed to view each of its two separate parts alone. We then needed to reassemble the total family to check our observations, validate ideas and impressions and begin to set the stage for the modification and healing of the split. As designed, our basic technique, utilizing multiple therapists, consists of a family session divided into three parts, or stages, and lasting between one and one-half to two hours.[3]

First stage. In this stage, the entire family, including the child in placement at Wiltwyck, is seen as a unit with two therapists participating as a team. The therapist of the child in placement is also present as auxiliary therapist and as a link for the child between the family sessions and the residential milieu.

Second stage. The family is then separated into two groups. One therapist takes the parents; the other therapist and the child's worker take the sibling group.

Third stage. Therapists and family reassemble.

We have since come to refer to the important post-session discussion among the therapists as the *fourth stage.*

We have now seen more than 60 families using this technique as a diagnostic tool in our intake procedure. For our research project, we have chosen seven of these families, each of which we have seen for a total of from 25 to 31 therapeutic sessions; we are now beginning therapy on a second group of six families.

The Family Functioning

The B. family is Puerto Rican. The father is bright, verbal, alcoholic, phobic and given to shifting from excessive love to excessive rage. The mother is slow and depressed, with psychosomatic symptoms, suicidal ideas and chronic resentment. They have four children. The two oldest boys show acting-out behavior. The ten-year-old girl shows psychosomatic symptoms and depression. The youngest boy, three, is a delightful hyperactive youngster. He wanders about from one spot to another, from one activity to another, seemingly not expecting any reaction from his parents. Every once in a while he seems to reach the limit of the permissible, at which time mother or father yells at him, slaps him or extends an inattentive hand to push him in another direction. The "moment" in which parental activity is elicited is unpredictable; one cannot see how the child's activity differs at this time. Sometimes the parents seem to "correct" him when the interviewers show some sign of annoyance.

This vignette, which repeats itself in many forms, seems to indicate a parental lack of reactivity to the children's actions, and suggests that the parents' reactions may be related to their own internal stress rather than to the action of the child. It is as if the interpersonal framework within which the child grows up were made of an elastic band: The child acts and gets no response; he acts again and again and the band gives, until it reaches the limits of its elasticity; he is then hit by all the rageful strength of the band snapping back to normal. The mode of parental response at this point is usually some form of violence. This phenomenon seems pervasive enough to merit status as in integrative force in the family. The violent action, if viewed over the long sweep of the child's development, is at least predictable in the sense that it will come. *When* it will come is unpredictable and, though long overdue, it has a somewhat reorganizing effect.

In the course of ego development, a child requires adequate parental response to his actions as signposts for an adequate evaluation of self. His evaluation of the correctness of his opinion or the adequacy of his performance requires the experience of coming up against discrete, interpersonal boundaries.[2] The child's self-evaluation develops by the confrontation of an "I" and a "you" in different situations through which the "I" experiences his impingement on the other and can correct, modify or reinforce certain aspects of behavior accordingly. Lack of reactivity on the part of the parent to the child's behavior creates a deficit in the child's awareness of his impingement on others. The child's behavior, verbal and nonverbal, is frequently responded to by the parent in a way that prevents the child's clear evaluation of himself or his performance, with the consequent development of uncertainty and confusion about his behavior, and apathetic withdrawal as a security measure.

This is illustrated by the following situation. The mother of the D. family (who has 12 children by eight different fathers) appears to treat her children as if they were an undifferentiated herd. They must all sing when she wants them to, regardless of the shame of the older children. She distributes cookies as a farmer throws feed to chickens, unmindful of age and differential needs. For most of the interview the children sit listless, only physically present. Every once in a while the mother addresses herself to some of them with a demand, a yell or a cry that "they" are making her varicose veins get inflamed. In response to such a contact, the child activates himself out of the autistic position he has been in up to that moment.

This quality of parental response pushes the child to his siblings for reflective appraisal, guidance, control and direction in how to cope with the familial and the outside world. The "parental siblings" to whom authority is implicitly or sometimes explicitly allocated by the parents or by the siblings, or both, become the source of reference for executive guidance. This sequence of insufficient and unpredictable parental response creates in the child the need to repeat the same action or increase its intensity until an acknowledgment of himself as the doer and, therefore, of himself as existing, is received. The need of *a* response becomes more vital than the nature of the response.

To repeat, at some point or other the parent will respond with an attempt at creating boundaries by violent and irrational interruption of the child's activity. The child experiences a deficit of response at one extreme of the continuum and violent response at the other extreme, with nothing between. It should be re-emphasized that this response of the parent is not clearly related to the nature of the child's action. The child's encounter with the reaction of violence is frequent, capricious and incomprehensible, and it creates in him the sense of being helpless. He experiences a violent world that he cannot modify by his own actions. The different intensities in the continuum of aggression are not perceived.

Also, since he cannot relate his experience meaningfully to his own behavior, his sense of participation *in* the event or *with* the other is impaired. The experience of being angry, for example, is articulated not as "I am angry," but "You are hurting me." Feelings become externalized and this militates against any clearly delineated grasp of the affective experience. This inability to learn from experience, which characterizes so many of these children, may be because many situations that happen to them they do not fully experience as happening to themselves. Children in these families tend to search for extreme dramatic stimulation, as if the stimulation must be multiplied before it is intense enough to make the child perceive that "this is happening to me" rather than "around me." This may add another explanation to the need for danger and adventure, and for much of the senseless cruelty often displayed in "delinquent" activity.

One of the most important forms of interaction within these families is the nurturing transaction. Parents' understanding of their parental role seems to rely heavily on their function as nurturers. This often seems true for both mother and father. "I am a parent" many times means "I am able to give." For a variety of reasons stemming from the cultural and experiential background of the parent, frustration in this role is perceived by the parent as personal failure and creates a loss of self-esteem. Between mother and child a contractual agreement appears to have been reached in which the child is being told, "You have the right to perpetual feeding." No qualifying clauses exist in this contract. Appropriateness of the child's demands, or need to delay satisfying them are not considered.

When a child makes a demand that is rejected by his parent, *both* parent and child feel it is a breach of contract. The mother responds with a sense of guilt in an implicit communication to the child that she has been a bad mother, and the child feels that he has been denied what is his due.

The child's response to being nurtured is, then, not one of gratitude or even the simple experience "I am being given something." It is rather "They owe it to me." When he is frustrated in his demands, or asked to delay them, his response is rage about "unfairness." He perceives the adult as a capricious denier. Within this framework he will attempt to manipulate this situation, to get what is "his own." He will steal "his own," with the feeling of doing justice by his own hand. These children's lack of a guilt response to stealing is often due to their feeling that they have simply repaired an injustice.

Often in these families a child's most predictable and differential areas of influence narrow down to one critical area, namely, his ability and power to "upset, make sick or even kill his parents." One of the most frequent symptomatic pictures produced by these families is the child who, though undeveloped in such skills as reading, writing, playing and bladder control, is overwhelmingly frightened of his belief in his destructive power against mother.

Mother's communication is full of variations on the theme. "You should help me, but you make me sick instead," and "I try my best but I am helpless and cannot control you." This type of communication leaves no room for alternative behavior. The child is not instructed about behavior that will make mother "well" again. He incorporates a self-image of evil omnipotence. This transaction leaves the children covertly or overtly afraid that they can kill their mother—obsessed with the fear that she may die, or devoted to her protection, or both. Thus the child is subjected to conflicting messages, "You are helpless and dependent on my nurturance for survival" and, "You have the power to hurt or destroy me, your source of survival." These two contradictory messages label the child as both powerful and weak. He cannot integrate such opposites. To avoid disorganization, he seems to select the message with most survival value, namely, that which offers power rather than helplessness.

The Therapy

From the start, it was apparent that we needed to take into account the sociological problems of these families, the problem areas of the family itself as a unit, and the intrapsychic operations of the individuals within the families.

The bridge across which interaction takes place in this field is verbal and nonverbal communication. Difficulties existing anywhere in the homeostatic field will be reflected in gaps and incongruities in the formation, transmission, reception and integration of messages, whether the distortion is in the individual, in the family, in the subculture surrounding the family or in the society within which the subculture operates. The family therapist, therefore, must work with these clearly observable and available interactional processes.

Various workers in the field, such as Ackerman, Bateson, Jackson and Virginia Satir, have stated this principle. Nathan Ackerman,[1] for example, has pointed out that in family therapy, "If a useful solution is to be found, intrapsychic conflict must be activated and reprojected into the field of family interaction. The longer the period of intrapsychic containment and isolation from the field of active personal interchange, the less probable it is that the pathogenic trend can be reversed." We have drawn heavily on the experience of these and other workers, and our experience with families has led us to agree fully with this point of view.

In our work with the first group of families in our project, three temporal phases developed; they cover the span of therapy. *Phase I* is the phase of induction and entry into the family system; *Phase II,* that of therapeutic work within the family system; and *Phase III,* that of disengagement and solidifying of the family's autonomy.

The problem inherent in the process of induction of these families into therapy deserves a paper in itself. The difficulty, however, boils down to operational distance—distance between sibling subgroup and parents, between individual family members, and most of all, between therapists and family. The therapists' first task is to fill these gaps. The three-stage multiple-therapist session provides an extremely useful tool for bridging this type of wide split within the family system. Intense conflicts and deep communicational barries between two or more family members sometimes will override all else and force isolation on the rest of the family. These conflicts can be worked with and the barriers circumvented more easily by separating the combatants or isolated ones, or both, from the rest of the family in the second stage.

It is extremely important to characterize the presenting problems as *family* problems *right from the start*. Failure to do so will result in widening the splits already present in the family system. When separations are made in the second stage of a session, the work done is always related to the family as a unit, and the content brought back into the whole family unit in the third stage.

Perhaps a gap even more difficult to close is that between the therapists and the family. We have used the whole gamut of techniques in our attempt to move into the family system. Among them, two deserve special mention.

Against the consistent background of insistence that the whole family come to our offices for their sessions, we have held one or several sessions in the home of the family, the number being determined by how quickly we can get the family to mobilize itself to come into our offices consistently.

The other meaningful technique evolved by necessity. The everyday problems of existence in these families are immense, and such emergencies as paying the rent, acquiring clothes for the children or food for the next week make up a large part of their lives. In order to work with them toward our goal of eventual autonomous family function, it was necessary to take an intense personal interest in these problems in an effort to extricate families from constant emergency operations. The families responded as if this were a new experience, as perhaps it was. We found ourselves paying for babysitters, for shoes for a child so he could go to school, and lending money to be paid as security on a new apartment or for a child's coat when he needed one, and the like. Although we were aware of the danger of supporting the collective dependency of the families in question, we found that such actions opened many doors and immeasurably enhanced our effort to enter the family system because our commitment was not suspect. We chose consciously to capitalize on this observation, and to worry about the additional difficulty of extricating ourselves later, in the phase aimed at development of family autonomy.

Our most demanding therapeutic task was to find ways to move into and work within the family system to combat its greatest handicap: the "global and undifferentiated" quality of these children's experiences, which gave them no chance to evaluate accurately their behavior and themselves. We had to help the members of the family perceive and articulate the ways in which they interacted and their mutual effect. Treatment, therefore, demanded the most active kind of participation in and interaction with the families. As therapists, we became models of differential responses. For example, when we felt angry, hurt or sad for a father who sat listless or laughed while his child insulted or openly lied about him, we expressed our feeling to the family. We explored also what was appropriate action to take in the light of such feelings. In the same way, we expressed our embarrassment, shame, hurt, happiness, surprise, interest or concern at what a child had to report. If necessary, we expressed what we felt were relevant attitudes to what was reported. We therapists sometimes disagreed, and survived. If the family did not make a point of this, we did. We were equally expressive of our pleasure upon finally understanding each other's views.

There were times when we incurred the family's anger, but we were willing to back up our value systems against their delinquent ones. We taught, intervened, showed affection; we were committed to the family's well-being and felt this gave us a right to a stake in its changing and thus we expressed our expectations and challenged the absence of a relevant mood or attitude. In other words, the characteristics of these families demanded a particular therapeutic impingement, one that could provide a framework of guiding signposts and feedback around which they could differentiate and articulate their experiences.

There were difficulties inherent in the nature of our families that made such efforts necessary. For instance, the paucity of verbal symbols available to many of the members of these families is at times incredible. In one family all negative affect is described by the same label, "I am *sad;*" all positive affect labeled as, "I am *happy.*" Verbal communication under these circumstances is often extremely simple, concrete and severely restricted. The therapist is, therefore, further handicapped in his attempts to increase awareness of intrapsychic and interpersonal events, since verbal tools are his main instrument.

At times, what seems to be a member's simple inability to verbalize an experience is, on the contrary, the result of a different modality of experiencing. A frequent instance of this occurred in the family sessions. Attempting to explore situations presented by a family member, one of the therapists would ask another member what he had perceived, thought or felt about the happening under discussion. Repeatedly, the answer would be, "I don't know." Incredulous (and frustrated), the therapist would come back with some statement such as, "You must have *something* to say about it," to which the response often was silence or some form of restless action. Looking back, it is embarrassing to see how long it took us to recognize that the "I don't know" was an honest answer.

It seems to us now that this kind of "I don't know" touches upon the phenomena in amnesia of young children described by Ernest Schachtel.[4]

The demand for a verbal, logical explanation of certain events requires the organization of the experience in discrete manageable units that can be discriminated against the background of other experience. This is contrary to the way in which experience has been integrated in the members of our families.

We have gradually found ourselves more able to differentiate between this lack of integration and the conscious or unconscious withholding of messages that have been integrated but, for reasons of say, anxiety, guilt or shame, have not been shared. Also, as therapy proceeds and our focus is maintained, events previously unattended by family members begin to be perceived and expressed with greater clarity.

We have previously mentioned the necessity of re-establishing appropriate parental function in the special areas of executive control and guidance. We have also referred to the need of appropriate use of nurturance. We have characterized these operations as central to the socializing functions of the family, and their re-establishment became the central goal in our therapeutic work. We found it was often necessary for the therapists to appropriate the role function of the parents in these areas during the family session in order to establish them (by demonstration) as needed ingredients of successful family function. One of the goals as therapy progressed was the gradual transfer of these functions to the parents. In the last phase of therapy, when the core issue was to establish family autonomy, parents were expected to take over these functions within the family, as well as without. The complex task of entering and withdrawing from the family system cannot be fully described here; it will be presented in detail in a forthcoming paper.

We are at present engaged in a systematic study of the structural and functional changes of the families as a result of therapy. A battery of specially designed tests was administered at the beginning and end of therapy and will be administered again in a follow-up six months after termination. Therapy sessions were all taped and their analysis will give us information relevant to family interaction, as well as a more detailed scrutiny of the therapeutic technique.

REFERENCES

1. Ackerman, N. 1958. The Psychodynamics of Family Life. Basic Books, Inc. New York, N.Y.
2. Festinger, L. 1954. A theory of social comparison processes. Human Relations 7: 117–140.
3. MacGregor, R. 1962. Multiple-impact psychotherapy with families. Family Process. 1(1): 15–29.
4. Schachtel, E. 1959. On memory and childhood amnesia. *In* Metamorphosis. Basic Books, Inc. New York, N.Y.

34. Disturbed Families and Conjoint Family Counseling

Otto Pollak

In recent years therapeutic encounters between disturbed families and individual therapists or therapeutic teams, consisting of two or more professional helpers, have attracted a great deal of practical and theoretical interest. A never-failing readiness for therapeutic experimentation has lead the professions of social work and psychiatry to shift diagnostic and methodological emphasis from individuals to families.

Origins of Family Therapy

More than 20 years ago it was observed that improvement in one family member was sometimes accompanied by deterioration in another.[1] This negative association between improvement in a family member who had been considered "sick" and deterioration in another who was considered "healthy" was observed also in the psychoanalysis of marriage partners and led to changes in techniques. One of the pioneers was Mittleman, who as early as 1944 drew attention to this phenomenon as well as to its therapeutic implications.[2] Later on, the effort to adjust therapy to the needs of both marriage partners in situations of marital disturbances brought about such approaches as collaborative therapy, concurrent psychoanalytic therapy, and conjoint marital therapy.[3]

Still later, family group sessions were introduced as a therapeutic method in situations in which the development of a child rather than the marital relationship seemed to be a problem. Well-known pioneers in this field are

Reprinted with permission of Child Welfare League of America, Inc., from *Child Welfare*, Vol. 46, No. 3 (March, 1967), pp. 143–49.
1. Mildred Burgum, "The Father Gets Worse: A Child Guidance Problem," *American Journal of Orthopsychiatry*, XII (1942), 475–485.
2. Bela Mittleman, "Complementary Neurotic Reactions in Intimate Relationships," *Psychoanalytic Quarterly*, XIII (1944), 479–481.
3. Bernard L. Greene, ed., *The Psychotherapies of Marital Disharmony* (New York: The Free Press, 1965).

Ackerman, Bell, Bowen, Jackson and Wynne.[4] In the course of this development, the adaptation of previously established therapeutic techniques to family group treatment lead ultimately to the form of family therapy in which a team of two or more therapists meets with the family group, so that a group of therapists meets a group of family members. This adaptation occurred first of all on a practical basis, largely because individual therapists meeting with family groups found it impossible to keep track of the multiplicity of two-way interactions occurring during the session. Furthermore, it proved to be even more difficult to keep track of the reactions of overtly nonparticipant family members to the two-way interactions that they witnessed. It was also found that the phenomena of countertransference could be better controlled if another therapist was present who—free from such dynamic engagement—could intervene correctively when he noticed elements of countertransference in the therapeutic intervention of his colleague.[5]

Family Therapy and the Family System

This development, based on experiences of clients and therapists in practice, led to theoretical clarifications. First of all, the negative reactions of certain family members to therapeutic improvement of other family members were explained by family system theory.[6] A system is an organization of parts so connected with one another that a change in one produces a change in another. Thus, on this interpretation, change in one family member must be expected to result in change in all other family members.

Change of a person as a result of individual therapy must produce changes in those family members who are not in treatment. In individual therapy this phenomenon can be accepted only if the therapist operates under one of two assumptions. The first is that the change in others is going to be beneficial. The second is that the need of the individual patient for improvement should be met and the therapeutic success maintained, regardless of the price in deterioration other family members might have to

4. *See* Nathan W. Ackerman, *The Psychodynamics of Family Life: Diagnosis and Treatment of Family Relationships* (New York: Basic Books, 1958); John E. Bell, *Family Group Therapy*, Public Health Monograph #64 (Washington, D.C.: U.S. Government Printing Office, 1961); Murray Bowen, "The Family as the Unit of Study and Treatment," *American Journal of Orthopsychiatry*, XXXI (1961), 40–60; Donald P. Jackson, "The Question of Family Homeostasis," *Psychiatric Quarterly*, XXI (1957, Supplement), 79–90; and Lyman C. Wynne, "The Study of Intrafamilial Alignments and Splits in Exploratory Family Family Therapy," in Nathan W. Ackerman, Frances Beatman, and Sanford N. Sherman, eds., *Exploring the Base for Family Therapy* (New York: Family Service Association of America, 1961) pp. 95–115.

5. John C. Sonne and Geraldine Lincoln, "Heterosexual Co-Therapy Relationship and its Significance in Family Therapy," in Alfred S. Friedman, *et al., Psychotherapy for the Whole Family* (New York: Springer Publishing Co., 1965), pp. 213–227.

6. Otto Pollak, *Integrating Sociological and Psychoanalytic Concepts: An Exploration in Child Psychotherapy* (New York: Russell Sage Foundation, 1956), Chapter IX.

pay. Family system theory would suggest that neither of these assumptions is safe, and that not individuals but relationships between individuals, and ultimately the system of such relationships comprised by the family, were treated.

To elaborate: we can assume that all family relationships serve two purposes, which are so organized that one cannot be met adequately without the other. These purposes are satisfaction in the here-and-now and preparation for the future. The satisfaction in the here-and-now is always based on complementarity of needs—complementarity based either on sex, age, or both. Where marital relationship is unsatisfactory, the relationships between the spouses and the children will be impaired, and where the relationships between the brothers and sisters are unsatisfactory, the relationships between the parents and the children will also be disturbed.

Deficient or excessive satisfaction in the here-and-now is likely to interfere with the preparation for the future. Developmental demand is always threatened by arrest: arrest is a frequent reaction to an excessive degree of dissatisfaction or satisfaction in the here-and-now that makes maturation a threat rather than a support of positive expectations. These phenomena may be concealed in a situation in which overt difficulties of one family member help other family members to conceal their developmental difficulties from themselves and one another. The sickness of one member may challenge the response pattern of another family member to produce behavior suggesting health and strength. It has frequently been observed that when a person has been taking care of a relative during long periods of illness, the recovery of the patient is followed by illness of the helper. It is the essence of a sick system that nobody can be healthy in it.

Disturbances of the Family System

Reasons for relationship sickness in the family can be conveniently grouped into two categories: deficit in family membership and failure in role performance on the part of the family members.

DEFICIT IN FAMILY MEMBERSHIP

In our society, families are often broken through divorce, leaving the surviving parent and children to cope with the problem of a missing spouse and parent. Families broken through death may also present a surviving mother and children with problems of a missing spouse and father, but are distinguished from the families broken by divorce by an apparent freedom from the feeling that they have failed in keeping the husband and father within the family group. Families who have lost a spouse through desertion probably experience the most difficult deficit, namely, failure in keeping the husband and father (or wife and mother), loss of his (or her) functions, and uncertainty over whether he (or she) will come back. Coping with the situation cannot even be based on the assumption that it has become definitive, and new arrangements cannot be made without concern about a return of the missing family member.[7]

Family therapy has usually been tried with complete families. It will be interesting, however, to explore its use with broken families, because it will be one way of bringing to the broken family the experience of witnessing mature relationships between an adult man and an adult woman in task performance related to all members of the family unit. For this reason the method of employing a team composed of a male and female therapist may be of special value in working with broken families.

The content of family therapy with broken families is likely to be different from that of family therapy with complete but disturbed families because it will include coping with problems of guilt, anger, and fatigue that will not occur in families with complete membership. Divorced persons will always ask themselves why they made the wrong choice, why they failed to keep their spouse in the marriage, and what efforts they should make to find a new spouse. Their children will ask themselves similar questions—why they were not important enough to keep their parent in the family home, why the parent who remains was unable to do it, and, probably, what new father (or mother) they will have to face if the parent should remarry. Anger about having been abandoned will probably also be present, and most dangerous of all, fantasies about replacement that no reality is likely to fulfill.

FAILURE IN ROLE PERFORMANCE

Wherever a role incumbent disappears from a role system, the incumbents of other roles are forced into taking over. They retain their old roles but have to assume in addition parts of the role that has been vacated. Not only does the remaining spouse have to take on realistic burdens, but he or she may also suffer from feelings of inadequacy due to a lack of opportunity to learn the new role through appropriate experiences. A divorcee may not have been a wage earner before, but she must now become one. A lone father has to provide suitable substitute mothering for his children. In the search for a new spouse, a person may have to engage in a quite unfamiliar courtship pattern. New conduct norms will have to be developed or accepted. The pressure on a mother to replace an absent father as a model for growing boys may also make itself felt and stimulate tendencies toward masculinity that may have been latent in her. Adolescent sons may be propelled into provider roles for a mother, or girls into wifely roles for a father, and thus suffer stimulation of repressed oedipal feelings.

Failure in role performance on the part of children is usually due either

7. Otto Pollak, "The Broken Family," in Nathan E. Cohen, ed., *Social Work and Social Problems* (New York: National Association of Social Workers, 1964), pp. 321–339.

to an arrest in the development of the parents or to an arrest in the development of the children themselves. A development arrest of the parents can also produce defensive reactions in children that may look like precocious development.

An example of developmental arrest in parents is often noted in those foster mothers who can take care of infants very well but lose many of their rearing skills when the children pass the stage of infancy. It is also a frequent occurrence for parents to react with disturbance to the adolescence of their sons or daughters. What seems to happen here is that the appearance of physiological maturity in a son or daughter awakens in the parents unresolved conflicts of their own development, particularly partial arrests that did not prevent them from child rearing but that do prevent them from letting the children separate from them in response to their own approaching adulthood. I should like to propose that arrests, or unwillingness to respond to the push of maturation, are not confined to the early stages of psychosexual development but can occur in any one of the eight stages of man.[8] Wherever a parent refuses to accept and respond to the next stage of the life cycle, his sons and daughters are likely to suffer, be they in the oral, anal, genital, or latency period; in pubescence, adolescence, adulthood, or even in senescence. Developmental arrest in a parent will make it difficult for him to let his children go and to respond to the demands of their own development. From the viewpoint of child welfare, certain consequences of these parental arrests have attracted attention. It has been pointed out, for instance, that the runaway girl is usually the child of a mother who tried to assume the dependency role of a child in the relation to her biological daughter, and thus pushed the child into the roles of wife and homemaker, stimulating her husband to look upon his daughter as a wife substitute, with the consequent arousal of incestuous urges. In such situations the girl frequently has no other defense than to run away from an impossible situation.[9] It is part of the classical theory of adolescence that juvenile delinquency and sexual acting out in girls is frequently a response to unfulfilled and unconscious wishes of the parents, who, by overstrictness and frequent warnings against immorality, keep the child's mind focused on sexual acting out. It may also be that such parental restrictiveness stimulates the hostility of the child to express itself by violating just those behavior norms that the parents abhor or at least claim to abhor.[10]

8. Erik H. Erickson, *Childhood and Society* (New York: W. W. Norton and Co., 1950), Chapter VII.
9. Ames Robey, *et al.,* "The Runaway Girl: A Reaction to Family Stress," *American Journal of Orthopsychiatry,* XXXIV (1964), 762–767.
10. Irene M. Josselyn, "The Family as a Psychological Unit," *Social Casework,* XXXIV (1953), 336–343.

Special Problems of a Foster Family

The special problems of a foster family seem to lie in the experience of intimacy without the correctiveness of incest taboo, in the demand for emotional commitment without the security of permanence, in the experience of sibling rivalry without the corrective of a blood relationship, and in the threat to parental autonomy that the claim of a real parent or the supervisory judgment of a caseworker may represent. In many instances the wish and readiness to take care of children other than one's own may simply be the expansiveness of libidinal feeling. There may be situations, however, in which the wish to take a foster child represents developmental arrest. A woman may need a child in an early stage of development for the gratification of her wish to take care of an infant, and to have the body contacts that such infant care demands from the mother. She, because of her own anal arrest, may wish to have children in her home whom she can toilet train. She may simply be a woman who cannot experience affirmatively the growth and development of her own children and, therefore, needs substitute children whose development has not progressed sufficiently to represent a threat to her.

To the husband of a foster mother, presence of a foster child can easily represent a reproach. He may feel that he has not provided enough children for his wife to satisfy her needs of maternity, or he may feel that he hasn't provided enough income to make the financial element of foster care irrelevant. Ultimately he may feel that, as a person, he does not satisfy his wife's needs sufficiently to keep her from needing an additional person.

In consequence, the presence of a foster child in a family may stimulate both libidinal and destructive urges in the foster father, the foster mother, and their own natural children. It may interfere with the self image of the foster father. It is, of course, recognized in child placement work that situations so loaded with stimuli for explosive personal experiences require supervision. Supervision itself, however, is anxiety-creating and must be coped with as an emotional experience that requires examination—it cannot be repressed, denied, or simply concealed. People who find themselves in such a network of threatening relationships are tempted to build around themselves fortresses of privacy in which, for the most part, they talk to themselves rather than to one another. They practically stop communicating with each other out of fear of revealing incestuous feelings, hostility, jealousy, and competitiveness. Therefore, one-to-one interviews between caseworkers and clients tend to expand the fortress of privacy rather than to establish or reestablish effective communication within the family.

It is at just this point that family group therapy can serve the foster family best. Breakdown in communication is usually accompanied by an attempt to carve up the available living space into areas of privacy. The individual family members try to have living space of their own that they do not have to share and where they can avoid even the semblance of communication. Husbands may withdraw to the basement, women to the kitchen, and children to the TV set. Couples who are unhappily married usually end up sleeping in separate rooms. Thus, physical separation aids and reinforces psychological separation. For people thus frozen in separation, family group treatment sessions establish first of all a new experience of sharing living space. With copresence in space comes the claim to communication and, with the family therapist present, a model of a person who responds positively to such claims.[11]

Special Problems of an Adoptive Family

Some of the difficulties outlined above with regard to foster parents may apply also to adoptive parents. Again we lack some of the correctives of impulse that are normally present in parents and siblings. No blood tie produces inhibition of response to sensual stimulation. No blood tie provides whatever control of sibling rivalry may be derived from it. On the other hand, there may be more concern over an equitable distribution of affection if adoptive parents have children of their own. It would seem that it is just this absence of certain controls and reassurance factors in foster and adoptive families that may make family treatment the treatment method of choice, particularly if the methodology followed contains two family therapists.

The Therapists as Models

In that case, the members of the family will have the experience of watching two persons coping with intimacy in an adult fashion. It has been pointed out by Warkentin[12] that psychotherapy is similar to marriage in being an experience of intense emotional intimacy. Intimacy means, according to its linguistic roots, "entering the fears of the other." The common usage of the term as referring to sexual closeness is not as unrelated to this original meaning as one might think at first. People brought up in the Judeo-Christian culture associate many fears with sex—fears about impulse release as such, fears about transference elements in the partner, and fears about their own hostilities. When they make a sexual contact, therefore, they make contact with their fears. This might not be true in other

11. Dwaine R. Lindburgh and Ann W. Womsek, "The Use of Family Sessions in Foster Home Care," *Social Casework*, XLIV (1963), 137–141.
12. John R. Warkentin, "Marriage—A Model of Intimacy in Our Society," in Otto Pollak and Alfred S. Friedman, eds., *Family Dynamics and Family Therapy—With Special Reference to Female Sexual Delinquency* (to be published by Science & Behavior Books, Palo Alto, Calif.)

cultures, but it certainly applies to western civilization. It also applies to psychotherapy, because the essence of the interaction between therapist and patient is the confrontation of repressed, denied, projected, and displaced fears that operate in the therapist as well as in the patient. When two therapists, one man and one woman, work as members of a team, they cannot help developing feelings for each other that approach intimacy, but being professionals, they can help each other to cope with these feelings instead of becoming victimized by them.[13] In the maturity of intimacy one not only recognizes the fears of the other, one also offers oneself as reassurance against these fears. In the experience of family therapy the two cotherapists enter each other's fears. If they are man and woman, the temptation to engage in sexual fantasies about each other will easily occur but will be recognized as something to be controlled and thus will furnish an important model for foster and adoptive families.

Other dynamics that have a healing effect and are specific to family therapy are the following. When people in a primary group such as the family build around themselves walls of psychological privacy, they also refuse to listen to others. They close themselves off from the rest of the family and spend their communicative potential in talking to and listening to themselves. The entrance of a family group therapist or a team of family therapists into this conspiracy of silence brings new experiences of talking and listening to the family members. First of all, the therapist shows by his behavior that he can assign priority to listening to others over listening to himself. Everybody in the family is being listened to and responded to by the family therapist. This experience alone opens the closed systems. It is perhaps even more dynamically significant that through being listened to by another who is not destructive, one gains a feeling of dignity for one's own suffering that improves the self-image.

If one's self-image is improved, if one is listened to with respect, one can afford to give the same response to the communication of others. One lends, thereby, additional dignity to their suffering, a dignity that is of a quality such as the therapist cannot provide. It is familial versus therapeutic response (i.e., it holds out a promise of lasting closeness), and suddenly a significant change has taken place. People who have not talked or listened to each other are being talked to and listened to by the therapist, and find themselves listening and talking to each other. Communication is restored, or perhaps established for the first time, and a strengthening discovery is made: one is not alone with one's suffering. Even when destructive urges are being expressed, one finds that other family members have similar urges, and the feeling of being cursed alone with such impulses disappears. One also discovers that one can verbally express destructive feelings without actually destroying and without being destroyed. In this

13. Sonne and Lincoln, *op. cit.*

way the members of the family are freed from the magical fear that verbalizing equals doing.[14]

Identification with the family therapist adds an element of therapeutic intent to the recovery of the familial potential for interaction. I think it has not been recognized sufficiently that the increasing number of therapeutic experiences that people have in our society enhances family life by adding these very elements of psychological healing and emotional nurture to the many other functions that family members have traditionally fulfilled.

When the specific problems of conflict, anxiety, and feelings of injustice that foster care and adoption may involve are brought into the realm of responsive communication, the foster family or adoptive family is established in the awareness of its membership as a community of destiny that has special coping tasks. These coping tasks require special understanding, as well as the development of special ego strength and special attitudes of empathy with the other family members. Suffering then becomes a challenge for growth.

Family Goals

Psychological and organizational growth requires goals. The family system is distinguished from the biological system of the individual person by the fact that the maturational push alone is not sufficient for securing adequate development. In consequence, the family therapist must have goals for the growth of the family with which the parents can learn to identify, and these goals must be concretely related to the experience of foster care and adoption.

A child in foster placement should probably have a goal of growth that would make him want to become a parent who would not have to place his children in foster care. A psychological problem in one's past can always be coped with by protecting others against suffering from similar experiences, and this is often the impulse behind foster parenting. This may be a shock to professional people who see foster care as a healing experience, and spend professional effort in trying to make it so. Still there are few among us who would not hope that children could grow up in their own parental homes and would not have to depend on foster care.

I would suggest that a goal for a foster mother would, in many instances, be the achievement of a state of personal development in which she does not have to be a foster mother, or better, would not have to be one for reasons of arrest in her own development, of financial need, or of marital dissatisfaction. In cases in which becoming a foster mother has been related to developmental arrest, the experience should be conceived as a regres-

14. Otto Pollak, "Entrance of the Caseworker into Family Interaction," *Social Casework,* XLV (1964), 216–220.

sion in the service of the ego, and a treatment goal would be the achieving of a new start for personality development that would lead beyond compulsive functioning on the foster mother level.

I would propose that the goal for an adoptive child would have to be the eventual growth into a person whose children would not have to be given up for adoption. Implied in this would be the liberation from a past that drives the child into a never-completed search for his own mother, and into self-questioning about his difference from children who were not given up for adoption.

For adoptive parents, the adoption presents a challenge to learn that having biological children and having adoptive children is not the same, and that adoption is not a substitute for procreation, but an experience in itself that must be lived out fully and adequately. Otherwise, the adopted child is exploited to make up for biological failure, and, since nobody can suffer exploitation without resentment, the attempt to make adoption a substitute for procreation is bound to fail.

One may wonder at this point what developmental goals can be posited for the natural children of a foster or adoptive family. I should like to suggest that, in a corporate society in which most people will have to make a living as employees, having an outsider in one's own group can be a valuable learning experience. In all large-scale organizations there are frequent transfers that introduce into established peer groups outsiders who either come and go, or have to be absorbed on a more or less permanent basis. Invariably an experience of intrusion is connected with these transfers, which are usually reacted to with feelings of injustice, hostility, or at least, resentment of complication. Such reactions, however, are usually self-defeating. If analogous experiences can be opened up for the children in the family therapy sessions, they may derive developmental gain in later life from these experiences.

For the man who is a foster father there is a growth challenge of a specific kind. It actually involves learning to be a husband whose wife does not need foster children for purposes other than helping these children. In other words, the goal would be that of becoming a husband who can meet the marital and developmental needs of his wife in such a fashion that she can decide about having foster children as an act of personal autonomy rather than as a response to needs that should have been met in other ways.

Concluding Comments

Every new venture in the methodology of helping is in danger of being oversold and overbought, since the possibility of failure is part of the human condition in professional life as elsewhere. No methodology, however therapeutically well-founded, is likely to bring unfailing success. Perhaps even more important, no methodology that becomes established remains as efficient as it was in the beginning. The zest of new therapeutic adventure gives the new form of treatment a special power, which is likely to diminish as the newness wears off. I should like therefore to close my paper with the following consideration: if child welfare workers tire of individual therapy as a major methodology, the time for family therapy has come. When they begin to become tired of family therapy, its value will be lost and new methodologies will have to be devised and put into practice. The helping effort, like other human efforts, knows no peace.

35. Group Therapy with Parents of Children in a Residential Treatment Center

ALVIN E. WINDER
LINDO FERRINI
GEORGE E. GABY

The practice of psychotherapy with the parents of children with emotional problems has received wide recognition in the child welfare field. Many such parent programs have been reported in the literature. These programs have been carried out in a variety of settings and with parents whose children come from a variety of clinical populations. This paper will deal with a specific population—the parents of emotionally disturbed children; a specific setting—the residential treatment center; and a specific therapeutic procedure—group psychotherapy.

The literature on residential treatment centers for emotionally disturbed children indicates that psychotherapy with parents is accepted both as philosophically sound and as good practice.[1] A recent report of 21 major centers reveals that parent counseling or psychotherapy on a regular basis is a part of the treatment program in all the institutions surveyed.[2]

Reprinted with permission of Child Welfare League of America, Inc., from *Child Welfare*, Vol. 44, No 5 (May, 1965), pp. 265–71.

1. Herschel Alt, *Residential Treatment for the Disturbed Child* (New York: International Universities Press, 1960).

2. Lydia F. Hylton, *The Residential Treatment Center: Children, Programs, and Costs* (New York: Child Welfare League of America, 1964).

Group psychotherapy with parents, however, is much less often reported. (Group psychotherapy is distinguished in this paper from group guidance, the former belonging to therapeutic processes, the latter to processes of parent education.) It has most generally been used with the parents of children in outpatient settings or with the parents of children suffering from a variety of specific disabilities.[3] Very rarely has it been reported as being used in the setting of a residential treatment center. The Hylton survey reports that only one out of the 21 centers studied uses group psychotherapy with parents.[4] Furthermore, this center had only one group with seven members. It should be added, however, that the literature is frequently a year or two behind actual practice. Recently, the authors heard that the Sweetser-Children's Home is using a group approach in working with parents.[5]

This paper is concerned with reporting the experience of two psychotherapy groups of parents of children with severe emotional disturbances who are resident in the Children's Study Home, Springfield, Massachusetts. This program was set up to meet several difficulties that had manifested themselves in the parents' relations with the Study Home. First, even though the parents were in individual casework treatment, they showed little motivation and strong resistance to change. Secondly, the agency staff felt that the parents had not accepted the help the agency was offering their children and that they had strong inner reservations about the value of the agency's help. Because of these reservations, there seemed to be some parental sabotaging of efforts to help the children. Therefore, the broad objective of the program was to help the parents identify the agency as being therapeutically valuable for their child. Specifically, the Study Home staff hoped for greater cooperation from the parents during the children's stay at the center. They further hoped that, through contact with the agency, the parents would improve their functioning as parents and increase their empathy for the needs and feelings of their children. Change in both the parents and the children could eventually make for successful return of the children to their family homes.

3. Edward G. Colbert, "Group Psychotherapy for Mothers of Schizophrenic Children in a State Hospital," *International Journal of Group Psychotherapy*, IX (1959), 93–98; Helen E. Durkin, *Group Therapy for Mothers of Disturbed Children* (Springfield, Ill.: Charles C Thomas, 1954); Mark Eshbaugh and James Walsh, "A Group Approach to Parents of Children in Trouble," *Children*, XI (1964), 108–112; Ruth Rothman, "Group Counseling with Parents of Visually Handicapped Children," *International Journal of Group Psychotherapy*, VI (1956), 317–323; S. R. Slavson, "Steps in Sensitizing Parents (Couples) in Groups Toward Schizophrenic Children," *International Journal of Group Psychotherapy*, XIII (1963), 176–186; Alvin E. Winder, "A Program of Group Counseling for the Parents of Cerebral Palsied Children," *Cerebral Palsy Review*, XIX, No. 3 (1958), 8–10.

4. Hylton, *op. cit.*

5. A personal communication from Eleanor L. Dotter, Social Work Supervisor, Sweetser-Children's Home, Saco, Maine; and Nicholas Fish, "Some Statistical Ramblings through Group Psychotherapy," unpublished paper (Saco, Maine: Sweetser-Children's Home, 1964).

Description of the Program

The group psychotherapy program was set up for two closed groups, which met separately for 12 sessions each. Group I met for an hour on Wednesday evenings, and Group II for an hour on Sunday evenings.

Group members were selected on the basis of parents' geographic proximity to the center, their willingness to participate in the group psychotherapy program, and the possibility of involving both parents in the group process. An initial letter was sent by the Study Home director to all parents residing within a 25-mile radius of the home (the home is located in the geographical center of the city of Springfield, Massachusetts). The letter expressed the goals of the group meetings, in the following terms:

> The Children's Study Home in our interest in serving the children and their families is initiating a series of parent group meetings for the purpose of working on the problems that parents have in relation to their child placed in the Children's Study Home. We know that you are interested in helping your child and that you are concerned about ways in which you can do this. This series is intended to work on this.

Later on, the letter stated:

> A number of parents with whom we have discussed this have already expressed interest in it, and I strongly recommend this program to you. You would be a member of one of these groups. Talk to your caseworker about it sometime before March 1st. We look forward to a helpful and interesting experience.

In almost all cases, it was explained to the parents that the group would not be a substitute for their individual meetings with their assigned caseworker. Twelve parents, seven mothers and five fathers, were selected for the group psychotherapy program. All were white, in their 30's, and belonged to either the upper-lower or the lower-middle socioeconomic class. Most had completed high school, and one of the fathers was a college graduate.

As might be expected, all of the parents manifested marked long-standing, firmly entrenched personality problems and defects. Of the seven mothers, three were grossly infantile, narcissistic, acting-out character disorders; two were rather fragile borderline psychotics (one with strong covert paranoic trends and an angry, phallic orientation; the other with clear-cut cyclothymic tendencies and a somewhat passive, fearful orientation), one suffered from a severe neurosis anxiety, and one is best described as passive and severely schizoid (there being no real suggestion of a potential or likely ego breakdown.)

The five fathers all exhibited major problems relative to passive-dependent longings and needs. Three are best categorized as inhibited, markedly passive-dependent, and somewhat schizoid. One is passive-dependent and, unlike the schizoid, capable of appropriate and genuine affective response. He tends, however, to be fearful of emotional intimacy, preferring to withdraw and isolate. The remaining father, out of his pervasive need to deny and defend against his strong underlying passive, homosexual propensities, is assertive (counterphobically intrusive), controlling, and hostile. He is very often difficult to deal with and, clinically, appears to be a "passive-aggressive personality, aggressive type."

The seven children of the 12 parents, four boys and three girls, ranged in age from 9 to 11. Four (two boys and two girls) were clearly schizophrenic. Another girl fluctuated between an acting-out, character-disorder orientation and a confused, hypomanic-like psychotic state. One boy was a severe impulse-ridden character disorder, and the remaining boy presented the multiple problems of a nonspecific aphasia, a significant but not clearly delineated hearing loss, and noteworthy passive-aggressive personality trends.

Two rules governed the assignment of parents to either the first or the second group. These were, first, placing husbands and wives in separate groups and, second, balancing the groups so that there would be approximately an equal number of men and women in each group. Each group met with a therapist and an observer. The therapist in the first group was a clinical psychologist with experience in working with parent groups. The therapist in the second group was a caseworker with experience in counseling parents in the residential treatment setting. A social groupworker was the observer in both groups. The two psychotherapists and the observer met weekly to discuss the group process and the progress of the parents. Agency staff were informed of the effects of the group psychotherapy on the parents through the caseworker's and the observer's reports at staff meetings.

Method Employed

The group psychotherapeutic approach that was used relied on the interpersonal relationship as the medium through which change was effected. Two levels of interpersonal relationships were present in the parent groups. These were the interaction of each member with the therapist and the interaction of the various members with one another. The major role of the therapist was to make selective use of these interactions, sometimes to encourage and sometimes to discourage them. In order to make selective use of the interactions, he had to understand the basic dynamics of group treatment. These involve the various ways (verbal and nonverbal) in which group members express their tensions. The communication of feelings by the group as a whole sometimes occurred in symbolic form, which is referred to in this paper as a group theme. The therapist also had to be able to understand and respond to nonverbal communications.

Group Attendance

Initially, six parents attended each group meeting. Group I had four members who attended regularly and two who attended sporadically. Group II had three whose attendance was regular and three whose attendance was irregular. Our experience indicates that regularity of attendance does not seem to be related to marital pairs.

In only one family did both husband and wife show poor attendance. The partners in two families had equal attendance, even though each member had to appear at a different time for his group session. In two families, one member attended regularly and the other irregularly. The member who was present in each of these families spoke of wishing that his or her spouse would attend. In both situations, the present members spoke of attempts by their spouses to actively dissuade them from group attendance. These attempts at dissuasion were unsuccessful in both cases. The force of the group seemed strong enough to reinforce the attending parents' motivations to make use of the group process.

Absence from the group sessions, but not from the casework sessions, was frequently felt by the staff to be the parents' way of asking the caseworker whether he approved of their participation in the group. Sometimes this was stated directly; one parent said, "I don't want to go to the group; I just want to see you." Sometimes it was stated indirectly. Another parent told her caseworker, "I talk about enough in the group; I have nothing really to say to you." Caseworkers were prepared to expect this kind of reaction. They understood that when the question arose, they should explore the feelings of the parent concerning group participation and that they should be careful to support the parent's participation in both the casework and the group programs.

Group Themes

Three major group themes—involving mistrust, loss, and defiance—have resolved themselves out of several questions the parents put to the therapist and to each other during the course of the 12 sessions. They asked the therapist and indirectly, through him, the agency: Are you honest in your stated wish to help us? Are you strong enough to withstand our demands? Will you retreat from helping us when you encounter our angry insistence that our demands be met? Do you have competitive values (as we do), which will lead you to reject us for producing an inadequate child?

To their fellow group members, the parents posed the following questions: Can you accept my expression of feeling over a continuous failure to have my demands met? Can you tolerate my criticism of how you handle your child, your family, the agency, me, the other group members, and the therapist? Finally, they asked each other: Can you understand if I become frightened and must stay away from the group meetings?

Initially, parents were very unsure of either the group's or the therapist's acceptance of them in relationship to their child. One parent summed up this theme and then showed his anxiety about whether he had presented an adequate image to the therapist:

> I saw George on a recent visit. Since January, his classwork has improved. He has done especially well in his figures and writing. Since he was little, we have accepted any improvement, even if he gained only an ounce. You're doing well for him, he likes it here. His flareups are less. I hope he continues to pick up. I don't know if that's what you want to hear about.

This initial theme of mistrust lingered through several sessions until it became clear that the therapist was not going to give advice defensively, lecture on child-rearing practices, or develop any punitive responses. As the group became more secure with the therapist's, and therefore the agency's understanding and acceptance, they were able to test each other. Are we willing, they asked, to tell each other our thoughts and feelings about our children? Midway through the group sessions, this problem was brought up through the medium of a television program.

> Mrs. Hogan asked, "Did you see the Eleventh Hour last night?" Mrs. Quinn had, and she said, "It was about an autistic child. Is that what they are really like?" Mrs. Jones said, "People want to know if that's how Carole is." "You mean they want to know if she is a nut?" asked Mrs. Quinn.
> Thoughtfully Mrs. Jones said, "He does a lot of things that Carole does, but he is further into another world. She doesn't really laugh or cry." Mr. Illing said, "I remember when George first cried." Mrs. Quinn countered, "Alice never did." "Carole has had tears in her eyes, but never cried," Mrs. Jones said.

This discussion of feelings about the child who shows no emotion led to a first admission on the part of these parents that their families gained some advantage in placing the child who did not feel. This represents a first handling of the theme of loss.

> A few minutes later, in the same session a parent said, "Sara was afraid she would be sent away also. Sometimes I'm happy that Carole is not home." Mr. Illing agreed: "It's easier for David to get along with George here. George used to knock the stuffings out of him." Mrs. Quinn said: "My mother said I never disciplined Alice enough. I think Donald is improving now that Alice is here."

Having spoken about their feelings and experiences concerning the placement of their children, the group seemed to develop a sense of cohesiveness. For the first time in these sessions, they began to express dissatisfaction with the agency. This criticism required a willingness to challenge the group therapist. The excerpt below shows that one of the parents, Mr. Illing, held back, but could not stem the tide of challenge and defiance. The theme of defiance is best illlustrated in this material from the 11th session:

> Mrs. Treynor said, "My son didn't have trouble at home." Mr. Illing suggested, "Maybe he gained something being here." Mrs. Hellweg interposed, somewhat sharply, "I don't know, I'm no nut; the caseworker did not believe me when I told him." Mrs. Quinn said, "Alice wouldn't tell her caseworker the truth; she really wants to come home now." Mrs. Hellweg agreed, "They are always picking on the kids here: don't do this, don't do that. The housemothers are too old. People that old shouldn't do that kind of work, they are too rigid."

Administrative Evaluation

Since the inception of the program to serve emotionally disturbed children, the professional staff of the agency have had as a major goal rehabilitation of the parents through casework, so that the children might be returned home as quickly as possible. It was considered most fortunate that the physical plant of the center was located in the city proper with easy access to public transportation. In assigning caseloads, emphasis was given to work with parents. In the agency's eagerness to preserve family ties, visiting policies were somewhat permissive, and visits took place as often as the parents wished. Few limits were set.

It soon became apparent that the goals the agency set for these parents were overly ambitious. The parents became increasingly hostile, and, in many instances, they sabotaged treatment. In two cases, the visiting pattern was destructive, and the consultant psychiatrist was able to show that the caseworker's guilt at having taken the child away from the parent was unresolved. It was because of concern over failure to rehabilitate parents and over the resulting lack of success in returning the children to their own homes that the agency turned to another treatment tool—group therapy.

At the conclusion of the first series of 12 sessions, we did a preliminary evaluation. During the group meetings, no evidence of treatment sabotage by the parents was detected. There was a diminution of overt hostility to the agency. These two highly encouraging changes in parent behavior can best be explained by an *esprit de corps* that the parents participating in the groups developed. For example, while the group therapy program was in process, the staff was able to put into effect new visiting policies designed to lessen the destructive impact of erratic visiting. The first two visiting days occurred during this period. Most of the administrative and professional staff were on hand for these visiting times. Refreshments were served. Parents, children, and staff participated in informal group games, and there seemed to be a relaxed atmosphere of friendliness and good will. The positive way in which parent group members responded to each other was especially noteworthy.

There was a change in the attitude of agency staff (possibly a lessening of the guilt of individual staff members), which could be seen when major shifts in treatment goals necessitated even further separation between two children and their parents. Staff members were able to take a forceful stand based on the needs of the child. Thus, it seems clear that, by providing a new vehicle to help parents, the staff of the Children's Study Home became able to deal with the parents in a much more constructive way.

It seems quite certain that the group therapy project will continue. The parents themselves sought and obtained a commitment from the agency for this. Much still needs to be worked through, however, and casework and group therapy goals need to be redefined and a method of communication developed between the therapists and the caseworkers. At this point, the staff is convinced that parental acceptance of treatment will be a necessary criterion for admission of a child.

Casework Evaluation

Caseworkers assigned to the parents report a major change in the parents' perceptions of them. Before the group therapy, some of the parents viewed the caseworker as a powerful authority with complete control over their relationship to the agency and to their children. The parents frequently responded to this perception by either being very submissive or very dependent. This behavior has a parallel in the initial group theme—mistrust. At first, the parents tried to tell the group therapist what they thought he wanted to hear.

Coincident with the change in parental attitudes in the group, the caseworkers reported that parents began to shift their emphasis in their meetings with the workers. One worker noticed that the parents seemed less clinging and less complaining. Another noted a change in the parents' use of the casework session. She observed that these parents spent less time unburdening their own problems on the worker and more time on joint planning for their children. A third worker reported that the parents assigned to him were more aware of themselves as persons and began responding as individuals and not just as parents. He felt that, through this change, their relationship to him was expressed less in stereotyped "parent" questions and became both more professional and more real.

Conclusion

The record of the 12 sessions reveals quite clearly that these parents were able, through the group method, to become involved with each other and with the agency to a much greater extent than they had through their previous agency contacts.

Their involvement seemed to stem, first, from their opportunity to test the group therapist to see whether he (as the agency's representative) could tolerate their ambivalent feelings toward themselves, their children, and the agency. Second, involvement developed out of the group identification that was the result of their successful testing experience. Third, it came out of the expression of negative feelings that they felt toward the agency's "inadequate" mothering of their children.

The caseworkers felt that both the stimulation the parents experienced in the group psychotherapy and the parents' increased involvement with the agency made their own contacts with the parents more realistic and more satisfying. The agency administrator noted decreased sabotage by parents of the treatment processes and signs of increased cooperation by them.

Because of the initial success of the program, group treatment will be further explored as a means of working through the parents' feelings about placement of their children, their identification with the treatment process, and their reactions to the improvement of their children's condition.

Index